PEOPLE AT WORK
Human Behavior in Organizations

Fifth Edition

PAUL R. TIMM
BRIGHAM YOUNG UNIVERSITY

BRENT D. PETERSON
FRANKLIN COVEY COMPANY

 South-Western College Publishing
Thomson Learning™

Australia • Canada • Denmark • Japan • Mexico • New Zealand • Philippines
Puerto Rico • Singapore • South Africa • Spain • United Kingdom • United States

People at Work: Human Behavior in Organizations, 5e, by Paul R. Timm & Brent D. Peterson

Publisher: DAVE SHAUT
Executive Editor: JOHN SZILAGYI
Developmental Editor: THERESA CURTIS
Marketing Manager: ROB BLOOM
Production Editor: ELIZABETH A. SHIPP
Manufacturing Coordinator: DANA BEGAN SCHWARTZ
Internal Design: LOU ANN THESING and KENT DESIGN
Cover Design: JOE DEVINE
Cover Illustration: ©ALEX GROSS/SIS
Photo Researcher: MARY GOLJENBOOM, FERRET RESEARCH
Production House: THE LEFT COAST GROUP, INC.
Printer: R.R. DONNELLEY & SONS COMPANY—WILLARD MANUFACTURING DIVISION

Printed in the United States of America
2 3 4 5 02 01

For more information contact South-Western College Publishing, 5101 Madison Road, Cincinnati, Ohio, 45227 or find us on the Internet at http://www.swcollege.com

For permission to use material from this text or product, contact us by
- **telephone: 1-800-730-2214**
- **fax: 1-800-730-2215**
- **web: http://www.thomsonrights.com**

Library of Congress Cataloging-in-Publication Data
Timm, Paul R.
    People at work: human behavior in organizations / Paul R. Timm,
Brent D. Peterson.—5th ed.
        p.   cm.
    Includes bibliographical references and index.
    ISBN 0-314-20041-X (hardcover : alk. paper)
I. Peterson, Brent D.   II. Title.
HD58.7.T55 1999   99-23191
658.4'092—dc21

This book is printed on acid-free paper.

Contents

Preface

It has been almost two decades since the first edition of this book was published. Although much has happened in the world of organizations since the early 1980s, the importance of human relations has not diminished. If anything, healthy, productive human relationships have become more important and challenging as our world shrinks. Today, more than ever before, we thrive and grow through our interdependence with humanity worldwide.

Among the changes, much remains the same. We still see evidence that people can develop the technical ability to solve almost any of the complex tasks facing humanity. Feeding people, cleaning up pollution, producing sufficient energy, and curing major diseases are within the technical grasp of people. The roadblocks to such accomplishments, however, lie in the problems of human relationships. Without cooperation, little can be accomplished; with cooperation, all things are possible.

This book is about people in the workplace. It focuses on the many psychological and social pressures that people experience when they interact with each other. But more importantly, the emphasis of the book is on you, the reader. Human behaviors and relationships play an important part in daily life. Understanding these relationships can help you accomplish your goals in all types of organizations.

Many of you are, or shortly will be, in a leadership position in which you deal with other people. We think you will find a great deal of information in this book that will help you succeed. We also believe you will find it enjoyable reading. The book includes examples and illustrations from a variety of sources, and each contributes to the overall flavor. You will find cartoons, illustrations, quotes, photographs, and even a few poems. These items are placed throughout the text to enhance your reading enjoyment and understanding of the subject.

We believe that this book should be read—and used; therefore, we have included self-evaluative exercises and learning projects. We encourage you to complete the exercises and use the techniques as you interact with other people. You may be pleasantly surprised at the results.

The fifth edition contains the following features to enhance the presentation of the material.

- Self-evaluation *Activities* are included for many themes such as leadership styles, motivation, and diversity.

- *Another Look* readings at the end of every chapter reflect current thinking on a variety of topics including management, organizational behavior, and human resource management.

- *Case in Point* readings at the end of every chapter explore typical issues encountered in today's organizations. Critical thinking and discussion questions are provided for each case.

In addition, the text provides *Objectives; Summary of Key Ideas; Key Terms, Concepts, and Names;* and *Questions and Exercises* to aid student learning and understanding.

To upgrade and enhance the fifth edition we have

- Added material throughout the book that addresses two critical issues: ethics and the impact of new technology.

- Streamlined the presentation of the material by combining related chapters and reducing the total number of chapters to 17.

- Updated the statistics and references to be more interesting to students.

- Assembled a comprehensive ancillary package including an updated and revised *Test Bank* and *Instructor's Manual;* new *PowerPoint Slides, Videos,* and a *Website.*

We have done our best to update and enhance—without tampering with— the feel and excitement created in the first four editions. We are certain that you will find this edition to be a true learning experience, one that will lead you to a greater understanding of *People at Work.*

Throughout this book we have used fictitious names for individuals and companies. Any similarity between those names and real people or organizations is coincidental and unintentional. The situations described in our cases and examples, however, are drawn from real-life experiences.

Preparing a textbook and accompanying ancillary package is truly a team effort. We especially wish to thank our editor, John Szilagyi, for his pushing and prodding the project to completion; and our developmental editor, Theresa Curtis, for her active and insightful involvement in the development of the manuscript. Special thanks go to our production editor, Libby Shipp, whose attention to detail has transformed our written words into the professional textbook you now hold. Their help was invaluable throughout the process.

In addition, we thank the professionals who reviewed earlier editions of the book and provided constructive suggestions for this revision:

Thomas R. Allen, Appalachian State University

Bob Amundson, Ulster County Community College

Hal Babson, Columbus State Community College

Kathryn Barchas, Skyline College

Bonnie Chavez, Santa Barbara City College

James Fellman, Hofstra University

Ron Herrick, Mesa Community College

Charleen S. Jaeb, Cuyahoga Community College

Donald N. Kelly, North Hennepin Community College

Jan Lauten, Rockingham Community College

David Leland, Red River Community College

Ron McDonald, DeVry Institute

Paula K. McNeil, Cameron University

Raphael Santos, Imperial Valley College

Reg St. Clair, Mountain Empire Community College

Nancy Stein, Red Rocks Community College

Wendy Stocker, DeVry Institute

Jerry Thomas, Arapahoe Community College

Linda Woiwood, Skagit Valley College

Richard K. Zollinger, Central Piedmont Community College

Furthermore, we appreciate the hundreds of instructors and thousands of students who used our first four editions and made this revision possible.

We acknowledge, too, the many people who inspired us to write this book. During our years of consulting, training, teaching, and working in business organizations, we have come to know countless people who have taught us important principles of human relations. Sometimes their teaching came through great example; sometimes their example taught us what not to do.

Paul R. Timm
Brent D. Peterson

Paul R. Timm   Brent D. Peterson

PART 1

HUMAN BEHAVIOR

Why Study Human Behavior in Organizations?

Bringing people together to work in organizations is a tricky process. Managers who describe their most frequent and challenging problems almost always place *people* problems at the top of their list. "They talk about their boss' poor communication skills, subordinate's lack of motivation, conflicts between employees within their department, overcoming employee resistance to departmental reorganization, and similar concerns," according to organizational behavior expert Steven Robbins.[1]

Understanding human behavior in organizations is the key to developing and maintaining good human relations.

More careers have been damaged by poor human relations skills than by any other cause. Having great technical ability but poor people skills is a formula for disaster. Knowing how to do a job isn't enough. Succeeding in any modern organization requires depending on others and knowing how to work with people. You seldom hear of a manager losing his or her job due to a lack of technical skills, but you regularly hear of people failing because they simply can't get along with others.

This book provides the background for developing skills in the crucial art of human relations. It identifies key forces and tools everyone needs to strengthen their relationships with others, especially in the work environment.

To understand and to relate constructively with people are the greatest of all human skills.

Just as an individual's personality is assessed by the way he or she interacts with others, so is an organization's culture—personality—shaped by its policies and behaviors.

An organization's personality is shaped by its human relations policies and behaviors.

Well-managed companies care about their people. Their actions say loudly and clearly that people are seen as the most important of all resources. Poorly managed companies may talk about human relations, but their actions belie their words.

Modern organizations are much more than offices and factories, plants and equipment. The soul of a company, hospital, government agency, or nonprofit group is the collective body of *people* who make it all work. The people who staff the offices, work on the production lines, sell the products, provide the services, and operate the machines give life to the organization and define its character.

Why Do People Love Some Companies and Hate Others?

In its annual feature "The 100 Best Companies to Work for in America," *Fortune* magazine[2] identifies companies where "workers sing their employers' praises and—although it's very un-90s—even declare pride in their corporate affiliation." What distinguishes these companies from the others? Concern for and involvement of their people.

Leaders in these organizations recognize and appreciate the human element by providing: inspiring leadership, great work facilities, and a sense of purpose. (The *Fortune* article appears on page 17–19.) In another publication,[3] researchers identify five key ways enlightened companies are creating better workplaces:

- More employee participation

- More sensitivity to work/family issues

- More two-way communications

The Study of Human Behavior in Organizations: A Key to Career Success

- What is the value of studying human behavior in organizations?

- Why do employees love working in some companies and not others?

- How does this area of study relate to other aspects of management?

- What is the significance of the Hawthorne studies to the field of human relations in the workplace?

- How do modern management approaches, such as systems theory, contingency management, QWL, and self-directed workgroups, rely on human relations skills to succeed?

- How can an understanding of human relations affect our personal and professional lives?

- Why are *caring* and *trust* the cornerstone values of human relations?

The answers to these and other questions are coming up next in Chapter 1 . . .

- More sharing of the wealth

- More fun

Clearly these factors all relate to the human side of businesses.

But is "a great place to work" also a productive business? *Fortune* magazine research concludes that "high morale and outstanding performance emphatically go together."[4] The most critical behaviors that can detract from a company's performance and profitability are employee productivity, absenteeism, and turnover.[5] Behaviors, of course, are linked to attitudes, and attitudes arise from a complex web of mental activities. How people feel about themselves, their leaders and coworkers, and their company will color their behaviors. Understanding some of these contributing factors can make us **"human-relations-smart."**

Many people are technically smart—they know how to do the technical aspects of their jobs—but are human-relations-dumb—unaware that simply knowing *how to do a job is not the key to success*. To produce results, most of us depend on others, and this requires knowing *how to work with people*. Before this can be done, many human relations skills need to be learned and practiced.

How Human Relations Smart Are You?

The following is a self-test that can give you a sense of how well you already practice some key human relations principles.

ACTIVITIES

HUMAN RELATIONS SELF-TEST

Although human relations skills are not as easy to identify or quantify as technical skills, they are extremely important to your career progress. The more you practice positive human relations, the less co-workers and superiors will misinterpret your goals, and the more supportive they will be.

Twenty human relations competencies are listed below. *Check only those you practice daily.* The exercise will demonstrate why it is difficult to be considered "human-relations-smart."

I consistently:

❏ Deal with all people in an honest, ethical, and moral way.

❏ Remain positive and upbeat even while working with others who may be negative.

❏ Send out positive verbal and nonverbal signals in all human interactions, including over the telephone.

❏ Refuse to be involved in any activity that might victimize another person.

❏ Build and maintain open and healthy working relationships with everyone in the workplace. I refuse to play favorites.

❏ Treat everyone, regardless of ethnic or socioeconomic differences, with respect.

❏ Work effectively with others, regardless of their sexual orientation.

❏ Permit others to restore a damaged relationship with me; I don't hold a grudge.

continued

ACTIVITIES

HUMAN RELATIONS SELF-TEST, CONTINUED

❏ Maintain a strong relationship with my immediate superior without alienating co-workers.

❏ Am a better-than-average producer while contributing to the productivity of co-workers.

❏ Refuse to initiate or circulate potentially harmful rumors.

❏ Maintain a good attendance record, including being on time to work.

❏ Show I can live up to my productivity potential without alienating co-workers who do not live up to theirs.

❏ Acknowledge mistakes or misjudgments, rather than hiding them.

❏ Refuse to allow small gripes to grow into major upsets.

❏ Am an excellent listener.

❏ Keep a good balance between my home and career lives so that neither suffers.

❏ Look for, and appreciate, the good characteristics of others.

❏ Keep my business and personal relationships sufficiently separated.

❏ Make only positive comments about those not present.

Score _____

(Add five points for each square checked)

A score of 70 or above indicates you are practicing a substantial number of recognized human relations skills; a score of under 50 suggests a review of current practices may be in order.

Source: Elwood N. Chapman, *Winning at Human Relations* (Los Altos, CA: Crisp Publications, 1989), p. 3.

A Brief History of People Management in Organizations

People at work were not always so valued as they are today. Today's sense of caring about individuals has evolved over many years. Many of history's great philosophers have contributed to our understanding of leadership and management. Machiavelli, a sixteenth-century Florentine statesman and political theorist, wrote *The Prince,* a cynical guide to ruling people. He assumed that all people were lazy and self-centered and that tricking them into working made good sense. He believed that the end justified the means. Indeed, we have come to associate his name with the process of manipulation. Thus an individual utilizing his principles is called **"Machiavellian."**

Throughout history, people were members of various classes. Some were rulers (kings, nobility, and trusted aristocrats) and many more were followers. If one assumed that people of lower social status should be subservient, management of them would likely rely on exerting power or force. Managers with such assumptions did not give much thought to human relations—after all, lower-class people were seen as barely human.

The eventual breakdown of the rigid class system with the advent of democratic thinking called for new and different ways to manage. The notion that people are "created equal and endowed with certain inalienable rights," as Thomas Jefferson asserted, was a radically different way of thinking about human relationships. Today's manager must be concerned with the "human element" instead of dictating to people as the ancient aristocrat did.

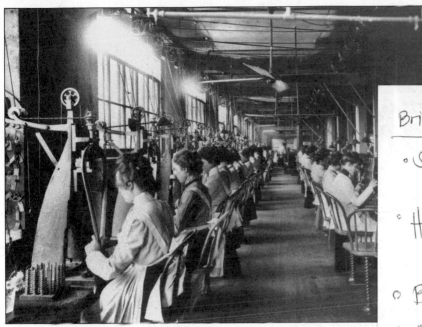

During the Industrial Revolution, many industries benefited from mechanization.

Brief History of Approaches to HR

- *Scientific management*
  — Frederick Taylor
- *Human Relations mngmt*
  — Elton Mayo
- *Behavioral movement*
- *modern mngmt theory*

Knowledge and understanding of someones behavior brings good human relations in the work area.

Good employee relations Increases productivity and satisfaction, which positively impact profit / success.

The Scientific Management Approach

By the late 1800s, the Industrial Revolution was picking up a great (pardon the pun). More and more jobs were being mechanized. Inv neers, and chemists were coming up with products people had o of. *Science* was being viewed as the great answer to most of hum lems, and managers were beginning to look at ways to apply scient to the study and improvement of work efficiency.

Although many researchers were involved with **scientific ma** Frederick W. Taylor is generally regarded as the father of this new management. Briefly, Taylor felt that through science, a careful worl ager could find the one best way to do any job. This right way wo from careful scientific observation, standardized measurements, and trial-and-error experiments.

People known as *efficiency experts* began to come into promine experts would carefully observe people at work (sometimes using a mo nological device, such as the motion picture), measure each moveme inc the tools being used, and even attempt to scientifically select the "first-class person" for the job. This was all done in search of the one best way to accomplish a task, and great improvements in efficiency often came about from these efforts.

During this search to study workers scientifically to improve management of them, supervisors sought to establish work rates, set standards of performance (all determined scientifically through observation), and define a full and fair day's labor for each task.

Taylor defined *management* as "knowing exactly what you want (people) to do, and then seeing that they do it in the best and cheapest way." To accomplish this, managers felt that they could simply replace people, the way we would exchange spare parts on a machine, and maintain or improve the output. This simplistic picture of human nature was the Achilles' heel of scientific management, as we'll see in a moment.

...ght the one best way to do any job.

The Human Relations Approach to Management

In the late 1920s and early 1930s, a new approach to management theory was born. A researcher named **Elton Mayo** and his associates conducted a series of experiments at the plant of the Western Electric Company in Hawthorne, Illinois. The **Hawthorne experiments** proved to be the transition point from scientific management to the early human relations style of management.

Mayo originally adhered to the scientific management approach. He and his associates had conducted many scientific investigations of such things as worker fatigue, the use of rest periods, changes in physical surroundings of the workplace, and their effects on worker output. In fact, Mayo's team was in the midst of a series of such experiments when a chance discovery gave birth to what we now call human relations.

A Chance Discovery at the Hawthorne Plant

Mayo and his associates were using experiments to study the relationships between the physical work environment and worker productivity when a breakthrough occurred.

Researchers discovered that something more than the physical work environment affected worker productivity.

The researchers were looking at the relationship between the brightness of light in the workplace and the efficiency of the workers, as measured by their output. They found that by making the workplace slightly brighter, they could increase output. So they cranked up a carefully measured increase in candlepower and found that the output increased even more. But being good scientific researchers, they also decided to check the other direction by reducing illumination. Output again went up. They reduced it even further. Output continued to *increase*! What was happening? They found that by either increasing or decreasing illumination, sometimes even dimming the lights to the brightness of a moonlit night, they almost always got *increases* in productivity. (See Figure 1.1.) Something that couldn't be accounted for in terms of their scientific measurements was taking place.

Paying attention to worker needs seemed to affect work output.

After considerable analysis, the researchers determined that the very fact that *the workers were being observed* by the research team seemed to affect their output. The workers enjoyed being the center of the research team's attention and responded by producing more. What resulted is now known as the

FIGURE 1.1 The results of the Hawthorne Studies, in which researchers measured the brightness of light (illumination) in relation to worker performance (productivity).

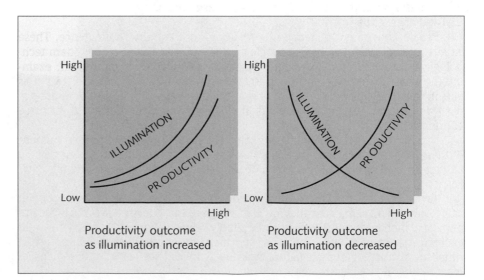

Productivity outcome as illumination increased

Productivity outcome as illumination decreased

Source: DILBERT reprinted by permission of United Features Syndicate, Inc.

Hawthorne effect, a situation created when managers or researchers pay special attention to workers that seems to result in improved worker output. But from a scientific management perspective, paying attention to people shouldn't have caused them to work better. After all, they weren't being *paid* any more money! Other forces must have been at work.

Mayo and his group hypothesized that the increased production resulted from changed social situations of the workers (they received more attention), modifications in worker motivation and satisfaction, and altered patterns of supervision. Social and psychological factors were seen as playing a major role in determining worker satisfaction and productivity.

Over the next decades, many other researchers studied the human relations approach. There emerged a genuine sense of "industrial humanism." Managers became increasingly aware of the importance of designing the work environment to reinforce workers' dignity. The human relationist soon concluded that most people were working for more than just money; other things motivated them.

Over the years, much research has focused on human behavior in the workplace. Among the findings of these studies are the following:

- Individuals are motivated by a wide variety of social and psychological factors, not just earnings.

- Worker behavior is affected by feelings, sentiments, and attitudes. People, after all, are not machines.

Social and psychological factors were found to play an important role in determining worker satisfaction.

People are motivated by a variety of things, not just money.

- Informal workgroups play an important role in determining the attitudes and performance of individual workers.

- Leadership behaviors that overemphasize the power to command workers should be modified. Allow workers to participate in decisions.

- Worker satisfaction is associated with productivity; satisfied workers are likely to be more effective.

- Communication channels were recognized as being important. Information flows not only through the formal organizational structure, but also in many informal ways.

- Worker participation in decision making is important to healthy organizations.

- Management requires effective social skills as well as technical skills; it is both an art and a science.

The Behavioral Movement Takes Management by Storm

By the 1950s and 1960s, behavioral scientists were busily conducting research and training programs in all types of businesses. Many of these researchers moved into business colleges and began teaching others their methods. Not since Taylor at the turn of the century has a new approach to study had such an effect on management. Some of the major impacts of the human relations approach on management are as follows:[6]

- The role of the manager became much more people oriented.

- Considering management as the problem in workers' lack of productivity opened up the whole question of incentives and source of motivation.

- Skills of supervision were expanded to encompass the ability to communicate, develop an understanding of others, and be effective in gaining cooperation.

- In organization structure, there was less emphasis on authority and a move toward power equalization.

- Leadership styles played down autocratic behavior and emphasized participation and freedom for subordinates.

- Organizations were viewed as social systems in which the informal relationships that emerged within the group were often more compelling than the formal rules of the company.

- The goal of the firm was viewed no longer as exclusively that of profit or efficiency. Fostering social goals became part of the measure of performance.

- The supervisor's role was not just to monitor operations but also to manage conflict and change.

Critics of Human Relations

Some critics labeled human relationists as "happiness boys" or "cow sociologists."

Despite the fact that the human relations approach to management has had a major impact upon management thought, there have been criticisms of it. Some people have called human relationists the "happiness boys" and criticized them for being so concerned with making contented workers than with emphasizing the importance of productivity. Also disparagingly referred to as "cow sociologists," human relationists are accused of wanting only to produce "contented cows," not productive workers. Others have criticized the movement for using certain human relations techniques, such as worker participation, to manipulate workers.

It would be unfair to end this discussion of the human relations school on such a negative note. Much of what we have learned—and continue to learn—through this approach has proved valuable to the study of people at work. Indeed, many chapters in this book will deal with principles learned through the research of human relationists that has been conducted in the last half century.

Where Management Theory Stands Today

Management thinking continues to evolve, of course. We will never reach a single ultimate theory to explain and predict all that managers would like to know. Recent trends have evolved into what might be called integrative approaches—theories that combine the best of what is known to try to cope with management challenges in today's world. These approaches recognize that our world is constantly and rapidly changing and that we are all more interdependent—dependent upon each other—than ever before.

> Modern management theory recognizes that our world is constantly changing and requires a combination of approaches to cope with management challenges.

The Systems Theory Approach

In the 1960s, a general **systems theory** emerged from a convergence of many sciences. A basic assumption was that nothing in nature exists in a vacuum—everything is interrelated with everything else at some point. *Systems* emerge from this interconnectedness. Every system has:

- Input
- Transformation
- Output

Any action taken affecting one system must have **ripple effects** on other systems.

For instance, the study of ecology uses systems theory to show interrelatedness. In the early 1970s, ecologists were successful in obtaining a ban on certain aerosol sprays because of the damage to the earth's ozone layer allegedly caused by fluorocarbon propellants. Many people were amazed that chemicals released by their underarm spray deodorants (input) could destroy the ozone (transformation), thus allowing more rays of the sun to penetrate the earth and perhaps cause additional skin cancer in people (output). The ecologists used a systems approach to explain interrelatedness in ways people never dreamed of.

Let's try another example. Suppose you set up a business to manufacture waterbeds. Your simplified organizational system might include the system shown in Figure 1.2 on page 12.

Systems theory holds, however, that such a description is grossly oversimplified and that managers must be able to account for interrelationships. What affects part of the system (i.e., a shortage of one raw material, a serious argument among workers, or a weakened market for finished products) affects the entire system and all interconnected systems.

Let's think for a moment about what we might learn about people at work from such a point of view:

- Mistreating one employee may result in "ripple effects" throughout the workforce. Supervisor-worker relationships are not isolated, one-on-one interactions.

FIGURE 1.2 A systems view of a waterbed manufacturer.

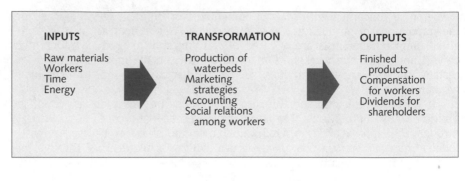

- A new business opening nearby may hire away your best workers unless something is done to retain them.

- Government regulations, enforced by agencies that are systems in themselves, can affect input, transformation, and/or output of your system.

- Organizations have multiple purposes, objectives, and functions, some of which will naturally be in conflict. Supervisors need to strive for a balance among the competing wants of subgroups.

Systems theory provides a more broad-based view of the management process than does a scientific or human relations approach taken alone. However, it has not yet produced as many specific techniques for managing people as have the scientific management (time studies, work measurement) and human relations (participation in decisions) approaches.

The Contingency Approach

Management theorists have been unable to agree upon one broad theory to unite the field—one approach that would be useful in all circumstances. This attempt may be an offshoot of Taylor's implicit belief that there is one best way.

The role of a manager in **contingency** or **situational theory** is different. This **contingency approach** accepts the idea that there is a need for, as the cliché goes, "different strokes for different folks." For example, the manager's job is like a golfer's. He or she faces two tasks: (1) determining where he or she is on the course in relation to the green, and (2) deciding what club to use to get the best results. Where you are and the tools you have available determine what must be done in that particular situation. There is no "one best way" applicable for all circumstances. Flexibility is called for in adjusting to changing conditions.

The primary emphasis of this approach is recognizing that no two situations are exactly alike since the world is in constant flux, and that different management actions are often called for in different situations; there are no easy answers applicable to any and all situations. We'll talk more about a contingency approach to leadership in Chapter 9.

The Quality of Work Life Approach

First introduced in the late 1960s, the **quality of work life (QWL)** concept refers to the degree to which work should provide opportunities to satisfy a wide variety of workers' needs.

The QWL approach seeks to make participation in work activities both gratifying and productive. Instead of breaking jobs down into mindless, repetitive tasks, advocates of QWL suggest redesigning workers' jobs so that they can complete a whole unit of work (such as assembling a whole product) instead of just

Contingency approaches stress the need to use different techniques in different situations.

performing isolated tasks, such as attaching one part of an assembly. Much more satisfaction arises from completing a whole job. Pilot programs in auto manufacturing plants showed impressive reductions in absenteeism and quality defects, and in other indicators of dissatisfaction when workers' jobs were redesigned in such ways.

One successful approach to redesigning jobs and improving the quality of work life has been the **quality circle.** This method uses employee participation to determine how jobs should be redesigned for the best results.

A quality circle is a group of eight to ten people who meet periodically (often once a week) to spot and solve problems in their work area. The idea of using small groups of workers to solve work-related problems was popularized by U.S. management consultants and then adopted by the Japanese after World War II. U.S. companies, stunned by dwindling productivity, then borrowed the idea back from the Japanese, who believe that such groups are partly responsible for their spectacular productivity gains since the war.

A quality circle selects and analyzes a problem, develops a solution, and presents its findings to management, which generally accepts the group's recommendations.

Based on the findings to date, quality circles appear to be quite successful, according to both management and labor.

The workers themselves (1) often share in any cost savings (some companies, for example, paid circle members approximately 10 percent of any cost savings), and (2) get a feeling of accomplishment from tackling a challenging task; therefore, they too benefit from the quality circles. On the whole, the circle idea appears to be an effective one for harnessing the performance-stimulating potential in a workgroup.

The Use of Self-Directed Workgroups

Self-directed workgroups (SDWs) have evolved from the idea of quality circles. In quality circles, employees are well trained in teamwork and problem solving, but they often have little power beyond calling attention to problems or suggesting ideas for change. SDWs go far beyond quality circles. As part of a SDW, employees are trained to use their skills daily to schedule, assign tasks, coordinate with other groups (and sometimes customers and suppliers), set goals, evaluate performance, and address discipline issues. Project management and participative management are SDW cousins, as each emphasizes sharing tasks and teamwork. SDW members contract to learn and share jobs usually performed by a manager. They do indeed self-manage.

The use of SDWs is based in the following beliefs:[7]

- *Employees are an organization's greatest resource.* Increasingly, organizations are giving employees more ownership and autonomy. They find that employees work harder and need less hand-holding when they have more control over their jobs and more freedom to choose how they will do them. Recent statistics indicate that organizations that encourage employee involvement are increasing productivity by 30 percent or more. Workers who participate in self-directed workgroups (self-managing teams) report higher motivation, increased self-worth, and greater pride in their work.

- *SDWs "self-correct" quickly.* Forward-looking organizations emphasize quality and excellence. They need skilled people who can perform several tasks and respond quickly to changes. SDW members are trained to "self-correct." In other words, they identify problems and correct them quickly. As organizations eliminate layers of management and staff to increase cost effectiveness and improve communication, SDWs are replacing managers by doing the job themselves.

- *SDWs provide today's workforce with a means of self-expression.* Intelligent people want psychological enrichment and control of their lives. One common complaint among employees is that they are frustrated in achieving organizational needs because management erects too many barriers. SDWs provide opportunities for people to be proactive and take responsibility for their actions. They are a logical way to group people who want to remain in an organization but value working creatively. As organizations struggle with the problem of too few people in the workforce, SDWs are serving as training grounds for learning multiple tasks.

The Bottom Line in Human Relations Today: Caring and Trust

As we move into the twenty-first century, a review of current problems in both public and private organizations reveals that there is an imperative need to continue to increase our understanding—and application—of the principles of human relations.

Some indicators suggest, however, that there is a reduced interest in other people; a self-centered attitude that disdains the need for cooperative interaction among people. In his well-known book on higher education, *The Closing of the American Mind,* Allan Bloom concludes that "students these days are pleasant, friendly, and, if not great-souled, at least not particularly mean-spirited. *Their primary preoccupation is themselves, understood in the narrowest sense* [italics added]."[8]

Virtually every book written about management success stresses the importance of good relationships among employees, managers, customers, and other stakeholders (others interested in the success of the company). The number-crunching, coldly analytical manager is inappropriate for today's organizations. Companies need people who care.

A sense of caring is the foundation of human relations success.

Indeed, it is the sense of **caring** about others that forms the foundation of human relations and organizational success. Buck Rodgers, former vice-president of marketing for IBM Corporation, describes this as "the glue that binds." He states that "the important thing [for effective organizations] is to get all your people, particularly the behind-the-scene ones, involved in working with the customer and developing a partnership relationship."[9]

A Working Description of Human Relations

When relationships are healthy, open, fun, and mutually rewarding, they enhance our lives.

So, what is this field of human relations in organizations? A sterile definition would satisfy few people, but some common characteristics are generally agreed upon.

First, human relations is a body of study that has deep roots. The need to increase cooperation among individuals has been present ever since the first human sought to do a job that was too big to do alone.

Second, human behavior in organizations has emerged as critical to success. People at work are not like machines with interchangeable parts. Factors other than the laws of physics are at work here.

Third, we now see human relations as an ever-evolving field of study involving virtually all aspects of human behavior as well as a few key *attitudes* that seem to relate to behaviors such as job satisfaction, morale, and organizational culture.

Source: DILBERT reprinted by permission of United Features Syndicate, Inc.

Finally, the root values underlying the study of human relations are *caring* and *trust*. The self-centered person will never master human relations. The successful manager knows that we win by helping other people win. We get what we want by showing others how to get what they want. All humanity is a part of a larger whole. And trust, cooperation, and mutual caring are critical elements in all success.

Ultimately, the relationships we create and maintain with others, whether at work or in our personal lives, are the treasures of our lives, the jewels of living. As Elwood Chapman says, "When relationships are healthy, open, fun, and mutually rewarding, they can enrich your life far beyond material possessions. Good relationships will sustain you in hard times."

Chapman goes on to caution that "interpersonal human dealings are fragile and demand tender loving care. Even when they seem strong, they can never be taken for granted. Those who become skillful at creating and maintaining ongoing positive relationships enjoy more successful careers and happier personal lives."[10]

People at Work can help you become human-relations-smart. We encourage you to undertake the journey with an open mind and a happy heart. We think you'll enjoy the experience.

Relationships we create with others are the treasures of life.

Summary of Key Ideas

- Managers often describe people problems as their most frequent and challenging difficulties.

- Understanding human behavior in organizations is central to the success of any cooperative effort.

- People consistently describe the best workplaces as those where people are valued and cared about, as manifest through such things as employee participation, sensitivity to work/family concerns, good two-way communication, and fun. These all relate to the human side of businesses.

- An organization's personality—its culture—is shaped by its policies and behaviors in human relations.

- Even with increasing emphasis on technology, the importance of understanding human behavior has never diminished.

- People in organizations were not always valued as much as they are today. The scientific management approach, for example, tended to take a rational, analytical look at industry. People were seen as physical parts of the overall machinery.

- Elton Mayo's Hawthorne experiments revealed the importance of understanding the human element in a broader sense: socially, psychologically, and physically.

- Modern management approaches, such as QWL and self-managing teams, require ever-increasing human relations skills.

- On a personal level, human relations skills can make the difference between success and failure in all we do.

- The object of this book is to help make you human-relations-smart.

- The underlying value in human relations is a sense of caring about others. Self-centered people find it more difficult to become human-relations-smart.

Key Terms, Concepts, and Names

Caring	Elton Mayo	Scientific management
Contingency approach	Quality circles	Self-directed workgroup
Hawthorne experiments	Quality of work life (QWL)	(SDW)
Human-relations-smart	Ripple effects	Systems theory
Machiavellian		

Notes

1. Steven Robbins, *Essentials of Organizational Behavior,* 5th ed. (Upper Saddle River, NJ: Prentice-Hall, Inc., 1997), p.1.

2. January 12, 1998, pp. 72–74.

3. Robert Levering and Milton Moskowitz, *The 100 Best Companies to Work for in America* (New York: Plume, 1996), pp. xiv–xv.

4. Linda Grant, "Happy Workers, High Returns," *Fortune* January 12, 1998, p. 81.

5. Robbins, p. 2.

6. Adapted from Howard M. Carlisle, *Management Essentials* (Chicago: Science Research Associates, 1989).

7. Robert F. Hicks and Diane Bone, *Self-Management Teams* (Los Altos, CA: Crisp Publications, 1990), p.5.

8. Allan Bloom, *The Closing of the American Mind* (New York: Simon and Schuster, 1987), p. 83.

9. Buck Rodgers, *The IBM Way* (New York: Harper & Row, 1986), p. 58.

10. Elwood N. Chapman, *Winning at Human Relations* (Los Altos, CA: Crisp Publications, 1989), p. 3.

Another Look: Why Employees Love These Companies

It isn't complicated: We found that most of the raves workers give their employers are based on just three corporate traits. For many companies they're within reach.

By now, most of us have been schooled to believe we'll spend the rest of our careers jumping from job to job, working ever harder to prove our mettle to cranky bosses, and getting promoted much less often than our predecessors. We've been told over and over that this Darwinian odyssey is the new workplace reality, bleak though it may be. Yet the cheerful employees of our 100 Best companies face a far different, far more benign daily work life. These workers sing their employers' praises and—though it's very un-'90s— even declare pride in their corporate affiliation.

Why? What makes employees not just like but love these companies? We looked hard and found three recurring traits that seem to explain a lot. The great majority of our 100 Best have at least one, and many have all three. The good news is, they're within the reach of just about any employer.

First, many of our 100 Best are run by a powerful, visionary leader. Superstar CEOs like Bill Gates of Microsoft, Andy Grove of Intel, and Larry Bossidy of AlliedSignal are among the most demanding bosses in business, yet workers seem to feel inspired rather than oppressed by them, non-celebrities running many lesser-known companies have the same effect. Second, many of these companies offer a physical work environment that employees adore. Third, these companies often frame their work as part of a deep, rewarding purpose that employees find fulfilling. Here's a closer look at how a few companies on our list wow their workers.

Inspiring Leadership

Exhibit A is Herb Kelleher, the Southwest Airlines CEO perched at the pinnacle of our 100 Best list. He spends his business life making sure his employees believe in him and in the operation he has muscled into the top tier of a savagely competitive industry. He smokes, he arm-wrestles, he drinks large quantities of Wild Turkey, he raps in music videos—and it is only slight hyperbole to say nearly all his employees worship the ground he walks on. But even he can't match the act of devotion displayed for Dave Duffield, the

"This is a company that understands that positive emotions can be good for the soul."
—Gloria Mayfield Banks, senior sales director, Mary Kay

founder and CEO of PeopleSoft, the software maker in Pleasanton, Calif. A few years ago employees formed a garage band and decided to call it The Raving Daves.

Remarkably, the well-worn story of Mary Kay Ash also retains its power to inspire. Those who know her well—and almost all who work for Mary Kay Inc. seem to think they do—describe her as a sort of corporate Everywoman: Pushed aside by her male superiors as a saleswoman in the 1950s, she quit her job and built a sales organization intended to empower other women.

Mary Kay's saga of how she grew her business and made a fortune is the chief inspiration for many of the 475,000 women who sell her products. "I was a secretary. I was not voted most likely to succeed in high school," says Lisa Madson, 37, who started selling for the company 11 years ago. "But she reaches so many people by talking about the potential that everyone has inside. And she's the living example."

Though Mary Kay herself is a millionaire many times over, the people who work for her marvel at her ability to remain accessible. Before she suffered a stroke in 1996, she used to invite employees to her home for tea several times a year. "I've sat on her

continued

Why Employees Love These Companies, *continued*

bed and had cookies at her table," says Gloria Mayfield Banks, 41, an executive senior sales director based in Baltimore. "It takes away the mystery when someone totally opens herself up to you like that."

The effective leader inspires employees not just to work hard and succeed but also to become miniversions of the leader. That seems to be happening at Mary Kay. "People understand that for Mary Kay, it was all about fulfilling a mission that was bigger than just her," say Janice Bird, 42, who works at corporate headquarters in Dallas. "They've increased their own self-esteem by being around her, and they want to pass that on to others the same way she did."

Knockout facilities

These may be the most persuasive way to tell employees they're valued. Top management at USAA, the San Antonio-based insurance and financial services company, demonstrates the value of wooing employees with an impressive corporate compound. "Anywhere you go in town, if you tell someone you work for USAA, they're impressed," says Jeannette Leal, a service adviser in the life/annuity service and claims department. "You become a part of this place, and it becomes everything that you're about."

The amenities begin with an on-site child care center. The facility can handle 300 kids, and there's car-seat storage for families where the mom drops off and the dad picks up. In Tampa, where the company also has a large presence, they've even thought to add industrial-strength fencing around the kiddie playground in case marauding alligators show up in search of snacks. "My wife and I visited ten or 12 day-care facilities all over town," says Raul Nevarez, 30, a USAA security officer. "There was no competition at all."

If you don't want to drive to work, the company sponsors a van pool. If you ruin your hose, you can pick up a pair at the on-site store. There's a dry-cleaning service, a bank, and several ATMs. Even the cafeteria food is tasty enough that, several years ago, employees began demanding dinner to go. At Thanksgiving they purchased 5,620 pies and 188 turkeys to take home to their families.

Then there are the athletic facilities. The three gyms are indistinguishable from those at many upscale health clubs, and one is open all night long.

Outside, employees compete in intramural leagues on basketball and tennis courts and softball and soccer fields. If you want to work on your backswing at lunch, there's a driving range too.

USAA employees clearly enjoy these breaks from their desks during the work-week, but they often return to the campus on the weekend with their families. "I enjoy bringing my kids here," say Donna Castillo, 34, a sales manager in consumer finance and auto service. "There are playgrounds where they can run around, and it's nice to take pictures of them here when the bluebonnets come out in the spring."

Amenities like these cost a company a lot, but they buy a lot too. "The facilities say that the company cares about us, that we're a valued asset," says security guard Nevarez. "People are dying to get in here. I have to go direct traffic when the parking lot at the employment center overflows. It makes me feel really good that I work for a company that is sought out like that, but it also means that I have to produce in order to earn the right to stay."

A Sense of Purpose

What sort of mission turns employees on? Well, it's not shareholder value, that's for sure. "I always try to make this very clear to analysts who cover our com-

continued

"I'm absolutely tied to my benefits here, and I also feel that what I'm doing is good in some larger sense."
—Lisa Shaw, body-care buyer, Whole Foods Market

Why Employees Love These Companies, *continued*

----

pany," says Bill George, 55, CEO of Medtronic, a medical-products company in Minneapolis. "Shareholder value is a hollow notion as the sole source of employee motivation."

Most of those analysts love Medtronic anyway, largely because its employees turn out so many great new gizmos that a full 50% of revenues come from products introduced in the past 12 months. Shareholder value? The company's total return to shareholders has averaged about 34% annually over the past decade. But that isn't what gets workers out of bed and into a lab coat in the morning. Rather it's the notion of helping sick people get well. Instead of concentrating on shareholders or doctors, workers at Medtronic concentrate on the people who will have the company's products implanted inside them.

This is hardly a new approach for companies in the health and medical industries. Employees at Merck, a perennial all-star in surveys of worker satisfaction, have long since memorized the mantra that the medicine is for patients, not profits. Medtronic finds novel ways to teach similar lessons, embodied in the company motto, "Restoring patients to full life." Its symbol is an image of a supine human rising toward upright wellness.

The resurrection imagery comes to life each December at the company's holiday party, where patients, their families, and their doctors are flown in to tell their survival stories. It sounds like the stuff of a made-for-TV tearjerker, but this is not PR gimmickry; journalists are generally not invited. Instead, it's the employees who are moved to tears year after year. "I remember going to my first holiday party, and someone asked me if I had brought my Kleenex," recalls Medtronic President Art Collins, 50, a strapping guy with a firm handshake who is generally not prone to crying fits. "I assumed I'd be fine, but then these parents got up with their daughter who was alive because of our product. Even the surgeons who see this stuff all the time were crying."

Improving human health, though in a much different way, was the deep purpose motivating John Mackey, 44, when he helped start Whole Foods Market, a chain of natural-foods grocery stores. That clearly stated mission has helped him draw motivated employees who are more educated than the average grocery worker. Take Lisa Shaw, 30, a Wellesley College graduate who works in Brighton, Mass., for one

of the company's Bread & Circus stores. "I remember going to a wedding after I graduated and seeing the looks on people's faces when I told them what I was doing, " she recalls. "I just hang on to the fact that my job is good in some larger sense. If people buy the sprouts, they're eating healthier foods, the farmer is doing well, and it's good for the planet because they're grown organically."

Such high-minded talk makes it tempting to dismiss Whole Foods employees as a bunch of hippies running an overgrown cooperative. But Whole Foods is a public company whose margins are roughly 50% higher than the average grocery chain's; its total return to stockholders over the past five years has averaged about 23% annually. And the people who work there make explicit connections between the company's financial success and its larger goals. "We're going to pass a billion dollars in sales this year," says Linda Fontaine, 38, the national tax coordinator at corporate headquarters. "All that means is that we've just made that much more of a difference in the world."

Blissed-out employees working in the best of economic times are fairly easy to please, of course. A better test of worker resolve comes when a company slams up against a serious crunch. TDIndustries, a specialty construction and service-repair business in Dallas, fell on hard times when building in that area practically stopped at the end of the 1980s. The company's bank had failed, and private investors wouldn't touch the place. So in 1989 CEO Jack Lowe took the problem to employees, who decided to terminate their overfunded pension plan. They could have put the $4 million thus liberated directly into their IRAs, but instead many of them elected to bet their retirement money on Lowe's bailout plan. All told, TDI employees put about $1.25 million back in the company in return for shares in an ESOP account.

A risky investment? Absolutely—but the value of those shares has more than doubled since then. Besides, it wasn't the money that people were worried about anyway. "Sure, we were fixing to lose a lot of our retirement funds if the company failed," says senior project manager Laura Price. "But the real fear was of having to go work for someone else."

Source: Ronald B. Lieber, "Why Employees Love These Companies," pp. 72–74. Reprinted from the January 12, 1998 issue of FORTUNE by special permission; copyright 1998, Time Inc.

Another Look: Make Work Fun

Geoffrey James's book *Business Wisdom of the Electronic Elite* looks at strategies used by top high-tech companies such as Microsoft, Compaq, Sun, Hewlett-Packard, and others. One section deals with how these kinds of companies seek to create a sense of community for their workers. One way they do this is by making work more fun.

Electronic Elite companies use direct communications and social interaction to create a feeling of community. But there's another element to community building that's very much a part of the world of the Electronic Elite—a sense of fun.

One company that carries this sense of fun to a delightful extreme is Sun Microsystems. In addition to Sun's sponsorship of sports activities, Sun has a tradition of April Fool's jokes, generally played by employees on their managers. For example, one manager at Sun discovered a replica of his office submerged in the bottom of an aquarium full of sharks.

One of the cofounders, Bill Joy, found his Ferrari parked in a shallow pond, replete with a bumper sticker reading "I brake for flamingos." Even CEO Scott McNealy isn't sacrosanct. He arrive one April Fool's morning to discover that his office had been turned into a one-hole, par-four miniature golf course.

What's important here isn't the silliness of the pranks, but the underlying cultural values that make these pranks acceptable. Because Electronic Elite organizations truly believe that work is supposed to be fun, they find occasions to make it so. It's also significant that the executives are the butt of the jokes. Can you imagine Andrew Carnegie, or General Electric CEO Jack Welsh for that matter, thinking it was not only funny, but appropriate, for their employees to turn a CEO's personal office into a golf course?

Source: Geoffrey James, *Business Wisdom of the Electronic Elite* (New York: Random House, 1996) pp. 70–1.

PART 2

PEOPLE

Human Perception and Human Relations

- What is human perception?

- What is the impact of human perception on people relationships?

- How does the perception/truth fallacy cause problems in human relations?

- What is perceptual expectancy?

- Why do fellow employees see the same situation in different ways?

- How can we help ourselves avoid the pitfalls of seeing situations inaccurately?

- How can awareness of differences in interpretation help us be more effective in dealing with others?

The answers to these and other questions are coming up next in Chapter 2 . . .

Why Study Human Perception?

Human perception is one of the most complex issues workers must address. What we see reflects our experiences, our expectations, and our interests. No two people see objects or ideas in exactly the same way. We perceive—that is, we make sense out of things—according to our own points of view. These different points of view can often cause trouble in human relations.

The purpose of this chapter is twofold: (1) to help us be more aware of the problems associated with the unique ways we each see the world, and (2) to helps us effectively deal with such problems. It is hoped that we will be better employees and more efficient members of society by becoming aware of such differences.

This chapter will help us understand an intangible and ambiguous human experience: perception.

The Perception/Truth Fallacy

Perception is the process of becoming aware of objects and other data through the medium of the senses. It is from our perceptions that we gain knowledge. The quality of that knowledge varies with the accuracy of our perceptions.

People have a strong tendency to believe that the way they see the world is closer to "the truth" than the way others see it. We tend to assume that people who see things differently from the way we do are wrong. This **assumption** leads frequently to misunderstandings and occasionally to major conflicts. One rule to keep in mind when dealing with people is this: *Do not accept all situations at their face value. The truth and what we see may not be the same.*

"We usually see only the things we are looking for—so much that we sometimes see them where they are not."

Eric Hoffer

Avoid assuming that you always see things accurately while others are more often wrong. The problem is that the things or events we perceive—accurately or not—become reality for us. We then act on these "truths" as we deal with other people.

Here's an example. Suppose you walk into the machine shop of a small company. Three people are there. One person is sitting next to a machine, leaning against the wall. Another is fixing a child's bicycle. The third person is talking on the phone to someone he addresses as "Honey." It is 9:30 A.M. on a Tuesday. What do your immediate impressions lead you to believe?

"A bunch of goof-offs," you say. "I'll bet their supervisor is away. I'd probably fire them if they worked for me!"

Misperceptions can lead to big mistakes.

Perhaps your perceptions are accurate. But if you act on this picture of "reality" without further investigation, you could be making a big mistake.

Here is what was really happening in that machine shop. The first employee had worked all night to get out a rush order. He hadn't slept in over 26 hours, and he was taking a 15 minute break. The second worker was taking time on her day off to work on the company-sponsored "Toys for Poor Kids" Christmas project. The man on the phone had also been at work through the night. This was the first chance he'd had to call his wife to see how their sick 4-year-old daughter was responding to new medications.

Does that change your perceptions of this scene a bit? What might have happened if you had just been appointed as a new supervisor and you'd ordered everyone "back to work"?

The point is this: *Don't take initial perceptions at face value.* Get as much information as possible before you firm up perceptions into opinions that influence your actions. A good way to avoid such misperceptions is to better understand how the perception process works. We'll examine this more closely in this chapter.

ACTIVITIES

YOUR POINT OF VIEW AFFECTS YOUR REACTION

How do you react to some everyday situations? How intense are your feelings about some typical events? Read each of the short incidents described below and select the word that best describes what your first reaction would be. Write the word in the space provided. You may use the same word more than once. Do not make an in-depth analysis of the situation; just read it quickly and give your first impression.

1. alarm	8. excitement	15. irritation
2. anger	9. fear	16. joy
3. concern	10. gladness	17. kindness
4. curiosity	11. gratitude	18. love
5. disapproval	12. happiness	19. resentment
6. disinterest	13. humiliation	20. sadness
7. envy	14. interest	21. worry

I.   While riding on the subway, you see a man with three small boys ranging in ages from about two to six. The boys run up and down the aisles, yelling and screaming. The father sits totally oblivious of the behavior of his kids.

_____

II. You are heading home after a hard day's work. You are passed on the freeway by a couple driving a car similar to yours. They are obviously close to each other; in fact, you worry that his hair tousling and her ear nibbling could cause an accident.

_____

III. While attending the company's family picnic, you overhear a child saying to his parent: "I hate you! You are so mean to me! I hate the way you treat me!"

_____

IV. At lunch time you decide to walk a few blocks for a quick sandwich. As you are crossing the street at a busy intersection, a car races through it, apparently trying to beat the red light. The car comes so close that you literally jump out of the way to avoid being hit.

_____

V.   You are on a committee for your service club to interview and select a citizen of the year. During the interview of candidates, you are informed that a real hero has been nominated and will arrive for an interview shortly. He saved a drowning child last summer and donated the reward money to create a CPR training program for youth leaders. He is kind and courteous.

_____

ACTIVITIES

Before considering your first responses, we'd like you to react to the incidents again, but from a slightly different point of view. Do the same as you did before: read the vignette and select the word that best describes your first response. Use the list of words below, writing the appropriate word in the space provided. Feel free to use the same words more than once.

1. alarm	8. excitement	15. irritation
2. anger	9. fear	16. joy
3. concern	10. gladness	17. kindness
4. curiosity	11. gratitude	18. love
5. disapproval	12. happiness	19. resentment
6. disinterest	13. humiliation	20. sadness
7. envy	14. interest	21. worry

I.   While riding on the subway, you see a man with three small boys ranging in ages from about two to six. The boys run up and down the aisles, yelling and screaming. The father sits totally oblivious of the behavior of his kids. They are on the way home from the hospital where his wife died after weeks of suffering from cancer.

_____

II. You are heading home after a hard day's work. You are passed on the freeway by a couple driving a car similar to yours. They are obviously close to each other; in fact, you worry that his hair tousling and her ear nibbling could cause an accident. The passenger is your spouse, and it is your car.

_____

III. While attending the company's family picnic, you overhear a child saying to his parent: "I hate you! You are so mean to me! I hate the way you treat me!" The child is your son, speaking to your spouse.

_____

IV. At lunch time you decide to walk a few blocks for a quick sandwich. As you are crossing the street at a busy intersection, a car races through it, apparently trying to beat the red light. The car comes so close that you literally jump out of the way to avoid being hit. The driver is your 80-year-old mother, who recently had an eye operation.

_____

V.   You are on a committee for your service club to interview and select a citizen of the year. During the interview of candidates, you are informed that a real hero has been nominated and will arrive for an interview shortly. He saved a drowning child last summer and donated the reward money to create a CPR training program for youth leaders. He is kind and courteous, but he was accused of sexually molesting your child, although evidence at the trial was insufficient to convict him.

_____

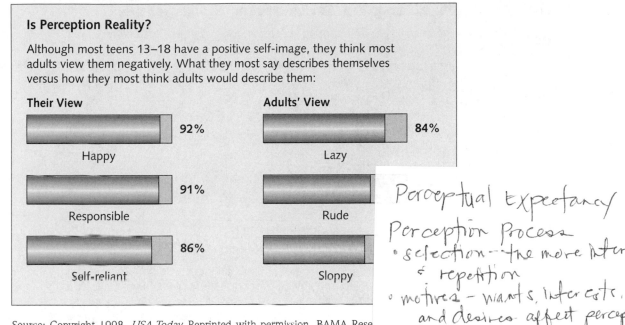

Is Perception Reality?

Although most teens 13–18 have a positive self-image, they think most adults view them negatively. What they most say describes themselves versus how they most think adults would describe them:

Their View

Happy — 92%

Responsible — 91%

Self-reliant — 86%

Adults' View

Lazy — 84%

Rude

Sloppy

Source: Copyright 1998. *USA Today.* Reprinted with permission. BAMA Rese...

Handwritten note:
Perceptual expectancy
Perception Process
• selection — the more intense & repetition
○ motives — wants, interests, and desires affect perception
○ organization — smells context affects awareness
○ Interpretation — analyzing the data (headlights perception)

Perceptual Expectancy

Magicians use it to fool us. Teachers and other professional com... it to preview the message they'll give us. Advertisers use it to ... new-car showroom. What is "it"? It's **perceptual expectancy,** t... ipation so natural to our everyday actions. We constantly make ... about how people, events, or things will be. Sometimes we are right; other times we are wrong. Occasionally we are deliberately misled.

Perceptual expectations create a mindset in us that causes us to anticipate future behaviors or events. For example, the new manager in a clothing company was described to her employees as very energetic, very autocratic, out to make money, cold, and standoffish. As you may suspect, the people who were going to be managed by this person felt some anxiety. Their perceptual expectancy was that they were going to have a new leader who would be pretty difficult to work for.

But when she took over, her demeanor, behavior, and treatment of the employees were exactly the opposite of their expectations. The workers were at first a little uncomfortable. Their expectations were *not* being met. "When is she going to get mean?", they wondered.

After getting to know the "truth" about this manager, the workgroup became very close and the organization functioned well. Fortunately in this case the negative expectations evaporated as the workers got to know the *real* new manager. But in many circumstances where workers have strong expectations about a new boss, barriers to communication and relationships can be difficult to overcome. The organizations and the people involved suffer.

The expectancies we have as a result of our perceptions influence the way we get along with others and the way we respond to them. This is the problem we face with perception.

> Our mindset causes us to anticipate future behaviors or events.

A Simple Reading Exercise

The triangles below contain some common sayings. Read them aloud.

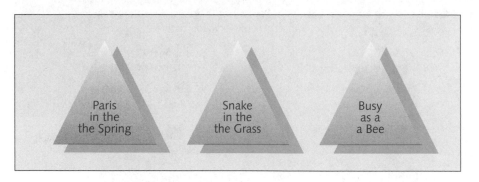

Now look at them carefully. In the first statement, you should have read, "Paris in *the the* spring." In the second statement, you should have read, "Snake in *the the* grass." In the third statement you should have read, "Busy as *a a* bee." If you did not read these statements accurately, you did not perceive the information correctly. If you misread the statements, your previous experience likely led you to expect to see only one *the* or *a.*

One way to reduce the number of mistaken perceptions is to become more aware of just how perception works.

Key Elements of the Perception Process

We said earlier that to perceive is to make sense out of things. Another way to describe perception is as a process of *attaching meaning to experience.* As we experience raw data through seeing, hearing, feeling, tasting, smelling, and the like, we mentally organize these sensations into something that has meaning for us.

Perception is the process of attaching meaning to sights, sounds, and other stimuli.

For example, let's say you are walking down a busy city sidewalk and see a crowd of people assembled near an intersection. As you get closer, you hear unusual sounds—the rhythm of steel drums. Eventually you assemble these sights and sounds and attach meaning: A street band is playing Jamaican music— an advertising gimmick for a travel agency.

First you pay attention to raw information: sights and sounds. Then you mentally organize these impressions into a meaningful event and label it "Jamaican street band." That's perception.

The perception process has four key elements: selection, motives, organization, and interpretation. Let's look at each of these.

Four key elements of the perception process are:

- **selection**
- **motives**
- **organization**
- **interpretation**

1. *Selection.*
   As we interact with people, we are constantly exposed to a barrage of meanings and innuendos. In fact, we become overexposed. We receive too much data to deal with. We select only key information from all the raw data. We select what seems important to us. Why do some messages seem more important than others? Intensity and repetition cause people to be attracted to some messages while they ignore others.

Intensity increases the probability of selection.

   The more *intense* a message, the higher the probability that we will attend to it. For example, at a cocktail party, the more boisterous and outgoing people have a greater probability of being heard. You may think a loud person is obnoxious or you may enjoy his or her antics, depending on your feelings toward the person. In either case,

(a)

(b)

(a) Which person is the tallest? What were your initial expectations?

(b) What do you see? A young woman? A grouchy old clown? Turn the book upside down and then respond again.

the probability is high that owing to the intensity of the person's actions, you will pay more attention to him or her.

People often pay more attention to an exceptionally tall or unusually short person than to a person of average size. Furthermore, the person with the loud Hawaiian shirt is difficult to forget—especially when the other partygoers are in business suits! Simply said, the intensity of the message in our environment has a direct impact on whether we perceive the message or not.

Repetition increases the chance of selection.

The rhythm of the steel drum music in the earlier example, as well as the unusually large number of people assembled, made you select this event for further investigation.

Just as people are attracted to a stimulus that is intense, they are also attracted to a stimulus *that is repetitious, that is repetitious, that is repetitious.* If we listen to a CD that skips, continuing to play the same message over and over again, we are very quickly attracted to the sound; we want to correct it before it drives us nuts!

Have you ever tried to block out of your mind the drip of a leaky faucet at night? Its maddening repetition holds your attention whether you want it to or not.

2. *Motives.*
Why do people do the things they do? We'll talk a lot more about this subject in the next five chapters. For now, it is enough to say that personal **motives**—wants, interests, and desires—affect perceptions.

Our motives can cause us to perceive one thing while ignoring others.

One young man had been driving across the country and was very hungry. On passing through a small town, he saw the sign over a Dairy Queen ice cream stand ahead. He drove up and jumped eagerly out of the car, only to discover that the sign actually said Dry Cleaner. His motive—to satisfy hunger—had led to a *mis*perception.

Similarly, if you had just been in a serious automobile accident, you would likely perceive the white-jacketed paramedic rushing to your aid as a fine person. Yet if you were not motivated by a need for medical help and you saw this same individual in a restaurant or shop, your perception might be totally different: "That person looks like a weirdo to me." Same person—different perceptions.

Our motives affect the ways we perceive.

3. *Organization.*
A perception is almost never of a single bit of raw data. Even the faucet dripping in the night is not taken alone. The *context* in which it

Perceptions make sense as we organize them.

occurs—late at night, you're trying to sleep, there are no other sounds in the house, you need to be alert in the morning for a big exam, and so on—adds to your awareness of the drip (and, in this case, the annoyance of it).

Likewise, the street band example begins to make sense as you put together in your mind the various perceptions: a large crowd, unusual music, and travel agency motive.

As we interact with people, we often organize our perceptions of them according to variables such as physical attractiveness, age, educational background, religion, and race. How much better might human relationships be if we did not organize people into groupings in this way? Once people are categorized in our minds, these perceptions can have wide-ranging effects on how we deal with people.

4. *Interpretation.*

Interpretation adds further meaning to perceptions.

Once we select and organize perceptions, we draw further conclusions about their meaning through **interpretation.**

Consider this example: A new and very attractive employee smiles at you. You are faced with the task of interpreting that smile. What does it mean? Is the smile out of politeness? Is it an indication of a romantic interest? Is it directed at the crazy sweatshirt you are wearing? Interpretation deals with the meaning you make of the smile.

Other Elements That Affect the Way We Interpret Situations

The following is adapted from *Looking Out/Looking In* by Ronald B. Adler and Neal Towne.[1]

- *Past Experience.*
  What meanings have similar events held? If you have been gouged by a landlord in the past, you might be skeptical about an apartment manager's assurances that careful housekeeping will ensure the refund of your cleaning deposit.

- *Assumptions about Human Behavior.*
  "Employees only do enough work to get by." "In spite of all their mistakes, our employees are doing the best they can." Beliefs such at these can shape the way a manager interprets an employee's actions.

Our moods—positive or negative—affect our interpretation of events.

Source: OVERBOARD reprinted by permission of United Features Syndicate, Inc.

- *Expectations.*
  Anticipation shapes interpretations. If you imagine your boss
  with your work, you will likely feel threatened by a request
  in my office Monday morning." However, if you imagine tha
  work is especially good, you weekend will probably be pleasa
  anticipate a great meeting with the boss.

- *Knowledge.*
  If you know that a friend has been jilted by a lover or had a
  ment with a friend, you will interpret his or her aloof behavi
  ently from the way you would if you were unaware of what
  pened. If you know that an instructor speaks sarcastically to a
  students, you will not be as likely to take his or her remarks

- *Personal Moods.*
  When you feel depressed or insecure, the world is a very diff
  than it is when you are confident. The same goes for happine
  ness, anger or bliss, or any other opposing moods.

Factors That Shade the Filters of Our Minds

In addition to the four key elements that affect perception (selection, motives, organization, and interpretation), other factors have also helped make us all unique individuals who perceive things differently. These personality influencers color the lenses of the "glasses" through which we see the world. Among them are heredity, environment, friendships and peers, and sensory organs.

Heredity

Heredity plays an important role in the way we see our world. We have little opportunity to choose our parents, our grandparents, or the families we come from. But our genes have a tremendous impact on whether we are able to see with 20/20 vision, for example, have hearing defects, are color blind, or are left- or right-handed.

It's hard to understand how the world looks to other people who have been endowed with different physical characteristics.

Environment

The **environment** in which people grow up directly affects how they see present situations. If you have grown up in a home where Mom and Dad are heavily involved in physical fitness and jogging, you are likely to see nonjoggers as people who do not care about their bodies and who tend to be overweight. If

A few other factors that influence our view of the world:

- Heredity
- Environment
- Friendships and peers
- Sensory organs

[handwritten margin notes:]
Affecting Perception
- Heredity
- Environment
- Friendships and Peers
- Sensory ~~Glans~~ Organs

In business, frequently we conform to an unwritten dress code.

you grew up in a small farming community, the way you see people who live in a large city is different from the way you see those who grew up as you did.

Some neighborhoods have a very pleasant feeling of community, of neighbors who care for each other. Some neighborhoods are marred by violent gangs, and people who live there constantly feel afraid to go outside. Our assumptions about people are likely to be very different depending on our home environment.

Friendships and Peers

People tend to see life in much the same way as their peers. In fact, a variety of studies have been done on the impact that peers have on their friends. The studies show that once a peer group has made a decision or taken a stand—even if that decision or stand is wrong—individual group members will frequently go along. This tendency to go along will depend on the strength of the group and the individual's desire to be a member of it.

Young people are particularly susceptible to **peer-group pressures.** Junior high schools are filled with kids who act, dress, and even think as they do primarily because of peer pressures.

Sensory Organs

Some people love the taste of liver, whereas others dislike it. Some enjoy the taste of wine or liquor, while others dislike it immensely. Taste buds affect perception. Likewise, a variety of smells affect us. A fragrance that is pleasant to one person may be unpleasant to another.

Smell, taste, tolerance for temperature changes, and tolerance for loud noises are examples of sensory differences. These too affect perceptions.

Our experience in teaching and training has taught us that the best way to help people deal with the problems of perception is to make them aware of the process and elements of perception. We hope that as you have read this chapter, you have had an opportunity to reflect on your own life and on the various problems that you have had in perceiving the environment in which you live and work.

A Summary: Six Blind Men and One Elephant

The well-known parable about six blind men who came to check out an elephant brings our discussion of perception to a close.

It was six men of Indostan
To learning much inclined,
Who went to see the elephant
Though all of them were blind
That each by observation
Might satisfy his mind.

The first approached the elephant,
And happening to fall
Against the broad and sturdy side,
At once began to bawl:
"Why, bless me! But the elephant
Is very like a wall!"

The second, feeling of the tusk,
Cried: "Ho! What have we here
So very round and smooth and sharp?
To me, 'tis very clear,
This wonder of an elephant
Is very like a spear!"

The third approached the animal,
And, happening to take
The squirming trunk within his hands
Thus boldly up he spake:
"I see," quoth he, "the elephant
Is very like a snake!"

The fourth reached out his eager hand
And felt about the knee:
"What most this wondrous beast is like
Is very plain," quoth he:
"'Tis clear enough the elephant
Is very like a tree!"

The fifth who chanced to touch the ear
Said: "E'en the blindest man
Can tell what this resembles most—
Deny the fact who can:
This marvel of an elephant
Is very like a fan!"

The sixth no sooner had begun
About the beast to grope
Than, seizing on the swinging tail
That fell within his scope,
"I see," quoth he, "the elephant
Is very like a rope!"

And so these men of Indostan
Disputed loud and long.
Each in his own opinion
Exceeding stiff and strong;
Though each was partly in the right,
And all were in the wrong.

JOHN G. SAXE

Summary of Key Ideas

- Our experiences, expectations, and interests influence what we see, and what we see may actually differ from the truth.

- Perceptual expectations occur when we see what we expect to see.

- The four key elements of the perceptual process include selection, motives, organization, and interpretation.

- Other elements that affect the way we interpret perceptions are experience, assumptions, expectations, knowledge, and personal moods.

- Factors that shade the filters of our minds are heredity, environment, friendships and peers, and sensory organs.

Key Terms, Concepts, and Names

Assumption   Peer-group pressures
Environment   Perception
Interpretation   Perception/truth fallacy
Knowledge   Perceptual expectancy
Motives   Selection
Organization

Questions and Exercises

1. Complete the following sequence; in other words, add the next letters to the sequence. Continue as far as you can.

   Z O T T F F S S E N __ __ __ __ __

   Do the same with the following sequences:

   S M T __ __ __ __

   J F M __ __ __ __ __ __ __ __ __

   Don't give up too quickly! Could you determine the sequences? If not, you may be having a perceptual problem. Your previous experience with words used in our instructions may have influenced your expectations. Or, your previous experience with letters in sequence might be messing you up. Look at the top of page 36 to see how to complete the exercise.

2. How do you see your instructor? Answer the following questions regarding your instructor and then check to see how accurate your perceptions are.

   a. Instructor's age?

   b. Instructor's marital status?

   c. What does the instructor do for a living?

   d. Instructor's political leanings?

   e. Instructor's educational background?

   f. Where was the instructor born?

   g. Instructor's favorite food?

    h. Instructor's favorite music?

    i. Instructor's favorite sport?

    j. Instructor's favorite novelist?

3. Explain how your heredity, sensory organs, and past experience may influence your perceptions toward the following:

Dogs	Auto mechanics	Snow
Company presidents	Middle-aged women	Textbook authors
Rhubarb	Hairdressers	Jogging
Retail clerks	Democratic Party leaders	Life
Advanced mathematics	Fashion designers	Death

4. Can you control your perceptions of events? Look at the figure below, and then answer the following questions:

    a. What do you see when you interpret the figure as a cooking utensil?

    Answer: _____

    b. What do you see when you interpret the figure as a weapon of war?

    Answer: _____

    c. What do you see when you interpret the figure as a person?

    Answer: _____

    d. What do you see when you interpret the figure as an animal?

    Answer: _____

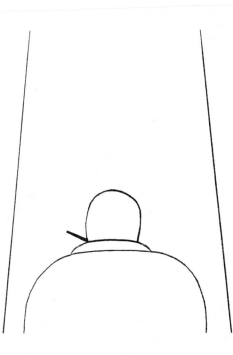

5. Answer the introductory questions at the beginning of the chapter.

Answers to Exercise 1:

Z O T T F F S S E N T E T T F:

Zero, One, Two, Three, Four, Five, Six, Seven, Eight, Nine, Ten, Eleven, Twelve, Thirteen, Fourteen

S M T W T F S:

Sunday, Monday, Tuesday, Wednesday, Thursday, Friday, Saturday

J F M A M J J A S O N D:

January, February, March, April, May, June, July, August, September, October, November, December

Notes

----

1.   Adapted from *Looking Out/Looking In,* 3d ed., by Ronald B. Adler and Neal Towne. Copyright © 1980 by Holt, Rinehart and Winston, Inc. Reprinted by permission of the publisher. For further ideas on how perception can affect work relationships, see Judith Jaffe, "Of Different Minds," *Association Management,* October 1985, pp. 120–24.

Another Look: On Recognition

I've been known to say, "I don't want any pats on the back—just put it in my check." Well, don't believe it. It's a crock! Regardless of how I may act, I do care a great deal what you and others think of me and what I do. Recognition *is* important to me. That's why I wear award pins, belt buckles, and the like; that's why I display trophies in my home; that's why I hang certificates on my wall.

Believe it or not, I'm looking for more from this job than just a paycheck. There's got to be more, 'cause I'm sure not gonna get rich on what I make! What *do* I want? I want to feel good about myself and the work I do; I want to feel like I really am an important part of this organization. And I tend to gauge my self-worth by others' perceptions . . . I often see myself through *your* eyes.

I fully realize that I don't do great work all the time. Some days I hit the bull's-eye, some days I'm in the outer rings, and once in a while, I miss the target altogether. I don't expect you to see me as a top-notch performer all of the time. But I do expect to be periodically recognized when I either go above and beyond the call of duty or just maintain good, solid performance over a long period of time. And the more you recognize my good work, the more good work I want to do. It's funny the way that works. I think it's all part of "human nature."

I know you're often so busy you probably don't think about recognizing me. And maybe you sometimes figure you don't get recognition yourself, so why should you give it to others? But if you'll just make a greater effort to let me know you appreciate me, I'll do my best to reciprocate. And I promise I won't complain about receiving too much praise!

Please understand how important this is to me. Walk awhile in *my* shoes.

Source: *Walk Awhile In My Shoes.* © Performance Systems Corporation, Dallas TX. Reprinted with permission. *www.walkthetalk.com*

Another Look: On How You Perceive Me

Someone once said, "If you want to be liked, don't become a boss." They were right! You just can't please everyone. If I've learned anything, it's that no matter what I do, inevitably somebody's gonna be chapped. That's a reality that comes with the job. I accept it. But there's another reality I'd like you to know about—a reality that comes with being human: I care what you and others think of me.

Do I sometimes *act* like I don't care? Sure! But with few exceptions, it's just that—an act. You see, convincing myself that I don't care (or at least trying to) gets me through difficult situations. It's what helps me follow through on what I believe to be right when the right thing is also the unpopular thing. If you're a parent, you undoubtedly understand what I'm saying.

I especially care what you think about me when it comes to honesty, integrity, and fairness. I'll bet you consider yourself a fair person. You probably take pride in that. Well, so do I. But occasionally I get a bum rap for being unfair in my dealings with employees. You hear one side of the story—without all the facts—and form an opinion about me. I know it and it bothers me, but I can't defend myself because the facts are usually confidential. So I take the rap . . . and pretend I don't care. But I do.

I fully understand that I must *earn* your trust and respect just as you must earn mine. And I'm working to do that. As I work on it, maybe you could give me the same benefit of the doubt that you would wish from me.

Before you judge me, try walking awhile in *my* shoes!

Source: *Walk Awhile In My Shoes.* © Performance Systems Corporation, Dallas TX. Reprinted with permission. *www.walkthetalk.com*

A Case in Point: "The New Consultant"

The following cartoon was used by a senior executive to introduce a newly hired team consultant to a group of middle managers in a large manufacturing company. The consultant had been hired to help develop stronger work teams in the company.

Questions

1. Generally, how will the middle managers respond to the new consultant?

2. What perceptions might the senior executive have regarding consultants?
3. What perceptions will the team consultant have of the senior executive?
4. Will all these perceptions influence the success of the consultant?
5. What perceptions might the cartoonist have of consultants?

Source: DILBERT reprinted by permission of United Features Syndicate, Inc.

A Case in Point: Lemkirk Trains New Employees

Harvey Lemkirk, a manufacturing plant foreman, was asked to teach a new employee how to run a machine. The new worker was a young man, a member of a minority race, who had been hired under a special program intended to train difficult-to-employ people.

Lemkirk, who did not sympathize with such special hiring programs, begrudgingly took the young man to the machine and instructed him how to run it: "Each time this metal part comes down this assembly line here, you pull it off, stick it under the press so that the edges line up here, and then push this foot pedal so the drill bit will come down and put the hole in the right place. Be careful to keep your hands away from the drill bit when you are doing it. Any moron should be able to do this. Got any questions?"

"No, sir," replied the new worker.

"Okay, then, go to it. And good luck. If you have any problems, let me know."

In the foreman's mind, there was little likelihood this employee would develop into a particularly effective worker. He had seen many minority employees hired under affirmative action who simply couldn't seem to cut it. And, frankly, he didn't understand exactly why it was like this. He treated them the same

as anyone else. In fact, he made it a point to use exactly the same language to explain this simple procedure to all new employees.

In a few days, Lemkirk's new employee fell seriously behind on both the quantity and quality of his work. Lemkirk was not surprised.

Let's look at how things worked for a second worker trained by Lemkirk:

The second new employee, a young man who Lemkirk seemed to think looked pretty sharp, was given essentially the same verbal instructions as the first worker. This new man, perhaps sensing that the foreman seemed to like him, took the "any moron should be able to do this" comment in stride and asked for a few clarifying pointers, which he got. Soon he was on his way to meeting his production quota just like the old pros who had been there for some time.

Questions

1. How did the perceptions of both Lemkirk and the first new employee influence the outcome of this situation?
2. How could either man change the situation?
3. How did perceptions affect the outcome for the second worker?
4. What perceptions were different?

Basic Principles of Human Needs and Motivation

- What is motivation and how can managers help people become and remain motivated?

- What does the organization achieve by getting its members to be motivated?

- What is motivation?

- What motivates *you?*

- Are there many different kinds of needs? Which ones motivate people best?

- How do people's expectations affect motivation?

- How does the hierarchy of needs affect the way people behave, according to Maslow?

- How effective is fear as a motivator in modern organizations?

- What are some harmful myths about the nature of motivation?

- What emerging motivators seem to be increasingly influential in today's organizations?

The answers to these and other questions are coming up next in Chapter 3 . . .

Some people have an oversimplified notion about what will motivate workers. They feel that by giving people extra wages, productivity will automatically increase. They are also convinced that paying special attention to workers will increase their motivation. Although any of these techniques may work in certain circumstances, none of them is a blanket solution.

In reality, motivation is a highly personal matter, and the influence a manager can have on someone else's motivation is quite limited. This chapter will explain some fundamentals of the motivating process.

Can you become an expert motivator?

Can a manager *really* bring about long-lasting motivation in workers? Before you answer yes, no, or maybe, take a careful look at the material in this chapter. You'll find a number of ideas about the nature of motivation and techniques for using the motives of others to get work done.

Can you become an expert motivator after reading this? Probably not. But you are likely to become more aware of what it takes to motivate. The best preparation for motivating others is like training in the art of painting: Get acquainted with the range of available techniques, train your judgment, experiment, and learn from the results.

Why Motivation Is the Manager's Challenge

One of the things that makes it so difficult for managers to instill **motivation** in others is the fact that *motivation itself is not visible or measurable.* What managers can see and measure is human *behavior* (productivity, quality of work, absenteeism, etc.). Motivation is a mental process. It is unique to every individual and extremely complex.

Whether or not motivation is taking place must be *inferred* from behaviors that are observed. Specifically, if you see a particular behavior taking place, you can make guesses about why the employee is acting that way.

Sometimes the relationship between the motivation and the behavior is pretty clear. For example, if you see a person leave the office and go to the company cafeteria for lunch (that's the behavior observed), you can assume that the person is motivated by hunger. Of course, you cannot see hunger, but you can see the behavior of getting some food. But even simple examples like this can be wrong. Maybe the worker goes to the cafeteria for social reasons—to talk with coworkers—even though he or she is not particularly hungry.

...es the motivation problem. Understanding the motivation of ... then doing something to affect that motivation are complicated ...at we cannot directly observe motivators. We can only observe ...rom that behavior presume what motivates it.

Handwritten notes in left margin:

The manager's Challenge:
- motivation itself is not visable or measurable.
- motivation is a mental process; it is unique to every individual and extremely complex.
- Behavior must be observed and interpreted.
- to understand what motives /needs are most likely to evoke productive behaviors in time.

nited Features Syndicate, Inc.

A Definition of Motivation

Motivation can be described as the need or drive *that incites a person to some action or behavior.* The verb *motivate* means to provide *reasons for action.* Motivation, then, provides a reason for exerting some sort of effort. This motivation springs forth from individual needs, wants, and drives. It provides a reason for behaving a certain way.

To motivate others involves a process of providing *motives for action.* Motivation, then, *provides a will to do or a reason for exerting some sort of effort.* This motivation springs from individual needs, wants, and drives.

We all constantly respond to needs, wants, and drives in our daily lives. When we first awake in the morning, we are likely to experience a need to satisfy hunger that has built up during the night. Most of us are motivated by wants such as career advancement, material goods, or pleasant relationships with others.

All *motivation, then, is directed toward some desired goal or reward.* We exert the effort to make breakfast because we anticipate the payoff: the satisfaction of our need for food. Likewise, we make certain efforts on the job because we anticipate the possibility of being rewarded with higher pay, status, praise, and the like. So, one key characteristic of motivation is that it is *goal oriented—focused on some desired end.*

Sometimes the desired payoff is the avoidance of something unple step outside for some fresh air to escape the stuffy office. Likewise, v motivated to seek a new job to reduce the stress we are experienc present one.

In this way, our motives show up in our behavior. That is, wh motivated, we *do* something that we might not do if we were not *Activity is the basic outcome of motivation.*

In this text, our focus is on **behaviorism**—an approach to psych assumes that observed behavior provides the only valid data of psych approach studies what people *do* and infers from those actions wl them to act that way.

Two Harmful Myths about Motivation

Two harmful myths about motivation are widely held:

1. that it can be gained from "motivational speakers," and

2. that it can be triggered simply with economic rewards.

Motivational speakers seldom if ever provide lasting motivation. A lot of advice is dispensed by motivational gurus about how to motivate employees and customers. Serious students of motivation recognize this as like worthless "snake oil" sold in a bottle. The value of pep talks (along with sales meetings, convention speeches, and posters or calendars with motivational messages) has been oversold. They may be entertaining and fun, but they are not permanently motivational. Lasting motivation comes from within the person.

Likewise, the notion that economic rewards necessarily trigger motivation is a gross oversimplification. According to this approach, all you have to do to get the behavior you want is to provide the right amount of money or other rewards. Economists assume that people act rationally in their own self-interest. However, as we all know, the perfectly rational human being does not exist. Each of us has a point after which extra money does not motivate us.

Dispelling these myths leads to an important lesson about motivation: motivation is not enthusiasm, and motivating a person only with money is not a guarantee of productivity. Lasting, persistent motivation comes from within; it is initiated and maintained by the self.

Motivation provides motives for action or reasons for exerting effort.

Motivation is directed toward some payoff.

What Managers Must Motivate People to Do

At the heart of any enterprise lies member motivation. To succeed, the organization, through its leaders, must help its people to be motivated to do the following:

1. Join and remain active in the group.

2. Produce dependable behavior—that which fulfills their designated roles and contributes to the planned, organizational tasks.

3. Innovate and adapt to changing organizational needs, going beyond their role requirements.

Creating conditions under which these kinds of behavior can flourish is the job of the effective manager. These conditions determine the extent to which motivation will occur.

Understanding the Nature of Motivation and Management

Understanding human motivation is a key to successful management.

Management is the process of getting productive work done with and through the efforts of other individuals. To do this effectively, the manager must answer this question: "What will motivate people to willingly work toward organizational goals?" The manager must predict, with reasonable accuracy, the kinds of behavior that result when different motivators are present. To make these predictions, the manager needs to understand what *motives* or *needs* are more likely to evoke productive behaviors in individuals at a particular *time*.

The better you understand motivation, the better you will be able to predict behavior accurately. You will come to know that when you as a manager do certain things, you might expect certain responses from the people you are managing.

Modern management approaches increasingly recognize that management is not *control* but *service.* The traditional management = control model implies that the real job of the manager is to control employee behavior. Employees who disagree with the manager and refuse to do something are "insubordinate" and dangerous.

Modern organizations, especially high-tech firms, have redefined the manager's job as one of service. With the **management as service** approach, a manager sets direction and obtains the resources employees need to get the job done. They *lead* but do not *run* the organization. Dissent is encouraged so long as it resolves itself with creative ideas.[1]

Emotions at the Root of Motivation

Human behavior is typically triggered by emotions. We do something because we feel an emotional catalyst. Three kinds of emotions can lead to ongoing behaviors or behavior changes:

1. Fear (we feel we *have to*)

2. Duty (we feel we *should*)

3. Desire (we feel we *want to*)

The motivation process is very complicated and unpredictable.

When motivated by fear, we behave because we *have* to. We are compelled to do something. Such motivation is short-lived.

When motivated by a sense of duty (or loyalty or obligation), we are responding because we *ought* to. For most people, this motivation is also rather short-lived.

When we respond to the emotion of desire, we act because we *want* to. This emotion provides for the strongest, most lasting motivation and behavior change—we do something because we truly love to do it.

What Motivation Is Not

We have discussed a number of things that motivation is. Now let's talk about some of the things it is not. We have already suggested *that motivation is not totally susceptible to outside control,* such as that exerted by an employee's supervisor. Motivation comes from within the individual. So the act of telling someone what to do or threatening someone is not, in itself, motivation.

Here are three more "nots" that apply to motivation:

1. *Motivation is not always based on conscious, "obvious" needs.* Some people are motivated by the darndest things! Although we managers may feel that we're providing ample rewards for employee behavior, in fact our efforts may not work. We cannot be sure that others will perceive the reward as worth the effort.

2. *We are sometimes motivated by forces we are not even aware of.* In recent years, there has been much concern about the ways some advertisers are using *subliminal* or subconscious appeals to get people to buy their products. Careful examination of magazine ads reveals sexual symbolism and suggestive illustrations designed to "grab" your unconscious mind, thus getting the sales message across.

   Sometimes people do not care to admit to subconscious motivations. A common example is the individual who has a low self-image and *prefers* to fail or do a poor job. By doing so, that individual reinforces his or her negative self-image. The effect is a somewhat perverse sense of satisfaction in realizing that "I was right all along about myself; I am a failure."

3. *Motivation is not the same as job satisfaction.* Some people are very satisfied on their jobs and yet are not motivated by the work. The manager who attempts to motivate employees by providing a more comfortable work environment, more friendly relationships, and even additional money may in fact be influencing **job satisfaction,** but not motivation. Employees may be satisfied but *not* motivated. Likewise, employees may be motivated but not satisfied. (This will be discussed further in Chapter 4.)

Motivation, then, is *not*:

1. totally susceptible to a supervisor's control, especially since it takes different things to motivate workers at different times;

2. always the same for all people; and

3. the same as job satisfaction.

One other "not" should be added to this list: *Motivation is not simple to understand or apply on the job.* It is far more complicated than it may appear at first glance. To use principles of motivation as a manager, one must become aware of some of the needs that motivate people at work.

The Best Indicators of Motivation

In most work situations, worker motivation (or lack of it) is expressed through behaviors, such as:

- Productivity—amount of work accomplished

- Quality of work

Motivation comes from within; it is not just telling someone what to do.

Why might some people prefer to fail?

TO BE RIGHT

High productivity and quality are good indicators of a motivated employee.

- Promptness
- Absenteeism
- Grievances expressed
- Accidents (as a result of carelessness)
- Turnover (number of workers quitting or fired)
- Agreement or disagreement among workers

Observing such behaviors, of course, may lead to errors of interpretation. We cannot always accurately identify specific motives from outcomes. For example, how can we know when a highly productive worker is being motivated by his or her pay or by some inner drive to be the fastest worker in the plant? The simple answer is that we can't know for sure. But understanding the nature of motivation can help us make more accurate guesses and probably be more effective at creating conditions that motivate people.

Can managers really expect to directly affect the motivation of others?

Remember, the motivation of individual employees can be *influenced* but cannot be *controlled* by organizational leaders, especially over the long run. Managers who think they have direct control on the motivation of others are probably being unrealistic. Managers can attempt to *influence individual motives,* but they cannot control the motivation of other people.

Everyone Has Motivating Needs

All people have needs, and they are unique for each person. Nevertheless, we all have some *basic needs.* All human beings need water, food, sleep, air to breathe, and a satisfactory temperature in which to live. Yet even among these basic needs, there are individual differences. Some people need more sleep than others; some eat more; some become acclimated to the cold or heat.

People also have a variety of **secondary needs.** Some would argue that these needs are really *wants.* These include the desire to be accepted by other people, the desire to achieve certain goals or objectives, and the need for prestige or status. Again, these vary widely among people.

The following theories seek to categorize and explain needs and motivators. Before you read on, complete the activity titled "Things That Motivate Me" below. We'll get back to it later.

Need for Achievement

David C. McClelland has spent a lifetime studying the human urge to achieve. His research has led him to believe that the **need for achievement** is a distinct human motive that can be identified in certain people. The need for achievement has been studied in a wide range of experiments. One typical experiment went something like this:[2]

Participants in the experiment were asked to play a ringtoss game. Their objective was to throw the rings so that they would hook on a peg. That was essentially the only instruction. The variable that the experimenters looked for was how close to the peg the individual subject stood when tossing the rings. The subjects could stand anywhere they wanted to.

Do some people have an exceptionally high need to achieve?

ACTIVITIES

THINGS THAT MOTIVATE ME

Circle the numbers of the *six* items from the following list that you believe are most important in motivating you to do your best work. Then rank the six selected items, with the most important item being 1, the second most important item 2, and so on.

1. ____ Having steady employment

2. ____ Being respected as a person

3. ____ Having adequate rest periods or coffee breaks

4. ____ Receiving good pay

5. ____ Working in good physical conditions

6. ____ Having a chance to turn out quality work

7. ____ Getting along well with others on the job

8. ____ Having a job close to home

9. ____ Having a chance for promotion

10. ____ Having an opportunity to do interesting work

11. ____ Receiving pensions and other security

12. ____ Not having to work too hard

13. ____ Knowing what is going on in the organization

14. ____ Feeling my job is important

15. ____ Having an employee council

16. ____ Having a written job description

17. ____ Being told by my boss when I do a good job

18. ____ Getting a performance rating

19. ____ Attending staff meetings

20. ____ Agreeing with the organization's objectives

21. ____ Having an opportunity for self-development and improvement

22. ____ Having fair vacation arrangements

23. ____ Knowing I will be disciplined if I do a bad job

24. ____ Working under close supervision

25. ____ Having a large amount of freedom on the job (not working under direct or close supervision)

After you have completed this chapter *and* Chapter 4 (not now!), compare your answers with others in the class.

Characteristics of people with a high need for achievement:

- **Prefer to work on the problem**
- **Gain satisfaction from achievement itself**
- **Appreciate concrete feedback**
- **Come from families where parents held high expectations**

Most people tended to throw randomly, first standing very close and later perhaps stepping back. The people with a high need for achievement seemed to carefully measure where they were most likely to get a sense of mastery—not too close to make the task ridiculously easy, or too far back to make it impossible. They set moderately difficult but potentially achievable goals.

McClelland found that people with a high need for achievement tend not to be gamblers. They *prefer to work on a problem, rather than leave the outcome to chance.* They don't mind taking moderate risks, but they want to have as much control as possible over the outcome.

Another characteristic of achievement-motivated people is that *they gain satisfaction from the accomplishment itself.* They do not reject rewards, but the rewards are not as essential as the achievement itself. Such people get a bigger kick out of winning or solving a difficult problem than from money, praise, or other rewards they may receive.

Another finding about these people is that they enjoy and *appreciate receiving concrete feedback.* They respond favorably to getting information on how well they are doing on the job. However, they tend to resent comments from supervisors about their personalities, their physical appearance, or other information not directly relevant to the work. They want task-relevant feedback. They want to know the score.

Finally, McClelland found that achievement-oriented people *are more likely to come from families where parents held high expectations for their children.* Some people tend to achieve because their parents expected them to.

From this description, one can see that achievement-motivated people would be very desirable in organizations. As managers, however, high achievers may be overly demanding or have unrealistically high expectations of others. This can result in leadership problems.

Need for Affiliation

Another need identified by McClelland is the **need for affiliation.** Some people have an unusually high desire to be accepted by others. *They tend to conform to what they believe other people want from them.* If the workgroup has high goals, effective work habits, and other organizationally desirable

Do some people have an exceptionally high need to be accepted?

Interaction with coworkers satisfies our need for affiliation.

characteristics, the group will tend to pull the individual member up to a high level of performance. Likewise, low performance can result from group pressures in the opposite direction.

Research on affiliation needs suggests that a common goal among people with a high need for affiliation is social interaction and communication with others. Such people dislike being alone.

In some cases, affiliative behavior is linked with the need to reduce anxiety. People may interact with others because they have fears or stresses that can be relieved in part by other people. It's the "misery loves company" idea. In other cases, individuals simply enjoy being with people.

Whatever the nature of the need for affiliation, the behavior it tends to produce is similar. *People with a high need for affiliation seek the company of others and take steps to be liked by them.* They try to project a favorable image, and they will work to smooth out disagreeable tensions in meetings and so forth. They help and support others and want to be liked in return.

Need for Power

McClelland's third need is the **need for power.** Some individuals have a strong need to win arguments, to persuade others, to prevail in every situation. These people are likely to be driven by a high need for power. They feel uncomfortable without it.

Do some people have an exceptionally high need to exert power?

The concept of a need for power is not new. As mentioned in Chapter 1, Machiavelli, a sixteenth-century philosopher and politician, was a master at using power to get his way. In fact, his name has become synonymous with a personality type that manipulates others. A strong power drive, however, is not necessarily undesirable or reflective of a character defect. In its positive sense, power can reflect the process by which persuasive and inspirational behavior on the part of a leader can evoke "can-do" feelings of power and ability in subordinates. Power can build confidence in people. The active leader who helps a group form goals and who helps the members attain their goals constructively uses power.

A strong power drive is not necessarily undesirable.

There is nothing wrong with having a high need for power, a high need for affiliation, or a high need for achievement. Each can be useful and productive to an organization. The key thing is for the manager to recognize the influence of these secondary needs on the behavior of employees.

Managers should strive to recognize the effects of secondary needs on people.

The Expectancy Theory of Motivation

Expectancy theory takes into account both personal needs and opportunities to fulfill those needs as it tries to explain and predict how and why people do what they do. This theory also contends that human beings are both emotional (seeking satisfaction of needs) and reasonable (thinking through what alternative action will satisfy needs) at the same time. Each person tries to predict, "If I do this particular thing, will it lead to that particular payoff for me?"

Victor Vroom is credited with developing an expectancy theory that considers these different needs and motivators (see Figure 3.1 on page 48).[3] In essence, the model states that an individual will expend effort (that is, will be motivated) when he or she believes that:

An expectancy model shows relationships between needs and motivation.

- the effort will result in favorable performance.

- favorable performance will result in a desired reward.

- the reward will satisfy an important need.

- the desire to satisfy that need is strong enough to make the effort worthwhile.

FIGURE 3.1 An expectancy model of motivation.

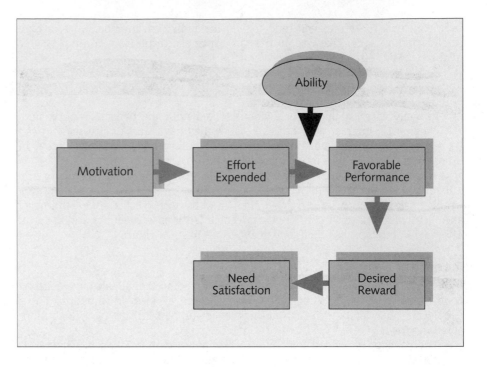

Notice that the model includes the variable *ability.* If an employee is motivated and expends effort but lacks in ability (skills, knowledge, training, etc.), he or she may fail to achieve favorable performance. Organizations bear some responsibility for seeing that employee ability is appropriate to the tasks required for "favorable performance."

Expressed another way, this model says that people ask themselves three questions in response to a motivator:

1. What's in it for me?

2. How hard will I have to work to get what's in it for me?

3. What are my *real* chances of getting that reward if I do what you (or they) want?

If a student wanted a grade of A for a particular course, for example, his or her *motivation* to study would be a function of:

1. how badly the student *desired* the grade, and

2. the level of *expectancy* that study would result in achieving it.

If a manager offers a sales representative a $500 cash bonus for selling 20 automobiles this month, the employee may or may not be motivated, depending on how he or she answers questions such as "Is $500 an appropriate reward for such an effort?" "How hard will it be to sell 20 cars?" or "If I do sell 20 automobiles, will the boss really pay me the $500?"

How Motives Change

People pay attention to their strongest need.

Motives do not always affect people equally. At any given time, many needs are competing for attention. People pay attention to the need with the greatest strength at that particular moment. This need most influences behavior at that

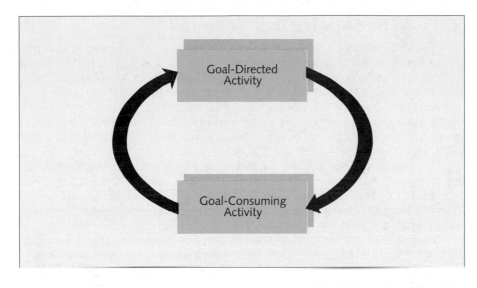

FIGURE 3.2 A continuous cycle can lead to long-term motivation.

time. Keep in mind that behavior or the activities people engage in are related to some sort of goals (conscious or unconscious). These goals are hoped-for rewards toward which motives are directed. The successful manager provides an environment in which *appropriate* goals are available for need satisfaction.

Management theorists make a distinction between goal-directed activities and goal-consuming activities. They suggest that **goal-directed activities** are motivated behaviors based on expectations that the goal is, in fact, attainable, worthwhile, and desirable. This ties in with the expectancy theory we just discussed. The need strength of goal-directed activities *increases* as a person engages in them. That is, as a person gets closer to some goal, the strength of the motivating needs increases. Anyone who has attempted to jog long distances might be aware of this principle. As one sees the last mile marker in a long-distance race, one tends to be even more motivated, knowing that the finish line is not far ahead. Students frequently experience additional motivation near the end of a course when the hoped-for goal of getting an A seems just around the corner. It seems to be human nature to want to sprint that last little distance and finish in a blaze of glory. This is the nature of goal-directed activity.

Goal-consuming activities, however, involve engaging in the goal itself. They are "consuming" activities (see Figure 3.2). A goal-directed activity might be going to a restaurant and ordering a pizza; the corresponding goal-consuming activity would be the act of eating the pizza. Unlike the need strength of goal-directed activities, the need strength of a goal-consuming activity *decreases* as one engages in it. The more pizza we eat, the less we are motivated by a desire for food.

Long-term, ongoing motivation occurs when people alternate between goal-directed and goal-consuming activities. Goal-directed motivation stimulates people to work for a desired reward. But if one never got to "consume" that reward—to relish its achievement—one would eventually tire of exerting the goal-directed effort. The expectation of goal attainment would evaporate, and the person would no longer have a reasonable target for efforts. Likewise, if someone engages only in goal-consuming behaviors and the goal is not challenging, lack of interest and apathy will develop and motivation will dissipate. The worker who is required to attain a productive level that is too easy to reach is not likely to be motivated by that aspect of the job.

A continuous cycle between goal-directed and goal-consuming opportunities is most likely to result in long-term motivation.

How do goal-directed and goal-consuming activities change as the objective gets nearer?

Should we switch between goal-consuming activities and goal-directed activities?

The Hierarchy of Needs

When a need has been satisfied, it no longer motivates—at least not for the time being. But let's look a little more closely at the common situation in which a need is only partially satisfied and is replaced by another. To understand that, we need to note the hierarchical arrangement of needs.

Abraham Maslow formulated his famous **hierarchy of needs** theory back in the 1940s. It continues to be a major contribution to the understanding of motivation. Maslow was one of a number of psychologists who sought to establish a list of "universal needs" that affect everyone.

In his research, Maslow saw that different needs work on people at different times and that some needs are more basic to all people than others. Until such **basic needs**—also called "lower-order needs"—are satisfied (at least to the extent that another need replaces them), "higher-order needs" cannot and will not motivate a person.[4]

Maslow boiled down his list of needs into five categories. These are physiological, safety, social, esteem, and self-actualization.

Physiological Needs

The human need for physical comfort is the most basic type of need, according to Maslow. Whenever we put on mittens in cold weather, replenish our body with food and water after exercise, or step outside for a breath of fresh air, we are seeking to satisfy these survival or **physiological needs.**

Most of us can understand how difficult it would be to pay attention to other types of needs if such basic needs are not met. Consider trying to concentrate on your studies, for example, while you are extremely hungry or very uncomfortable in a hot, stuffy room. These unsatisfied physiological needs are likely to dominate your thoughts and behavior, even though you'd prefer to concentrate on your higher goal of studying effectively.

Safety Needs

The next level of needs in Maslow's hierarchy deals with safety and security. Included in **safety needs** are such things as freedom from fear of physical danger, the need for self-preservation, and the concern for the future. In the early years of the industrial United States, many workers were no doubt fearful of injury or even death on the job. These concerns in part led to the organization of labor unions and other pressure groups. Once their immediate physical needs are taken care of, people turn to the need for self-preservation and to thoughts about the future.

People respond to the need for security in a number of ways. We may quit a job we view as being too physically dangerous. We may be especially motivated to observe certain safety precautions to reduce the chance of accident and injury. We may save some money from paychecks for the eventuality that income may be cut off. And we may do a number of other things to reflect our concern for self-preservation and our concern for the future. Once we feel reasonably secure, still higher needs become primary motivators.

Social Needs

People are social animals. We have a need for **belonging**—acceptance by other people. In modern society, there are few real hermits.

Social needs, like any others, vary widely among different individuals. Some of us do prefer to be left alone, but most people have a basic yearning for meaningful relationships with others. We need only look at people who are imprisoned, such as the POWs in Vietnam, to recognize how much affiliation is needed. Many of these prisoners relate that after being kept in isolated captiv-

---

Maslow's hierarchy of needs was a major contribution to our understanding of motivation.

Why was Maslow's theory such an important step in improving our understanding of motivation?

We cannot be motivated by higher-level needs if these most basic needs are not met.

We may quit a job we see as too dangerous.

Most people need good relationships with others.

ity for months and months, they were finally permitted the opportunity to communicate with other prisoners. They reacted ecstatically to the fulfillment of this need. As another example, studies have shown that employees who work away from others, such as bank tellers who work in isolated, drive-in banking facilities, tend to be less satisfied on the job. They typically cite the lack of interaction with other employees as a source of their dissatisfaction.

Esteem Needs

People have varying needs to be recognized by others and to have clear self-images. We all like to receive "strokes" that tell us, "Your efforts are recognized, and you are regarded as a person of value." Organizational rewards can often fill these **esteem needs.** Even subtle rewards, such as private offices, carpeting, or a more desirable location in a workroom, can convey this recognition and sense of worth to individual employees. Unfulfilled esteem needs can very quickly lead to dissatisfied employees.

Recognition and rewards can satisfy our need for esteem.

Such things as organizational titles, or status symbols such as a new automobile and expensive clothing, are attempts to meet our esteem needs.

Self-Actualization Needs

Maslow coined the term **self-actualization** to identify the highest level of needs that motivate people. This is described as the need to maximize one's potential. According to Maslow's theory, the individual who has achieved a reasonable degree of satisfaction in the four lower-level needs can now focus energies on self-actualization. The result is usually a high degree of professional development and accomplishment. The artist who produces her very best painting and the author who creates what he regards as a literary masterpiece are examples of self-actualized people.

Self-actualization arises from doing your very best.

The employee who seeks to satisfy self-actualization needs strives to produce their best possible on the job. This employee is best motivated by supervisors who are supportive by providing an environment where self-directed work may take place.

We All "Live" at Different Need Levels

Maslow's theory has become a cornerstone in the literature of management and psychology. The key to its value lies in its recognition of the ever-changing needs that motivate us all. One implication of Maslow's theory is that we all "live" at different levels of existence; we find our most consistent needs to be at one or two levels.

In general, we are motivated most strongly by our strongest unfulfilled needs. Those of you who are reading this book are likely to be successful individuals. You are likely to be either a manager or training to become a manager. By and large, you find your lower-order needs easily satisfied, so you concentrate on higher ones. This is not to say that you are not occasionally motivated by physical hunger or desires, but you are not compelled to seek satisfaction from hunger as a *primary* activity of your day. Physical needs, safety needs, and probably your social needs are generally satisfied. Your need satisfaction efforts focus on the higher-order needs, such as esteem and self-actualization.

Remember, however, that other people are not in exactly the same position. To assume that all workers are likely to be motivated by higher-order needs may not be true. Some low-level employees are most motivated by survival and security needs.

ACTIVITIES

Maslow's hierarchy of needs shows that all humans have the same basic needs. How do these needs get satisfied in the average job? Put an X on the level where you think you spend most of your time. Are you at the survival level or closer to self-actualization? Or do you operate mostly in the security or esteem levels?

Look again at the triangle. Circle your X and then place new Xs with the initials of others you work with where you think they fit.

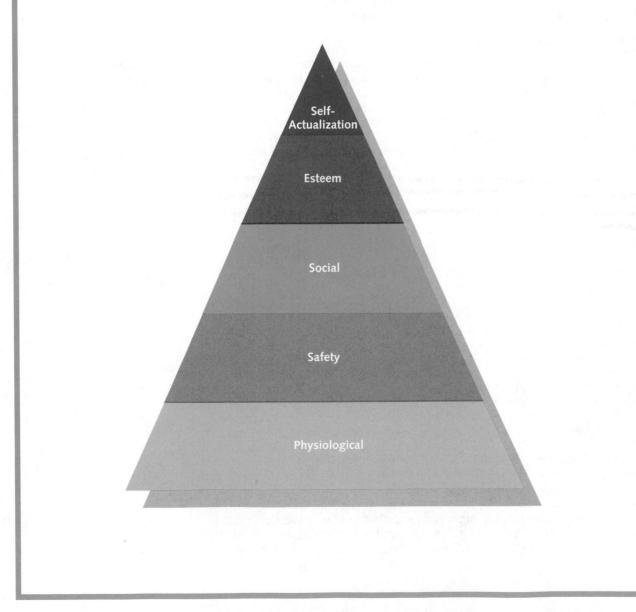

In this chapter we've talked about human needs and how the ⌐
motivation. Each theory described suggests ways to better understand
pens as people experience and respond to different needs.

Although these theories suggest that people at times seem to b
external forces, we do not mean to minimize free will. Human be
like the salivating dogs or rats in a maze so often used in psych⌐
ments. We maintain a higher sense of values, which can and ⌐
our behaviors. We are not totally self-centered nor constantly seek
gratification. We often develop a larger sense of worth by giving of
a larger, common good.

Indeed, employees in the best companies gain need satisfac⌐
highest of human goals: the desire to produce excellent product⌐
for their fellow human beings. In short, they are motivated by a ⌐
pose.

As mentioned in the reading at the end of Chapter 1 (pp. 1⌐
ees in health and medical industries want more than profits. T⌐
since memorized the mantra that medicine is for patients, not p⌐
device manufacturer Medtronics "finds novel ways to [motivate e⌐
the company motto, 'Restoring patients to a full life.'"[5]

New thoughts about what work should be:
◦ fulfilling and fun
◦ job security
◦ life balance

The Growing Trend Toward Self-Actualization

The 1990s was a decade marked by many shifts in what had been traditional
thinking about people and work. One important shift was that people came to
look at work as a source of more than just financial income. In their book *Re-inventing the Corporation,* John Naisbitt and Patricia Aburdene explain the
trend this way:

> There is a new ideal about work emerging in America today. For the first time,
> there is a widespread expectation that work should be fulfilling—that work
> should be fun.
>
> Thirty years ago, that would have been an outrageous notion. . . . Neverthe
> less, people know intuitively that work ought to be fun and satisfying, even
> when it is not.
>
> Today . . . the same forces which are re-inventing the corporation are trans-
> forming this deep human need into a realistic expectation in the workplace. The
> economic demands of the information society together with the new values of
> the baby boom generation are fostering the "work should be fun" idea.[6]

A second shift in traditional thinking lies in the ways people view job security. Today, relatively few people can expect to join a corporation upon graduation from school and remain securely there until retirement. With so many companies being restructured, taken over, or simply going out of business,
old-fashioned job security with a big corporation is largely a myth.

As a result, more people are recognizing that job security is achieved by
developing excellent and marketable skills. A sharply increasing number of people are starting their own businesses. Entrepreneurs often gain feelings of control over their own destiny and freedom that are not available in traditional organizations.

Another shift is that people are rethinking the broader issue of balancing
career and other life activities. People need to feel fulfilled in all areas: career,
family or relationships, self-development, and so forth. People are increasingly
recognizing the need for self-management and **life balance.**

As one author put it, "We have the same amount of mental energy and the
same number of hours in a day as people of other generations and other locations, but we have so many more demands, so many more things. We live in

Today, work is seen as more than just a source of income.

the first time and place in the world's history and geography where challenges stem not from scarcity but from surplus, not from oppression but from options, and not from absences but from abundance."[7]

Psychological theories help us understand much of what motivates, but they cannot explain all human behavior. The challenge to those who would seek to motivate others is to understand what has been known to work in some situations and to make judgments about what may be helpful in the future.

In Chapter 4 we'll suggest some things that supervisors and managers can do to create a climate in which individual needs can be satisfied and motivation can flourish.

Summary of Key Ideas

- Management is the process of getting productive work done with and through the efforts of other individuals; thus, understanding human motivation is essential for managerial success.

- Motivation comes from individual needs, wants, and desires, which provide motives for action. Motives are the reason for exerting effort.

- Motivation itself is not visible; we can only infer that it has occurred by observed behaviors.

- Two harmful myths confuse the issue for many: the belief that lasting motivation can be generated by a pep talk, and the belief that motivation can always be triggered by money or rewards.

- Managers can best provide a motivating environment by seeing their job as service (to employees) rather than control (of employees).

- Emotions are at the root of motivation. Three emotional categories can result in desired actions: fear, duty, or desire. Desire is the strongest of these.

- Motivation is *not:* under the control of managers, the same for all people (one size does not fit all), or the same thing as job satisfaction.

- Research on human motivation has shown that characteristics of people vary depending on their need for achievement, affiliation, and power.

- Victor Vroom's expectancy theory of motivation helps explain the interaction between needs and motivation.

- A major contribution to motivation theory is Abraham Maslow's hierarchy of needs, which includes (in ascending order) physiological, safety, social, esteem, and self-actualization needs.

Key Terms, Concepts, and Names

Basic needs
Behaviorism
Esteem needs
Expectancy theory
Fear = motivation
Goal-consuming activity
Goal-directed activity
Job satisfaction
Life balance

Management as service
Abraham Maslow
Maslow's hierarchy of
  needs
David C. McClelland
Motivation
Need for achievement

Need for affiliation
Need for power
Physiological needs
Safety needs
Secondary needs
Self-actualization
Social needs
Victor Vroom

Questions and Exercises

1. List several examples of each of Maslow's five levels of needs.

2. What are some of your key personal goals? What are the key goals of the organization you work (or have worked) for? Are they compatible?

3. Summarize McClelland's description of the person with a high need for achievement. To what extent does this describe your own behaviors and attitudes? (If you don't fit this description very well, don't feel bad. Only a tiny percentage of all people studied by McClelland's researchers fit the "high-achiever" profile exactly.)

4. How well do you fit the description of one having a high need for affiliation? How well do you fit the description of a person having a high need for power?

5. Summarize in your own words Vroom's expectancy theory of motivation. Cite examples that support or seem to contradict this theory.

6. To what degree do you agree that people today are rethinking their ideas of security and self-actualization? Give examples.

7. Answer the introductory questions at the beginning of this chapter.

Notes

1. Geoffrey James, *Business Wisdom of the Electronic Elite* (New York: Times Books/Random House, 1996), p. 24.

2. David C. McClelland et al., *The Achieving Society* (Princeton, NJ: Van Nostrand, 1961).

3. Victor H. Vroom, *Work and Motivation* (New York: Wiley, 1964).

4. Abraham Maslow, *Motivation and Personality* (New York: Harper & Row, 1954).

5. Ronald B. Lieberman, "Why Employees Love These Companies," *Fortune* January 12, 1998, p. 74.

6. John Naisbitt and Patricia Aburdene, *Re-inventing the Corporation* (New York: Warner Books, 1985), p. 79.

7. Linda and Richard Eyre, *LifeBalance* (New York: Ballantine Books, 1987), p. 16.

Another Look: The Dysfunctional Concept of Fear = Motivation

Probably the most dysfunctional concept of traditional corporate culture is that it's appropriate, even beneficial, to control workers with fear. If the function of management is to control worker behavior, and the way to view employees is as children, then management needs a tool with which to keep the children in line. And, historically, that tool has been fear.

In the past, and today as well, many managers hold the threat of firing or demotion over employees' heads. The message is clear: "Work hard or you're outta here!" The tone was set in the nineteenth century. Anyone who refused (or was unable) to work 14-hour days, seven days a week, was unceremoniously dismissed, only to be replaced by another—to the manager—faceless, nameless laborer.

The all-too-obvious strong-arm tactics were abandoned by the mid-twentieth century. IBM, for example, became known for its policy of lifetime employment. Once you were hired by IBM, you had a steady job for the rest of your life, as long as you followed the rules. IBM, like other companies that promised such security, has been unable to deliver on that promise. Recent changes in the economy have made the concept of a steady job nothing more than a memory. Millions of workers have lost their jobs as a result of downsizing, rightsizing, outsourcing, and reengineering. This resurgence of insecurity in the workplace has reawakened the fear of joblessness in many workers in all fields.

Fear makes companies less competitive and adaptable, and causes workers to become less, rather than more, productive. When people are afraid, they will avoid taking necessary risks.

Source: Geoffrey James, *Business Wisdom of the Electronic Elite* (New York: Random House, 1996), pp. 113–114.

isn't this a lie? walmart holds employees to low hours to not have benefits...?

A Case in Point: People Power at Wal-Mart

Long before "empowerment" became a corporate buzzword, Wal-Mart employees were empowered, not just allowed, but encouraged to make decisions, take risks and, yes, even make mistakes in the cause of customer service.

Who makes the customer Number One? "Our People Make the Difference!"

At Wal-Mart, our people make the difference for each other, too.

"Our division's mission for our associates is to 'Get' them, 'Keep' them and 'Grow' them," said Coleman Peterson, Senior Vice President of the People Division. "Everything we do comes out of our basic Wal-Mart principle of 'Respect for the individual.'

"And when we put all that together, it translates into great service to the customer."

In addition to an industry-leading array of health and other benefits, Wal-Mart offers associates a variety of incentive programs. Most of these incentives are based directly on the performance of an associate's store or division—improvements in profits, reduction in shrink, etc. Virtually all Wal-Mart associates are eligible for some type of performance-based incentive plan.

From an associate's point of view, the equation is obvious: Better service to the customer means better profits, which means higher incentives and increased shareholder value. And yes, Wal-Mart associates care deeply about shareholder value, because so many are shareholders themselves. Our associates are kept informed about the stock price, so everyone understands the connection between Wal-Mart's performance and their own financial success.

Last year, the total company and every division but one met or exceeded its maximum profit improvement goals. As a result, a record level of payout was awarded to associates. We believe there is a direct correlation between record incentive levels and the company's record-setting performance last year.

Even traditional associate benefits also show the Wal-Mart touch. They provide the best available service at the lowest possible price.

"We have health plans to fit anyone's budget," said Tom Emerick, Vice President of Benefits. "I'm proud to say that we have a health plan, with no lifetime caps. Very few benefit plans will cover a major health problem as well as ours.

"And yet, thanks to diligent negotiations with providers and the great work our associates do in controlling costs, our total cost of benefits is below industry averages."

Perhaps the biggest benefit news in fiscal 1998 came when we rolled out our 401(k) savings plan,

continued

People Power at Wal-Mart, *continued*

which has been so well received that we expect it to become the largest such plan, in number of participants, in the United States.

The 401(k) plan, which provides a tax-deferred opportunity to save for retirement, came about after associates suggested it in Wal-Mart's "Grass Roots" communications program. This year, Wal-Mart divided the company's annual contribution equally between the Profit Sharing and 401(k) plans.

Nowhere is the link between associates' interests and the success of the shareholders more visible than in the Profit Sharing program, which has 70 percent of its assets invested in Wal-Mart stock. "Thanks to the 73 percent increase in the stock price, the Profit Sharing plan's assets increased 57 percent in the last year," said Chief Financial Officer John Menzer.

That's what can happen when Wal-Mart people, the best in the retail industry, focus on creating value for customers, shareholders and the company as a whole.

Questions

1. What specific motivators are described in this case? List as many as you can find.
2. How might these motivators be classified using Maslow's hierarchy?
3. Does this case depict an accurate picture of Wal-Mart's relationship with its associates (employees)?
4. If you know people who work at a Wal-Mart store, interview them about the realities of their jobs. Are they motivated by management's efforts? Do they feel a sense of satisfaction in their work? Overall, do they agree with this description of "people power"?

Source: Wal-Mart Annual Report, 1998

A Case in Point: You Call This Fair Play?

"Can you believe this?" exclaimed Frank during the morning coffee break. He had been reading a copy of the daily newspaper. "It says here that the city garbage collectors' new contract calls for a minimum pay of $38,000 a year! I can't believe I'm reading this!"

Frank wasn't the only person upset after reading that. "That really burns me up," interjected Rosalee. "I work my tail off at this factory 40 hours a week, and I don't make anywhere near that much money. What do those guys think they are trying to prove?"

"If a garbage collector is worth thirty-eight grand, then I'm worth more than that," exclaimed Jose as he pounded on the table. "We need to do something about this. Let's go talk to Charlie and demand some raises."

Coincidentally, Charlie, their supervisor, walked into the break room about this time. "What are you demanding now?" he asked calmly. All three of the workers immediately started telling him about the newspaper article reporting the garbage collectors' pay.

"I can see why you folks might be a little upset. Let's cool off a bit and talk about this at our meeting later on today," said Charlie. "But don't get your hopes up."

Questions

1. What do you think is motivating these employees to complain about their pay?
2. Discuss the employees' complaint in terms of Maslow's hierarchy of needs.
3. Assume that the average earnings of each employee are $19,000 a year. If you were Charlie, what would you say to these employees at the team meeting this afternoon?

Creating a Motivational Environment

- What is empowerment, and how does it relate to goals and motivation?
- What happens when people's goals are blocked from achievement?
- What is cognitive dissonance, and why is it so uncomfortable?
- How do programmed limitations cause us to fall short of goals?
- How can managers realistically influence motivation?
- What is the key to a motivating climate?
- How can job enrichment provide motivation for workers?
- Are there any surefire ways to motivate?
- What role can performance reviews play in motivation?
- What is motivational faith?

The answers to these and other questions are coming up next in Chapter 4 . . .

Empowerment became a buzzword in the 1990s. The process of empowerment involves giving—or helping people discover—the power within themselves to satisfy their needs and wants.

For empowerment to flourish, organizational leaders need to create conditions for motivation. This is done in large part by removing the stumbling blocks to satisfaction of employee needs. In this chapter, we'll talk about what happens when people's needs are unmet and suggest ways that the manager can help develop a climate where workers can be motivated—and empowered.

The needs that trigger motivation are highly individual in nature. No two people experience exactly the same feelings or desires.

Because understanding human motivation is a key to successful organizations, it is useful to know what happens when people's needs are blocked.

What Happens When Goals Are Blocked?

When our goals are blocked, we usually respond with one or more of these behaviors:

- Coping
- Substitution of another goal
- Repression, retaliation, or resignation
- Fixation or obsession
- Rationalization
- Cognitive dissonance
- Frustration

What happens when a goal seems both achievable and desirable, but for some reason we are blocked from attaining it? Typically, we respond with one or a combination of the following behaviors.

Coping

Coping means that people struggle and contend with the problem, often by trial and error, until they achieve some degree of satisfaction. One approach to coping is to simply adjust to that which we cannot control. For instance, when prices of a product go up sharply, people cope by buying a cheaper substitute or buying less. This is one way of coping with a blockage (in this case, a loss of purchasing power).

Substitution of Another Goal

Another response to a blocked goal is to seek out a substitute goal. The basketball player who realizes that success at a major college is not likely because he or she is a foot shorter than all the other players may try a different sport. The worker who sees no opportunity for promotion may change jobs.

Workers who can't find goal satisfaction on the job channel their efforts into off-the-job goals. The active civic club member or the avid hobbyist may be substituting such activities for job-related satisfactions.

Repression, Retaliation, or Resignation

Simply giving up the pursuit of a goal is another option. Some people *repress* their goals or force them to the back of their mind. Occasionally, people *retaliate* against the person or force that is blocking achievement of the goal. The citizen who fights city hall or the upset employee who files a grievance with a labor union may be retaliating.

Retaliation often takes other forms in business. Unhappy employees take more sick days, tell others what a lousy company they work for, or sometimes even sabotage work output.

While retaliation is almost always destructive, *resignation* can be either destructive or healthy. When being resigned to blocked goals fosters a sense of helpless resentment, it is, of course, detrimental. When employees are resigned to an uncontrollable goal blocker and make the best of a less than ideal situation, they may simply have a realistic view of the world. Such a view can be healthy.

SHOE   JEFF MacNELLY

Fixation or Obsession

A consistently unhealthy response to a blocked goal is **fixation** or **obsession.** This involves focusing on the goal and continuing to "beat one's head against a wall" in a futile effort to accomplish the blocked goal. Such behavior differs from coping behaviors in that the person who is fixated seldom tries any new approaches to the problem. The person becomes obsessed but also becomes incapable of rationally working toward the goal.

Some argue that an obsession can be a positive thing, like an obsession for excellence or for quality. Perhaps. But in those contexts, the word *obsession* is being used as a synonym for a drive or ongoing effort. Obsessive behaviors imply an *irrational* pursuit, not a conscious, sustained, thoughtful effort.

Rationalization

The attitude that "I didn't really want to achieve that anyhow" illustrates **rationalization.** A response to a blocked goal may simply be to very convincingly tell ourselves that we didn't really want to obtain that goal anyhow.

Another form of rationalization is to identify scapegoats. Here, we blame an outside force over which we have no control—such as the economy or our competitor—for blocking our goal achievement.

Cognitive Dissonance

Leon Festinger developed a psychological concept in the 1950s called **cognitive dissonance.**[1] His theory deals with the ways people respond to new information or experiences, especially those that differ from what was previously believed to be true.

We all develop a complex network of attitudes and emotions based on our experiences against which we evaluate new information or experiences. If the new data fit what we already "know," there is no problem. The network is reinforced and strengthened. If, however, we experience something that seems inconsistent with what we already "know," an imbalance is created in our minds. Something just doesn't seem to fit.

People seek a balance in their thoughts and experiences.

According to Festinger's theory, people seek a balance or an equilibrium between their thoughts and experiences. Put another way, people want the world to make sense to them. When people feel some psychological discomfort, they will act to deal with it.

One's response to dissonance can be any of the following:

1. Ignore it.

2. Discount the new information or experience.

3. Change your attitudes or behavior.

Here's an example of cognitive dissonance. Suppose that your supervisor has been riding you pretty hard and seldom seems to have a good word for anything you do. You are convinced that she dislikes you—and the feeling is mutual. This is information already "known" to you.

One day, you overhear this same supervisor vigorously arguing for a big raise for you! She is telling the boss that you are definitely the best worker in the department and that you have a lot of promotion potential. This new bit of information (the overheard conversation) doesn't fit with what you already "know" (that your supervisor thinks you're a bum).

Cognitive dissonance theory would suggest that you'll probably change your view in some way. Perhaps you'll adjust your thinking: "Maybe my supervisor really does appreciate me. Maybe she's not so bad but just has trouble expressing appreciation to others."

Or you may adjust for this dissonance by thinking, "My supervisor's just trying to throw her weight around and impress the boss with her apparent 'concern' for workers. The raise for me is not really important. This is just an attempt at a power play."

Frustration

One final result of blocked needs is individual **frustration.** Frustration exists within the mind of the person. Frequently, blockages that people perceive, and are frustrated by, are **programmed limitations** that people have in their own minds.

Mental limitations become real when we accept them as such.

We all have programmed our self-perception of what we can or cannot achieve. A blocked goal may serve to reinforce those limitations, even though the only blockage is in our own mind. Some interesting stories are told about such mentally programmed limitations.

What are programmed limitations?

For example, elephants used in setting up circus tents are trained to have certain programmed limitations from a very early age. When an elephant is very small (say, only a half ton or so), it is tied with a very heavy rope to a large stake. Although it may frequently pull and tug at that rope, there is no way it can get away from the stake. When this elephant gets older and much more powerful, easily strong enough to pull up such a stake, it does not do so. In fact, some circus trainers simply put a leg iron around the elephant's foot with no rope attached at all. Simply having the leg iron in place causes the elephant to stay put. The animal "knows" it cannot wander.

Other examples of programmed limitations are found in the world of sports. Before 1954, people generally believed that no human being could run a mile in less than four minutes. Then Roger Bannister broke the "magical" four-minute mile. Within only a few months, several other people also ran a mile in less than four minutes. The limitation seemed to have been a socially dictated "belief" rather than a real, physical barrier.

Advocates of the "power of positive thinking" see such programmed limitations as sources of frustration. The frustrations that grow out of goal blockages only serve to reinforce these limitations.

How Managers Can Influence Motivation

While understanding the nature of motivation and some of its effects on people is very useful, even more important is knowing how to create situations where motivation can work for managers and for their organization. The following paragraphs describe several ways that a manager can use the information in this chapter to help empower employees to become motivated.

Managers can influence motivation by doing the following:

- **Having realistic expectations**
- **Communicating about wants, needs, and goals**
- **Understanding the difference between motivators and maintenance factors**
- **Creating a motivational climate**
- **Using the reward system**

Have Realistic Expectations

Managers cannot force people to be motivated. Their input to the motivating situation is limited and, at best, bears indirectly on the performance of others. This does not mean that they should ignore opportunities to help people motivate themselves. What managers can most profitably do is seek to understand what motivates the individual employee at a particular time. And there is only one realistic way to do that: communicate.

Communicate about Wants, Needs, and Goals

The effective manager seeks to understand what motivates others through *listening* and encouraging free expression of employee wants. Because motivation is goal oriented, managers and their employees must *clarify* organizational and workgroup goals, as well as the individual objectives of the employee. Managers need to see where each person fits. In most cases, individual wants and goals can mesh effectively with the needs of the organization.

Kenneth Blanchard and Spencer Johnson described a simple but effective goal-setting process in their book *The One Minute Manager*.[2] The six steps to setting and using goals are as follows:

1. Agree on your goals.
2. See what good behavior looks like.
3. Write out each of your goals on a single sheet of paper using less than 250 words.
4. Read and reread each goal, which requires only a minute or so each time you do it.
5. Take a minute periodically during your day to assess your performance.
6. See whether or not your behavior matches your goal.

Managers and workers get on the same wavelength by clarifying goals.

By talking through this process and coming to agreement about the desirability and description of goals and their related behaviors, managers and employees get on the same wavelength and can move toward goal accomplishment.

Communication consultant Charles E. Beck[3] reminds us of the importance of feedback in the motivation process.

> As a motivational force, feedback is perhaps the most significant communication element. Organizations need performance systems based on formal reviews to track long-term performance accomplishment; however, employees need feedback more frequently than just the annual review. The feedback should also be multidimensional, not merely limited to a very specific task. In other words, feedback should take into account more of the total person rather than a minor segment of the individual's performance. Such an approach recognizes the individual nature of motivation—managers cannot rely on the generic motivators but must respond to an individual employee.

Beck goes on to say that we create a motivational environment by giving feedback on forms of individual performance such as:

Action	Teamwork
Creativity	Communication
Decision making	Leadership
Proficiency	Accountability
Adaptability	Development

"Hey! The carrot's for the horse!"

Managers can use frequent informal feedback with employees that frees both participants from the bureaucracy and "red tape" of the organization; nevertheless, such happenings may bring mixed results. Supervisory feedback is a form of control and superiority, thus inherently creating a defensive environment. Employees in the feedback situation may be reluctant to ask questions and clarify impressions. Furthermore, informal feedback may create a greater disparity between the subordinate's perceptions and the intentions and overall credibility. Because *interpretation* plays a significant role in the feedback process, setting up a supportive communication climate provides the backdrop for effective feedback communication between manager and employee.[4]

Understand the Difference between Motivators and Maintenance Factors

Frederick Herzberg put forth a **two-factor theory of motivation.** He suggested that the things that can motivate people appeal to the higher-order needs as described by Maslow.[5] These include opportunities for achievement, recognition, challenging work, responsibility, and advancement. Many managers, however, spend a great deal of time trying to motivate people by appealing to their lower-level needs. For instance, providing people with more comfortable work environments, more money, an office with a view, or even pleasant relationships with supervisors can, and probably will, lead to worker *satisfaction.*

The two-factor theory identifies motivation and satisfaction as two different, and often unrelated, things. Where working conditions are tolerable or better, managers waste a great deal of time trying to motivate people using satisfiers. If minimum satisfiers are not met, however, workers can be highly dissatisfied, and this can have disastrous effects on their productivity.

One critic of Herzberg's work, Abraham K. Korman, feels that this research erred by assuming that most, if not all, individuals are at the higher-level needs.[6] That criticism may be valid, because people do function at different levels of needs. Otherwise, the theories of Maslow and Herzberg support each other. As shown in Table 4.1 on page 66, motivators relate to the higher-level needs. Similarly, dissatisfiers, or what Herzberg called **hygiene or maintenance factors,**

Herzberg's two-factor theory of motivation contrasts motivators and hygiene or maintenance factors.

The two factors are satisfaction and motivation. They are not the same.

relate to lower-level needs. Herzberg contended that only appeals to the higher-level needs can be motivating. Efforts to stimulate workers through the lower-level needs will, at best, simply reduce the probability of worker dissatisfaction.

The sensitive manager recognizes that to motivate people, the work itself—the job being done by the individual—must generate some degree of interest and provide some opportunity for the individual to attain self-actualization.

TABLE 4.1   *A Comparison of Maslow's and Herzberg's Theories*

MASLOW	HERZBERG
Higher-Order Needs	***Motivators***
Self-actualization	Work itself
	Achievement
	Responsibility
Esteem	Recognition
	Advancement
Lower-Order Needs	***Hygiene or Maintenance Factors***
Social	Interpersonal relations
	Technical supervision
Safety	Company policy and administration
Physiological	Job security
	Working conditions
	Personal life

Create a Motivational Climate

To create a motivational climate, there must be openness between managers and subordinates. Each must have a clear understanding of both the organization's goals and, to the degree possible, the individual employee's goals. The manager must be flexible, creative, and receptive to new ideas from subordinates. The only way this can be conveyed is through effective communication and positive interpersonal relationships.

Sometimes employees find it difficult to express personal goals. Many have never considered what their life objectives are. Effective supervisors will help employees formulate their goals through discussion and training. These efforts can pay off handsomely in motivating organization members.

One effective way of creating a motivational climate is through **job enrichment.** According to Herzberg, job enrichment is a process where, through talking together, subordinates and their supervisors come to an understanding of how the job could be made more meaningful.

The manager's primary task is to create a climate of trust, so that a subordinate will feel comfortable in offering suggestions about the nature and scope of the worker's job. Once the trust is created, the supervisor and worker can systematically discuss the nature and duties of the subordinate's job with suggestions of how that job could be enriched—that is, how the *responsibilities* of the job can be increased. Most, but not all, people are motivated by more responsible jobs over which they have control.

Openness between managers and subordinates is a key to a motivating climate.

Job enrichment means increasing job responsibility.

ACTIVITIES

WHAT MOTIVATES YOUR EMPLOYEES?

Think of yourself as a manager. (Use your part-time or full-time job as a point of reference.) If you were the manager, would you know what your employees really want? Their answers could surprise you. A survey of 2,000 workers and their immediate supervisors found that what managers think employees want and what employees really want are often at opposite ends of the spectrum.

Rank the following most common motivators in terms of how effective they would be for motivating you and your employees:

Motivator	Ranking for You	Ranking for Your Employees
Money	_____	_____
Job security	_____	_____
Promotion	_____	_____
Personal development	_____	_____
Working conditions	_____	_____
Interesting work	_____	_____
Loyalty from the company	_____	_____
Tactful disciplining	_____	_____
Appreciation	_____	_____
Flexibility about personal needs	_____	_____
Feeling informed	_____	_____

In responding to the survey, managers consistently saw themselves as being motivated by different factors than their employees. They felt that the best ways to motivate employees were the traditional trio of motivators: job security, financial rewards, and job advancement.

The problem is that the traditional motivators are scarce resources for a company. There is not an unlimited amount of these to pass around. They cannot always be provided. So the majority of employees would remain unsatisfied if these were the supervisor's primary means of motivation.

Everyone Can Be a VIP

There is some good news, however. The survey also asked all the employees in the company to say what really motivated them. They picked a very different set of motivators as most effective. In fact, the traditional trio of motivators were the bottom three of their list. The primary motivators of the empowered workplace are what we call the VIP motivators:

Validation

- Respect for employees as people
- Flexibility to meet personal needs
- Encouragement of learning, growth, and new skills

Information

- Knowing why things are being done
- Getting inside information about the company

Participation

- Employees having control over how they do their work
- Involvement in decisions that affect them

Validation: _____

Information: _____

Participation: _____

Source: Adapted from Cynthia D. Scott and Dennis T. Jaffe, *Empowerment* (Los Altos, CA: Crisp Publications, 1991) and reprinted from Elwood N. Chapman, *Winning at Human Relations* (Los Angeles: Crisp Publications, 1989), p. 3. Used with permission.

The Role of Performance Reviews in Motivation

Regular **performance reviews** (also called **performance appraisals**) can provide a basis for employee motivation—if handled well. Often, however, these reviews become uncomfortable rituals for employees and managers alike, leading to satirical "guides" like the one shown in Table 4.2.

TABLE 4.2   *Guide To Employee Performance Appraisal*

PERFORMANCE FACTORS	FAR EXCEEDS JOB REQUIREMENTS	EXCEEDS JOB REQUIREMENTS	MEETS JOB REQUIREMENTS	NEEDS SOME IMPROVEMENT	MINIMUM REQUIREMENTS
Quality	Leaps tall buildings with a single bound	Must take running start to leap over tall buildings	Can leap over short buildings only	Crashes into buildings when attempting to jump over them	Cannot recognize buildings at all
Timeliness	Is faster than a speeding bullet	Is as fast as a speeding bullet	Not quite as fast as a speeding bullet	Would you believe a slow bullet?	Wounds self with bullet when attempting to shoot
Initiative	Is stronger than a locomotive	Is stronger than a bull elephant	Is stronger than a bull	Shoots the bull	Smells like a bull
Adaptability	Walks on water consistently	Walks on water in emergencies	Washes with water	Drinks water	Passes water in emergencies
Communication	Talks with God	Talks with the angels	Talks to himself	Argues with himself	Loses those arguments

Regular performance reviews are vital to the management of people.

An effective appraisal session with employees can clarify expectations and objectives for both supervisors and workers and can provide a base for supportive, mutually beneficial relationships. A poorly prepared or improperly conducted performance review can undo in an hour all the good manager-employee relationships that have developed over a period of months or even years.

Ideally, periodic performance reviews combine information *giving* with information *getting*. They are not talking *to* subordinates, they are talking *with* subordinates. The manager's role is, and must be, that of an evaluator, but the review should not be judgmental in matters going beyond the work context. Statements such as "Your sales order accuracy needs to be improved" would normally be appropriate in an appraisal interview. Statements such as "You need to change your hairstyle and stop living with your boyfriend" would be out of line. Stick to work-related valuations.

An effective performance review can accomplish the following:

1. Let employees *know where they stand.*

2. *Recognize and commend* good work.

3. Provide workers with *directions* on how they could best improve their work.

4. Develop employees in their present jobs by suggesting ways to *enrich* or *enlarge* their tasks.

5. Identify *training opportunities* so employees might be qualified for higher-rated jobs.

6. Let subordinates know the direction in which they may *progress in the organization.*

7. *Record* results of the department or unit as a whole and show where each person fits into the larger picture.

8. Officially *warn* certain employees that they must improve.

While employees receive valuable information from an effective performance appraisal, leaders also gain. Unfortunately, some people responsible for performance appraisals often assign low priority to them because they are unaware of the benefits. Managers and supervisors report the following advantages of an effective appraisal:

Advantages of effective performance reviews:

1. Performance appraisals give me valuable insights into the work being done and those who are doing it.

2. When I maintain good communication with others about job expectations and results, opportunities are created for new ideas and improved methods.

3. When I do a good job appraising performance, anxiety is reduced because employees know how they are doing.

4. I increase productivity when employees receive timely corrective feedback on their performance.

5. I reinforce sound work practices and encourage good performance when I publicly recognize positive contributions.

6. When I encourage two-way communication with employees, goals are clarified so they can be achieved or exceeded.

7. Regular appraisal sessions remove surprises about how the quality of work is being perceived.

8. Learning to do professional performance appraisals is excellent preparation for advancement and increased responsibility.[7]

Supervisors must be aware of possible stumbling blocks to effective performance reviews. Certain attitudes on the part of the supervisor can set the stage for failure. Among those are the following:

Stumbling blocks to effective performance reviews:

1. *Failing to accept the subordinate as a person, unconditionally.* A fundamental respect for the worth of people is required for effective performance appraisals to take place. This does not mean that the manager accepts the subordinate's behavior or value system. Instead, it means that the subordinate's potential and intrinsic worth to the organization are recognized.

2. *Being overly concerned with why the subordinate behaves as he or she does, rather than with what can be done to improve.* Overemphasizing specific causes tends to elicit excuses by the subordinate. When this approach is carried too far, the manager may be playing amateur psychologist. Diagnosing a psychological condition and giving it a label such as "poor self-image," "lack of aggressiveness," or "too hot-tempered" can lead to self-fulfilling prophecies. Once a manager has identified a problem in such a way, he or she is likely to see more and more evidence that supports the diagnosis as correct. The manager will selectively pay attention to examples of hot temper or apparent lack of self-assurance so he or she can say, "Aha—just as I thought!"

3. *Harboring an underlying belief that appraisal sessions should be used to punish the employee.* If you find yourself thinking, "Wait till the performance review—I'll get that SOB then," you are missing the point. Confrontational review sessions are seldom productive. The wise supervisor pays special attention to creating a supportive climate so that performance reviews result in improved performance as well as evaluation.

Fostering Motivational Faith

Alan L. Wilkins talks about building **motivational faith** in his book *Developing Corporate Character.* People will be motivated to the extent that they have faith in their organization and belief in its future.

> Employees use their understanding of history, the promises made to them, and their own predisposition to trust others to decide how much effort they will give to the organization. If they have faith in the fairness and in the ability of the organization and in their own ability to make valued contributions, then they are very likely to be motivated to work for the good of the organization. They assume that their own excellent contributions to the organization will be rewarded appropriately. They therefore spend little time worrying about how to protect themselves and work hard to cooperate with others to make the organization succeed.[8]

Wilkins goes on to describe the elements of motivational faith:

1. *Faith in the fairness of leaders*—belief that management plays fair and gives equal opportunities.

2. *Faith in the fairness of employees*—belief that other workers carry their share of the workload.

3. *Faith in the ability of the organization*—belief that it can deliver on its leaders' promises.

4. *Faith in one's own ability*—belief that one's job will make a difference and that one has the capability to do what is asked.[9]

Use the Reward System

A key management tool is the allocation of rewards. What you reward others for is what you get more of. The rewards or resources that a manager can allocate include such obvious things as pay, benefits, and promotions but also some other things that are more subtle. For example, virtually all supervisors can dispense the reward of *verbal* approval to their employees. Each time supervisors tell employees that they are doing a good job or "stroke" them for some special efforts they have made, they are using part of the organizational reward system.

Likewise, rewards managers can provide may take the form of qualities that people want from their jobs. One survey found that the following ten qualities were most sought after. Arranging for workers to do any of them can be construed as creating a motivational environment.[10]

1. Work for efficient managers

2. Think for themselves

3. See the end result of their work

4. Be assigned interesting work

5. Be informed

6. Be listened to

7. Be respected

8. Be recognized for their efforts

9. Be challenged

10. Have opportunities for increased skill development

Managers need to be conscious of the systematic ways in which they reward people. In an ideal world, rewards would never be haphazardly distributed. But this is not the way it is. Managers are not perfect. In fact, it is not unusual for managers to reward behavior that is actually counterproductive to the organization. This topic is discussed in depth in Chapter 10.

Empowerment and Unblocking Goals Boost Self-Esteem

People spend one-third of their waking lives at work. For many, the workplace is the most important community they live in. Empowerment builds and enhances self-esteem. People who feel good about themselves give more to their work. They are also physically healthier. The outcome is healthy people in healthy places.

In situations where people are not free to work at their maximum effectiveness and their self-esteem is constantly under attack, stress claims, illness, and absenteeism go up. Morale goes down. Productivity plummets. We can look at health, productivity, and satisfaction with work as three interlocking circles:

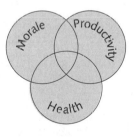

Workers need to be encouraged to find their satisfaction in how well they do their jobs. The key to motivation in an empowered environment is to understand that what gives people the most personal satisfaction is doing a good job. When people are given information, skills, tools, and responsibility, they thrive. Self-esteem is enhanced when people are allowed to exercise more judgment in their work.

Self-esteem is nurtured by achieving goals. The successful organization needs to create a structure and a climate in which people may be successful. Unblocking goal achievement leads to empowerment, which leads to healthy organizations.

Caution: There Is No Easy, Surefire Way to Motivate

A final thought about motivation is offered by organizational psychologists Daniel Katz and Robert L. Kahn. They suggest three ways that people oversimplify their thinking about motivation in organizations and thus get into trouble.[11]

1. People tend to rely too heavily on the use of *blanket motivation*—the same approach to motivating all organization members. "What's good for the goose is good for the gander" may work on fowl—but not on people.

2. People believe in a concept of *global morale*—an overall assessment of organizational spirit without regard to individual differences. The *average* depth of a river may be only four feet, but that doesn't mean someone can walk across it.

3. People tend to emphasize *motivation of the individual* while neglecting the formal structure of the organization. They fail to account for the ways the organization itself affects the individual members. An enthusiastic worker in a poorly designed job—one with too much or too little work to do, for example—soon gets *de*motivated.

Avoiding such oversimplifications can be very difficult. Because efforts to motivate don't always bring about the desired results, the manager must be able to tolerate a degree of frustration. Indeed, the only managers who can hope to succeed are those who can deal with uncertainty, aggravation, and ongoing battles that are never won but only fought well. *Employee motivation (and self-motivation, too!) requires constant managerial attention.*

Summary of Key Ideas

- Empowerment grows when stumbling blocks to satisfying employee needs are removed.

- The seven responses to blocked goals are coping; goal substitution; repression, retaliation, or resignation; fixation; rationalization; cognitive dissonance; and frustration.

- Although managers cannot actually motivate anyone, they can influence motivation by having reasonable expectations, communicating wants and goals, understanding the difference between motivators and maintenance factors, creating a motivational climate, and using a reward system.

- Frederick Herzberg's two-factor theory describes factors that motivate (e.g., recognition, challenging work, and responsibility) and those that satisfy (e.g., work environment, money, and relationship with peers).

- Three ways in which people oversimplify motivation are by relying on one motivational program, failing to account for individual differences, and neglecting structural barriers to motivation.

- Performance reviews can be motivational if handled effectively.

- Empowerment can boost employee self-esteem, leading to better morale, productivity, and health.

- People develop a sense of motivational faith based on their belief in (1) the fairness of leaders, (2) the fairness of employees, (3) the ability of the organization, and (4) their own ability to contribute.

Key Terms, Concepts, and Names

Cognitive dissonance

Coping

Empowerment

Leon Festinger

Fixation or obsession

Frustration

Frederick Herzberg

Hygiene or maintenance factors

Job enrichment

Job satisfaction questionnaire

Motivational faith

Performance review (appraisal)

Programmed limitations

Rationalization

Two-factor theory of motivation

Alan L. Wilkins

Questions and Exercises

1. Review your answers in the activity "What Motivates Your Employees?" Discuss why you ranked the items as you did. How do your rankings compare with those of your classmates? What might account for differences? To what extent are you motivated by maintenance factors? By motivational factors?

2. Think of a recent example where one of your personal goals has been blocked from achievement. (We all have occasional blockages, so don't feel bad.) How, specifically, did you respond to that blockage? What alternatives might you have used?

3. We've discussed the concept of programmed limitations in this chapter. Do you believe that we are limited by such things? If so, suggest some other examples of this process. If not, how might the examples we've suggested be explained?

4. Think of a job you have worked on. How, specifically, could that job be enriched?

5. Why are openness and faith between managers and subordinates the keys to creating a climate for motivation?

6. Describe your experience with performance reviews. What was positive? Negative? How could they have been improved?

7. Answer the introductory questions at the beginning of this chapter.

Notes

1.   Leon Festinger, *A Theory of Cognitive Dissonance* (Stanford, CA: Stanford University Press, 1957).

2.   Kenneth Blanchard and Spencer Johnson, *The One Minute Manager* (New York: Morrow, 1982), p. 34.

3.   Charles E. Beck, *Managerial Communication: Bridging Theory and Practice* (Upper Saddle River, NJ: Prentice Hall, Inc., 1999), pp. 238–239.

4.   Ibid., p. 239

5.   Frederick Herzberg, B. Mausner, and Barbara Snyderman, *The Motivation to Work,* 2d ed. (New York: Wiley, 1959).

6.   Abraham K. Korman, *Organizational Behavior* (Englewood Cliffs, NJ: Prentice-Hall, 1977), especially pp. 140–145.

7.   The survey was conducted by the Public Agenda Foundation and is reported in Twyla Dell, *An Honest Day's Work* (Los Altos, CA: Crisp Publications, 1988), p. 13.

8.   Alan L. Wilkins, *Developing Corporate Character* (San Francisco; Jossey-Bass, 1989), p. 27.

9.   Ibid., pp. 28–29.

10. Cynthia D. Scott and Dennis T. Jaffe, *Empowerment* (Los Altos, CA: Crisp Publications, 1991), p. 46.

11. Based on Daniel Katz and Robert L. Kahn, *The Social Psychology of Organizations,* 2d ed. (New York: Wiley, 1978).

Another Look: Treating People Right

Success starts inside, but it doesn't mean much until you draw others in. They key is to be fair—to treat people right. To treat people right, you have to master three fundamentals: caring, teamwork, and support.

Caring

Caring is feeling what another person feels. Some people call it empathy. Genuinely caring about people usually leads to success. And successful people widen the circle of people they care about more and more as they grow older. Mary Kay Ash of Mary Kay Cosmetics once told me something that helps her: "Pretend that every person you meet has a sign around his or her neck that says, 'Make me feel important.'"

Just before Christmas one year, I went to a Wendy's restaurant in Albuquerque, New Mexico, to film a TV adoption segment with two youngsters. The little girl, who was about seven, had a fresh scar where her father had walloped her with a beer bottle. As we ate lunch, the girl and her older brother, who was about nine, finally started to look me and an old friend who was with me in the eyes. We talked about how important it is to stick together when you don't have other family. And then the boy said something I'll never forget: "I don't want to be adopted with her. Just look at her ugly scar!" The boy knew his sister's appearance would turn off many possible adoptive parents.

My friend—who is smart in a low-key way and who made it big-time building a business over the years—reached into his wallet and pulled out two crisp $100 bills. "You kids," he said in a quiet voice, "don't have any money to buy Christmas presents. So I want you to buy some Christmas presents, but there is a catch. You can't buy anything for yourself. Think hard about what your brother or sister might like or need and buy that instead. Write me a letter about what you got each other." That one-minute course in caring outdid the best universities anywhere. The kids made up. In January my friend received a letter about what they bought each other, and he sent a copy to me. The kids got adopted. As I hear it, they're quite a team, and their new parents are proud of them—because of the way that they care for each other.

Teamwork

Teamwork is the starting point for treating people right. Most people think that teamwork is only important when competing against other teams. I don't. Competition is only part of the teamwork picture. In most things we do in life, people have to work together rather than against each other to get something done. So, I think win-win situations and partnerships are the most important part of teamwork. The best teams in the world are the ones that help people become better and achieve more than they ever thought they could on their own, so it's no mystery that teamwork is such a big part of success.

One place people learn teamwork is in families. Children get their first teamwork lesson from the way they watch their parents behave toward each other. If you're a parent, you are also a teacher of teamwork—good or bad—every day. Your offspring learn from what you do.

The people I work with have become my family, too. Throughout my career, these "second families" have taught me a lot about teamwork. For example, on Monday morning, August 24, 1992, Hurricane Andrew slammed into South Florida. And yet, all but three of our 21 restaurants in the area were open for business by Friday of that week.

We had employees who lost homes and cars, but nearly all of them came to work. Yes, they were loyal employees, but there's another reason that they came to work. When your life has turned into chaos, people like the stability of a job and being part of a team. This experience drove home the importance of teamwork. A hurricane may rob you of your home, but it can feel good on the dreary, lonely morning after a catastrophe to come home to a team.

Support

Caring is what you give people who can help themselves but who need a partner to open a window or push aside a roadblock. Support is real help, commitment, and effort. Support is "teamwork plus." Support is also sharing feelings and insights with other people. The best way to get support is to give it. It is amazing what can be done when you treat people with respect.

Support is also easier if things aren't too complicated. The simpler you can keep it, the better you

continued

Treating People Right, *continued*

can execute it. If you want to give and get support, it's a lot more likely to come and keep coming if the rules are simple and clear than if they are fuzzy and complicated.

We have all heard of "vicious circles," and most of us have been trapped in a few of them. But what if we get the arrow pointed in the other direction and start putting some "vicious circles" into motion?

Think of others and never let them repay you, but ask that they anonymously repay their debt to you to someone else.

DAVE THOMAS
Founder of Wendy's International

Source: Reprinted from Ken Shelton, ed., *Best of Class* (Provo, UT: Executive Excellence, 1998), pp. 211–212.

Another Look: Motivating Part-Time Employees: What Works

It's hard to motivate part-time employees. They often do low-level work, have little chance for advancement, and are treated as outsiders by full-time employees. So how do managers overcome these problems and turn their part-time staff into a potent force? Here are some proven methods:

- **Orient them properly.** Take 15 minutes to describe job duties and go over the basic rules, e.g., are personal phone calls allowed? *Important: Avoid confusion by clearly identifying who is allowed to give the part-time worker assignments.*

- **Assign a mentor.** Even after proper orientation, part-time workers will be confused. Assign them a full-time worker to be a mentor. The part-time worker will feel more like part of the team, and the mentor will feel good about the added responsibility. *Important: Pick someone who is patient and has the time to answer questions.*

- **Mix up the workload.** Don't overload part-time workers with "grunt" tasks only. It's a common temptation to assign all low-level work to part-time employees. Don't! It's demoralizing. *Important: Find out what specialized skills the part-time worker has, and take advantage of them.*

- **Eliminate any hard feelings** between part-timers and full-timers right from the start. Make sure full-time employees know why you're bringing in part-time help—and that their jobs are not being threatened. *Important: Sell them on the idea that this is going to make their jobs easier.*

- **Offer flexible hours.** Many part-time workers have special situations that require them to work only part-time. Use that to your advantage. By allowing flexible work hours, you'll retain your part-time workers longer, eliminating the need for costly retraining. *Important: Make sure part-time employees clear all scheduling conflicts in advance, to avoid confusion.*

- **Offer financial incentives.** Most companies don't offer part-time workers bonuses. That's a mistake. Set up a bonus plan based on company revenues. Give them a reason to get excited about their jobs. *Important: Offer part-time employees a higher wage than standard. It will prevent competitors from raiding your employees and forcing you to retrain new ones.*

Source: Adapted from *Law Practice Management,* The American Bar Association. Used with permission.

A Case in Point: Foster's Bluebird Territory

At first, Xonyx Corporation was hesitant about hiring Kris Foster. She was attractive and bright, but her education seemed totally unrelated to the competitive business world. She had graduated from a small liberal arts college and had majored in, of all things, humanities.

At the time Foster applied for the job of sales representative, the corporation was under considerable pressure to hire more women. Other women had been employed in the past, but most had not worked out very well. But Foster was different. In her first full year in her sales territory, she made seven thousand dollars more than any other first-year sales representative. Top management was happy to see her succeeding and wanted to give her every opportunity.

Xonyx Corporation is a major manufacturer and distributor of office products. Its word processors, copiers, and duplicators are well known for high quality and very good service. Each sales representative covers a geographic territory. He or she is responsible for following up on the present customers to make sure their equipment needs are being met and for getting additional sales within that area. Often this follow-up requires frequent visits to the offices of customers and potential customers.

Occasionally, sales territories are realigned to meet an increasing demand for Xonyx products. Although every effort is made to give each sales representative an equal opportunity to make commissions, some territories are simply more lucrative than others. Foster's territory, for example, includes several large office complexes. In addition, a major corporation will soon locate in her territory. Other sales representatives on the team good-naturedly kidded her about having a "bluebird" territory: "The bluebirds just come floating in the window bringing her little orders." And, in fact, Foster did receive many more orders over the phone than did the other sales reps.

After a while, though, the ribbing became less good-natured, and the references to her bluebird territory started getting under Foster's skin. She felt she had to work just as hard for each order as did any other sales rep. The situation was aggravated further when the economy took a downturn, and many of the other sales reps had considerable difficulty in meeting their quotas.

Just this morning, Foster came into your office and appeared to be very upset. She recognized that her sales results for the last two months were far lower than in the earlier part of the year. But she seemed to be agitated by something more than just her results.

After a short discussion with you, her manager, in which she expressed her frustrations, Foster shrugged her shoulders and went back to work. But she hinted in her comments that she may not want to stay with the company too much longer. You are concerned about this. She is a good producer, and her long-term relationship with the company would be very beneficial.

Questions

1. What do you think motivates Foster?
2. What types of needs are being fulfilled or being left unfulfilled on her job?
3. How would you, as her manager, help her overcome this slump?
4. What long-range issues need to be addressed to maintain high morale, job satisfaction, and productivity for your sales team?

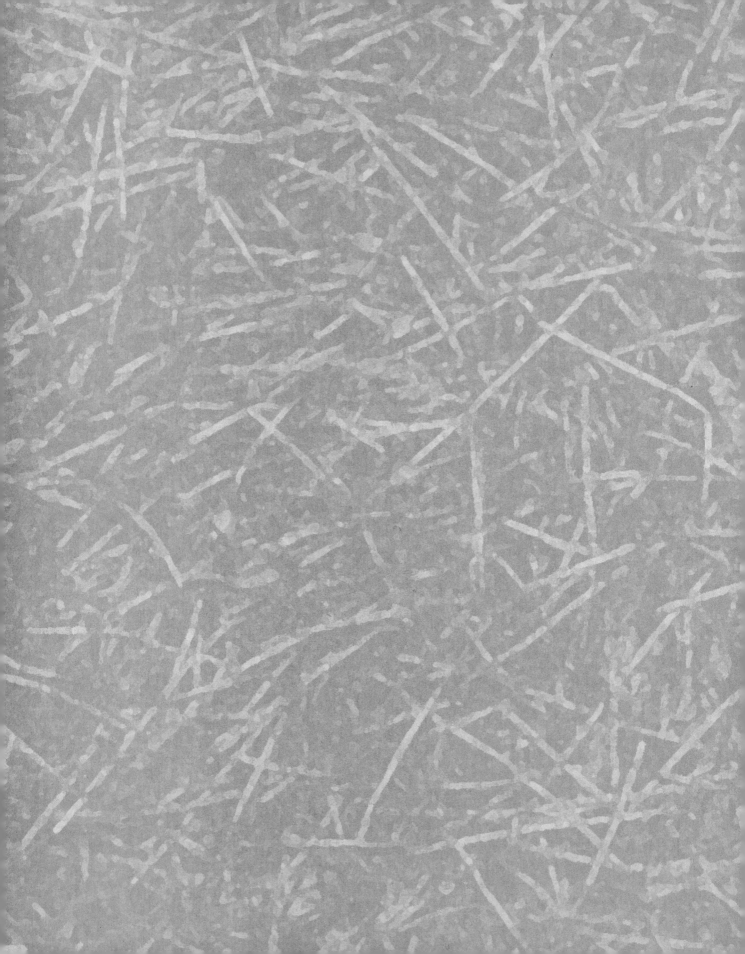

PART 3

ORGANIZATIONS

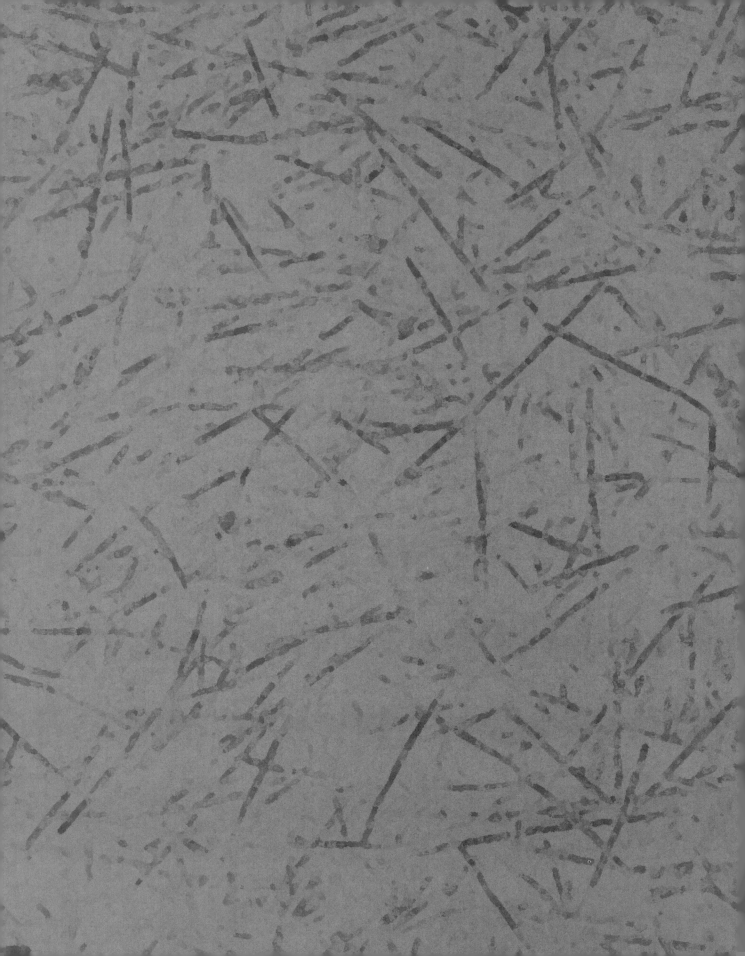

Organizational Structure

- Why do people form organizations?

- What trade-offs must people face as they join or are pulled into organizations?

- Is there one best way to design an organization?

- What features of organizations can be designed by managers?

- What are hot groups or communities of practice?

- What are the six principal types of departmentalization?

- In what ways do organizations seek to control individual behavior?

- What are some modern alternatives to traditional organization patterns?

- What is a virtual organization?

The answers to these and other questions are coming up next in Chapter 5 . . .

In this chapter, we introduce some of the basic concepts of organization theory—issues that affect people at work. We focus on characteristics of organizations—the arrangement of people and resources.

We begin with a warning: Organizations tend to be far more complex than they appear. Neat pyramids of little boxes tell us very little about organizations.

Likewise, comparing organizations to machines (well oiled or otherwise) is an oversimplification. Such a **mechanistic view of organizations** implies that if something goes wrong, one can simply replace the malfunctioning "part" and—voilà!—the machine purrs on once again. But people are not interchangeable parts.

Organizations are far more complicated than machines.

Human organizations are far more complex than any machine. Human interaction is influenced by countless factors: intelligence, social skills, experience, attitudes, emotions, and technical abilities, just to name a few. And no two people are alike.

The One Best Way to Organize: An Elusive Creature

Is there an *ideal* way to build an organization? The search for that elusive butterfly, "the one best way," has been going on for a long time.

In the nineteenth century, Max Weber thought he had found the perfect organizational system. He called it bureaucracy. In a purely theoretical sense, bureaucracy probably could work. But as we all know, the term has now become synonymous with organizational ineffectiveness.

Indeed, no one organizational structure can be perfect for every situation. Just as no two people are exactly alike, neither are any two organizations the same. Every one has its own unique purpose and task. Each has its own distinct culture, or set of acceptable behaviors and values. Therefore, to say that a certain "perfect structure" could be imposed on any organization would be unrealistic.

How Organizing Is Beneficial to Employees

Picture this scene: You have signed on with Moose Lips Corporation, a manufacturer of camping equipment. On your first day, you arrive at the plant, but no one there tells you what you are expected to do. You notice that other people come to work whenever they wish, take long coffee breaks, and generally seem to wander around aimlessly. The work they occasionally do accomplish seems to be of poor quality. No one seems to care much.

Lack of organization is frustrating to workers.

This behavior could get very frustrating, especially if you want to be an effective worker—if you want to contribute to the company's goals. The chaotic situation would lead to very little job satisfaction for you. And the company's objectives—if there were any to begin with—would very likely not be met. (All this probably explains why you don't see Moose Lips products in the stores!)

Organizing seeks to reduce such confusion. It helps members of an organization understand what they are to do, whom they are to report to and receive instructions from, and how their efforts relate to the company's objectives. An effective organizational pattern helps employees gain job satisfaction.

How Organizing Is Beneficial to Companies

Organizations exist for the purpose of accomplishing things that cannot be done by individuals working alone. From the day the earliest cave dweller discovered that a large boulder could not be moved by one person and that the help of others was needed, people have organized their efforts. As the tasks at hand became more and more complicated, the organizational structure also became more complex. Today, with such enormous tasks as building elaborate missile systems, nuclear power generators, water conservation systems, and ambitious space exploration programs, the need for sophisticated organizations is greater than ever.

> The fundamental reason for any organization is to accomplish work that cannot be accomplished by one person working alone.

The benefits of organizing do not, however, come free. People pay a price when they join or form an organization.

Trade-offs: The Price of Organizations

We are all members of many organizations. In our modern world, we all spend a major portion of our lives in some sort of organized activity. At birth, we are introduced to an organization called the hospital staff. Within a few days, we actively join an organization called the family. For the rest of our lives, our needs and wants are fulfilled directly or indirectly by organizations. Manufacturing, farming, mining, and distribution organizations bring products to satisfy material needs. Schools, churches, clubs, and informal social groups serve needs for information, understanding, personal growth, and affiliation. Governments are organized to provide essential services for the public good.

About 90 percent of us work in organizations. In contemporary society, there are few real hermits. Being a recluse from organizational life is difficult, if not impossible.

> Ninety percent of us work in organizations.

Nevertheless, people pay a price to join or exist in organizations. The price is some personal freedom. People cannot do everything they wish once they are members of organizations.

> People pay a price for the benefits of an organization: some freedom.

In the largest organization of which we all are members—society—the price of membership is conformity to social standards. As citizens, we agree to obey the laws, even though we may not want to obey them. Failure to obey the laws, even ones we disagree with, results in punishment.

When we enroll in school, we agree to behave in organizationally acceptable ways—even though we may prefer to act otherwise. We're quiet when we'd rather talk; we sit still when we'd rather jump up and down.

For every organization of which we are members, the trade-off is some decrease in personal freedom—some restraint on what we might like to do—in exchange for the benefit that organization provides.

How Organizations Seek to Control People

One important aspect of an organization's design is the way **controls** are imposed on its members. The number and types of controls used vary.

> What are some examples of organizational controls?

Examples of organizational controls include budgets, interviews, quality inspections, performance reports, product specifications, time clocks, and checks on progress toward goals. The controls imposed on the assembly crew producing a nuclear missile would be very different from those imposed on traveling journalists for *National Geographic* magazine.

In the missile production crew, the tasks would require strict adherence to specifications, safety procedures, and instructions from the engineers. Imagine what disastrous consequences could result if a crew didn't follow assembly instructions precisely: the crew could start a new (and final) world war with a single mistake! Strict controls, such as frequent inspections, engineering tests, and detailed work rules, would be essential in the missile assembly process.

On the other hand, the tough missile assembly rules could never fit the creative atmosphere needed for effective journalism. Here the task requires adherence

FIGURE 5.1 Each organization must find a workable fit between these elements.

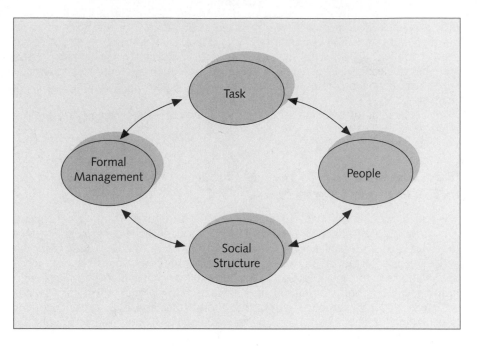

to facts—but not to strict and detailed production inspections. Lives are not usually at stake in writing magazine articles. Besides, if a supervisor from *National Geographic* frequently hovered over the journalists' desks, the independent-minded writers might quit because the close control was intrusive and insulting.

Clearly, the type of organizational structure and controls must *fit* the people, social structure, and task of the organization (see Figure 5.1). However, most organizations follow a similar evolution in structure.

Line and Staff

When organizations first emerge, all members are likely to be **line workers.** The line organization is made up of workers and their supervisors who are directly involved in producing the goods or services that the organization exists to produce.

Line workers produce the goods or services.

Let's say that you have set up shop to manufacture and sell hang gliders. At first, only three people are involved in producing your brand of hang glider, the Gooneybird. Demand for your product is strong, and you all work long hours to keep your distributors stocked with Gooneybirds. You are all line workers.

Eventually, you add more workers and decide to specialize. Some employees build the frames; others install the fabric shell. You set up separate departments. One group focuses on buying raw materials, another is in charge of shipping the Gooneybirds to dealers, and so on. To this point, all workers can still be classified as line workers; they are all involved in the *primary* task of your company—the manufacture and sale of Gooneybird hang gliders.

Finally, the organization grows so large that it needs *specialized assistance.* When one of your customers flies a Gooneybird off a mountainside and is injured on the canyon floor, you see a need for a legal staff to fight the resulting lawsuit. The number of your employees increases, and your line supervisors are spending too much time hiring, explaining company benefits, and so on. So you need to add staff functions like a personnel department.

Staff personnel advise and assist the line organization. They have special expertise, but they normally do not have authority to tell line managers or

As the organization soars to new heights, differentiation becomes necessary.

workers what to do. They offer advice; they do not give orders. Typically, the larger and more complex an organization, the more staff employees it will have.

In addition to the staff-line distinction, other factors affect the design of an organization.

Staff personnel advise and assist the line organization.

Factors That Affect Organizational Design

At least five key factors play a major part in determining the design of an organization: task specialization, task integration, chain of command, location of decisions, and distribution of and access to information.

Task Specialization

One important question in organizational design is "How specialized should each position or job be?" Organizational designers would say, "How 'differentiated' should the organization be?" Let's look into this more deeply.

Going back to the hang glider company example, we can see how **task specialization** might work in two different ways. Suppose the success of the Gooneybird hang glider has been so great that the company is now a major manufacturer. Such a company would become more differentiated; task specialties would emerge. One group of workers would deal full-time with the process of procuring raw materials. Other specialized areas might be the quality control inspectors, the research and development staff, the sales staff, and the like.

The result is that each of these specialized groups becomes expert in dealing with a specific segment of the organization's overall mission. Each group may become so expert—and isolated from other parts of the organization—that the differentiated unit may develop different ways of thinking and even different emotional orientations as it works in those specialized areas. Sometimes its members get carried away and lose sight of the larger organization's intentions.

If the organization becomes too differentiated, the right hand may not know what the left hand is doing. Salespeople may aggressively sell Gooneybirds, while production people are turning out many more of your new, improved model, the Albatross. The specialized purchasing department may buy a ten-year

Five key factors affect the design of an organization:

- Task specialization
- Task integration
- Chain of command
- Location of decisions
- Distribution of and access to information

Efficiency results when specialized tasks are carefully coordinated.

The greater the specialization, the greater the need for integration.

Span of control is the number of people reporting to a manager.

Tall organizations permit managers to work with employees on an individual basis.

Tall organizations may have more communication problems, resulting from the many levels information flows through.

Managers may have difficulty getting to know all their workers in flat organizations with a large span of control.

supply of fabric, while your research people have just discovered a cheaper but stronger substitute product.

Task specialization affects the organization's efficiency in another way. Mass-production techniques, especially the use of assembly lines, are based on the notion of task specialization. The thinking is that as a person repeats a relatively simple procedure over and over again, he or she becomes very efficient at accomplishing that task. This efficiency can pay off for the organization so long as there is adequate coordination of this job with other related tasks. This leads to the next feature of organizational design: **task integration.**

Task Integration

Job specialization as just described can be very useful to the organization so long as its benefits can be *integrated* into the overall organizational talk. The degree of effectiveness of this coordination is another feature of organizational design over which managers have some influence. Once task specialization has occurred, coordination must take place to ensure a smooth operation.

In successful firms, the states of integration and differentiation go hand in hand. The more differentiation there is, the greater the need for collaboration and coordination.

Picture a manufacturing operation where one section is assembling the electronic parts for portable radios and the other is producing cases for them. If the group producing the radios' "innards" assembles six hundred units a day while the other group can only produce three hundred cabinets to house them, the result will be an unbalanced operation. The manager's function here would be to balance the amount of work between the two groups—preferably without sacrificing efficiency. This coordination is a typical organizational design function.

Chain of Command

The arrangement of organizational authority is known as the **chain of command.** It determines who reports to whom. The size of an organization and the number of levels of authority—how many different "ranks" you have—determine the shape of that organization. Some organizations are described as "tall"; others are "flat." Each supervisor's **span of control** helps determine the organization's shape. The span of control indicates how many people report to an individual supervisor. In a **tall organization,** *few people report to each manager,* but there are many levels of management. In a **flat organization,** the span of control is quite broad; *many people report to a given manager.* Figure 5.2 illustrates these two organizational arrangements.

Each type of structure has advantages and disadvantages. The task, the total number of employees, and several other factors can affect the shape of an organization. When the span of control is narrow (as in a tall organization), each supervisor or manager can work on an individual basis with subordinates. The manager who has, say, five people reporting to him or her can get to know and work closely with each employee.

Tall organizations may have more communication problems. As information flows from level to level in a tall organization, messages get distorted. The more levels, the greater the distortion problem. A message from the top executive officer of the company coming down the organization through many levels is at a far greater risk of being distorted than is the same message in a flat organization.

The flat organization with a wide span of control (where one supervisor has many subordinates) poses some other communication and coordination problems. Typically, a manager in a flat organization may have difficulty developing a close relationship with the workers—there are too many people to get to know.

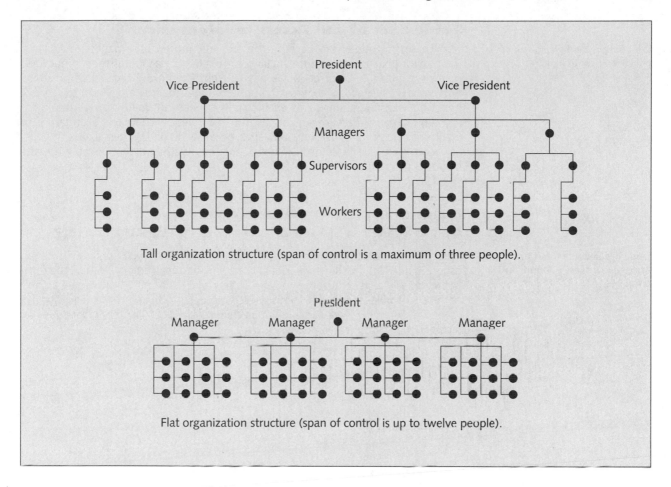

Tall organization structure (span of control is a maximum of three people).

Flat organization structure (span of control is up to twelve people).

Furthermore, when the organization has few different levels, there may be less incentive to work for promotions. The organization that has, say, only three different levels of authority offers fewer opportunities to advance. This may affect the worker's motivation.

FIGURE 5.2 Tall and flat organization structures. Note: Each dot represents one worker.

Location of Decisions

Who makes important decisions in the organization? This question can in part be determined by the organizational design. Some organizations employ *centralized* **decision making** at a very high level. Even relatively routine decisions are made only by top-level management. Other organizations create subunits where decisions may be made. These units may be called **profit centers** and may exist as separate entities for organizational decision making. They plan their own strategies, carry out plans, and are totally responsible for the outcomes of their own efforts.

As discussed in Chapter 4, job enrichment—which is becoming more widespread in organizations—deals with increased responsibility and decision making. Organizations are frequently allowing workers, even at lower-level jobs, to make decisions relevant to their jobs. However, job enrichment is difficult when the tasks to be done are highly specialized or closely regulated. For example, the worker on a timed assembly line has little opportunity for creativity or personal decision making on that job. This limitation in part accounts for the criticism of assembly lines as dehumanizing.

Profit centers are subgroups responsible for their own decisions.

Distribution of and Access to Information

Information can be a source of power and control.

Modern organizations are becoming more and more "information intensive." This means that the need for crucial information is becoming more important to the organization. Information is power. People who are located in positions where they have access to great amounts of information are likely to control organizational functioning. This form of power need not follow the formal organization chart. In many organizations, for example, an executive secretary to a top-level manager may be very powerful because he or she has access to organizational scuttlebutt—informal information—as well as control over who gets in to see the boss.

Departmentalization: Another Approach to Organizing

Large organizations can be broken down into subunits in six ways.

Departmentalization involves grouping together similar types of activities and responsibilities into sections, divisions, branches, or departments. We use the term *department* in a general sense to refer to any such subunit of the organization.

We can break down the large work organization in one of at least six different ways, or we can use a combination of the six. The principal types of departmentalization are as follows:[1]

1. Function
2. Territory
3. Product
4. Customer
5. Time
6. Equipment or process

Function

The most common way to break down work is by **function departmentalization.** Specialized needs of a company are met by specialized departments such

Bookstores display their merchandise to appeal to a wide range of customers.

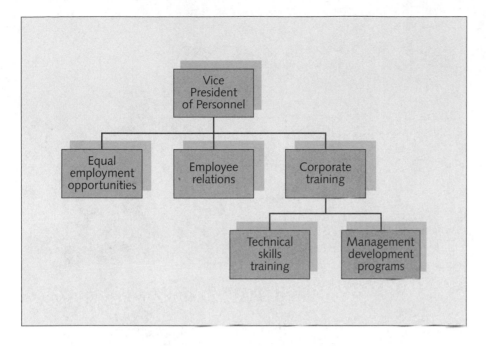

FIGURE 5.3 Function departmentalization.

as research and development, finance, human resources, marketing, and manufacturing.

Large, complex organizations often create many functional divisions with subfunctions under each. For example, the function called *human resources* may eventually add further specialized units, such as equal opportunity employment, employee relations, and corporate training. Even these areas may be further departmentalized, as illustrated in Figure 5.3.

Territory

Some firms organize along *territorial* or *geographic* lines. Local banks, for example, often find they can serve their customers better and gain more customers by establishing branch banks in different neighborhoods. Similarly, companies set up regional offices around the country or around the world to be closer to their customers, suppliers, or transportation facilities. These are examples of **territory departmentalization.**

Product

As organizations grow, they often broaden their lines of products or services. A cosmetics manufacturer may expand into costume jewelry; a food distributor may add a line of paper products. Creation of a jewelry division or paper products division may now make sense. Employees in such divisions can focus their attention on the unique characteristics of their specific products. This is one of the benefits of **product departmentalization.**

Customer

The type of customer served provides another opportunity for departmentalization. Some organizations set up specialized sales forces that sell only to major industrial accounts or to government agencies.

Department stores often create divisions based on the customers served. A bargain basement may serve cost-conscious buyers, while a catalog service offers a wide range of goods to people who prefer not to come to the store. These are examples of **customer departmentalization.**

FIGURE 5.4 Departmentalization on several levels.

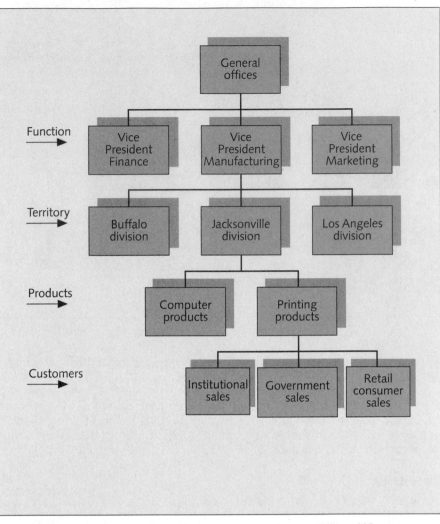

Source: Adapted from Stan Kossen, *Supervision* (New York: Harper & Row, 1981), p. 225.

Wise companies clarify their marketing niche—the specific people at whom they target their sales effort—to maximize productivity. If the target market is senior citizens with above-average income, the company wastes no time on teenagers.

Time

Some organizations work around the clock. The use of shifts is an example of **time departmentalization.** Sometimes a completely different organization with different reporting relationships and responsibilities goes into effect during, for example, the graveyard shift (midnight to 8 A.M.). Equipment breakdowns may be reported directly to the maintenance manager at night, rather than to a lower-level supervisor, as on the day shift.

Equipment or Process

The nature of the equipment or process used provides another common departmentalization opportunity. For example, in a modern printing plant, one department may produce only four-color printing on high-speed presses, while another may print one-color work or do binding, camera work, platemaking, or some other specialized process. This is an example of **equipment or process departmentalization.**

Not all firms use all these types of departmentalization, but often a firm will use several. An organization chart illustrating the combination of several forms of departmentalization is shown in Figure 5.4.

Although departmentalization such as we've described often provides for a more streamlined organization, it can have drawbacks. Perhaps the major one is that departments tend to become competitive and sometimes uncooperative. These smaller work units often fight for their "fair share"—or perhaps a bit more—of the organization's resources. They also tend to blame other departments for foul-ups or delays.

Departmentalization can have drawbacks.

Modern Alternatives to Traditional Organizations

In recent years, companies have often experimented with organization patterns that differ from the traditional ones described thus far. Among these innovations are work teams, matrix organizations, outsourcing, and "communities of practice."

Work Teams and Individual Autonomy

One attempt to overcome the drawbacks of traditional organizational structures is a return to small **work teams or workgroups.** The workgroup in such cases is an autonomous group of employees who are collectively responsible for their output. Perhaps a classic example of this approach was carried out by two Scandinavian auto manufacturers beginning in the 1960s. Work at the Saab and Volvo plants in Sweden was redesigned so that different work teams are responsible for specific installations on the car (for example, the entire electrical system, controls, and instrumentation). One first-level supervisor and one industrial engineer or technician oversee two or four teams. Supervision focuses primarily on overall quality and on making certain that each team has the necessary equipment.[2]

A number of other manufacturing organizations have also begun to use small work teams, sometimes giving them the responsibility for building an entire

Some work teams build entire products from the ground up.

Small, autonomous work teams can offset the drawbacks of larger, traditional organization structures.

product from the ground up. The result of these **self-directed groups** has been, for some employees, additional opportunities, responsibilities, and a higher level of motivation. Quality of the products produced by these teams has been generally very good.

Carrying the team approach one step further, some organizations allow individual workers to build an entire product from the parts provided. Here the manager's responsibility is simply to see that necessary parts are available and to check the quality. One organization using this approach is the Western Electric Corporation, where some employees build electronic switchboard systems from the ground up. The firm's television advertisements extol the virtues of this return to individual craftsmanship and describe the assembly process as a "virtuoso performance." Opportunities for personal satisfaction do exist in such an arrangement, even though not all workers may be ready to be master craftsmen.

Matrix Organizations

A **matrix organization** may be used as an alternative design for the overall company structure or for special projects. The matrix design is organized around function and basically replaces the **pyramid structure** of traditional management organizations. For example, a school's faculty organization might be organized in a matrix design. The functional areas of education—that is, the various subjects taught—could form one axis of the matrix, with the instructors forming the other axis (see Figure 5.5).

This faculty's organization could be shifted or revised each term or school year to match the school's varying needs with the instructors having the most applicable training. For example, in the first year, Mrs. Parker heads the math instruction for both seventh and eighth grades. In the second year, Mrs. Parker shifts to take over science instruction, having taken advanced courses in science during the summer. Now Ms. Jones and Mr. Davis take over seventh- and eighth-grade math instruction to fill the void created by Mrs. Parker's shift to teach science. In addition to working in their functional subject areas, all faculty members report to the principal's office on administrative issues.

A matrix form of organization is often used when special projects must be undertaken. For example, in the aerospace industry, companies create teams made up of employees from different departments for special short-term projects. One such company may want to prepare a major proposal to bid for a government contract. A team is pulled together including engineers, drafters, financial specialists, technical writers, and artists. A project director becomes their boss for as long as they work on the project. When the proposal is completed, the workers return to their regular departments and report again to their departmental bosses.

FIGURE 5.5 A school's matrix organization.

Organizational Resources (Instructors)	Organizational Needs (subjects)					
	Grade 7 History	Grade 8 History	Grade 7 Math	Grade 8 Math	Grade 7 Science	Grade 8 Science
Mrs. Parker						
Ms. Jones						
Mr. Davis						

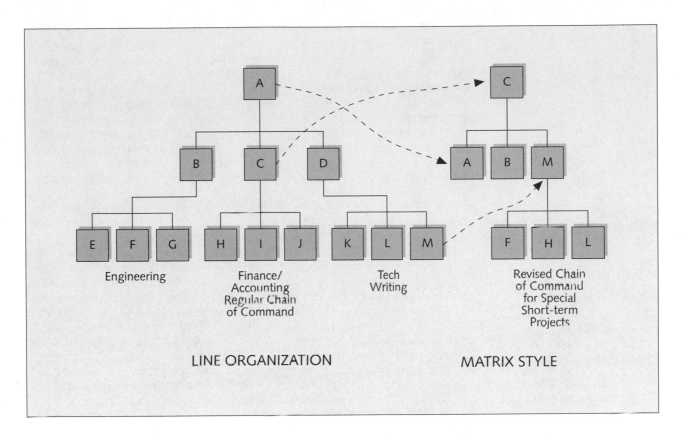

Engineering

Finance/
Accounting
Regular Chain
of Command

Tech
Writing

Revised Chain
of Command
for Special
Short-term
Projects

LINE ORGANIZATION   MATRIX STYLE

In some cases, people of lower rank in the formal organization become bosses in the matrix team. Figure 5.6 shows how person C becomes temporary boss over person A when representatives from various functions are assembled into a project team.

A project manager is chosen to coordinate the effort of this work team but may have no *permanent* authority over these workers. In effect, the matrix organization is a separate entity superimposed on the larger organization. The project leader may temporarily supervise employees who are above, below, or on the same hierarchical level.

Once the project is complete—say, the government bid document is prepared and submitted—the project team is disbanded, and the workers return to their original departments.

Although specialized teams assembled into matrix organizations can be very effective, they also have some disadvantages. For one thing, matrix organization members usually continue to report to their permanent department supervisor as well as to the project leader. This violates an old principle of organizations called **unity of command**—the belief that each individual should report to only one boss.

If the matrix approach is to be successful, both project supervisors and permanent supervisors must resolve any conflicts in their orders to subordinates. The employee must not be required to choose between managers.

Probably the most important determinant of satisfaction in a matrix is a worker's flexibility and self-confidence. Rigid or insecure employees are likely to be uncomfortable in such an arrangement.

FIGURE 5.6 A matrix organization.

The matrix becomes a separate entity superimposed on the larger organization.

Matrix organizations violate the unity-of-command principle.

The flexible, self-confident worker will be most comfortable in a matrix.

Hot Groups and Communities of Practice

While most organizational structure is consciously created, subgroups often emerge spontaneously. In some cases these groups are a response to a pressing problem or issue; they sprout up to seek a solution. These are sometimes called **hot groups or hot teams.**

Hot groups are not formally defined or empowered by management; they spontaneously come together to tackle a common issue. Their members are dedicated and committed to the group's goal. Roles and responsibilities within the group change and shift continuously. There is no formal leader; instead, leadership flows from person to person. They are not controlled by management but need management's blessing in the form of autonomy and leeway to pursue their cause.

At times, hot groups can be disruptive to the organization. They may seem arrogant toward other parts of the organization, and they may bend the rules. However, their value lies in their inventiveness and energy.

Thomas Stewart's breakthrough book, *Intellectual Capital*,[3] explains a similar type of informal organization in a particularly useful way. He speaks of "communities of practice" where people with a similar interest come together without formal structure. Business examples may be the copier repair people who share ideas on how to deal with a sticky repair problem. Social examples are people who meet to enrich their lives through study, discussion, religious experience, charitable service, hobbies, or the like. (An excerpt from Stewart's book appears later in this chapter.)

The important thing to remember about both hot groups and communities of practice is that, for them to succeed, management should "bug out." Attempts to formalize (for example, scheduling a regular idea-sharing meeting each week) only damage the spontaneity and flexible nature of the group. Such informal subgroups add much to the texture and effectiveness of companies. Managers should value and encourage such organic interaction.

From Pyramid to Circle

Bureaucratic or rigidly structured organizations are marked by highly specialized functions, clear departmental boundaries, limited job descriptions, and close supervisory control to make sure that the work gets done. Cynthia Scott and Dennis T. Jaffe see modern organizations moving away from pyramid structures to "circles" that permit greater employee empowerment. They see the following as characteristics of the pyramid:

- Decisions are made at the top.

- Each person is clearly responsible only for his or her job.

- Change is slow and rare and comes only from the top.

- Feedback and communication come from the top down.

- Movement and communication between divisions is minimal.

- If you do your job, you can expect job security and promotions as the organization expands.

- People focus attention upward, and the person above you is responsible for your results.

- Managers say how things are done and what is expected.

- Employees are not expected to be highly motivated, so it is necessary to keep tight control over their behavior.

Until recently, most organizations operated roughly according to those principles. But now, more organizations are evolving into a new organizational environment characterized by high commitment, high involvement, and self-management. One way to look at the shift toward empowerment is to think of two basic ways to structure the organization.

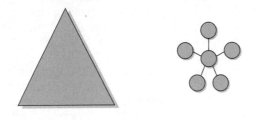

The traditional organization is the pyramid, while the new, empowered organization looks more like a **circle** or a **network.** The new organizational form is called the circle or network because it can be viewed as a series of coordinating groups or teams, linked by a center rather than an apex.

However, do not confuse a flattened organizational structure with the philosophy of empowerment. Empowered individuals can and do thrive in hierarchical structures, and many flattened organizations have traditional employees. Empowerment and hierarchies are not mutually exclusive management/organizational philosophies. Both are prevalent and necessary in business today.

The following are characteristics of the circle:

- The customer is in the center.

- People work cooperatively to do what is needed.

- Responsibility, skills, authority, and control are shared.

- Control and coordination come through continual communication and many decisions.

- Change is sometimes very quick, as new challenges come up.

- The key skill for an employee, and a manager, is the ability to work with others.

- There are relatively few levels of organization.

- Power comes from the ability to influence and inspire others, not from your position.

- Individuals are expected to manage themselves and are accountable to the whole; the focus is on the customer.

- Managers are the energizers, the connectors, and the empowerers of their teams.[4]

Outsourcing and Virtual Organizations

One of the most dramatic changes in modern organizations is the use of outsourcing to do the company's functions. In traditional companies, we had departments to fulfill most if not all functions: sales, manufacturing, accounting, human

resources, training, and so on. Some organizations today eschew as many functions as possible and instead hire outside firms to do them all. In a sense they
create **virtual organizations,** organizations that are really a confederation of
independent service providers.

The major advantage of a virtual organization is that the company need not
own or maintain facilities and functions that can soak up a lot of cash. You could,
for example, create a virtual organization by calling a staffing agency to get the
workers you need (the agency will handle recruiting, hiring, payroll, benefits,
and so on), hiring another firm to produce a product, another company to distribute the product through their sales force, another firm to handle accounting,
and so on.

This kind of organization is being used quite frequently in small, entrepreneurial firms. It obviously cuts down the need for large capital investment. Futurists see modified versions of the virtual organization becoming widespread. Traditional companies with a large, permanent employee base will soon be replaced
by more adaptable structures consisting of three groups (Figure 5.7).[5]

Core Employees

In the first group, critical functions will be retained by a small core of relatively
permanent employees with broad skills allowing them to tackle a variety of jobs.
Core employees are those who make lifelong learning and ongoing skill development a priority in their lives. They function to create and shape the vision of
the organization.

Supplemental Employees

A second, larger group of available employees will be added or eliminated quickly
as needed. Supplemental employees will be retained through contract or temporary services to meet shifting work levels. The technical skill level of these

FIGURE 5.7 Organizational
structures will be more adaptable
in the future.

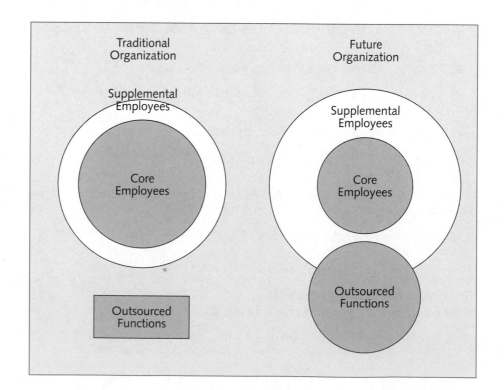

people will be dramatically higher than today's "temps." They will be technicians, managers, and even executives who will be contracted as supplemental workers.

Outsourced Work Functions

Finally, more work will be farmed out to a third group: other companies or professionals. Examples of outsourced work functions may be accounting, legal, human resources, and transportation functions. Some companies may even farm out manufacturing.

What communication skills are likely to be critical in each of these groups? Core workers will need to communicate and coordinate across **functional disciplines** and be, as mentioned earlier, constantly learning. They must be good at asking the right questions, seeking out the right information, and learning new disciplines, largely on their own. This type of worker would readily read a book or manual, and apply the information to his or her ever-expanding work responsibilities.

Effects of Technology on Organizations

Finally, traditional organizational structures can be drastically changed by adapting to changing technology. Many manufacturing organizations are becoming more aware of the economic advantages of using robots to accomplish organizational work. The cost of human labor is often extremely high when compared with the operating costs of the increasingly available, electronically guided machines. Although few people think that machines will entirely replace human labor, machines do pose an alternative for some firms.

The cost of human labor is often far greater than the cost of machines.

Another impact of technology is increased sophistication in communications. Today, a growing number of people are members of organizations but never have any physical contact with their fellow members. Via computer networks, modems, fax machines, and the like, more people work at home or other widely dispersed locations. The organization is based almost entirely in the commonness of purpose, not in any physical structure.

Up to this point, we've emphasized (1) factors that determine a need for organizations and (2) factors that shape organizations from within. But organizations also are shaped by outside forces, some of which they may have little control over.

Other Forces That Organizations Must Face

Organizations do not exist in a vacuum. They are constantly interacting with many different environmental forces. These forces include the society in which they exist, the political climate, and the availability of needed resources, all of which provide opportunities and challenges to organizational leaders.

Organizations have recognized that they need not be simply *acted on* by their environment. Frequently, an organization may do better to reach out and try to influence environmental forces. For example, many corporations have become very active in the political arena. Their intent is to affect legislation that in turn affects their businesses. So, instead of sitting back and having the government act on the organization with regulations and legislation, organizations reach out and attempt to influence those governmental actions.

Organizations realize the value of reaching out to influence their environment.

Similarly, organizations are sensitive to social problems and changes. Many companies have initiated aggressive social action programs. In part, they do this

Organizations seek to influence social changes, political actions, sources of resources, and so forth.

to avoid government regulation, But in many cases, they simply recognize the public relations and societal benefits of such activities.

For example, some major companies, such as Xerox, IBM, and Wells Fargo, offer their employees **social service leaves of absence.** Under this program, selected employees are given full pay and benefits while they perform volunteer service for a year or more. Often the volunteer service is coordinated through a social services agency or charitable group. The advantages for the company are public recognition as well as a program that can boost employee morale and help workers gain new skills.

The idea of influencing the environment is not new. Early manufacturers recognized the importance of controlling resources for their companies. Near the beginning of the twentieth century, Ford Motor Company bought mines, foundries, and railroads to ensure that raw materials for its automobiles would not be interrupted. Today, many organizations contribute generously to colleges and universities to ensure a continued supply of trained labor.

The point is that few organizations can sit back and be acted on by external forces. It makes sense for them to reach out and to activate, influence, and control important forces such as government, social pressure groups, and suppliers of vital materials.

Summary of Key Ideas

- Organizations are complex social systems that provide order and direction for individuals through a structure that helps the organization accomplish its goals.

- With organization come some necessary limitations on personal freedom.

- Despite the years of research on how to organize, no one has found one best way that is appropriate in all situations.

- People are controlled in varying degrees by the formal management controls, task requirements, and social structure of an organization.

- Line employees are concerned with production of the organization's goals or service, while staff personnel provide assistance and counsel to the line employees.

- Five factors affecting organizational design are task specialization, task integration, chain of command, location of decisions, and distribution of and access to information.

- Departments may be organized by function, territory, product, customer, time, and equipment or process. Any combination of the six may also be found.

- Four modern alternatives to traditional organizations are work teams, matrix organizations, hot groups, and communities of practice.

- Virtual organizations are created by outsourcing most of a firm's functions.

- Modern organizations are moving away from pyramid structures toward circle or network structures.

- People are often connected via communication technology and have no physical contact with the organization.

Key Terms, Concepts, and Names

Centralized decision making
Chain of command
Circle or network organizations
Controls
Customer departmentalization
Equipment or process
    departmentalization
Flat versus tall organizations
Function departmentalization
Functional disciplines
Hot groups or hot teams
Line workers
Matrix organizations
Mechanistic view of organizations

Product departmentalization
Profit center
Pyramid structure
Self-directed workgroups
Social service leaves of absence
Span of control
Staff personnel
Task integration
Task specialization
Territory departmentalization
Time departmentalization
Unity of command
Virtual organizations
Work teams or workgroups

Questions and Exercises

1. Describe some ways in which specific organizations reach out to influence their environments. How effective are they? How could they do more?

2. Draw up an organization chart for your school or organization. Show any departmentalization. Explain whether the organization is tall or flat. How could it be rearranged?

3. What are some of the effects of a tall organization? of a flat organization? How are these types of organization structures likely to affect workers on the job? Which type of organization would you prefer to work in? Why?

4. Describe a case in which work teams, matrix organizations, and virtual organization structures would be effective.

5. Read the "Another Look" articles on the following pages. Then answer the introductory questions at the beginning of this chapter.

Notes

1. The discussion of departmentalization was adapted in part from Stan Kossen, *Supervision* (New York: Harper & Row, 1981), pp. 224–229.

2. Edgar F. Huse, *The Modern Manager* (St. Paul, MN: West, 1979), p. 353.

3. Thomas A. Stewart, *Intellectual Capital: The New Wealth of Organizations* (New York: Currency/Doubleday, 1997).

4. Cynthia D. Scott and Dennis T. Jaffe, *Empowerment* (Los Altos, CA: Crisp Publications, 1991), p. 12.

5. Paul R. Timm and James A Stead, *Communication Skills for Business and Professions* (Upper Saddle River, NJ: Prentice-Hall, 1996), p. 12.

Another Look: How to Build Human Capital: The Role of Community

When the CEO says "people are our most important asset," he's speaking of people who know how to serve customers in ways that give the company an edge. Considering human capital in these terms sheds new light on how to build it, and on the process of capitalizing individual knowledge to create an organizational asset.

If the term "community of practice" wasn't invented at the Institute for Research on Learning, that's where it's most often bandied about. IRL's mission—to study how people learn—makes it a center for basic research for the Information Age. The fundamental finding in IRL's work is that learning is a social activity: However romantic the image of the scholar bent over his desk in a pool of lamplight, learning happens in groups.

That's an insight with huge—and problematic—implications for managers. Not every group is a learning place. You can't take a dozen people at random, give them a pot of coffee and a box of doughnuts, and expect them to learn something. Groups that learn, communities of practice, have special characteristics. They emerge of their own accord: Three, four, twenty, maybe thirty people find themselves drawn to one another by a force that's both social and professional; they collaborate directly, use one another as sounding boards, teach each other, strike out together to explore new subject matter. You cannot create communities like this by fiat, but they are easy to destroy. They are among the most important structures of any organization where thinking matters; but they are, almost inevitably, subversive of its formal structures and strictures.

Communities of practice are the shop floor of human capital, the place where the stuff gets made. Brook Manville, a consultant at McKinsey & Co., defines a community of practice thus: "A group of professionals, informally bound to one another through exposure to a common class of problems, common pursuit of solutions, and thereby themselves embodying a store of knowledge." Most of us belong to more than one, and not just on the job: The management team; the engineers, some in your company and some not, trying to cram more circuits onto a wafer of silicon; the church choir. Different communities might have concerns that overlap. Trying to solve a problem for his church choir—how could they mark the day's hymns without damaging the

hymnals by dog-earing or paper-clipping pages?—led tenor Arthur Fry to conceive the product that became Post-it notes, developed by a community of adhesives experts at 3M.

IRL's Etienne Wenger points to several traits that define communities of practice and distinguish them from other groups. First, they have history—they develop over time, indeed "you can define them in terms of the learning they do over time." Second, a community of practice has an enterprise, but not an agenda; that is, it forms around a value-adding something-we're-all-doing. It could be a gang seeking to carve a place for itself on the streets, or a district sales office wanting to be the best doggone district office in the company; it could be people who don't work side by side but share a mission, like antitrust lawyers, Alcoholics Anonymous groups, or copier repairers who exchange tips at the water cooler. Third, the enterprise involves learning; as a result, over time communities of practice develop customs, culture—"a way of dealing with the world they share."

Perhaps most intriguing, communities of practice are responsible only to themselves. No one owns them. They're like professional societies. People join and stay because they have something to learn and something to contribute. The work they do is the joint and several property of the group—"cosa nostra," our thing.

These traits give communities of practice a distinct place in the ecology of the informal organization. Project groups and teams have a charter and report to a higher authority: Even if they have no box on an organization chart, they have an agenda, a deadline, accountability, a membership list. A community of practice is voluntary, longer-lived and has no specific "deliverable" such as a report or a new product. Affinity groups and clubs—the salesmen who play poker every Friday night—are about fellowship rather than work. Grapevines and other networks may support your work, but are not central to it.

Communities of practice are so obviously present in our daily lives that we don't usually notice them. When we do, however, the implications are anything but quotidian. Communities of practice perform two main jobs of human capital formation: knowledge transfer and innovation. James Euchner, a vice president of Nynex's research and development

continued

How to Build Human Capital: The Role of Community, *continued*

department, began thinking about them when he was puzzling over why some groups at Nynex were quick to adopt new technologies, others not. For example, some groups needed, on average, seventeen days to set up data services for customers. Euchner hired an anthropologist to learn why they took so long. She found that different departments involved in the process never communicated informally and, as a result, didn't understand one another's roles and needs and couldn't solve problems together. When she and Euchner put the workers together in the same room, they created an environment that allowed informal groups to form around various tasks, which soon grew into a full-fledged community of practice. Result: a mutual sense of purpose and a sharing of ideas that cut the time to provision data services to just three days.

Euchner found himself face to face with a challenge communities of practice pose: Organizational learning depends on these often invisible groups, but they're virtually immune to management in a conventional sense—indeed, managing them can kill them. A study by three academics—Ronald Purser of Loyola University in Chicago and William Pasmore and Ramkrishnan Tenkasi of Cleveland's Case Western Reserve University—shows why. The professors followed two product-development projects in the same big American manufacturer. One, a major upgrade of a key technology, was rigorously managed and relied on big fortnightly meetings to keep everybody up to speed; the other, a radical innovation, was scarcely managed at all: The professors called it "self-organizing . . . informal . . . egalitarian." The former slogged; the latter soared; the main reason, Purser et al. found, was that the formal structure of the first group erected barriers to learning. Chief among them: failure to use already-available knowledge, withholding important knowledge because of mistrust or conflicts between groups, holding discussions from which key people were missing, failure to take heed of important information from other divisions or the business environment, and divergent values between groups. Essentially, the formal structure of the first group prevented people from talking; the second group was full of places where people felt free to speak up.

If they can't manage communities of practice, managers can nevertheless help them. How?

Recognize Them and Their Importance

They're relatively easy to spot within a department or business unit, like those copier repairers; harder to see are communities that cross lines. Look for jobs that exist in different functions, business units, or geographic areas. Plant or office managers, sales reps, metallurgists, MIS weenies—from Abilene to Aberdeen, these have common enterprises; all probably do some knowledge sharing; they would benefit from closer contact.

In Silicon Valley, National Semiconductor has encouraged communities of practice by giving them semiofficial status. It set up a Communities of Practice Council, in which half a dozen communities are currently members, among them a group of technologists who focus on designing computer chips for communications signal processing, another exploring wireless computing, a third specializing in design for manufacturing. These are all critical technologies for many different lines of business at National Semiconductor—so it's vital that expertise isn't bottled up inside one business unit. The Communities of Practice Council helps them by offering technical support (such as designing internal Web pages) and lobbying for funds to, for example, fly an outside expert to company headquarters to speak to a group. Though they don't show up on the org chart, these professional associations are recognized as important by top management; one has even taken on responsibility for reviewing all microchip designs developed by different business units.

Give Them the Resources They Need

Communities of practice don't need much in the way of resources: Let them build an intranet, use the conference room from time to time, put an occasional get-together on the expense account, bring in a speaker. Company communications systems are usually laid out along existing departmental lines—and thus are inimical to brainstorming, floating trial balloons, and other informal means of sharing problems and ideas. Brevetting people to work for a time in another business unit or department can also help. For the company, there are major benefits from connecting people who may otherwise unknowingly duplicate each others' efforts or walk away from projects that are too big to undertake single-handed.

continued

How to Build Human Capital: The Role of Community, *continued*

Fertilize the Soil, But Stay Away from Actual Husbandry

Says Valdis Krebs, a Los Angeles consultant who helps businesses solve organizational design problems by mapping networks to reveal how work really gets done: "Fund them too much, and you'll start to want deliverables. You won't get what you want. You'll get what the community wants to deliver." That's because these groups are motivated by their enterprise—this thing we're all learning about. For them, boundaries exist to be crossed, just as mountains exist to be climbed. Information wants to be free.

That's the subversive part. Stanford professor Stephen Barley puts it: "As communities of practice proliferate, occupational principles begin to compete with administrative principles." A person's responsibilities to the communities of which he is a member sometimes conflict with each other, and with the rules and interests of the company he works for.

Watch a bunch of scientists at a convention: They swap secrets like street vendors opening their jackets to flash contraband Rolexes. In the late 1980s, Eric von Hippel, a professor at the Sloan School of Management at MIT, studied how manufacturing process engineers in the steel minimill industry traded proprietary information even with direct competitors. With so much to learn in their relatively young business, the steelmakers—from companies like Nucor and Chaparal Steel—evidently figured that sharing secrets was a fair price for progress. Says Von Hippel: "It happens everywhere. The standard corporate view is you're giving away the store, but the fact is, if others are cooperating and you decide not to, you fall behind."

Another Look: Dr. Peter Drucker Tells All about the Network Society . . . the New Structure of Business

On the eve of World War I, less than one-fifth of the U.S. labor force worked for an organization, primarily as blue-collar workers in small family-owned enterprises. The vast majority of people, by contrast, worked for a "master" or "mistress."

By the 1950s, employees of large organizations dominated every developed economy—as blue-collar workers and managers in industry . . . as civil servants in giant government agencies . . . as nurses in rapidly growing hospitals . . . as teachers in even-faster-growing universities.

The best-selling books of those years were jeremiads about the "Organization Man" who puts loyalty to the organization above everything else.

Few people then doubted that by 1990 almost everyone in the work force could be employed by an organization, and probably a big one.

They were wrong.

A much larger proportion of adults now participate in the US labor force than they did 30 or 40 years ago. Most—especially the great majority of educated people—do indeed work for an organization.

But increasingly they are not employees of that organization. They are contractors, part-timers and temps.

Recently I ran a three-day seminar for some 300 alumni of one of the major graduate business schools—mostly highly successful people in their late 30s or early 40s. Practically every one of them worked for an organization—but barely half as employees. Fewer still expected to spend their entire working lives as employees of an organization.

Not Enough to Do

One participant—a 45-year-old metallurgist—was an executive of a *Fortune* 500 company only five years ago. Today he is on his own and retained by five companies, one of them his former employer.

"There simply wasn't enough to do for me in the old company," he said. "It has a serious metallurgical problem only three or four times a year. The rest of the time, I wrote memoranda. Now, when that company has a metallurgical problem I dive right in . . . as a full-time member of the team and as its leader.

continued

Peter Drucker Tells All, *continued*

But I stay only until we've licked the problem. I work the same way for my other four clients."

Full-Time Temps

Then there was the 38-year-old information specialist who works as a "permanent temp" for a number of state agencies in the Midwest.

There was the executive of an "outsourcing' firm who described herself as an "itinerant member of top management" in the 20 large hospitals for which her company keeps the books and does housekeeping and maintenance.

There was the engineer on the payroll of a "temporary-help" firm who works as plant manager for large companies—usually on a three-year contract whenever such a company builds and runs in a new plant; the woman physician who works as a "temp" in setting up emergency departments in hospitals; and a former college dean who works as a "full-time temp"—for a year at a time—setting up and running college fund-raising campaigns.

New Relationships

In the US, the number of temporary-employment agencies doubled to 7,000 in 1994 from 3,500 five years earlier. Perhaps half, if not more, of this growth is in agencies providing professionals—all the way up to senior managers.

Relations between organizations themselves are changing just as fast. The most visible example is "outsourcing," in which a company, hospital or government agency turns over an entire activity to an independent firm specializing in that kind of work. Hospitals have been turning over maintenance and housekeeping for many years now; increasingly they are also outsourcing their data processing and business management.

Outsourcing information systems has become routine for businesses, government agencies, universities and hospitals.

On one day in March, two such ventures were announced. The largest hospital company in the US, Columbia/HCA, announced that it had outsourced the purchasing and maintenance of all diagnostic instruments in its 300 hospitals to General Electric Co.'s Medical Systems. And IBM announced the formation of a new business (called NetWorkStation Management) to purchase, maintain and manage the many thousands of personal computers in large companies.

In another 10 or 15 years, organizations may be outsourcing all work that is "support" rather than revenue-producing, and all activities that do not offer career opportunities into senior management. In many organizations, a majority of the people might be employees of an outsourcing contractor.

The Power of Alliances

Even more important may be the trend toward alliances as the vehicle for business growth. Downsizing, divestitures, mergers, acquisitions—these dominate the headlines. But the greatest change in corporate structure—and in the way business is being conducted—may be the accelerating growth of relationships based not on ownership but on partnership—joint ventures . . . minority investments cementing a joint-marketing agreement or an agreement to do joint research . . . seminormal alliances of all sorts.

Japanese computer makers are gaining access to software technology by buying minority stakes in high-tech Silicon Valley firms.

Large American and European pharmaceutical companies gain access to research in genetics, medical electronics and biotechnology by buying minority stakes in start-up firms or by going into partnership with small, independent asset managers.

And there are any number of even less formal "alliances"—most of them unreported—like the one between the world's leading designer of microchips, Intel, and Sharp, a major Japanese manufacturer. Intel will do the research and design . . . Sharp, the manufacturing. Each company will separately market the resulting new products—and apparently neither firm is investing a penny in the other.

In telecommunications there are the "consortia" in which three or more big established telephone companies—one American, one English, one Swedish, for instance—team up to obtain licenses for cellular-phone services all over the world, or for cable TV or to buy into an old government monopoly about to be privatized.

One reason the trend toward partnerships is accelerating is that no one company, not even the

continued

Peter Drucker Tells All, *continued*

telephone giants, has enough money to swing the deal alone. A more important reason is that no one company has the needed technology. And in many parts of the world, such as coastal China and Malaysia, business cannot be done except through a joint venture or an alliance with a local partner.

Size Isn't Everything

In 1967, the world's business best-seller was *"Le Défi Américain"* ("The American Challenge") by Jean-Jacques Servan-Schreiber, a French journalist. It predicted that by 1985 or 1990, the world's economies would be owned and run by a mere dozen or so huge American multinationals producing some 90% of the world's manufactured goods. Even earlier, in 1955, the "Fortune 500" had made bigness the measurement of business success.

By the time Servan-Schreiber published his book, the tide in the world economy had already turned. Both the Europeans and the Japanese were giving the Americans a run for their money. A few years later, the growth dynamics in the US economy (and soon after in the European economies) began to shift toward the medium-sized company. But still, the basic structures of organizations and of employment seemed to remain what they had been for decades. Now both are changing rapidly.

Earning Trust

Even if 20 years hence the majority of managers and professionals are still employees of the organizations they work for, the psychology of the work force—especially of the knowledge work force—will largely be determined by the large minority who are not employees of that organization. This means that organizations had better stop talking about "loyalty." They will have to earn the trust of the people who work for them, whether these people are their own employees or not. Even the professional or executive who has no intention of leaving the company's employ will know that there are opportunities outside—many already know that, even in Japan.

And even professionals or executives who would much prefer to stay with the company they now work for will know that there is no such thing as "lifetime employment" anymore. Even in government service, where lifetime tenure has been the rule, radical downsizing is surely going to occur in all developed (and in most emerging) countries.

Conversely, individual professionals and executives will have to learn that they must take responsibility for placing themselves, both within their organization and outside of it. This means above all that they must know their strengths.

Most résumés I get—and I get several from former students every day—list the jobs the person has held. A few then describe the job the person would like to get.

Very few even mention what the person has done well and can do well.

Even fewer state what a future employer can and should expect from that person.

Very, very few, in other words, yet look upon themselves as a "product" that must be marketed.

The Network Society

Equally novel are the demands partnerships and alliances make on managing a business and its relationships. Executives are used to command.

Even Japanese "consensus management" is one way to get acceptance by the organization of whatever the higher-ups have decided should be done—and so is the much-touted "participative management."

But in a partnership, one cannot command. One can only gain trust. Specifically that means that one must not start out asking, "What do we want to do?" The right question is, "What do they want to do? What are their objectives? Their values? Their ways of doing things?" *Again:* These are marketing relationships—and in marketing one starts with the customer rather than with one's own product.

I asked participants in that alumni seminar a few months ago what to call this new organization and its society. At first they said: "Call it free-form." But then they reconsidered and said: "Call it the *Network Society."*

Source: Reprinted by permission of the author. First published in *The Wall Street Journal* on July 1, 1995. © Peter R. Drucker, 1995.

A Case in Point: Moto-Wiz Goes Matrix

Sandra Dudley was generally happy in her job as an electrical engineer working for a medium-sized, but rapidly growing, specialized motors manufacturer. She had been with Moto-Wiz for eight months, having been hired fresh out of college. She had a good boss, one who was very careful in giving her clear instructions for each task assigned to her. But she now got the impression that all that would soon change.

Moto-Wiz had been invited to bid on a government contract for specialized plastic motors to be used in the armament system of the new B-2 bomber. Winning the contract could result in enormous profits for Moto-Wiz. It would be, by far, the company's largest contract.

Top management had decided to set up a special team to prepare a proposal, complete with design specifications to be submitted. They assigned as project director a man from the research and development department. Dudley was selected for the project, along with people from marketing, finance, technical writing, and the art department. The project was to be completed in 30 days. This would require a lot of overtime and a lot of very hard work.

Dudley knew the project manager vaguely, but the rest of the team members were unknown to her.

She was more than a little uncomfortable about the upcoming project.

Questions

1. How do you think Dudley is likely to react to this new assignment?
2. As Dudley's department head, what would you do to help her in this change in her work arrangement?
3. What could the project director do to help employees like Dudley be successful in this matrix organization?
4. What are the probable advantages and disadvantages faced by Moto-Wiz in its decision to use a matrix organization?
5. How might the matrix organization affect work climate, employee satisfaction, and worker motivation?

Training and Development: Yourself and Others

- What are the basic steps for bringing about change in people's lives?

- What is the difference between attitudes and behaviors?

- Why is dissonance important in the process of change?

- What role do trusted people play in the change process?

- What role do life experiences play in the change process?

- What are the differences between training, education, and development?

- What are the differences between the three areas of development focus: job, individual, and organization?

- What is the role of employee development in organizations?

The answers to these and other questions are coming up next in Chapter 6 . . .

Phil grew up on a large ranch in a sparsely populated area of the West, where he enjoyed such activities as riding a horse, camping under the stars, and playing with his dog. His father was constantly pushing him to leave home and attend a university: "You'll grow up to be a bum! You've got to go to college and get educated. If you want to be a success in this life, you need to be better than me!"

Phil would ponder his father's statements and usually reply, "I don't want to go to college, I don't need a college education to work on the ranch." When Phil's father could see that his begging wasn't working, he decided to bribe Phil. He offered him a new horse trailer if he would go to college for one semester. His hopes were that Phil would enjoy the university so much that he wouldn't want to come back to the ranch until he finished his education.

Phil decided a horse trailer was worth one semester at college. He entered a large university on the Pacific coast with a gigantic group of first-year students. The smallest class he signed up for had 50 students in it. He did not enjoy being with a lot of people, but he started to have positive experiences.

Just before he took his first examination, a young woman named Jennifer started sitting next to him in class. He was a bit embarrassed but said, "Hi, I'm Phil."

She looked at him and said, "Hi, Phil, my name is Jennifer." She looked at Phil's boots and said, "You must be a cowboy."

"Yes, I'm in the rodeo club," he replied.

She in turn said, "I was a rodeo queen in my hometown."

"Well, let's go riding," Phil said.

"I'd love to," Jennifer responded.

While they were horseback riding, they decided to study together for their first test. They studied together and both of them received A's on the test. Suddenly, Phil was starting to get some very positive feelings about attending college. He was getting good grades, and he had met a great young woman.

Furthermore, he met one of the outstanding rodeo stars who had always been his favorite. The rodeo star told Phil, "You really made a wise decision. Riding and messing around rodeos the rest of your life is not the way to go. You need to have managerial experience; you need a background in business so you can more effectively run the ranch."

Needless to say, Phil said he would stay in college and get his degree. He was very satisfied that his father had bribed him by giving him a horse trailer. After all, he now had a horse trailer, and in a few years he would have a college degree.

Getting Started: Bringing About Change

The way people act is the result of what they think.

Phil's story illustrates the change process in human beings. There are a variety of ways to bring about change in the lives of people.

The way people act is the result of what they think or the **attitude** they hold. Phil came to college because he was bribed by his father. His attitude was that attending college was bad and that staying home on the ranch was good. However, at school he received positive reinforcement or feedback on his schooling experience, which caused him to change his attitude. He liked Jennifer, he aced the test, and a respected person told him that being at school was important. His attitude changed to be in accordance with his behavior. We can diagram this as shown in Figure 6.1.

Attitudes are opinions and the positive or negative feelings people associate with those opinions. Attitudes predispose people to behave or act the way they do. For example, if you feel that attending college is good (attitude), then you will likely attend college (behavior).

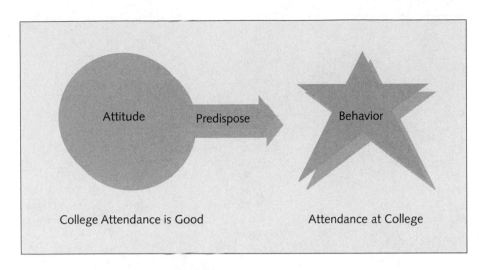

FIGURE 6.1 A model of change.

When managers deal with employees in organizations, the principles are the same. To change someone, begin by dealing with the person's behavior or attitudes. One can try to change the attitude, or one can try to change the behavior.

There are many theories about attitude change. One of the more famous deals with **cognitive dissonance.** This theory states that dissonance occurs if attitudes and behaviors are dissimilar. It is difficult to change someone whose attitudes and behavior are in agreement. However, if a manager can create within an employee a difference between behaviors and attitudes, the employee will reduce the dissonance by changing either the behavior or the attitude, so the two will match.

Dissonance is the feeling one has when doing something in which one does not believe.

Phil came to the university in a dissonant state. His attitudes and behavior were not similar. He was open for change. Two things could happen to reduce his dissonance: (1) he could leave school and retain his attitude that school was bad, or (2) he could change his attitude to "school is good" and stay at school.

If we want to change people, we can create dissonance in them.

Change: A Slow Process

Experience with people in organizations shows that after dissonance is created, two major steps can help a person change: (1) introduction to new and **credible people** and (2) introduction to new experiences. The impact that people and new experiences have on us is exemplified by the story of Phil. Having a rodeo rider he trusted and respected say he was doing the proper thing by being in school had a very positive impact on him. After he met Jennifer and they became friends, she too had an impact on him. These credible people helped him change. Furthermore, the new experiences of being in school, being involved in the rodeo club, and doing well on his test were positive change experiences.

Helping people change is often a slow process.

The impacts of experiences and people are not always positive. Suppose Phil came to school and flunked the first test, and as the teacher handed it back to him she said, "That's one of the poorer scores on the test." Or suppose Jennifer turned to Phil, sniffed the air, and (in a big-city way) said, "You must be a cowboy. Don't you ever clean your boots?" Or suppose Phil didn't become a member of the rodeo club. Or suppose that when Phil met his favorite rodeo star, the cowboy said, "Boy, you've made a big mistake, you're just wasting your time going to college. You ought to be out on the rodeo circuit making money." If these things had happened to Phil, his attitude about not going to school might

FIGURE 6.2 How people and experiences affect change.

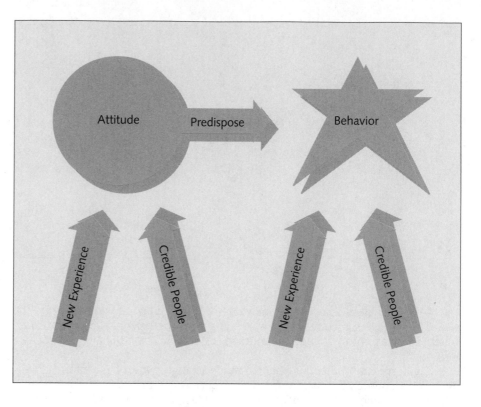

have been strengthened. At the first available opportunity, he might have left school, never to return.

People and experiences have a tremendous impact on us. Figure 6.2 shows how this works. The diagram points out that change can be made by dealing with either the attitude or the behavior. However, new experiences and credible people must be present to bring about change.

If you are concerned about the behavior of an employee and wish to influence that person to do what you perceive as best for the organization, then introduce the employee to as many new experiences and credible people as possible who can reinforce your point of view. For example, let's say one of your male employees is having difficulty accepting his new female boss, and the feedback he is getting from his associates and the people he trusts is that women should be in the home and not on the job. He could snub his new boss completely, and the work of the office might not get completed. If you want to change this employee's attitude and behavior regarding his boss, introduce him to new credible people. Bring in employees who feel that women's rights are extremely important. Remember, this approach won't work unless the male employee trusts and believes in the people who speak to him. Furthermore, give him as many new experiences as possible that point out that the boss's efficiency, not gender, is what matters. Make certain the female supervisor provides positive work experiences for the male employee.

Changing Yourself

Changing oneself is as important as changing others.

Even more important than bringing about change among your employees is bringing about change in your own life. The process is the same for you as for anyone else. For example, if you wish to quit cigarette smoking and your experiences with smoking are positive, you probably won't quit. If close friends tell

"It's worse than we thought—
there's going to be random testing for *competence*."

Source: Sidney Harris

you that smoking the new low-tar brands is okay and evidence doesn't seem to indicate that they are harmful then you will likely be reinforced to continue.

If you wish to change, listen to people you trust who are against smoking and give yourself new experiences with cigarette smoking that are not positive. Visit someone who has smoked a pack of cigarettes a day most of his or her life and who has undergone lung surgery to remove a cancerous growth. This could give you negative reactions, both from the experience of the visit and from the person you visited.

Whatever the situation, whether personal or organizational, if you want to change your behavior, you must be aware of the kind of people with whom you associate and the kinds of experiences you are having. They both have a tremendous impact on what you do and what you think.

We have talked about how you get started in bringing about change. You need to be aware of your attitudes and your behaviors and the impact that people and experiences have on you. The next section of this chapter covers how people can continue to reinforce themselves after they make an initial change.

Learning Is a Lifelong Process

After making a change, continued progress and **development** are important. How does one continue this process? In his book *Developing Human Resources,* **Leonard Nadler** offers some good ideas about learning approaches to help people develop more effectively.[1] He advocates three major areas of focus: (1) the job, (2) the individual, and (3) the organization (see Figure 6.3).

Learning is a lifelong process.

FIGURE 6.3   Areas of focus.

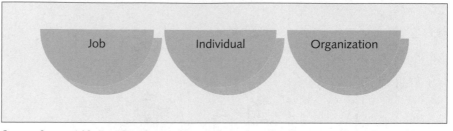

Source: Leonard Nadler, *Developing Human Resources* (San Francisco: Jossey-Bass, 1989).

Human resource development is important for all organizations.

Each of these areas of focus requires a different type of learning development (see Figure 6.4). For development needs associated with the job, Nadler discusses **training.** Training is development associated with learning human and technical skills to make the employee more effective on a specific job. Nadler relates individual development to **education.** Education is the process of an employee becoming well rounded and generally developed. **Organizational development** means developing employees to be able to adapt and progress with the organization.

These three areas of focus and the three types of learning together create a complete concept of human resource development (see Figure 6.5).

FIGURE 6.4   Types of development.

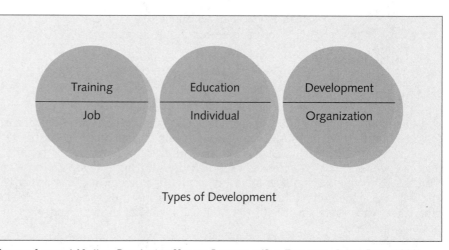

Source: Leonard Nadler, *Developing Human Resources* (San Francisco: Jossey-Bass, 1989).

FIGURE 6.5   The concept of human resource development (HRD).

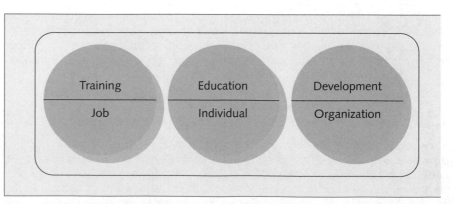

Source: Leonard Nadler, *Developing Human Resources* (San Francisco: Jossey-Bass, 1989).

Human Resource Development

Each person who belongs to an organization can strengthen and develop himself or herself for specific jobs, for individual needs, and for changing organizations. We will now discuss the importance of the three types of human resource development (HRD) and how they can help people maintain themselves.

Training

Training includes activities that improve job performance. It helps make a person more employable or promotable within the organization and teaches basic skills. It is specific learning and focuses directly on basic activities. For example, a typist may be trained to move from the typing pool to a secretarial position. A laborer could be taught to drive a truck to qualify as a driver. Training teaches people new basic techniques and introduces them to new methods related to their jobs. We all need to improve ourselves for our jobs at all times by being as effectively trained as possible.

Rapid technological changes place increased demands on management and labor. The rapidly changing workplace requires a workforce that has a greater range of skills than were needed a generation ago. A recent research project revealed five key basic skills that employers say are needed in today's workplace and should be addressed in current training programs.

1. How to learn

2. Listening and oral communications

3. Problem solving and creative thinking

4. Interpersonal

5. Organizational effectiveness and leadership[2]

Each skill area might well be addressed in both education and training programs.

What is the difference between training and education? Nadler explains it as shown in Figure 6.6. Training and education use essentially the same varieties of behaviors to reach their goals. They also use the same kinds of human resource development experiences. However, their goals are different. Although **training** on a particular job can usually be transferred to other, similar jobs, the goal of training is to learn very specific behaviors or skills. The goal of education, on the other hand, is to learn a variety of behaviors and skills so one can deal with different situations in the organization. Training focuses on a specific job activity, and education focuses on teaching a person to be effective from a broad perspective.

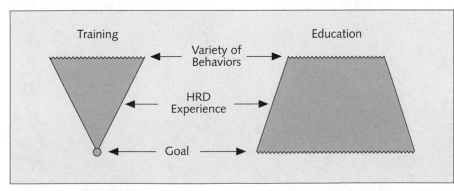

FIGURE 6.6 Contrasting training and education.

Source: Leonard Nadler, *Developing Human Resources* (San Francisco: Jossey-Bass, 1989).

Education

Employee education is the responsibility of the employee, not the organization. Employees who wish to seek career advancement or even remain competitive in their current position will be wise to continue their education. Although a high school diploma was sufficient for most entry-level jobs a generation ago, many employers today are seeking (and finding) applicants with college degrees for most jobs. Many people with less than a college degree are finding it difficult to compete in the high-tech environment of business.

Because of this demand for higher education levels, a variety of special courses, high school and college programs, and nontraditional learning experiences are available in most parts of the United States and Canada for people who wish to improve their ability to deal with work organizations and life itself. The emphasis has shifted from technical or job-related training only to employee education, which is often experiential and focuses on improving the student's appreciation for life and people. As employees gain wider experience, more maturity and understanding, and a better appreciation for life and people, they have greater opportunities for advancement. To become educated, as well as trained, should be a goal for every member of society.

Development

The basic function of training is to help people improve their performance on specific jobs. Education is geared to helping people prepare for life in general and for general careers or vocations. Employee development helps employees prepare for individual growth and advancement with growing organizations. It helps employees better understand and cope with changes in the organization.

Education and training focus on the individual employee. Employee development, on the other hand, focuses on the organization. Its purpose is to create a workforce that is geared to the needs of the organization, oriented to the future, looking for change, and able to adapt to change while maintaining effectiveness and efficiency.

Specific models have been designed to facilitate the achievement of development goals. One such model, a design for **organizational development**

Organizational training prepares workers to handle specific job situations.

through the involvement of employees (ODIE), focuses on an organization's vision, mission, and goals. It requires that employee groups identify obstacles that keep them from achieving organizational goals, quantify the identified obstacle, set a performance level, and take steps to achieve it.

What is the ODIE model for organizational development?

The ODIE model illustrates that employee development is a serious and essential undertaking for organizations that hope to maintain a competitive edge in the business world as we approach the twenty-first century. Its application is likely to result in improvements in (1) productivity, product or service quality or both, cost containment, business development, and technological advancement; (2) the quality of work life; and (3) organizational development knowledge.[3]

We have pointed out the importance of change in your life and your employees' lives. And we have reviewed the importance of training, education, and development within the organization and within the individual. Now ask yourself, "Am I in a situation where I need to change? If so, how should I go about making change?" What kinds of training do you need to be effective in your job? How can you better educate yourself for your job? Do you need more active involvement with your organization as it grows, develops, and changes? In summary: (1) what do you or your organization need to change? and (2) what do you or your organization need to learn? The one certainty of life is change. Employees who are not willing to change and learn new information will be less likely to succeed as organizations grow and develop in the future. Where do you stand?

Personal Coaching

This training delivery system has only recently appeared in corporations. Each of us has been personally coached at one point in our lives—sports, dance or music lessons, our parents—but the formalization of the coaching process is finding great success in organizations.

A personal coach is selected or assigned to an individual for a predetermined amount of time (8–12 weeks is the average length for coaching programs). Once a week or so, the employee speaks to the coach (either face-to-face or over the phone) about issues or challenges at work. The coach provides guidance, advice, motivation, and accountability, while the employee benefits from individualized, relevant, just-in-time learning.

Some of the areas that personal coaches can address with great success include goal setting, leadership skills, customer service, and time management.

As technologies advance, telephone coaching will be replaced with Internet or real-time audio/video computer uplinks. Whatever the medium, personal coaching will continue its newfound success in shaping the individuals and corporations of tomorrow.

Summary of Key Ideas

- Attitudes affect one's behaviors; thus, to change a person's behavior you often must first change his or her attitude.

- Although changing a person's behavior is a slow process, the two major steps that can help the process are introducing the person to new and credible people and introducing the person to new experiences.

- Nadler advocates three areas of development: the job, the individual, and the organization. He combines each of these areas with training, education, and development.

Key Terms, Concepts, and Names

Attitude

Cognitive dissonance

Credible people

Development

Education

Leonard Nadler

Organizational development

Organizational development through the
 involvement of employees (ODIE)

Personal coaching

Training

Questions and Exercises

1.   Answer the introductory questions at the beginning of the chapter.

2.   Differentiate between training, education, and development.

3.   Give a personal example from your life that illustrates the change process.

Notes

1.   Adapted from Leonard Nadler, *Developing Human Resources,* 2d ed. (Austin, TX: Learning Concepts, 1979), pp. 37–90.

2.   Anthony P. Carnavale, Leila J. Gainer, Ann S. Meltzer, and Shari L. Holland, "Workplace Basics: The Skills Employers Want," *Training and Development Journal* 42, October 1988, pp. 22–30.

3.   Peggy Tollison, "Meet 'ODIE,'" *Journal for Quality and Participation* 12, March 1989, pp. 82–88.

Another Look: Grasping the Learning Organization

Today's successful organizations are ones where constant learning is occurring. Enlightened employees at all levels know the importance of constant improvement by discovering and applying new ideas. This process requires good communication.

Knowledge for individuals and organizations typically evolves through four *stages of learning*. Notice how the stages relate to communication skills.

Stage 1: You Aren't Aware That You Don't Know.

To understand this point, consider the example of an energetic 2-year-old boy who wants to ride a bike that he sees his older brother riding. He doesn't know, however, that he doesn't know how to ride it. All he says is, "Mommy, I want to ride the bike." Most people in business who do not receive detailed feedback about their communication skills are at this state of unconscious incompetence. They simply are not aware of their interpersonal communication habits.

Stage 2: You Are Aware That You Don't Know.

Here you learn that you are not competent at something. This often comes as a rude awakening. For example, a 2-year-old boy gets on a bike and falls off. He has immediately gone from stages 1 to 2 and knows that he does not know how to ride a bike. A writer whose tone is offensive or a speaker whose mannerisms are annoying makes this shift to stage 2 when the problem is pointed out and accepted as true. A company climate of openness where honest criticism is given freely and with sincere intent, and where people are willing to accept criticism without undue offense, helps us move into stage 2.

Stage 3: You Work at What You Don't Know.

At stage 3, you consciously make an effort to learn a new skill. Practice, drill, and repetition are at the forefront. This is where most learning occurs. It takes effort and work. The little boy carefully steers, balances, and pedals, and thinks of what he is doing, step by step. The writer or speaker consciously works at changing a distracting habit. An employee takes the time to develop proficiency with new communication media, such as e-mail, the Internet, and various software programs.

Stage 4: You Don't Have to Think about Knowing It.

Here the skill set happens automatically at an unconscious level. For example, a little boy rides his bike without even thinking about it. He can whistle, talk, sing, or do other things with his mind at the same time. A speaker with a distracting habit who has learned to overcome it through practice doesn't have to concentrate on not doing the distracting habit. The business writer feels comfortable in composing a memo or letter.

People and learning organizations evolve through these stages constantly as they adapt to the realities of our fast-changing world.

What Does a Learning Organization Learn?

What do learning organizations learn that other organizations do not? Learning organizations learn

- to use learning to reach their goals
- to help people value the effects of their learning on their organizations
- to avoid making the same mistakes again (and again)
- to share information in ways that prompt appropriate action

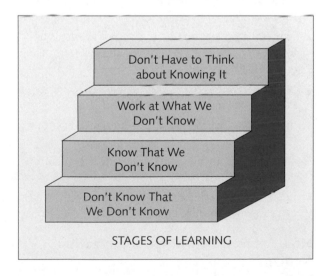

Don't Have to Think about Knowing It

Work at What We Don't Know

Know That We Don't Know

Don't Know That We Don't Know

STAGES OF LEARNING

continued

Grasping the Learning Organization, *continued*

- to link individual performance with organizational performance
- to tie rewards to key measures of performance
- to take in a lot of environmental information at all times
- to create structures and procedures that support the learning process
- to foster ongoing and orderly dialogues
- to make it safe for people to share openly and take risks.

What Does a Learning Organization Look like?

A learning organization

- learns collaboratively, openly, and across boundaries
- values *how* it learns as well as *what* it learns
- invests in staying ahead of the learning curve in its industry
- gains a competitive edge by learning faster and smarter than competitors
- turns data into useful knowledge quickly and at the right time and place
- enables every employee to feel that every experience provides him or her a chance to learn something potentially useful, even if only for leveraging future learning
- exhibits little fear and defensiveness; rewards and learns from what goes wrong ("failure" learning) and right ("success" learning)
- takes risks but avoids jeopardizing basic security of the organization
- invests in experimental and seemingly tangential learning
- supports people and teams who want to pursue action-learning projects
- depoliticizes learning by not penalizing individuals or groups for sharing information and conclusions.

How Does a Learning Organization Evolve?

What are the first steps to becoming a learning organization? A budding learning organization can begin by

- questioning current assumptions about learning

- getting an outside perspective
- tying the goal of becoming a learning organization to its organizational vision
- finding or creating a champion in top management
- looking for the "pain" in the organization—the place where more effective learning could help
- articulating learning-organization ideas plainly
- rewarding group as well as individual learning success and failure
- finding an external enemy to spur greater cooperative learning
- finding ways to collaborate internally in and unhampered by boundaries.

Better Learning and the Bottom Line

What connections do trainers, line managers, and consultants see between organizational learning and organizational profitability?

When organizational learning directly addresses operations—for example, as with training for TQM—people are less likely to question the positive connection between organizational learning and profitability. The same could be said of any training initiative targeted at improving organizational productivity and performance.

Focus groups addressed the connection between organizational learning and profits by contrasting the positive effects learning has on profits with the negative effects that occur when no learning takes place.

Consider, for example, the effect on the bottom line of unsolved customer problems or missed new-market opportunities. Compare those scenarios with the bottom-line gains that would be realized if a company learned to solve customer problems or exploit new-markets.

Participants suggested ways that organizational learning can increase profits. Organizations can use learning to better their bottom lines by

- using action learning to solve business problems or seize business opportunities
- reflecting on learning experiences, such as asking what prevented or permitted seeing better solutions
- improving processes by learning from more knowledgeable people
- developing awareness of the gains that can be squeezed from mistakes and successes

continued

Grasping the Learning Organization, *continued*

- -

- shortening competitive cycles, as in developing new products more quickly

- helping management to recognize learning as a factor that affects the bottom line

- increasing individual and group accountability for learning

- leveraging key learning points, such as learning to acquire the most critical data, not all data.

Source: Gene Calvert, Sandra Mobley, and Lisa Marshall, "Grasping the Learning Organization." Reprinted from *Training & Development.* © June 1994 the American Society for Training & Development. Reprinted with permission. All rights reserved.

Another Look: The Training Myth

- -

If you aren't satisfied with the results you've been getting from your employee-training programs, maybe it's because you've been doing the wrong kind of training.

It's amazing, when you think about it, how little our ideas about employee training have changed in the past 40 years. The entire business world has been turned upside down, but most of us continue to look at training as a specialized activity. We think people won't learn unless you take them off the job, sit them down, and put them through a step-by-step instruction program, complete with "coaches," workbooks, videos, whatever. Then we complain that training is too expensive and doesn't deliver the promised results.

Most learning doesn't happen that way—in business or anywhere else. I can tell you all there is to know about bass fishing. You can read every fishing magazine, study every fishing book, and watch Jimmy Houston haul them in every Saturday morning on ESPN. But it won't mean much until you go out on a lake and start throwing a lure. When you feel that first bite or have that first backlash, then you'll begin to learn about fishing.

I'm not saying that formal instruction is worthless, just that it's overrated. According to a recent authoritative study conducted by the Center for Workforce Development, up to 70% of what employees know about their jobs they learn informally from the people they work with. Formal training programs account for 30% or less.

Those findings aren't as surprising as they may seem at first glance. Think about your own company. When you bring in new people, you probably give them some kind of orientation. You explain their benefits and tell them what's expected on the job. But who gives them their real orientation? How do

they find out what's really expected? They learn, all right, but not in any formal training session.

The point is that job-related learning goes on whether or not we're aware of it. People learn through a whole series of events that most companies don't even recognize, so they never figure out how to leverage the process. They don't see how much training you can do outside a formal training program.

I'll give you an example. We have a young manager who's responsible for a business doing about $20 million in annual sales. Last year his business sprang a leak. He'd brought in several new product lines, and sales were growing, but as his volume went up his gross margin began to slide. I asked the manager what was happening. He said he thought his expenses might be running a little high on the new lines.

"Which lines and which expenses?" I asked. He didn't know. In his weekly financial reports, comparable expenses from different product lines were mixed together, so he couldn't pinpoint the exact cause of the problem. He seemed to be hoping it would just go away.

So what do you do in such a situation? There are two typical responses. One is to do nothing, except maybe give a lecture on watching costs. Then, if the problem turns into a crisis, you hold the manager accountable. The other response is to focus single-mindedly on getting the problem resolved. So you send in your fix-it person to find out what's really going on. Either that, or you do it yourself.

But there's a third option, a learning option, and that's the one we chose. I told the manager to go back and find out exactly what was causing his margin to shrink. "How do I do that?" he asked.

"There's only one way," I said. "You have to break the numbers down."

continued

The Training Myth, *continued*

It didn't take long for him to figure out that most of the losses were coming from one product line, which accounted for about $1.2 million of his sales. That was a mystery, because the line is a simple one. All it involves is repackaging engine components. We buy them from the manufacturer, put them in boxes with some washers and gaskets, seal them up, and ship them out. How could we lose money in the deal?

The manager did an analysis and was stunned by what he found. It turned out he was losing all the money in the packaging. When he added up what he was spending on labor, cellophane, boxes, and so on, he discovered that the packaging was costing $16 per unit—and we had it down for just $4 per unit. In other words, we were losing $12 on every box we shipped.

It was a big mistake. The loss on the line had come to $40,000 for the previous year. At our usual margins, we would have earned about $85,000 on it. So our failure to price the product correctly had resulted in a profit swing of $125,000 in that year alone.

Unfortunately, the damage was already done, but at least we got something for our money—namely, a manager's education. In the course of diagnosing his margin problem, that manager learned more about running a business than we could have taught him in hours of classroom instruction.

I'm not referring only to the lessons he learned about the pitfalls of combining costs or the need to break down problems. More important was the opportunity we had to plant some seeds, to begin developing in this manager qualities that must eventually become part of his daily existence—a passion for numbers, a hunger to find out where he's making or losing money, constant curiosity about what's really going on in the business. There is no formal program that can instill those instincts and emotions. People acquire them informally or not at all.

That's one of the great benefits of informal learning. It develops a kind of knowledge you can't teach in formal training programs. Yes, it's important that people have certain basic skills—the ability to read, write, and do arithmetic, for example. Assuming people have those tools, however, you don't need a classroom to teach them about business. They can learn more, and they can learn faster, if you integrate the teaching into the normal, day-to-day functions of the business.

That is, in fact, exactly what we've tried to do with *The Great Game of Business,* our system of open-book management, which includes a whole series of mechanisms designed to teach people about different aspects of our business. But you don't need a fully developed management system to leverage the informal learning process. What's important is to recognize the teaching opportunities. It's not hard. Once you begin looking for them, you'll find them all over the place.

For example, every company I know has trouble allocating funds for employee activities—sporting events, parties, community projects, and so on. For many CEOs it's a major source of frustration. You try to please everyone, but somebody always comes along with another idea or request after the money's already been divvied up. Then you're the one who has to play Solomon. You can't win.

Our idea was to turn the problem into an informal training program. We set up an employee-activity committee composed of frontline people from various departments. We give them $5,000, and they decide how to spend it. In the process they learn a lot about the difficulties of managing—how hard it is to be fair, how unreasonable some people can be, how important it is to communicate.

Every six months we ask people to agree or disagree with 14 statements, such as "At work, your opinions count" or "Those of you who want to be a leader in this company have the opportunity to become one." When the scores come in low in one area, we turn them over to a committee that investigates the problems and comes up with solutions. The next survey tells us how successful the committee has been. In 18 months, we saw morale scores improve an average of 20% in one of our plants. And who do you think served on the committee? Our front-line employees, of course.

It's all part of our effort to promote continuous learning throughout the company. We believe everyone at Springfield ReManufacturing needs to be learning continually if we're going to keep growing, providing opportunities, and taking care of people's wants and needs. In this economy, there isn't any alternative.

A Case in Point: COACH

Louise is a manager in a department with more than 100 people. Though she is competent technically, many of her staff find her difficult to deal with on a personal level. When her boss approached her about her management style, Louise contacted the HR department to see whether it could give her some coaching assistance. Sally was assigned to work with her.

Contract

Sally met with Louise to become acquainted and discover her coaching needs. She gave Louise some options to think about and got her okay to talk with Louise's boss about his views. Sally and Louise agreed to meet later to decide how to proceed. At that meeting, Louise said she wanted to use "360 feedback" to learn how people in her department view her as a manager. She agreed that she'd share the results with her boss and that she'd work with Sally to address issues that arose in the feedback.

Observe and Assess

Next, Sally used a 360 instrument and conducted semi-structured interviews with Louise's staff. Sally found that they had respect for Louise's technical skills, extensive experience, and analytical abilities. But they resented her arbitrary decision-making style, abrasive and critical manner, and unwillingness to delegate meaningful responsibilities. Many feared her and would just try to get through the day rather than use their abilities and contribute fully.

Constructively Challenge

Sally didn't look forward to presenting the information to Louise, though she knew she had to. The meeting was uncomfortable, but Sally was able to present the feedback clearly and directly without sugarcoating it. She also tried to be gentle and supportive. To clarify some points, Sally used her own observations to help Louise understand why people perceived her the way they did.

Handle Resistance

Despite Sally's care in presenting the assessment, Louise wasn't consistently receptive. At one point, Louise criticized her staff, saying that their perceptions were biased, that they were envious of her position, and that they were upset about organizational problems that had little to do with her. Louise also challenged Sally directly, saying that she was unprofessional because she took the staff's side and was "taken in" by disgruntled people with an ax to grind. Sally handled the resistance by not taking it personally and by realizing that it's a typical response to hearing negative information about oneself. Sally pointed out gently that Louise might be using those rationales to discount information that she found disturbing.

After some discussion, Louise acknowledged that possibility and decided to address her issues head-on. They agreed that she would attend a class on delegating and participative management, and have several coaching sessions with Sally to work on some of the more difficult problems.

Louise did attend class and meet with Sally for coaching. Though she didn't find it easy, Louise was able to make some significant changes in her behavior. She also said that she was proud to be able to handle some difficult management situations differently than she would have in the past. After six months, Sally did a follow-up assessment with Louise's staff. She found that some issues remained, but they reported that Louise's management style had improved considerably. People also said that her department was more productive and less tense.

Questions

1. What does the acronym COACH represent?
2. How does personal coaching help us learn and change?
3. What are your feelings about personal coaching? Could it help you learn and be more effective?
4. Give your impressions of Louise. Why do you suppose it was difficult for her to work with a coach?

A Case in Point: Eager Mike McHugh

One Monday morning Mike McHugh, a recent college graduate, walked into the sales office as a new sales trainee. Ron Noel, the zone sales manager for a business machines company, was there to greet him. Noel's area covered three counties, and ten sales representatives reported to him. The large volume of sales in his area was attributed to recent population growth; industries were finding this section of the state very attractive.

Noel has collected several sales reports, catalogs, and pamphlets describing in detail the types of office equipment sold by the company. After a pleasant chat, he gave McHugh the collected material and showed him his assigned desk. Soon afterward, Noel excused himself and did not return. McHugh spent the day reading over the material, and at 5 PM he went home. This was the entire "training program."

Questions

1. What can be said about Noel's training program?
2. In light of the information presented in the chapter about training, education, and development, does McHugh really need any more training than he received from Noel?
3. If you would suggest more training, what would it be? What approach do you think would be most effective?

Source: Jack Halloran and George L. Frunzi, *Supervision: The Art of Management,* 2d ed. (Englewood Cliffs, NJ; Prentice-Hall, 1986), p. 275. © 1986. Adapted with permission of Prentice-Hall, Inc., Englewood Cliffs, NJ.

The Human Side of Organizations

- How do the ways people really act create an informal organization?

- What is mentoring, and what implications does it hold for an organization?

- What is organizational climate, and how can we measure it?

- How do values of the organization's culture manifest themselves?

- What three "c-words" help us understand the human side of organizations?

- Why is it important for a manager to recognize the effects of organization structures on employees?

The answers to these and other questions are coming up next in Chapter 7 . . .

We looked at reasons for organizing and the pros and cons of various organizational structures in Chapter 5. Next, we'll look more closely at *human* aspects that determine organizational effectiveness. Organizations are never as clear-cut and mechanical in reality as they appear on paper. Organizational charts can be misleading.

The human side of organizations—the ways people *really* interact—creates an **informal organization.** Organizations and suborganizations (departments, work teams, and the like) develop personalities of their own. An informal organization arises, and it often contradicts the established "real" organization.

For example, a simple formal organization chart might look like Figure 7.1 But *informal* reporting patterns may look quite different. The president's secretary may be far more influential (in part because he or she can control access to the president), and the accounting manager may seldom make a move without checking with the marketing manager. The informal organization chart might look like Figure 7.2 on page 125.

Managers who assume that the formal organization chart accurately describes all reporting arrangements may be in for a surprise. Often the real power resides in people who do not occupy key spots in the organization. Consider the case of the chief executive officer (CEO) of a medium-sized company whose office workers "ran" her. She lightheartedly introduced her secretary to outsiders as her "boss." While everyone laughed during such introductions, workers within the company knew there was much truth to the designation. The secretary had been with the company longer than the CEO, and it was the secretary who made sure everyone in the office followed procedures her way. It was even said that vice presidents occasionally fetched the mail or a cup of coffee for the CEO's secretary—the boss's "boss." For a glance at where this informally powerful secretary fits in, see Figure 7.3 on page 125.

> The **informal** organization may look quite different from the formal one.

> Often, the **real** power resides in people who do not hold formal leadership positions.

Factors That Can Give People Informal Authority

Many factors tend to give people informal authority in organizations. In the preceding case of the CEO's secretary, **seniority** (years with the company) and familiarity with company procedures provided a basis for her power. Other important factors might include access to other powerful people in the organization, aggressive or intimidating behavior, experience in the area of the organization's work, professional expertise, and general credibility among peers. Clearly, looking at the boxes in a company's organizational chart doesn't tell us who *really* has power and influence.

FIGURE 7.1 A simple formal organization chart.

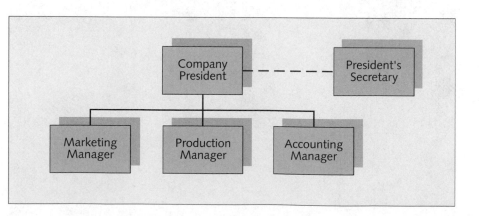

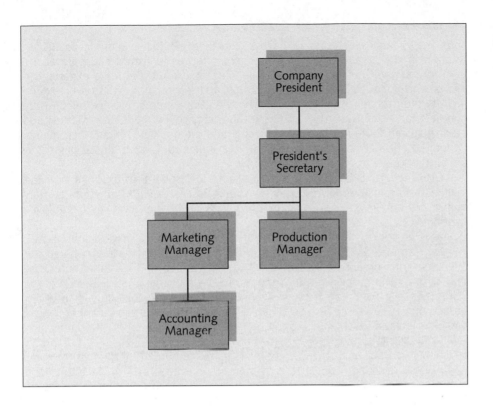

FIGURE 7.2 An informal organization chart.

Seeing others attempting to gain or use informal authority in organizations upsets some people, who call it "company politics," "brown-nosing," "empire building," and so on. While we don't encourage anyone to aggressively seek power in this way, we do believe it cannot be avoided. People naturally create informal alliances and relationships with each other—sometimes in an ethical way, sometimes in an attempt to manipulate.

Many factors tend to give people informal authority in organizations.

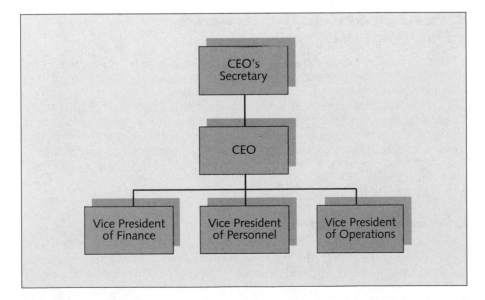

FIGURE 7.3 The boss's "boss"—an informal organization chart.

Mentors and Informal Authority

Mentors can convey informal authority on their protégés.

Some new employees seem to have a knack for finding a mentor, or helper-teacher, in the organization. Such employees form friendships and enjoy common interests with more experienced people. As a result, the more experienced and powerful mentors provide contacts, tips, and recommendations for their own favorite (and usually younger) friends or protégés. A mentor-protégé relationship may last for years. Many top leaders in business, government, the military, and other fields attribute much of their success to a mentor who helped them along. Others complain that such relationships are unfair to those who are passed by for promotions that are given to protégés.

Mentoring has been so helpful to people that some organizations now formalize this typically informal activity. Managers are assigning mentors to new employees and even explaining mentoring skills in the company's employee handbook.

A 1996 survey showed that more than a third of large corporations (AT&T, Federal Express, GM, J. C. Penney, and DuPont among them) had initiated formal mentoring programs. By late 1998 it was hard to find a sizable enterprise that didn't claim to be deep into mentoring[1] with varying degrees of success. But mentoring itself can have an impact on formal organizational structure. *Forbes* magazine writer Dan Seligman talks about the "certain blurriness about the main point: Why is such counseling no longer entrusted to the young person's supervisor but considered someone higher up's job? [When he posed this question to an official at the Society for Human Resource Management, he was told,] `Well, there are a lot of crappy supervisors out there'."[2] The implication of this, says Seligman, is that senior management is supposed to help junior management (supervisors) do their job, which sounds like a poor use of senior management's time.

This problem notwithstanding, mentoring seems to build increased loyalty to the company and reduces turnover among bright young employees. Ironically, mentoring, which began as an informal aspect of an organization's culture, may be losing its effectiveness when it is formalized. Assigning people to mentor young employees without regard to common interests, values, or personality often does not work. On the other hand, if executives choose to only mentor employees who are just like them—young versions of themselves—they leave the company open to charges of discrimination.

Organizational Climate and Morale

Organizational climate is often hard to define.

Climate arises from the members' impressions of the work environment.

Climate is a rather slippery concept to define. This is true whether one is referring to the weather (just exactly how does one describe the climate of, say, Chicago?) or to the environment within a company.

Organizational climate arises from a composite impression of such things as the way managers treat their workers, the corporate "philosophy," the work atmosphere, and the types of objectives the organization is chasing. A key point to keep in mind is that climate arises from the perceptions and impressions of the people who work in the organization, not directly from some way of organizing or managing the work. "Morale" or the general sense of well-being arises from this climate.

Components of Climate

One pioneer researcher who has studied the concept of climate extensively is **W. Charles Redding.** His work over decades of professional experience has been instrumental in developing our current thinking about this rather ambiguous concept. Redding identifies five components that, taken together, determine the organizational climate. These are

1. The degree to which management is *supportive* of its employees' efforts

2. The extent of *participative decision making* used

3. The degree of *trust* employees have in management

4. The amount of *freedom to communicate* openly

5. The firm's degree of emphasis on *high performance goals*[3]

Climate in Exceptional Companies

The classic book *In Search of Excellence,* by Thomas Peters and Robert H. Waterman, cites numerous climate characteristics of the exceptional company. Among them were organizational systems designed to:

- produce lots of winners by boosting employee self-worth

- celebrate the winning once it occurs

- make extraordinary use of nonmonetary incentives—especially "hoopla" and applause

- permit people to feel that they have control over their own destinies

- encourage fertile talk and an "action bias" (they *do* things; they don't talk ideas to death)

- encourage "fluid" organizations with many ways of communicating informally

- promote open communication where people get in contact with each other regularly

- encourage friendly, internal competition[4]

These qualities can be considered a major part of the organization's climate. They also constitute critical dimensions of the organizational *culture,* which we will describe in a moment.

What Would an Ideal Organizational Climate Be Like?

It is unlikely that there is a perfectly "ideal" organization anywhere on Earth. But we do feel, and the research supports, that the following are essential to a strong organizational climate:

1. *Trust.* Personnel at all levels should make every effort to develop and maintain relationships in which trust, confidence, and credibility are sustained by statement and act.

2. *Participative decision making.* Employees at all levels in the organization should be communicated to and consulted with on organization policies relevant to their positions. Employees at all levels should be provided with avenues of communication with management levels above theirs for the purpose of participating in decision making and goal setting.

3. *Supportiveness.* An atmosphere of candor and **supportiveness** should pervade relationships within the organization, with employees being

> Six factors are essential to a strong organizational climate.

Work stations are arranged in a circle at the Central Intelligence Agency's operations center to provide easy access to information for all team members.

encouraged to say what's on their minds regardless of whether they are talking to peers, subordinates, or superiors.

4. *Openness in downward communication.* Except for necessary security information, members of the organization should have relatively easy access to information that relates to their jobs, that affects their abilities to coordinate work with other people or departments, and that deals broadly with the company, its organization, leaders, and plans. This is known as **downward communication.**

5. *Listening in upward communication.* Personnel at all levels in the organization should listen with open minds to suggestions or reports of problems. Information from subordinates—**upward communication**—should be viewed generally as important enough to be acted on.

6. *Concern for high performance goals.* Personnel at all levels in the organization should demonstrate a commitment to high performance goals (high productivity, high quality, low cost), as well as a high concern for other members of the organization.

Trust among organization members is the most important ingredient of a good climate.

The Most Important Climate Factor: Trust   Of all these items, which seems to be the most important? Research indicates that the single most important ingredient of good organizational climate is **trust** among organizational members.

Traditional organizational structure, with its heavy emphasis on hierarchy and control over people—implying a low level of trust—seldom produces a good organizational climate. More flexible organizations can build better trust.

Culture in Organizations

Closely related to climate is **organizational culture.** The values and norms of the most influential leaders—formal *or* informal leaders—become adopted by most members of the organization. This whole set of pervasive values, norms, and attitudes is called the *culture* of the organization.

When you join an organization, no one hands you a printed description of its culture. In fact, it may take days, weeks, or months to learn a culture well enough to describe it.

Why is culture so important—and how does one discover what an organization's culture is? Culture constitutes rules and norms that determine who will succeed, fail, gain power, or gain influence in an organization. Employees who are working for a company while ignorant of its culture are like foreigners trying to drive autos in a distant land without any knowledge of the traffic laws there. They haven't taken the time to learn the rules.

While the "rules" of a culture are usually unwritten, they are still enforced. One must learn them by asking questions and observing what behaviors are practiced by those who are rewarded or promoted. Asking "What would I be expected to continually do in this company to eventually be promoted to vice president?" would probably help one learn about a culture. The rules, expectations, and acceptable behaviors in an organization are its outward manifestations of its "private" culture.

Let's look at an example that took place in a Goodyear auto service center. A newly hired mechanic named Jim was told that *"superior service to the customer"* was the creed of the whole shop. Jim's supervisor emphasized that if he would just remember this, Jim would do as well as any mechanic in the company.

Being well trained in auto mechanics, Jim worked hard to please customers during his first morning on the job. When the lunch break came, he was exhausted. Jim was happy to see that there were no customers in sight, and his supervisor shut several doors to the service stalls. Taking his sack lunch and a soda pop, Jim found a clean spot on the shop floor, sat down, and began to eat. He was glad it was lunchtime, as his legs ached from standing all morning.

But as soon as Jim had seated himself comfortably on the shop floor, his supervisor startled him with a curse and loud yelling—directed straight at Jim! "What? Get off your butt, Jim! I thought I told you there's never any sittin' around here. Imagine what would happen if the regional store director stopped by and saw you just sittin' there!"

Jim was shocked! Jumping up, he protested to his supervisor that he had worked harder than any other mechanic that morning, that his legs were tired, and that the shop had no chairs in it. Then his supervisor explained that it "just didn't look right" to have a uniformed mechanic sitting on the shop floor—even during lunch break. Jim learned that one had to go into a back room or outside to be able to sit.

The unwritten rule about never sitting on the shop floor was an outward manifestation of the values and norms of the service center. Workers always had to appear to be actively in the service of the customer. That was a big part of the culture. The "no sitting" rule was merely an outward sign of the culture's internal value. Jim learned about the culture in the service center the hard way. If another mechanic had just given him a few hints, Jim could have avoided this unpleasant experience on his first day at work.

Alan L. Wilkins, a leading authority on organizational cultures today, explains why learning a culture is so important for new employees:

> For the new employee, learning the organization is like learning how to fit in and avoid major blunders in a foreign culture. When traveling in a foreign country, it is of course useful to have a map which shows you how to get from one

The "rules" of a culture are often unwritten but are still enforced.

Every organization develops a culture of its own.

place to another. However, avoiding social blunders and really understanding the foreign culture requires another kind of map—a social map. You need to know how to get where you want to go socially. . . .

Shortly after starting a new job, most new employees learn that the policy handbook and the standard operating procedures only go so far. New employees soon learn that there are exceptions to the rules. Some rules can be violated without great repercussions and others are sacred. Even more important, the new employee learns that certain ways of thinking and acting (we are a "conservative company," "look busy," "don't kill a new product idea") are really more important to know than rules.[5]

Organizational Character: Going Beyond Culture

A third "c-word" (after climate and culture) is also useful in understanding the human side of organizations. Alan Wilkins prefers the term *character* to *culture*. He feels that culture has been overused and "trivialized because so many have written about 'managing culture,' 'managing myths,' or 'creating meaning' without serious attention to just how difficult it is to manipulate these complex social processes. [In addition] culture has been used to talk about almost everything organizational, and it has therefore lost much of its special meaning."[6]

Organizational character may be described as ideas, beliefs, and hopes of people both inside and outside the organization about the appropriate role for the organization and about how it should fulfill that role. Character is created from the skills, habits, and personal commitments that make fulfillment of these role expectations possible.

An organization's character is created from its people's skills, habits, and personal commitment.

Specifically, Wilkins identifies the following components of organizational character:

1. *Shared vision:* a common understanding of organizational purpose; a sense of "who we are"

2. *Motivational faith:*

   - in the fairness of the leaders and others

   - in the ability of personnel and the organization

3. *Distinctive skills:* the tacit customs, the networks of experts, and the technology that add up to the collective organizational competence.[7]

The "corporate character" approach to understanding organizations is relatively new, and its usefulness remains to be seen. Nevertheless, the focus on these key components seems to be promising as we seek to better understand a complex, yet vitally important, dimension of organizations.

Organizational character arises from a shared vision.

Organizational Ethics

An implicit element underlying climate, culture, and character is the company's collective sense of right and wrong—its ethics. An ethical organization attracts and nurtures ethical employees; a shady operation prone to ethical lapses or shortcuts encourages such behavior in its people.

Management writer Kenneth Blanchard and personal motivation expert Norman Vincent Peale say that

> Ethical behavior is related to self-esteem. We both believe that people who feel good about themselves have what it takes to withstand outside pressure and to do what is right rather than do what is merely expedient, popular, or lucrative. We believe that a strong code of morality in any business is the first step toward success. We believe that ethical managers are winning managers.[8]

Rules for Ethical Behavior

Almost every decision has ethical implications. The "right" thing to do often isn't clear.

To "do the right thing" begins with thinking rightly, say authors Robert C. Solomon and Kristine Hanson.

To think ethically means to steer your thoughts toward *compliance* with the rules, *contributions* you can make, and harmful *consequences* to avoid. Solomon and Hanson distill their study of ethical thinking into the following eight rules:[9]

1. *Consider the well-being of others, including nonparticipants.* Follow the golden rule, without sacrificing your own interests. As far as is reasonable, contribute to the general good and avoid consequences that hurt others.

2. *Think as a member of the business community, not as an isolated individual.* Business has rules of priority and fairness that allow it to prosper. Respecting contracts, paying debts, and selling decent products at a just price underpin the business community's existence.

3. *Obey, but do not solely depend on, the law.* Ethical thinking goes beyond mere legal compliance. Many things that are not illegal, such as taking advantage of trust, are unethical.

4. *Think of yourself and your company as part of society.* Business people are citizens, and business thrives because it serves society. Business is subject to the same ethical rules as the rest of society. Ignore social problems and you invite government regulation.

5. *Obey moral rules.* These are unqualified commands—no exceptions, even for busy executives on the cusp of a profitable deal.

6. *Think objectively.* To think from a neutral perspective is essential to determine whether an action is truly right and not just rationalized self-interest.

7. *Ask "What sort of person would do such a thing?"* Ethics is the upkeep of your personal and company character—your "good name."

8. *Respect others' customs, but not at the expense of your own ethics.* The hardest ethical dilemmas involve not a conflict between ethics and profits but one between two ethical systems. "When in Rome . . ." is a good rule of thumb. But if following a community's customs violates your moral values, stick to your own principles.

The collective adherence to ethics determines an organization's character—and success.

Dealing with the Human Side of Organizational Change

Organizational structures are not fixed and permanent. If anything, they are more flexible and changeable now than ever before in history. No set of skills can be used forever. The needs of people and organizations change constantly. Wise leaders recognize and appreciate this need for change. Wise managers also deal with the human side of the inevitable change process.

Even relatively minor organizational changes can lead to disruptions, friction, and heavy expenses. By nature, people tend to resist change. They see threats in the unknown and are usually more comfortable with the status quo.

When it is necessary to change the structure of an organization (either a whole company or small subgroups within a company), the process must be carefully planned and executed. Two experts in such change, Cynthia D. Scott and Dennis T. Jaffe, offer these basic guidelines:

Organizational change must be carefully planned and executed.

1. *Have a good reason for making the change.* Changes are not fun. Take them seriously. Be sure to understand the reasons making the change necessary.

2. *Involve people in the change.* By being involved, people understand the need for changes and are less resistant to them.

3. *Put a respected person in charge of the process.* The change leader should be seen in a positive light by the people to be affected by the change.

4. *Create transitions management teams.* Assemble a team to plan, anticipate, troubleshoot, coordinate, and focus the change efforts.

5. *Provide training in new values and behavior.* Guide the people through the new ways things are expected to be done.

6. *Bring in outside help.* An objective, third-party consultant can often anticipate unforeseen problems and reinforce the direction you want to go.

7. *Establish symbols of change.* Encourage the development of newsletters, new logos or slogans, and/or recognition events to help celebrate and reflect the change.

8. *Acknowledge and reward people.* As change begins to work, take time to recognize and recall the achievements of the people who made it happen.[10]

How Does Organizational Structure Affect People at Work?

Organizational structures contribute to employee perceptions of the work environment. Climate, culture, and character are heavily influenced by opportunities to communicate and by the trust engendered by such interactions. Traditional organizations, with emphasis on controlling people's behavior, seldom develop feelings of trust, which are a critical part of organizational climate and employee morale.

In summary, the manager needs to be aware of the trade-offs encountered when making decisions about organizational design. The astute manager will continue to seek greater understanding of and sensitivity to how organizational issues affect human beings.

Managers need to be aware of the trade-offs encountered when changing organizational structure.

Summary of Key Ideas

- The informal organization is structured more around personalities and norms than around organizational positions and procedures.

- Five contributors to informal power are seniority, access to key organizational people, aggressive behavior, experience, and credibility among peers.

- Redding's five components of organizational climate are supportiveness, participation in decision making, trust, open communication, and concern for high performance goals.

- The eight characteristics of excellent companies identified by Peters and Waterman are considered part of an organization's climate.

- Culture includes the pervasive values, norms, and attitudes for the whole organization; climate, then, is one aspect of organizational culture.

- Corporate character is defined by shared vision, motivational faith, and distinctive skills.

- A sense of organizational ethics is a foundation upon which managers can build trust and morale.

Key Terms, Concepts, and Names

Downward communication
Employee involvement
Informal organization
Mentoring
"Mop Bucket Attitude (MBA)"
Organizational character
Organizational climate

Organizational culture
W. Charles Redding
Seniority
Supportiveness
Trust
Upward communication
Alan L. Wilkins

Questions and Exercises

1. Pick a particular job with which you are familiar. How could it be redesigned using one or more of the alternatives to traditional design? What would be the effects on the people involved? on the organization?

2. Why is it important for the manager to be aware of organizational culture?

3. Does the notion of organizational character seem potentially more fruitful than the concept of organizational culture? Defend your view.

4. Defend or argue against the following statement: Absolute fidelity to a clear sense of ethics is critical for corporate success.

5. Imagine that you see a need to reorganize the department you manage in XYZ Corporation. Assume that your boss gives you the go-ahead. How would you go about implementing a change?

6. Answer the introductory questions at the beginning of the chapter.

Notes

1. Dan Seligman, "Down with Dyading," *Forbes* November 2, 1998, p. 109.

2. Ibid.

3. W. Charles Redding, *Communication Within the Organization* (New York: Industrial Communication Council, 1972), p. 139ff.

4. Thomas J. Peters and Robert H. Waterman, *In Search of Excellence* (New York: Harper & Row, 1982).

5. Alan L. Wilkins, "Business Stories," *Exchange* Fall 1981, p. 26.

6. Alan L. Wilkins, *Creating Corporate Character* (San Francisco: Jossey-Bass, 1989), pp. xi–xii.

7. Ibid., p. 3.

8. As cited in Paul R. Timm and James A. Stead, *Communication Skills for Business and Professions* (Upper Saddle River, NJ: Prentice-Hall, Inc., 1996), p. 114.

9. Excerpted from Robert C. Solomon and Kristine Hanson, "Use These Eight Rules of Ethical Thinking," in *The Prior Report* 10, No. 5a (1994), p. 9.

10. Cynthia D. Scott and Dennis T. Jaffe, *Managing Organizational Change* (Los Altos, CA: Crisp Publications, 1989), p.9.

Another Look: The Perils of Culture Conflict

Every society, be it a tropical isle or an Exxon, develops a distinctive culture. Your advancement or even survival depends on figuring out whether you fit in.

On the Micronesian island of Pohnpei, one measure of a man's status is his ability to contribute enormous yams to the village feasts. If someone does this consistently, his fellow villagers will praise both his skill as a farmer and the supernatural powers at his command, and often he will be elevated to a titled position. Contributing foods other than yams might be nice, but wouldn't enhance his status. All that matters is yam size.

Using labor-intensive techniques, the men of Pohnpei sometimes cultivate yams exceeding nine feet in length and requiring up to 12 people to carry them. Frequently the yams are adorned with leaves, and the biggest ones have to be held together with mud so they don't collapse in pieces. These "show yams" are rarely eaten. Indeed, after a night's work in the feast house, a prize yam will often be reburied in somebody's garden. Why? So that it can grow larger, of course.

Many Pacific islanders attach ceremonial significance to yams. Some emphasize size; others emphasize number and quality. But even Western cultures have their "yams"—things that are valued less for their inherent qualities than for the meaning the culture assigns them. Nations do this, and, yes, so do corporations. Especially in an era of entrepreneurship like ours, in which companies are as different from one another as their individualistic founders, identifying the yams of a particular company's culture before you sign on is now a matter of career survival.

Kathy Wheeler learned this the hard way in 1992, when she left Hewlett-Packard for Apple Computer. An engineer by training, Wheeler was one of three managers running a 40-person product-design team at HP when she was recruited. Wheeler liked HP, but the Apple job promised her sole responsibility for a product team and a corresponding bump in salary.

Though Apple's headquarters were just two miles from Wheeler's old office, to hear Wheeler tell it, she might as well have moved to Pohnpei. Wheeler had felt comfortable with the "yams" of HP culture: collaboration, consensus seeking, rock-solid engineering ability. Those were the qualities HP prized, and Wheeler had them big. At Apple, she says, everything was different. Suddenly she encountered a culture that exalted heroes and admired slick user interfaces. Those who got ahead were not for the most part the most skilled engineers but rather the "evangelists"—brash marketers of Apple products to the outside world. Before long, Wheeler says, she was deeply unhappy. "When you're used to being valued for one set of accomplishments," she says. "and what's actually being valued are accomplishments you either don't feel comfortable with or just aren't able to deliver on, the discomfort is pretty profound." Fourteen months after arriving at Apple, Wheeler returned to HP, notwithstanding Apple's efforts to keep her. "I admire Apple to a large extent," she says. "But I wouldn't work there again because of the cultural issues."

One reason many job hunters don't spend enough time selecting for culture is that they're not quite sure what it is. Anthropological definitions can run a page in length. But a corporate culture can be defined succinctly as a set of behaviors or qualities that are valued not because competition forces all successful companies to value them, but simply because . . . well, because that's the way things are.

One way to figure out the culture of a corporation, says Jennifer Chatman of the University of California at Berkeley's Haas School of Business, is to identify the personality traits and behaviors that those who thrive in the company have in common. Such traits will emerge in evolutionary fashion, says Dan Cable of the University of North Carolina's Kenan-Flagler Business School. As we all know, managers tend to hire others like them—people they feel comfortable with—and employees tend to accept jobs at places where they expect to feel comfortable. At the same time, employees who don't hit it off with their bosses quit at higher rates, and those who fit in splendidly get promoted faster. Moreover, the personal values of the ones who stay the longest have more time to be molded by mentors, fellow employees, training programs, and company reward systems. Gradually, from the actions of all these forces, emerges a culture: an agglomeration of values and practices that are shared by anyone who matters at the firm.

For example, true to Wheeler's experience, Hewlett-Packard has elevated egalitarianism to

continued

The Perils of Culture Conflict, *continued*

something of a fetish. Everyone in a company-owned building works in a cubicle—including CEO Lew Platt, who, not surprisingly, works in a very large cubicle. And every company car in the U.S., Platt's included, is a Ford Taurus. As HR directors can tell you, a well-defined culture can be an enormous hindrance to a firm if the market changes underneath it and the culture fails to keep pace. Susan Bowick, HP's head of HR, says the company's commitment to decision by consensus has been a disadvantage in some of the fast-moving markets the firm has entered.

One measure of the importance of culture at a company is the amount of time its top executives spend worrying about it. Shaping the company culture, says Dave Arnold of Heidrick & Struggles, a top headhunting firm, is "one of the main missions facing most top human resources executives today." Rob Goffee and Gareth Jones, two British professors of organizational behavior, have recently published a book offering a new typology of firm cultures. In *The Character of a Corporation* (HarperCollins), they set up a two-by-two matrix in which a company's degrees of sociability and solidarity are rated. Sociability is general friendliness among employees, while solidarity is the more hard-headed kind of cooperation that even people who don't like one another demonstrate when they have an overriding goal. Goffee and Jones see certain personality types fitting into particular culture types—for example, high-sociability but low-solidarity cultures attract extroverts with "low needs for structure or certainty."

Company culture is at least as important for employees as it is for managers. That's because many managers despair of ever changing a company's culture from the top down, but canny employees are free to select a company whose culture is compatible with their personal values. Doing so, says Chatman, can make a big difference in their careers. In a study of accounting firms she conducted, Chatman found that new employees whose personalities suited the firm's culture were about 20% less likely to leave their jobs in the first three years than those whose values-sorting test results suggested a poor fit. They also performed better and were more satisfied with their work.

Employees interested in achieving a good match face a two-part task. First, they must figure out their workplace priorities—those values and traits most basic to their identities, whether by birth or upbringing.

Second, they must identify the companies where those qualities are most abundant and prized.

You can address the first task by making a list of the ten values that are most characteristic of your ideal workplace and the ten that are least characteristic (see box).

The second task is tougher, since companies won't always be completely candid about their cultures. Still, even before you decide to apply for a job at a particular company, you can make some educated guesses about its culture just on the basis of its business strategy, says Ed Gubman of Hewitt Associates. For instance, if you're a "people person," service-oriented companies such as Nordstrom or Home Depot are better bets than efficiency-obsessed commodity producers like Cargill.

But don't, Chatman warns, fall into the trap of stereotyping a culture on the basis of its firm's industry. When Chatman studied the accounting profession in the mid-1980s, the employees of Touche Ross (now Deloitte & Touche) picked informality as their firm's No. 1 value among Chatman's 54 items. At Arthur Andersen, informality ranked dead last. How much more varied can you get?

Company websites are a rich source of clues, say career experts. You also might want to see whether reports on the companies you're curious about have been published by Wet Feet Press (www.wetfeet.com) or Vault Reports (www.vaultreports.com). The two services sell company dossiers geared to job applicants.

When it comes time to visit a company, bear in mind that you can learn a lot just from nonverbal artifacts: What do the work spaces look like? How are employees dressed? Most important, what are they doing—standing around chatting or sitting alone in their offices? The most telling artifact of all is the company's compensation system. Does it pay people for performing well over a long period, or is compensation tagged to yearly or quarterly goals? Chatman recalls the case of a financial services firm that bragged about the nifty 360-degree evaluation scheme it had implemented to promote teamwork. But Chatman realized this was all hot air when she learned that the new system played no part in promotions or pay.

For more nuanced information, make sure you interview people at all levels—especially peers—in every department where you might be spending significant amounts of time. And don't forget to speak with former employees who were at your level. Other good information sources are the company's suppliers and its

continued

The Perils of Culture Conflict, *continued*

WHAT DO YOU VALUE AT WORK?

The 54 items listed below cover the full range of personal and institutional values you'd be likely to encounter at any company. Professor Jennifer Chatman and others use this list to study cultural preferences. Divide it into two groups: the 27 that would be the most evident in your ideal workplace, and the 27 that would be the least. Keep halving the groups until you have a rank ordering, then fill in the numbers of your top and bottom ten choices. Test your fit at a firm by seeing whether the company's values match your top and bottom ten.

Top Ten Choices _____

Bottom Ten Choices _____

The Choice Menu

You Are:

1. Flexible
2. Adaptable
3. Innovative
4. Able to seize opportunities
5. Willing to experiment
6. Risk-taking
7. Careful
8. Autonomy-seeking
9. Comfortable with rules
10. Analytical
11. Attentive to detail
12. Precise
13. Team-oriented
14. Ready to share information
15. People-oriented
16. Easygoing
17. Calm
18. Supportive
19. Aggressive
20. Decisive
21. Action-oriented
22. Eager to take initiative
23. Reflective
24. Achievement-oriented
25. Demanding
26. Comfortable with individual responsibility
27. Comfortable with conflict
28. Competitive
29. Highly organized
30. Results-oriented
31. Interested in making friends at work
32. Collaborative
33. Eager to fit in with colleagues
34. Enthusiastic about the job

Your Company Offers:

35. Stability
36. Predictability
37. High expectations of performance
38. Opportunities for professional growth
39. High pay for good performance
40. Job security
41. Praise for good performance
42. A clear guiding philosophy
43. A low level of conflict
44. An emphasis on quality
45. A good reputation
46. Respect for the individual's rights
47. Tolerance
48. Informality
49. Fairness
50. A unitary culture throughout the organization
51. A sense of social responsibility
52. Long hours
53. Relative freedom from rules
54. The opportunity to be distinctive, or different from others

continued

The Perils of Culture Conflict, *continued*

corporate customers. But before all that are questions you should put to just about anyone you talk with about the company: What kind of people seem to succeed there? What particular aspects of their behavior are celebrated? And what sorts of behavior bring failure? The answers will tell you volumes about the firm's shared values—that is, about its culture.

Before you walk into an interview, try to prepare other questions that will ferret out whether the firm shares your top ten and bottom ten priorities. Career counselor John McDorman urges clients to ask questions that call for examples, since the answers can't be easily faked. For instance, if you're particularly concerned about work-life balance, you might ask your interviewer to tell about a time when an employee's personal commitments conflicted with the immediate needs of the company, and how that dilemma was resolved. George Bailey, formerly of Watson Wyatt, recommends another line of questioning that's often fruitful. Especially if you're a manager,

ask how the yearly budget is handled: It's a case study in how the firm resolves conflict. And Chatman advises job seekers to ask about the company's founders, its early history, and its folklore. Firms, like people, often reflect their formative experiences, even many years later.

Chatman recalls a Federal Express folk tale about a delivery guy who had been given the wrong key to a FedEx drop box. So he loaded it into his truck and took it back to the station, where they were able to pry it open and get the contents to their destination the following day. At FedEx, this employee is remembered as a hero. At the U.S. Postal Service, Chatman suggests, someone who uprooted a mailbox from a sidewalk would probably be regarded as a lunatic, if not a felon.

Another Look: No Ifs, Ands or Buts, Office Cubicles a Pain

The office tour was nearly complete. I'd met my new coworkers. I'd been shown the copy room, the break room, the bathroom. Only one thing was left. We turned the corner and my supervisor swept her arm out like a model on "The Price is Right." But instead of a new car, she gestured towards a small, dreary enclosure roughly the size of a veal pen. "This will be your cubicle!" I scanned my cell: decor by Huxley, chair by de Sade, window by Gates. I let out a deep sigh. I knew I was in for some serious life-sucking.

The cubicle is the most nefarious innovation in workplace design since the time clock. They make you think it's a big deal—as if you're getting the corner office or a company car—when it's really just a transparent labor-maximizing strategy.

The walls shut you off from other people. Not so you can concentrate, but so you don't waste the company's time talking. But the walls offer only the illusion of privacy. You can't see the faces, but you—and your supervisor—can hear everything. One day, I listened to a coworker melt down over some personal mini-tragedy. For several minutes, I listened to him argue with a telephone operator. He kept saying, "I'm not at a phone I can do that on!" I think he

wanted to make some sort of collect call. I guess he was afraid to use the company's long distance (a Company Man—how quaint). Finally, he lost it. He started asking for the operator's supervisor's name, and it sounded like he was holding back tears of rage. "Who does she report to? Well, if anything has happened, you'll be hearing from me, my lawyer, and . . . and everyone." Everyone? They won't be hearing from me, dude. It was pitiful. And how can you respect a guy after you hear him betting next week's salary on the Raiders with one of those off-shore bookmakers? And give six points! My coworkers will never be able to look at me the same way again.

Karl Marx believed that the factory jobs of the Industrial Revolution alienated the workers. That was small-time compared to the lonely hypnosis of the new information industry, where the only interface is the 1,024 by 768 pixels of flickering dullness. A lot of people make a feeble attempt to combat the crushing modularization by decorating their cubes with pictures from home and other reminders of life outside the walls. I shun this practice. Cube-decorators are lifers—they've accepted their fate as career keyboard drones. They're hanging on to the

continued

No Ifs, Ands or Buts, Office Cubicles a Pain, *continued*

archaic ideal of a Ward Cleaver business world, complete with Christmas bonuses, personal secretaries, and pension plans. They haven't realized that we are careening towards a labor market characterized by total free agency. A world of COBRA and transferable 401(k)s. A world where loyalty to the company is as extinct as the corporate ladder.

There is, however, something worse than the demeaning lack of privacy. Something worse than the mind-numbing effect of a weekly 40-hour sentence inside a uniformly gray box. I'm not a doctor, but I believe the medical term for it is "Butt Pain." After a year and a half of sitting virtually motionless for 8 hours a day, I can no longer sit anywhere for long without an ache radiating down my left leg. I'd trade in my Butt Pain for Carpal Tunnel Syndrome in a second. After all, I can always stop typing. I know I'm not alone. The next great labor movement in this country will focus on one goal: a more comfortable office chair. Let's just hope it's not a sit-down strike.

Source: Reprinted from Rob Hughes, "No Ifs, And or Buts, Office Cubicles a Pain," *The Daily Herald*, Provo, Utah, September 19, 1998, p. A2. Used with permission.

A Case in Point: Wendy's Successful "Mop Bucket Attitude"

After feasting on success for more than 15 years, Wendy's Old Fashioned Hamburgers restaurants developed heartburn in the mid-1980s. Costs soared, sales dropped, and formerly enthusiastic analysts waxed gloomy about Wendy's prospects, convinced our company had lost focus.

I came on as president in 1986 and found we had indeed lost our focus—on people. We had such a fear in our hearts about numbers, about the power of computer printouts and going by the book, we'd managed to lose sight of our customers and employees both.

There's a special purgatory for service businesses that forget their business starts with people. What happened to us was typical: Managers weren't getting the respect they needed and were passing their frustrations along to the crew. The crew, feeling unappreciated, made the customer feel the same. And the customers voted with their feet—as customers are wont to do.

As sales fell, store labor was cut and sales fell ever further. Morale took a nose dive, quality became spotty, and consistency in operations was nonexistent. It was time, clearly, to heave the charts and the printouts and to concentrate once more on the basics. Beginning with the most basic tenet of them all: **Mop Bucket Attitude, or M.B.A.**

Mop Bucket Attitude says that all the business sophistication in the world pales before the "wisdom" of a clean floor. Fancy price-cost tabulations or quarterly earnings have no meaning to the customer, but quality food, variety, and atmosphere do. Those had traditionally been our strengths, and they hadn't lost one bit in value; we just weren't playing to them any more. With our priorities now firmly in hand, we turned to our employees.

Ours is an industry once defined by high employee turnover. It was viewed as normal if not inevitable. We questioned that view, and decided the best way to become the customer's restaurant of choice was to become the employer of choice. Our plan on this front was two-pronged: to work harder to develop the potential of the people we already had, and to move aggressively to attract and retain the best people we could.

We began by raising employee training to uniformly high standards, seeing that everyone, from the newest kid on fries all the way up to the manager, received the same basic training. (Previously, anyone with two weeks on the job might train the last person in the door.) Then we worked to make "manager" truly a status position, giving managers more control and latitude in day-to-day decisions.

Still, we knew young people of ambition might forsake us the first chance they got for "real" jobs with benefits to match. So we improved base compensation, offered a package of top-flight benefits and a cash bonus paid out each quarter. We created an employee stock option plan called "We-share" to give our employees a larger stake in the company. And, reflecting the special concerns of our founder, Dave Thomas, we included paid leave and reimbursed medical and legal costs for company employees who adopt children.

It worked. Our turnover rate for general managers fell to 20% in 1991 from 39% in 1989, while

continued

Wendy's Successful "Mop Bucket Attitude," *continued*

turnover among co- and assistant managers dropped to 37% from 60%—among the lowest in the business. With a stable—and able—work force, sales began to pick up as well. To win back repeat business, though, we would have to concentrate not just on this transaction, but the next.

We know it's easy to increase store traffic and sales short term. You flood the market with coupons, let fly with a few specials, maybe go for a splashy new ad campaign. But if you get customers in the door and disappoint them, it's a disaster. Not only must you offer customers quality, value, and a pleasant experience: You must offer it consistently.

With the aim of increasing consistency throughout the 3,800 Wendy's restaurants world-wide, we launched "Sparkle" in 1989—a program that is part incentive, part strategy for elevating standards and measuring quality, service, and cleanliness on a daily basis. We refocused our managers and crew to look at their restaurants from the customer's point of view.

We also looked at our menu lineup and added more products to the premium side of the business, an acknowledged area of our strength. At the same time, we reached out to our cost-conscious customers with a Super Value menu of nine items priced at 99 cents—not just on Wednesdays or for a "limited time only," but every day of the year.

The customers who'd deserted us began to come back. I won't say it was a flood; more of a trickle at first. When we started these programs in 1987, we made just five cents a share. In 1991, by contrast, we reported earnings of 52 cents a share. Amid flat sales in the rest of the industry and a recession that wouldn't go away, Wendy's realized a 31% rise in earnings last year for a profit of $51 million—its best year since 1985.

I wish I could say there was some kind of magic wand behind all of this. In fact, the "magic wand" approach was the first thing to go. The main reason we have sustained 12 consecutive quarters of sales gains over the prior year—and look to continue it into the next 12 and beyond—is because we returned to the solid, unmagical principles of management that put us on the map in the first place.

These are the principles that focus on people—and never go out of fashion.

Questions

1. What actions by management indicate an awareness of the importance of the human side of organization?
2. What can we learn about people in organizations from this case?

Source: Reprinted from James W. Near, *Wall Street Journal,* April 27, 1992, p. A16. Used with permission.

A Case in Point: The Electronic Games Division

The electronic games division of Toys R Fun Corporation, a large toy manufacturer, was organized along functional lines. Each department, or function, worked pretty much on its own. There were departments of research, new product design, manufacturing, marketing, finance, and human resources. The division manufactured a variety of electronic games, all of which were selling quite well. It was somewhat less successful at coming up with competitive new products in this fast-changing industry.

Because the division had experienced some turbulent business conditions and had seemed to lose much of its competitive edge, the general manager called in a consultant to discuss what he saw as problems in intergroup relations. The manager felt that there were too many conflicts among the various

groups. He believed those conflicts were hindering the division from keeping on top of the very rapidly changing market. Specifically, he was afraid that the conflicts were hampering the division's product development efforts, efforts that required coordination and cooperation among all the functional groups.

A university-based consultant, Arlene Steinberg, came to the organization and decided to do a thorough analysis before she made any recommendations. Her efforts included interviewing virtually every manager in the plant, administering questionnaires to many of the workers and supervisors, and carefully analyzing the organizational structure of the plant.

Steinberg found that the division was highly specialized and that the managers and others were

continued

The Electronic Games Division, *continued*

highly motivated. But the overall design of the division needed to be improved. The primary coordination of departments was through the division manager, who held frequent meetings with his top staff to discuss and coordinate all product development activities in the division. This was not sufficient, however. Poor intergroup relations were symptoms; poor organizational design, Steinberg concluded, was a cause. The different functional groups simply were not communicating with each other.

The consultant suggested that a new organizational structure be tried. She suggested that new product developments be carried out by teams made up of one or more individuals from each of the different functions in the plant. This, she felt, would bring about better coordination.

The consultant stayed on to train key people who would coordinate and assemble these teams for new product development. The project teams designed all phases of the new products, including design, financing, and marketing. Once a team's project had been launched, the team itself was disbanded and people went back to their own organizations. Typically, this took about six months.

Two years after this reorganization, follow-up studies were done to see if the new system was working. It was found that in the year after the implementation of the program, nine complex and highly profitable new products had been developed. This compared with a total of five new products in the previous five years. The friction among groups apparently had been reduced, morale was better, and the company's profits were up.

Questions

1. What were some of the key organizational design problems with the old way that Toys R Fun was working?
2. What principles of effective organizational structure had been violated by the old way of doing things?
3. Specifically, how did organizational design seem to affect the people involved in this company? How did the design changes affect the way people interacted and communicated?

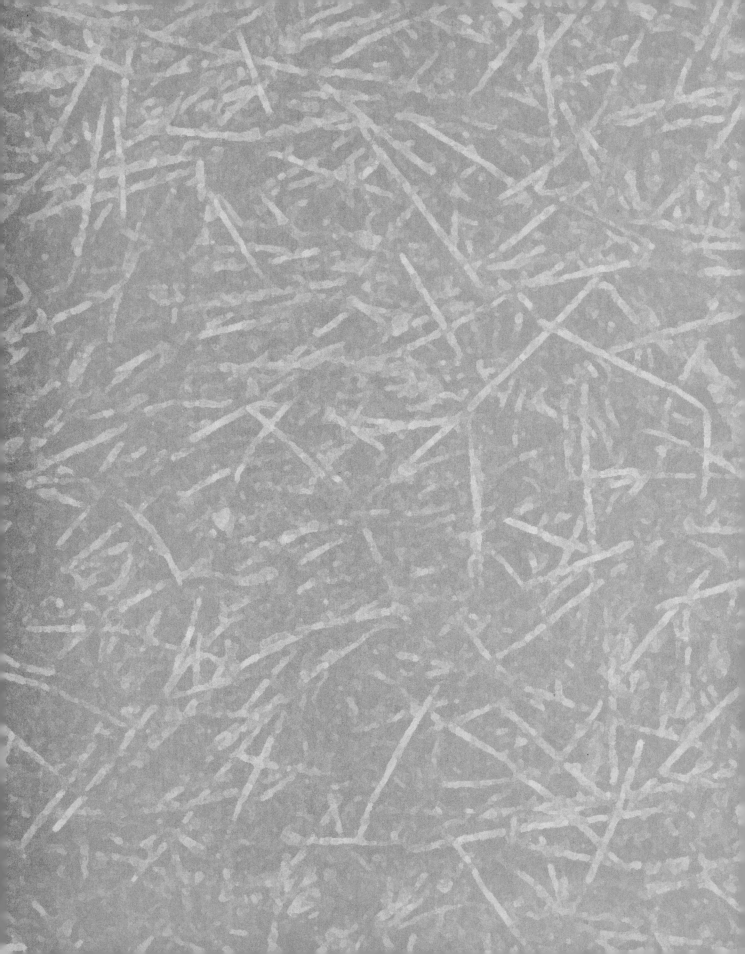

PART 4

LEADERSHIP

The Driving Force: Leadership

- Are there certain personal characteristics that make someone a good leader?

- What is the difference between management and leadership?

- What do followers expect from their leaders?

- Are leaders born or made?

- What personal characteristics will eliminate someone from consideration for leadership positions?

- What four factors most influence the leadership situation?

- How do assumptions or expectations affect leadership style?

- What did Douglas McGregor mean by Theory X and Theory Y?

- What is a self-fulfilling prophecy, and how can it affect leadership?

- What is power, and how can it influence leadership?

- What are some popular myths about leadership?

The answers to these and other questions are coming up next in Chapter 8 . . .

Leadership. It's a term we apply to the movers and shakers of this world—the people who have the amazing power to get others to do things. We see Teddy Roosevelt charging up San Juan Hill, and Norman Schwarzkopf and Colin Powell orchestrating Operation Desert Storm. We see Gloria Steinem actively advocating women's equality for three decades. We see Jesse Jackson uniting minority voices that might have gone unheard. We see professional athletes leading antidrug campaigns and AIDS-prevention efforts. We see courageous leaders in political, moral, religious, and educational causes. Our lives are constantly bumping against people we designate as true leaders.

But true leadership does not require news media exposure. Great leadership happens every day in millions of contexts. We have true leaders among parents, students, teachers, citizens, and people in all walks of life.

In this chapter, we present an overview of the nature of leadership. In the following chapter, we'll show you how to develop an effective leadership style.

Understanding Leadership

So much is currently being written and discussed about leadership that it is easy to become confused trying to figure out what ideas are really most helpful. A short visit to the Internet and one of the current Internet bookstores will help you quickly discover how many new books have been written on leadership. Do they all say the same thing? No!

Three current leaders in the leadership field are **Stephen Covey, Peter Senge,** and **Tom Peters.** They each speak and consult about leadership throughout the world. They do not say the same things, but they are somewhat similar. Covey's book *The 7 Habits of Highly Effective People* has sold ten million copies. *In Search of Excellence* by Tom Peters has sold five million copies. Senge's work *The Fifth Discipline* has sold two million copies. The sheer number of copies sold of these books shows how strong the interest in leadership is. Covey talks about Principle Centered Leadership, while Senge calls for Conceptual Leadership. In this chapter, we will present ideas about the nature of leadership by illustrating a variety of different ideas.

Stephen Covey

Tom Peters

Peter Senge

Leaders Require Willing Followers

A young man walks into the late-night convenience store, pulls out a pistol, and orders the clerk to put her hands over her head.

"Open the cash register," he commands, "and then walk into the storage room."

The clerk does exactly what she's told. The man locks her in the back room, scoops the money out of the cash drawer, and pours himself a large cherry cola Slurpee.

"Stay in that room for ten minutes," he shouts as he heads for the door, "or I'll blow your head off." He jumps into his car and roars off.

Is this armed man a leader? He did get the clerk to do what he wanted, didn't he?

Yes, he did, but he used *coercion* (actually, direct threat) rather than *leadership*. Leadership of the type we are concerned with in organizations cannot be based on threats—at least not over the long run.

A leader is a person who has in some way gained the loyalty of others who are *willing* to follow. The willingness to follow arises from people's perceptions of the leader's position and personal characteristics. Sometimes people are "thrust into positions of leadership." More often, they earn the right to lead by developing useful skills and attributes. Alluding to such skills, Henry Ford made this often-quoted observation: "The question 'Who ought to be boss?' is like asking 'Who ought to be the tenor in the quartet?' Obviously the man who can sing tenor."

What Do Followers Say They Want Their Leaders to Be?

Several ideas have been presented about leadership. What do you think a good leader should be? What does leadership mean to you? Following is a short questionnaire. Fill in your answers and then turn the page to discover how other people like you have described what they think a leader should be.

"The greatest mistake made in selecting managers is to become impressed with an individual's ability to do things himself as opposed to getting things done through other people. The best managers are those who get things done through other people."

E. B. Barnes
President
Dow Chemical Company

People earn the right to lead by developing skills and aptitudes.

ACTIVITIES

A LEADER IS . . .

Complete the following statement by selecting single words or short sentences that describe the important characteristics of a leader.

A Leader Is One Who:

1. _____

2. _____

3. _____

4. _____

5. _____

ACTIVITIES

A recent study was completed by the Franklin Covey Center for Research where a question similar to the one you have just completed was asked. The Center for Research evaluated more than 37,000 responses to this question from people in organizations across the U.S. These responses were all received during 1997 and 1998. Most types of organizations were included as well as most levels of administration. Following is a summary of their responses. The categories were created by content analyzing all the responses. The percentages simply represent the percent of responses to each category. Compare your responses to these.

A Leader Is One Who:

Category	Percentage of Response
1. Effectively **Communicates**	22.1%
2. Exhibits **Integrity**	19.2%
3. Enjoys **Teams**	14.8%
4. Is **Visionary**	10.2%
5. Makes **Decisions**	7.2%
6. Demonstrates **Caring**	5.6%
7. Always **Models**	5.5%
8. Shows **Dedication**	5.3%
9. Effectively **Motivates**	3.8%
10. Exhibits **Expertness**	3.5%
11. Is **Courageous**	3.0%

Source: Reprinted from Brent Peterson and Mike Wuergler, *Characteristics of Effective Leaders: Analysis of the Principle-Centered Leadership Profile from Over 37,000 Responses* (Salt Lake City: Franklin Covey Company, International Leadership Symposium, 1998). Used with permission.

There were some surprises in the study referenced in the activity above. The Center had expected many more responses in the expertness category and fewer in integrity. Basically, the results seem to indicate that employees want their leaders to:

1. *Effectively Communicate*
   The ability to effectively communicate is the most important skill employees would like to see in their leaders. It is important to note that the

words employees used to describe effective communication deal with interpersonal communication. Employees want a leader who listens to them and works with them well in a one-on-one situation. The word "communicator" was most often chosen to describe what an employee wants in a leader.

2. *Exhibit Integrity*

This seems to be a trait employees would like to see more of in their leaders. "Trustworthy" and "honesty" were the second and third most used words to describe the ideal leader, along with "integrity," "ethical," and "truthful." Employees want a leader they know tells them the truth and is trustworthy.

3. *Enjoy Team Work*

This attribute is characterized by words such as "team" and "team player." Employees clearly want to work with a leader who enjoys being with people and working with them as a team. It can be inferred that employees are saying, "We want a leader who is one of us."

4. *Be Visionary*

The responses indicate that employees want their leader to be creative and goal oriented in creating a vision for the work team. Words that were used to describe this attribute were "visionary," "goal," "proactive," and "creative." Employees like a leader who gives the team his or her vision and then works with them to attain the vision.

5. *Make Decisions*

There were only four words stated more than 3,000 times; "decision" was one of them. It is obvious that this is a very important aspect of leadership to the employees. Other words in this category included "problem solver," "planner," and "organized." Employees want a leader who can make decisions.

6. *Demonstrate Caring*

This category comes from a long list of similar words suggesting that employees want a leader that cares for them. The key words that make up this attribute are "caring," "compassionate," "serving," and "concerned." At first it seemed that these words should be included in the communication category or maybe the team category, but after much consideration, the researchers made this a unique category. Employees want to feel that someone in the organization cares about them.

7. *Be a Model*

The words selected by the employees in this category suggest that they want a leader who is a good example to them. They want a leader they look up to, one who is a "model," a "coach," a "mentor." Much is expected of a leader. This category is somewhat like the character category. Again, the researchers kept it separate because it is unique and it deals with the importance of how modeling influences others' behaviors.

8. *Be Dedicated*

The words selected in this category indicate that employees want a leader who is not afraid to work. The words used were "willing," "committed," "dedicated," "hard working." It seems that employees want a leader who works hard and is dedicated to the importance of what the team is trying to accomplish.

9. *Be a Motivator*

This category is difficult to label; the words used stressed motivating others and being enthusiastic about it. Employees feel that good leaders should be motivational in the approach they take to leading. It is interesting to note, however, that only 3.8 percent of the words the employees selected fell into this category.

10. *Be Expert*

The words listed in this category include terms such as "knowledgeable," "competent," and "intelligent," and were only mentioned 3.5 percent of the time. In light of other research and other information regarding leadership, such a small percentage is quite surprising. Employees want their boss to be an expert, but they are much more concerned with the boss's character and ability to communicate effectively.

11. *Be Courageous*

Unexpectedly, the word "courage" came up frequently in this study and hence was included. Employees seem to be supportive of a leader who shows courage and tenacity.

Are Leaders Born or Made?

Although now mostly discredited, the "born leaders" school of thought once prevailed. For many years, social scientists attempted to define specific personal traits or characteristics in individuals that made them effective leaders. This research approach was based on the underlying assumption that leaders are somehow different from ordinary people. If these differences could only be identified, people would be able to "scientifically" select the best leaders. One early study indicated that tall people tended to be better leaders than short people. (Napoleon would have been surprised to hear that!) Other studies looked at such attributes as general intelligence, self-confidence, persuasiveness, and intuition as they relate to leadership.

Are leaders somehow different from ordinary people?

Several problems arose from this avenue of study. For one thing, some of the labels for the traits being studied were unclear. Just how does one define something like *intuition* or *attractiveness?* A more important criticism of this research approach is that the findings were largely inconclusive when applied to different leadership situations. An effective sales manager may not be successful as a railroad crew supervisor. A military commander may function poorly as a cleric or as a political leader.

Are there any universal leadership traits?

Social scientists who saw the need to study individual situations began to regard the search for *universal* leadership traits as virtually worthless. Before we write off more than 50 years of the **traits approach to research studies,** however, let's consider a massive review of such studies prepared by Ralph Stogdill. Stogdill's analysis of almost 300 studies concluded that leaders, when compared with nonleaders, possessed some almost universal characteristics. They were almost always goal-directed, venturesome, self-confident, responsible, tolerant of stress and frustration, and capable of influencing others. Stogdill also concluded that when a person has only one or two of these traits, it's impossible to reliably predict whether that individual will be a good leader. For example, a self-confident, goal-directed person who does not also possess several other leadership characteristics could not automatically be assumed to be a good leader. However, when a combination of most of these characteristics was present, they tended to indicate a personality appropriate to the person seeking the responsibilities of leadership.[1] This result, although completed nearly 25 years ago, seems to be quite similar to the current Franklin Covey Company research.

Perhaps one reason some people discredit the traits approach to leadership studies is that it seems to imply that a leader either does or doesn't have the desired characteristics—an implication that questions the value of leadership training. If you have leadership traits, you don't need the training; if you don't have them, the training probably won't help. That could be depressing for those who don't have the "right" traits.

Clearly, the trait studies have problems. But to completely deny the existence of some prominent leadership traits could be an over-correction. Although personal traits do not in themselves make a leader, they are part of the larger, more complex set of forces working in any leadership situation.

Does leadership training do any good?

Factors That Affect Leadership Success

Social science research has not been overly successful in predicting who would be a good leader. It has, however, been successful in determining the kinds of factors that affect leadership success.

Among these are the personal characteristics or traits we've already discussed. But at least four other factors are equally, if not more, important:

Four factors, in addition to the leader's personality traits, affect leadership success.

1. Leader's expectations or assumptions about human behavior
2. Nature of the task(s) to be accomplished
3. Leader's power
4. Leader's style

Assumptions about Others: You Get What You Expect

We all tend to make assumptions about other people we encounter. The leader is no exception. Leaders see their subordinates, as a group or individually, in favorable, neutral, or negative ways. More specifically, they *assume* that their subordinates can and will do some things but cannot or will not do others. These perceptions are likely to change, but the assumptions leaders hold about others affect the ways they work with them. These leadership attitudes, or expectations of how others will react, affect how one leads others. In a very real sense, people act in certain ways because one expects them to.

Theory X and Theory Y   In 1960, **Douglas McGregor** published a classic book in the field of management titled *The Human Side of Enterprise*. The book was based on considerable research about human nature and human motivation.

"Effective leadership must comprise many elements, three of which are essential—integrity, enterprise, and service; and of these, integrity is first among equals."

Rawleigh Warner, Jr.
Chairman of the Board,
Mobil Oil Corporation

Source: OVERBOARD reprinted by permission of United Features Syndicate, Inc.

McGregor found that leaders in organizations tended to hold a set of assumptions about their followers, which he labeled **Theory X.*** These assumptions were by and large negative:

1. Work is inherently distasteful to most people.

2. Most people are not ambitious, have little desire for responsibility, and prefer to be directed.

3. Most people have little capacity for creativity in solving organizational problems.

4. Motivation occurs only at what Maslow called the survival and security levels.

5. Most people must be closely controlled and often coerced to achieve organizational objectives.

Most traditional managers seemed to hold Theory X assumptions.

McGregor felt that these assumptions were held by most traditional managers. He questioned, however, whether or not they are really true. Can one realistically say that most people are basically lazy, or that they are self-centered and have little concern for organizational goals? McGregor thought not. He then developed an alternate set of assumptions, which he labeled **Theory Y:**

1. Work is as natural as play, if the conditions are favorable.

2. Self-control of the individual is often indispensable in achieving organizational goals.

3. The capacity for creativity in solving an organization's problems is widely distributed throughout the organization.

4. Motivation occurs at the belonging, prestige, and self-fulfillment levels, as well as the survival and security levels.

5. People can be self-directed and creative at work if properly motivated.[2]

Don't be confused by the letters X and Y. McGregor intentionally used these nondescriptive names to avoid implying that one set of assumptions is absolutely better than the other. Although Theory X does represent a more pessimistic view of people, Theory Y is not always preferable or more appropriate. For this reason, McGregor avoided calling the two approaches "good" assumptions versus "bad," or "pessimistic" versus "optimistic."

The point of McGregor's work is that the assumptions we hold about others affect the way we behave toward them. A manager who holds Theory X assumptions is likely to treat people very differently from the way a manager who holds Theory Y assumptions would treat people. Although the assumptions themselves do not *cause* a manager to act in a particular way, they do *influence* the behavior of that manager.

If a manager subscribes to Theory X's rather pessimistic view and believes that people basically dislike work and will try to avoid it whenever they can, he or she is likely to act to prevent them from avoiding work. The result is closer supervision and probably a more dictatorial style. If, however, a manager subscribes to Theory Y assumptions and sees others as *potentially* enjoying their work, he or she will try to help them do so. If a manager views workers as having imagination and creativity on the job, he or she will likely give them opportunities to exercise that creativity. So, outlook affects management style.

---

*Over the years, the label Theory X has led to some confusion. It is not really a theory—in the sense of a set of guidelines that explain and help people predict—but is rather a *listing of key assumptions* that people hold with regard to others. These assumptions are paraphrased here for easy reading.

Don't assume, however, that the manager who holds Theory Y assumptions is *necessarily* the nice, easygoing leader. By the same token, don't assume that the Theory X manager is a dictator or an ogre. Some managers who hold Theory X assumptions are very friendly and very nice to their workers. Often this friendliness is based on a paternalistic attitude—a sense of "I'll take care of you, you're not bright enough to take care of yourself."

Theory Y managers are not always nice.

McGregor believed that most people have the *potential* to be mature and self-motivated workers. However, don't jump to the conclusion that Theory Y expectations are always appropriate. Some people simply do not live up to their potential. Positive assumptions do occasionally lead to disappointments. But by and large, giving the benefit of the doubt seems to be a good managerial approach.

Theory X managers are not always bad.

The sets of expectations described by Theory X and Theory Y are *attitudes* or *predispositions* toward people. As with other attitudes, we develop them in part through our experiences. Although holding Theory Y assumptions about people may be useful, be aware that some people will let you down. Don't let the few sour your assumptions about the many.

People develop Theory X and Theory Y assumptions based on experience.

Some workers do drive managers to Theory X assumptions. But few managers can be driven to where they don't want to go. Look into yourself. Do you want to think the best of others? Or is it more comfortable to subconsciously use disappointments of the past as excuses for holding negative assumptions about others?

The only way to reap the benefits of positive assumptions about others is simply to make the Theory Y assumptions guides to your behavior. Stick to them, don't attach conditional clauses, and probably your workers will eventually respond by living up to your expectations.

How can you make Theory Y work?

Self-Fulfilling Prophecies   Theory X assumptions tend to be based on a rather pessimistic view of subordinates. Theory Y is more optimistic. Business leaders who have sought to apply McGregor's concepts contend that the only way one can confirm Theory Y assumptions is to go ahead and use them. The whole secret to applying Theory Y is to make those assumptions and give them an opportunity to prove useful. As one industrialist has put it (and as more than one great spiritual leader has stated in slightly different words), "Make the same assumptions about others that you make about yourself, and then behave accordingly."

Psychologists have been very interested in the effects of expectations on people's behavior. Robert K. Merton, Robert Rosenthal, and others extensively studied such **self-fulfilling prophecies.** They found that our expectations of others seem to *cause* those others to behave in certain ways.

People are just beginning to understand the concept of the self-fulfilling prophesy. No one fully understands all the forces at work. Expectations may be transmitted to others through subtle, nonverbal cues. Perhaps once one gets an idea, one's brain works overtime to seek confirmation of it. Perhaps a worker's behavior is not really so bad, but a manager may go out of the way (unconsciously) to gather examples that better "fit" with a preconceived negative opinion of that worker.

People who have studied self-fulfilling prophecies recommend that we all withhold judgments on other individuals as much as possible—that we keep our expectations rather loose and not let our assumptions about what a person can or cannot do interfere with the way we work with that person.

How can we avoid negative self-fulfilling prophecies?

Task to Be Accomplished

The nature of the work that needs to be done also has an impact on choosing appropriate leadership styles. In the military service, for example, leadership training tends to emphasize an autocratic style. This style seems to be based on

Assembling automobiles is high in task structure and affects the leader's style.

Theory X assumptions about the nature of people. It seldom recommends opportunities for participation in decision making. At least this is the popular view of the military leader accustomed to following orders.

This style of leadership may be used because the nature of the military task is unique. Few other jobs openly suggest that followers may be called on to give the ultimate sacrifice: their lives. There is little time for participative decision making on the battlefield.

On a more day-to-day level, the nature of the tasks being accomplished by a company also affects appropriate leadership styles. If the organization is primarily concerned with assembling or manufacturing something, the work to be done is clearly identified and easily measured. For example, the manager may ask the worker to insert wheels on skateboards or bumpers on automobiles. The job is clearly designed and not very flexible. A job with this degree of clarity is referred to as being high in **task structure.** The step-by-step details permit little variation in how the work is to be done.

A clearly defined, step-by-step job is high in task structure.

In other situations, tasks may be much more vague—low in structure. Some organizations such as research laboratories, universities, public relations firms, or governmental review boards carry out tasks that are much less well defined. The supervisor on the assembly line seldom needs to be overly concerned with defining exactly *what* is to be done, but leaders in think-tank organizations spend a great deal of time doing so. So the nature of the task does affect the leader's job and style.

Typically, the higher one goes in the organizational hierarchy, the less task structure one finds. Top managers spend more time conceptualizing—thinking about what should be done—than actually doing or directing the job.

The Leader's Power

Leaders can have two types of power: personal and position.

Leaders bring two types of power to any situation: *personal* power and *position* power. **Personal power** given to an individual is based on how others perceive that individual. It usually emerges when one is seen as having expertise, skills, ability, or other characteristics that the group considers important. There is a natural attraction to people with high personal power.

Position power is conferred on an individual by someone in a higher level of authority. It depends on rank, position, status, ability, or a combination of these to provide others with rewards or punishments. In short, position power is *authority.*

The newly announced political candidate may run initially on personal power (personality, appearance, experiences, and so on), until position power in the form of endorsements and party nomination is granted. After being elected, the officeholder has position power (having been legitimately selected by the voters), which adds significantly to the potential for leadership effectiveness.

Think for a moment about these two forms of power. Some characteristics of personal power are

- It is incremental—it grows as people see the individual exercising it well.

- It can be expanded over time.

- It can be shared. Holders of personal power can give of their credibility and power by showing that others are with them

Authority or position power is more formal and cannot be "grown":

- It is limited by the "job description."

- It cannot normally be shared.

- It works best when used the least.

Successful leaders exert their authority sparingly. To do otherwise conveys a dictatorial attitude of "Do it this way because I'm the boss." The leader using personal power would convey an attitude of "Do it this way because you recognize my experience, judgment, and ability."

The Leader's Style

The final determinant of leadership success is **personal style.** This is a vague term. Styles can be as unique as the individuals who develop them. But one thing is certain: Style is heavily influenced by the other three factors we've already discussed—expectations, the tasks to be accomplished, and power. In the next chapter, we focus on how to develop styles.

The Myths of Leadership

The whole subject of leadership is permeated with myths. In sum, it would be useful to puncture a few of those myths.[3]

Myth 1: Leadership Is a Rare Skill

Reality:

- Nothing could be farther from the truth; everyone has leadership potential.

- There are millions of leadership roles throughout the world, and many are filled by capable leaders.

- People may be leaders in one organization and followers in another.

- Leadership opportunities are plentiful and within the reach of most people.

A wide range of people can become leaders.

Myth 2: Leaders Are Born, Not Made

Reality:

- Biographies mislead by sometimes portraying great leaders as unpredictable superhumans with unique charisma and almost mystical genius.

- Leadership is not a gift of grace too abstract to be defined, much less learned.

- Because the title of leader is often attributed to those whose actions take place in the most dramatic realms of human endeavor (for example, Mahatma Gandhi, Napoleon, Evita Perón, Winston Churchill, Joan of Arc, Nelson Mandela), we sometimes assume they were destined to lead.

- This myth perpetuates myth 3.

Leadership is exercised in everyday situations, not just during great conflict.

Myth 3: Leaders Are Created by Extraordinary Circumstances and Great Events

Reality:

- This myth would have us believe that leaders emerge suddenly, during times of great conflict and chaos, as did Martin Luther King, Jr. This is true only sometimes.

- This myth limits the opportunities for leadership still further. It indicates that leadership is only associated with some sort of grand cataclysm or rise and fall of power; we have no opportunity to exercise leadership skills under normal circumstances. But leadership is exercised by all kinds of people in all kinds of situations every day.

Myth 4: Leadership Exists Only at the Top of an Organization

Reality:

- We feed this myth by focusing on top leadership when organizations have thousands of leadership roles available to employees.

- Corporations are moving in the direction of creating more leadership roles through empowerment and self-directed work teams within the organization.

True leaders empower others.

Myth 5: The Leader Controls, Directs, Prods, Manipulates

Reality:

- This is perhaps the most damaging myth of all.

- Leadership is not so much the exercise of power itself as the ability to empower others.

- Leaders align their energies with others: they pull, rather than push; they inspire, rather than command.

- Managers may command people, use a system of rewards and punishments, and maintain control through intimidation—but a leader's tools are very different.

- Some managers try to substitute management for leadership.

- Often organizations are overmanaged and underled.

- Management is never a substitute for leadership.

Myth 6: Leaders Are Charismatic

Reality:

- Some are, most are not.

- There are always a few leaders who correspond to our fantasies of "divine inspiration" and "grace under pressure" (for example, John F. Kennedy), but most leaders are all too human—fallible, flawed, with no particular charm that separates them externally from their followers.

- Charisma is the result of effective leadership—not the other way around. It is often the ability to articulate the felt needs of an emerging group of people.

Myth 7: It Is Immoral to Seek Power

Reality:

- Those who recognize that power is a key requisite for change may feel revulsion toward it.

- Power has been maligned and misunderstood.

- Power is often associated with greed and selfish ambition.

- Power is associated with those who abuse and misuse it, rather than with those who use it wisely.

- We confuse power with subjugation and control. In doing so, we reject power, whether consciously or unconsciously, and thereby restrict our own opportunities for leadership.

- Power is a means to an end.

- Power is energy, and as with any form of energy, its value lies in how we use it. Until used, power is neutral—it is neither benign nor corrupting.

We all have opportunities to be leaders. All that's really required is that we cultivate some willing followers. Whenever we attempt to lead—that is, to get someone to do what we require—we choose from various tactics available to us. The use of physical threat, as in the convenience store holdup case, is not leadership; it's coercion. It will not produce lasting results.

Managers must evaluate the effects on their followers' freedom resulting from orders or requests. The dictator permits no freedom for subordinates; the participative leader permits a great deal. There is a place for both approaches—and for all those in between. The exact place is determined by the leader's and the follower's personality traits, the leader's expectations and assumptions, the nature of the task to be accomplished, and the leader's power.

Summary of Key Ideas

- There are many points of view about leadership. Learning as many ideas as possible regarding leadership can help a person be a more effective leader.

- Leadership and management are not the same. There are many differences between leaders and managers. However, leaders generally focus on people and managers focus on tasks.

- A leader is a person who has in some way gained the loyalty of others who are willing to follow. The willingness to follow arises from people's perceptions of the leader's position and personal characteristics.

- Employees seem to indicate they want leaders who communicate effectively, have a high degree of integrity, and enjoy working as a team.

- The personality characteristics or traits of a leader are only one of the factors that contribute to effective leadership. Other factors include the leader's expectations about human behavior, the leader's power, and the nature of the task.

- Douglas McGregor believes that people's actual behavior is often consistent with the way we expect them to act; that their behavior may not reflect their full potential, and that people develop their Theory X or Theory Y assumptions based on their own experience.

- To reduce the possibility of self-fulfilling prophecies, we should withhold judgments as much as possible, keep our expectations loose, and avoid letting our assumptions about a person interfere with the way we work with that person.

- The two types of power that a leader brings to any situation are personal power based on the individual's personal style and position power based on the authority conferred by the organization.

- The study of leadership has been permeated with many myths.

Key Terms, Concepts, and Names

Stephen Covey

Douglas McGregor

Myths of leadership

Personal power

Personal style

Tom Peters

Position power

Self-fulfilling prophecies

Peter Senge

Task structure

Theory X

Theory Y

Traits approach to leadership studies

Questions and Exercises

1. List and describe three characteristics that followers would suggest are important in their leader.

2. Describe several situations where expectations seem to have affected outcomes. (These examples need not be related to on-the-job activities.)

3. Why is it important to differentiate between management and leadership? What is the difference?

4. How can leaders apply Theory Y assumptions? To what degree is the approach realistic?

5. Interview a leader in an organization in such a way as to determine that person's assumptions about his or her subordinates. To what extent could this person's comments be regarded as Theory X or Theory Y assumptions?

6. Think of a situation in which you feel that others expected you to fail or succeed. How did their expectations influence your behavior?

7. Read and discuss your reactions to the following "Another Look" articles.

8. Read the following two "Case in Point" articles, and then answer the introductory questions at the beginning of this chapter.

Notes

1. Ralph M. Stogdill, *Handbook of Leadership* (New York: Free Press, 1974), pp. 81–82.

2. This summary of McGregor's assumptions is adapted from Paul Hersey and Kenneth H. Blanchard, *Management of Organizational Behavior,* 3d ed. (Englewood Cliffs, NJ: Prentice-Hall, 1977), p. 55.

3. SyberVision Seminar Systems, *Leaders: The Strategies of Taking Charge,* based on the work of Warren Bennis and Burt Nanus (Pleasonton, CA: SyberVision, 1989).

Another Look: Warren Bennis on Becoming a Leader

Leaders, Not Managers

I tend to think of the differences between leaders and managers as the differences between those who master the context and those who surrender to it. There are other differences, as well, and they are enormous and crucial:

- The manager administers; the leader innovates.

- The manager is a copy; the leader is an original.

- The manager maintains; the leader develops.

- The manager focuses on systems and structure; the leader focuses on people.

- The manager relies on control; the leader inspires trust.

- The manager has a short-range view; the leader has a long-range perspective.

- The manager asks how and when; the leader asks what and why.

- The manager has his eye always on the bottom line; the leader has his eye on the horizon.

- The manager imitates; the leader originates.

- The manager accepts the status quo; the leader challenges it.

- The manager is the classic good soldier; the leader is his own person.

- The manager does things right; the leader does the right thing.

To reprise Wallace Stevens, managers wear square hats and learn through training. Leaders wear sombreros and opt for education. Consider the differences between training and education:

Education	Training
inductive	deductive
tentative	firm
dynamic	static
understanding	memorizing
ideas	facts
broad	narrow
deep	surface
experiential	rote
active	passive
questions	answers
process	content
strategy	tactics
alternatives	goal

Education	Training
exploration	prediction
discovery	dogma
active	reactive
initiative	direction
whole brain	left brain
life	job
long-term	short-term
change	stability
content	form
flexible	rigid
risk	rules
synthesis	thesis
open	closed
imagination	common sense

The Sum: Leader	Manager

If the list on the left seems strange to you, it's because that isn't the way we are usually taught. Our educational system is really better at training than educating. And that's unfortunate. Training is good for dogs, because we require obedience from them. In people, all it does is orient them toward the bottom line.

The list on the left is of all the qualities that business schools don't encourage, as they opt for the short-run, profit-maximizing, microeconomic bottom line. Bottom lines have nothing to do with problem-finding. And we need people who know how to find problems, because the ones we face today aren't always clearly defined, and they aren't linear. Modern architects are moving away from the divinity of the right angle to rhomboids, to rounded spaces and parabolas. For a leader to develop the necessary competencies, he must start to think about rhomboids.

Leaders have nothing but themselves to work with. It is one of the paradoxes of life that good leaders rise to the top in spite of their weakness, while bad leaders rise because of their weakness. Abraham Lincoln was subject to fits of serious depression, yet he was perhaps this country's best president, guiding this country through its most severe crisis. On the other hand, Hitler imposed his psychosis on the German people, leading them through delusions of grandeur into the vilest madness and most horrific slaughter the world has ever known.

What is true for leaders is, for better or for worse, true for each of us: we are our own raw

continued

Warren Bennis on Becoming a Leader, *continued*

material. Only when we know what we're made of and what we want to make of it can we begin our lives—and we must do it despite an unwitting conspiracy of people and events against us. It's that tension in the national character again. As Norman Lear put it, "On the one hand, we're a society that seems

to be proud of individuality. On the other hand, we don't really tolerate real individuality. We want to homogenize it."

Source: From *On Becoming a Leader* by Warren Bennis. Copyright © 1989, 1994 by Warren Bennis, Inc. Reprinted by permission of Perseus Books Publishers, a member of Perseus Books, L.L.C.

Another Look: Peter Drucker on Leadership and Management

Galagan: You've written about management and leadership, but much more about the former. How do you define the difference between them, and which one do you think is more important for success in the knowledge economy?

Drucker: This is largely a misunderstanding. I have written a great deal about leadership, starting with my earliest management book, *Concept of the Corporation,* which came out in 1946. In *The Practice of Management,* written in 1954, there is a whole chapter called "The Spirit of an Organization" that deals primarily with leadership. And I wrote the very first book on leadership in organizations, *The Effective Executive,* which came out in 1966 and is still a best-seller. And since then, I have published quite a bit on leadership.

I know something that today's writers on leadership mostly do not know or want to know. I come out of political science and, therefore, I know what every political scientist has known since Aristotle 2,400 years ago: Leadership has to be grounded in a Constitution. Otherwise, it quickly becomes irresponsibility. The people who knew that best were the founding fathers of the American Republic, and especially the authors of *The Federalist Papers*—which is still by far the best book on leadership.

Leadership grounded in charisma, which is what so many writers today want to advocate, inevitably becomes misleadership. I am amazed that today's prominent writers on leadership do not seem to realize that the three most charismatic leaders in all recorded history were Hitler, Stalin, and Mao. I do

not believe that there are three men who did more evil and more harm.

Leadership has to be grounded in responsibility. It has to be grounded in a Constitution. It has to be grounded in accountability. Otherwise, it will lead to tyranny. When I look at the last 30 to 50 years—I've been around that long—without exception, the charismatic leaders—whether in business, government, or religion—have ended in failure and disgrace. And they have left a legacy of mismanagement and chaos.

The test of any leader is not what he or she accomplishes. It is what happens when they leave the scene. It is the succession that is the test. If the enterprise collapses the moment these wonderful, charismatic leaders leave, that is not leadership. That is—very bluntly—deception.

I have written, I would say, as much about leadership as most of today's prominent experts on the subject, but I have always stressed that leadership is responsibility. Leadership is accountability. Leadership is *doing*—to use the title of one of my most popular articles and one that is quoted again and again.

And as for separating management from leadership, that is nonsense—as much nonsense as separating management from entrepreneurship. Those are part and parcel of the same job. They are different to be sure, but only as different as the right hand from the left or the nose from the mouth. They belong to the same body.

Source: Excerpted from *Training and Development.* © September 1998 the American Society for Training and Development. Reprinted with permission. All rights reserved.

Another Look: Four Pioneers Reflect on Leadership

Warren Bennis talks with three CEOs about the leadership lessons they've learned from important people in their lives.

The Global Institute for Leadership Development hosts an annual Emerging Leader Program that brings together people who will help lead their organizations into the future. One of last year's Lessons of Leadership panels was hosted by Global Institute co-chair and University of Southern California professor **Warren Bennis** and featured Herman Miller chairman emeritus **Max DePree,** Motorola chairman of the executive committee **Bob Galvin,** and Levi Strauss chairman of the board and CEO **Bob Haas.** Here are excerpts of their conversation.

Bennis: With all the changes you've seen and expect to see, what one fundamental truth of management still applies?

Galvin: Integrity hasn't changed as being a supreme requirement. And I consider trust to be the greatest motivator.

DePree: I agree with Bob on the matters of integrity and trust. I would add that trust takes a lot of moxie and commitment to build. It takes a long time, and you can lose it overnight.

Haas: I think there are two essential things. The first is the value of people, and the second is the importance of values. None of our enterprises are worth anything—Motorola's great technology, Herman Miller's brilliant design, Levi's innovation and heritage—without our people. People are what make it happen. So, as a leader, I focus on enabling and encouraging people.

DePree: We're becoming more interdependent. The way that you focus on people is by learning how to establish and nurture relationships. Technology is wonderful, but it's not sufficient. Relationships are the things that enable technology and all our other skills.

Bennis: How do you build trust in large institutions?

Haas: I don't think there is such a thing as a large organization. I think there are organizations that *behave* like large organizations.

Our work experience is as intimate as our work groups. Leaders create an environment that is intimate and defines how an individual feels about the larger enterprise. We [Levi Strauss] have 36,000 people in over 60 countries around the world. That's a huge, sprawling enterprise. There are pockets of it that feel enormously personal and exciting, and where bonds of trust and mutual commitment are characteristic. There are other parts of it that are grinding, dull, impersonal, and horrible, and I think all of us recognize that picture in most of our enterprises. Our goals as leaders are to amplify the intimacy of every work group.

Source: Excerpted from *Training & Development.* © July 1998 the American Society for Training & Development. Reprinted with permission. All rights reserved.

A Case in Point: Liar, Liar, Pants on Fire

The behavior of the people at the top—not their insincere pronouncements—has the biggest impact on the attitudes of the nation.

Not long ago, the chairman of a large company hired me to help the president of one of his company's entrepreneurial units. The parent company was siphoning millions every year from the young business unit, and the chairman was convinced that the guy running the show was a genius. But the company was facing a sexual-harassment suit as a result of the genius's behavior. My job was to help stop this fellow from continuing to sexually harass women in his employ.

"Look," the genius said to me during our first meeting, "I don't need your help. I'm going to trial on these sexual-harassment charges, and I'm going to lie. What's more, my two top executives have agreed to lie for me. Hell, I could tell all my workers that I'm intending to lie under oath, and it wouldn't make a damn bit of difference. Cash, stock in the company, they're what matter today. What makes you think integrity matters? President Clinton dances around the truth daily. If integrity mattered, Dole would be president."

The genius reasoned that if the President could get away with his alleged bad behavior, then why couldn't he? But the genius missed the point. A chief executive may adhere to the mandate "Do as I say, not as I do," but most people behave according to the principle that actions speak louder than words. Psychologists call that social-influence theory. You want to know how leadership works? Throw out the mission statements; don't bother with values statements; just look at how the company leader behaves and you'll know with 100% certainty how the employees will act and feel about their employer and their employment status.

If your employees know you to be corrupt, their attitude toward work will be shaped by what you do, your mission or values statement be damned. When people at the top of an institution behave in a self centered, narcissistic way, their "screw the rules" attitude is likely to be emulated by all they come in contact with.

There are psychological consequences for living the life of a hypocrite, and there are business consequences as well. Consider the number of start-ups that soar to initial-public-offering viability, only to crash and burn when key employees pocket their stock and seek greener pastures. Or worse, they stay put, parading around in "Screw you, I'm vested" T-shirts, thumbing their noses at company loyalty.

When you lie and believe there will be no consequences for your leadership status or your bottom line, if your key workers are spineless and mercenary too, then you may be correct. Lawyers will tell you that the courts are so full of pathological prevaricators that judges and arbitrators have come to believe that everyone who stands before them is at least mildly disingenuous. The CEO who lies and cheats, however, should remember this: the liar's punishment is not that he is not believed, but that he can believe no one else. That's the true consequence of amoral leadership.

Questions

1. Why would the authors have included this case in the nature of leadership chapter? What is the point of the article?
2. "Hell, I could tell all my workers that I'm intending to lie under oath . . . Cash, stock in the company, they're what matter today. What makes you think integrity matters?" What are your reactions to this statement? Is it true? Do you believe leaders can lie and get away with it?
3. Do you believe that if company leaders lack integrity it carries over to all other employees in the company? Justify this answer to yourself and at least one friend.
4. Compare the way you answered these three questions to the way you responded to the activity regarding what you want in a leader. Do your answers match your reactions to the activity?

Source: Republished with permission of *Inc.* magazine, Goldhirsch Group, Inc., 38 Commercial Wharf, Boston MA 02110. *Liar, Liar, Pants on Fire.* Dr. Steven Berglas, August 1998. Reproduced by permission of the publisher via Copyright Clearance Center, Inc.

A Case in Point: Understanding Your Employees

Immediately after college, Karen had joined the telephone company in its management training program. She had been identified as a potentially "fast-track" manager and had been working in the Miami office for only four months when an opening for a unit manager came about. At first, the district manager thought about hiring someone from outside or transferring a more experienced manager. But because Karen was already available and to avoid recruiting or moving costs, he decided to let Karen have a chance at the job. In the new job, she would have seven supervisors reporting to her. Each supervisor directed five or six customer service representatives who talked directly to customers all day.

Shirley, the most experienced of the supervisors, had been filling in as acting manager for the past few weeks. She seemed to know pretty well what she was doing, and because of her many years working in the office, she knew each employee well.

The first day on the job, she sat down with Karen and briefed her on which employees were indifferent, which were plain lazy, which were marginal performers, and which had personality problems. Her list seemed to include almost all the employees! Along with her assessment of the workers, this supervisor gave Karen some tips on how to "handle" certain members of the staff. The two women spent all morning discussing these things.

Usually, Karen diplomatically turned a deaf ear to this kind of advice. But because she was so new on the job and knew no one in the office, she was more susceptible to suggestion. Although Shirley seemed pretty negative, Karen felt that generally the advice was probably sound. This office was going to need quite a bit of shaping up, concluded Karen.

Questions

1. How would the advice received from this experienced supervisor be likely to affect Karen's management style?

2. What would you do in a similar situation if an employee gave you some unsolicited appraisals of all the workers who were to report to you?

3. How do the potential problem of self-fulfilling prophecies and the discussion of McGregor's Theory X and Theory Y apply in this case?

Developing a Leadership Style That Works

- Why is the manager's choice between decisiveness and participation so important?

- What are some potential advantages to be gained from employee participation in decisions?

- What are some potential disadvantages of participation?

- Which leadership style is right?

- What is the difference between task and maintenance activities?

- What is Fiedler's leadership contingency model, and how can it be used?

- What key ingredients determine an employee's or group's development level?

- What does Likert mean by the linking-pin function of management?

- Why are feedback and flexibility important for leaders?

The answers to these and other questions are coming up next in Chapter 9 . . .

Congratulations! You've just been elected president of the Discovery Club, a service organization. You've been active in the club for several years and feel strongly about the importance of its goal: to strengthen relationships between students and the community via civic service projects. You have lots of good ideas, and now you are in a position to get things rolling in a new direction. But you're a little concerned about being a "boss." What kind of leadership should you use?

In the previous chapter, we discussed the nature of leadership and emphasized key variables that affect the leadership process. In this chapter, we suggest some ways to apply such information in leading others. Before we go on, however, let's look at your potential as a leader. Answer the questions in the following "test" of your leadership potential. Be honest.

ACTIVITIES

MANAGEMENT/LEADERSHIP ASSESSMENT SCALE

This survey describes 20 practices that are commonly demonstrated by excellent managers and 20 commonly demonstrated by effective leaders. Please read all statements carefully. Then decide as a manager/leader the priority you would assign each practice or characteristic. Indicate your decision by circling the appropriate number.

	Priority				
	Highest	High	Important	Modest	Low
1. Gets tough when needed.	5	4	3	2	1
2. Speaks well to groups.	5	4	3	2	1
3. Establishes consistent, clear discipline line.	5	4	3	2	1
4. Attracts others to message that is given.	5	4	3	2	1
5. Provides environment conducive to a feeling of cohesiveness.	5	4	3	2	1
6. Communicates sense of "being in charge."	5	4	3	2	1
7. Has full backing from those reporting to her/him.	5	4	3	2	1
8. Converts employees into followers.	5	4	3	2	1
9. Strives to win by allowing employees to also win.	5	4	3	2	1
10. Attracts others to join his/her group.	5	4	3	2	1
11. Provides important rewards to staff.	5	4	3	2	1

continued

ACTIVITIES

MANAGEMENT/LEADERSHIP ASSESSMENT SCALE, CONTINUED

	Priority				
	Highest	High	Important	Modest	Low
12. Utilizes sources of power in a sensitive, consistent manner.	5	4	3	2	1
13. Shows compassion.	5	4	3	2	1
14. Strong track record for making solid and decisive decisions.	5	4	3	2	1
15. Good listener.	5	4	3	2	1
16. Formalizes and "stages" communication announcements.	5	4	3	2	1
17. Expresses thoughts clearly.	5	4	3	2	1
18. Prudent risk taker.	5	4	3	2	1
19. Keeps employees fully informed.	5	4	3	2	1
20. Articulates an inspiring mission.	5	4	3	2	1
21. Highly ethical.	5	4	3	2	1
22. Generates a feeling of pride in followers.	5	4	3	2	1
23. Delegates effectively.	5	4	3	2	1
24. Ties short-term work goals to mission.	5	4	3	2	1
25. Shares large and small victories with staff.	5	4	3	2	1
26. Gets others caught up in his/her positive force.	5	4	3	2	1
27. Makes work enjoyable.	5	4	3	2	1
28. Creates active tempo.	5	4	3	2	1
29. Maintains positive, upbeat attitude.	5	4	3	2	1
30. Highly energetic; not "desk bound."	5	4	3	2	1

continued

ACTIVITIES

	Highest	High	Priority Important	Modest	Low
31. Admits mistakes.	5	4	3	2	1
32. Good negotiator; knows when to compromise.	5	4	3	2	1
33. Follows logical steps in making decisions.	5	4	3	2	1
34. If she/he resigned, others would consider following.	5	4	3	2	1
35. Consults with others in making decisions.	5	4	3	2	1
36. Builds commitment to his/her cause.	5	4	3	2	1
37. Uses management role with sensitivity.	5	4	3	2	1
38. Stands firm on principle.	5	4	3	2	1
39. Respected by employees when authority is used.	5	4	3	2	1
40. Communicates a power image.	5	4	3	2	1

All of the above practices that are found in effective *managers* have odd numbers. Those practices not always found in managers but *usually found in leaders* have even numbers.

Please add up all the numbers you circled in the *odd*-numbered statements and enter into this box:

Management Practices

Please add up all the numbers you circled in the *even*-numbered statements and enter into this box:

Leadership Practices

continued

ACTIVITIES

MANAGEMENT/LEADERSHIP ASSESSMENT SCALE, CONTINUED

Possible Interpretation

1. If your score in the Management Practices box on page 168 is higher than your Leadership Practices score, this may be an indication that becoming more familiar with Leadership Practices may improve your status as a manager either now or later.

2. If your score in the Leadership Practices box is 80 or above, it would appear you are getting a signal that you are "ready" to take on a stronger leadership role.

3. If your score in the Leadership Practices box is between 60 and 80, it may be a signal that you are "getting ready" to move into a leadership role.

4. If your Leadership Practices score is substantially under your Management Practices score, it may be an indication that leadership, at this time, may not be for you.

5. Please list any additional interpretations that you make from the results of your assessments.

    _____

    _____

    _____

    _____

    _____

    _____

    _____

Source: Elwood N. Chapman and Patricia Heim, *Learning to Lead* (Menlo Park, CA: Crisp Publications, Inc., 1995), pp. 7–9.

Your Leadership Style: Decisive Versus Participative

Four general styles of leadership are autocratic, consultative, participative, and laissez-faire.

Probably the most important problem most managers face is that of creating an appropriate balance between *decisiveness* and *participation*. Ultimately, managers need to make decisions. Once a problem has been carefully thought through, being decisive is a great virtue. Nevertheless, the chief advantage of having others participate in decision making is that the decision arrived at by group participation is more likely to be accepted. Resistance to new ideas is greatly reduced when people have had a chance to participate in decisions. In practical application, this is what is known as "getting employee buy-in," or seeking ownership of the decision.

The way one mixes decisiveness with participation opportunities says much about one's general leadership style. Keep in mind that most managers adjust styles depending on the people they are leading and on other issues that we'll talk more about later.

Studies of leadership suggest that there are at least four commonly recognized styles: autocratic, consultative, participative, and laissez-faire (see Figure 9.1). All but the autocratic style are regarded as democratic to some degree in that the followers participate in leader decisions.

Autocratic

Leaders who use the **autocratic style** are decisive and permit little, if any, follower participation in the decision-making process. Such individuals simply weigh the information, make the decision, and impose that decision on their followers. This may sometimes be necessary, such as in an emergency. If a restaurant patron is choking on food and you are the only person who knows the Heimlich maneuver, it's appropriate for you to jump in and take charge. Likewise, in warfare, military leaders make command decisions, some of which are not popular.

Successful autocrats (and there are some) make short-term expectations clear and leave no doubt about the rewards of conforming and the costs of not conforming. Then they deliver the rewards or punishment as promised.

FIGURE 9.1 Degrees of leader decisiveness and follower participation under four leadership styles.

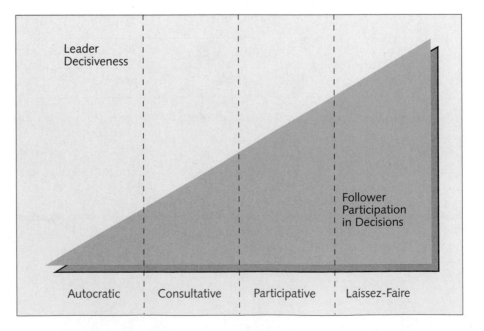

Source: DILBERT reprinted by permission of United Features Syndicate, Inc.

In most organizations, the consistently autocratic leader is disliked and ultimately becomes ineffective. People spend a great deal of energy attempting to get around or defeat the purposes of the autocratic leader.

Consultative

Leaders who use the **consultative style** tend to be fairly high in decisiveness but allow followers more participation in the decision-making process by letting them assume more responsibility for their own future and preparing them for greater responsibilities within the company.

Laissez-Faire

Loosely translated from the French, **laissez-faire** means "let them do anything they want to." Using the "laid-back" laissez-faire style, a leader may have happy employees but not productive ones— although, again, there are exceptions. When subordinates are self-motivated and highly interested in what they are doing, this free-rein style may be appropriate. Under this approach, the leader acts principally as a representative of the workgroup. The leader's job is to ensure there are resources necessary for the group to accomplish its tasks. In essence, the leader is saying, "You know what needs to be done and how to do it, so I'll keep out of your way. Let me know if you need anything."

A certain type of follower is needed to work effectively under laissez-faire leadership. Workers who are both self-motivated and experienced enjoy such

A laissez-faire leader represents the group and obtains the resources it needs.

hands-off leadership. Workers who are not so sure of themselves may resent what they perceive as a lack of direction, or they may simply avoid doing anything productive. Later in this chapter we will show how you can determine if this style is likely to work for you.

The autocratic leader uses a top-down approach.

The consultative or laissez-faire leader does more to serve and support the followers in a bottom-up manner:

Participative

Is a participative style always best?

A manager using the **participative style** is likely to work from Theory Y assumptions. Participative leaders assume that subordinates are creative and have worthwhile ideas that can be applied on the job. They seek out insights and ideas and use them—usually *before* a decision has been made.

Tremendous advantages can arise from participation. More and better ideas can emerge. Resistance to changes is likely to dissipate. And in general, the work climate and employee morale can improve with group involvement.

Participation has disadvantages, however, especially when overused. Some decisions do not lend themselves to a participative approach. For example, decisions about individual compensation or about highly personal matters should not be discussed widely. Similarly, decisions that need to be made quickly often cannot be made with a participative approach.

In addition, the leader must keep in mind that participation can be expensive. It ties up a number of people in meetings (which too often are poorly run), and the costs in time and money can be enormous. Nevertheless, the quality of decisions reached may well offset these costs.

A participative style spreads the responsibilities of leadership among all involved. This can pay big dividends in developing your workers by allowing them to assume more responsibility for their own future as well as preparing them for more responsible positions within the company.

Some argue that the bottom-up versus top-down philosophy is what distinguishes leadership from management. A leader is one who serves and supports others (bottom-up), while a manager pushes down an agenda of work to be done.

Circumstances dictate the appropriate leadership style. For instance, in an emergency the leader is likely to be autocratic.

Which Style Is Best?

The question is, "When should the different leadership styles be used? What works best?" Before we can answer that, we need to review some of what has already been covered and add a few more ingredients to the soup.

To determine which leadership style is likely to work best, one must understand **situational variables** (factors in the environment that are likely to change). One such variable is the mixture of task and maintenance activities needed by the workgroup.

Getting the Job Done Versus Feeling Good About It

In any work situation, two types of activities are influenced by the leader: **task activities** and **maintenance activities.** Task has to do with *what* the group is doing; maintenance is concerned with *how* the group members do it. Clarifying workgroup goals is primarily a task activity, while establishing a pleasant, creative, supportive work climate is mostly a maintenance activity.

Most leaders understand their task roles; they see a job to be done and know they're responsible to see that it is accomplished. Some, however, underestimate the importance of maintenance. One can go too far with either activity, and the degree of emphasis is an important management judgment.

Although the task activities get the job done, neglect of maintenance can lead to serious dissatisfaction that could undermine the entire process. The manager who rams through a solution may face group resentment that eventually will more than offset the "victory." And sometimes maintenance activities are the most important outcome of a meeting, making participants feel good about the opportunities for affiliation and participation in group work. The manager who is sensitive to a healthy balance between getting the job done and making that experience rewarding to the workers is likely to be more successful in the long run than one who overemphasizes one factor. Group members will appreciate an appropriate mix of task and maintenance efforts. They are far more likely to go along with the manager who balances these activities.

The manager who rams through a decision may face resentment that offsets the "victory."

The Leadership Contingency Approach

Fiedler sees three key leadership variables:

- **Leader-member relations**
- **Task structure**
- **Position power**

Fred E. Fiedler developed a **leadership contingency model** that helps determine the best leadership style by looking at three variables: **leader-member relations, task structure,** and **position power.**

Fiedler's research suggests that the degree to which a leader should emphasize task versus maintenance activities can be determined by the **favorableness of the situation.** This he defines as "the degree to which the situation enables the leader to exert his or her influence over the group."[1]

In the most *favorable situation,* the leader

- is well liked by the group
- is directing a clearly defined task
- has recognized status or position power

In an *unfavorable* situation,

- the leader is not well liked
- the task is unclear
- the group does not recognize the leader's right to power

Some mixture of positives and negatives would put the leader in a **mixed situation.**

Fiedler's research concludes that when the situation is either very favorable *or* very unfavorable to the leader, the leader would do well to stress task activities and not be overly concerned with relationship activities. When the situation is intermediately favorable, the leader needs to be more concerned with the building of good relationships (see Figure 9.2).

Stated simply, when the situation is highly favorable (you are liked, the task is clear, and you have position power), you can afford to be a little bossy. Likewise, when the situation is highly unfavorable (you are disliked, the task is ambiguous, and you don't have position power), you might as well be bossy—you have little to lose. But when the situation is somewhere in the middle (you

FIGURE 9.2 Fiedler's leadership contingency model.

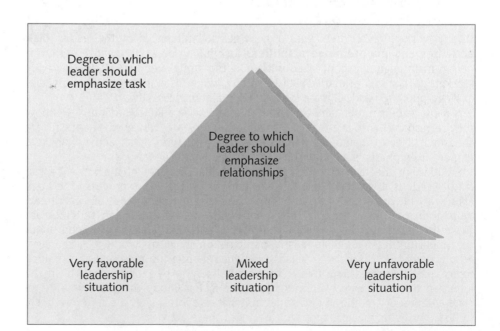

are liked but the task is unclear and you have only moderate position power), you'd be wise to stress maintenance activities—that is, relationship building.

A skillful leader should be capable of switching emphasis as needed. As changes appear in, say, task clarity and relationships with group participants, a marked increase in situational favorableness may call for a shift in emphasis from maintenance (building rapport and so on) to task activities.

A skilled leader switches emphasis from task to maintenance as needed.

Situational Leadership: Getting at the Best Approach

Management theorists **Paul Hersey** and **Kenneth H. Blanchard** have built on the ideas of Fiedler and a number of others to develop their **situational leadership theory (SLT).** According to their approach, a leader can determine an appropriate mixture of relationship building and task directing to increase the probability of effectiveness. "To determine what leadership style is appropriate in a given situation, a leader must first determine the **development level** of the individual or group in relation to a specific task that the leader is attempting to accomplish through their efforts."[2]

What is development level? According to SLT, the development level of a person or group can be diagnosed by considering four characteristics of the group *in relation to the specific job the group is called on to accomplish.* These characteristics are as follows:

Development level is determined by four characteristics.

1. The capacity to set high but attainable goals

2. The willingness and ability to take on responsibility

3. Education, experience, or both, relevant to the task

4. Personal maturity on the job in combination with a psychological maturity or self-confidence and self-respect

These characteristics can be categorized under two headings: *competence* and *commitment.*

Let's look at an example. You have been asked to lead a committee to recommend a marketing strategy for a new product line. In gathering information about those who will work on the committee, you determine the following:

1. The participants have a good record for reaching ambitious yet realistic targets for themselves (commitment).

2. The participants have shown an eagerness to work on the committee and to take responsibility for marketing this new product line in a vigorous manner (commitment). If the product goes over well, they expect to get credit; if it flops, they expect to shoulder the blame.

3. Each participant has been in on the new product development from the ground floor. The participants know how the product is made and why it's built the way it is, and they have a good idea of potential markets based on past experience (competence).

4. The participants are seasoned professionals in their fields. They are interested in success, and they have proven track records (competence).

The preceding committee is at a very high development level. But what if the team consists of quite another group? Let's say that the participants

1. tend to take excessive risks (have a record of "biting off more than they can chew")

2. want credit if their plan works but won't accept blame if it fails

3. have never worked on a committee like this one before

4. are "rookies" in this business

Under this second set of circumstances, the leader's job is likely to be quite different. The second group's development level is very low.

FIGURE 9.3 Situational leadership.

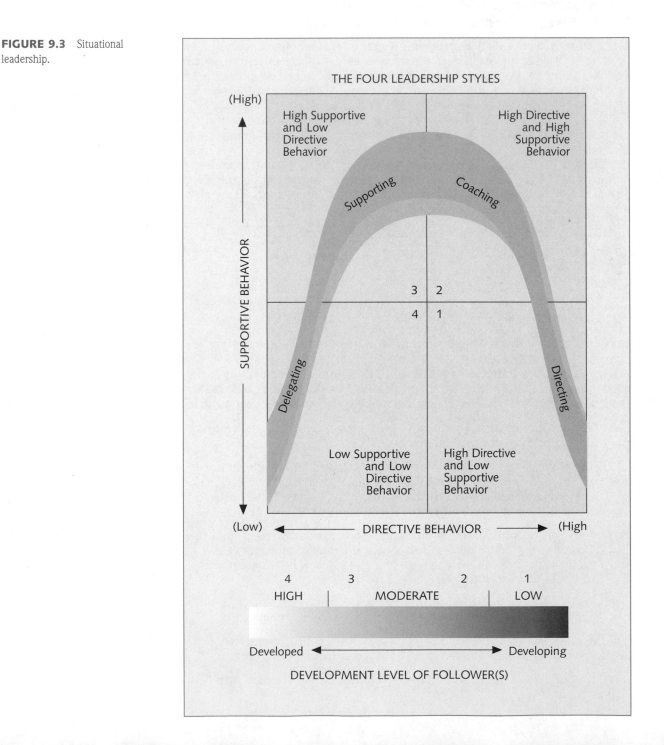

THE FOUR LEADERSHIP STYLES

(High)

High Supportive and Low Directive Behavior

High Directive and High Supportive Behavior

Supporting

Coaching

SUPPORTIVE BEHAVIOR

3   2
4   1

Delegating

Directing

Low Supportive and Low Directive Behavior

High Directive and Low Supportive Behavior

(Low) ◄——— DIRECTIVE BEHAVIOR ———► (High

4   3   2   1
HIGH   MODERATE   LOW

Developed ◄———————————► Developing

DEVELOPMENT LEVEL OF FOLLOWER(S)

Most groups are likely to fall somewhere in between these two examples. Figure 9.3 (on page 176) indicates how the effective leadership style would be determined. Once the development level of the participants is identified (or realistically guessed at), "the appropriate leadership style can be determined by constructing a right (90-degree) angle from the point on the continuum that represents the development level of the follower(s) to a point where it intersects the [curve] in the style-of-leader portion of the model. The quadrant in which that intersection takes place suggests the appropriate style to be used by the leader in that situation with follower(s) of that maturity level."[3]

Or we could say that the leader's predominant behavior changes in relation to the group's development level. The leader also tends toward a different leadership style under each condition, as illustrated in Table 9.1.

TABLE 9.1 *Workers' Development Level Affects Leadership Style and Communication Approach*

TASK–RELEVANT MATURITY LEVEL OF THE GROUP	LEADERSHIP STYLE	PREDOMINANT BEHAVIOR OF THE LEADER
1. Low	Autocratic	Directing
2. Moderately low	Consultative	Coaching
3. Moderately high	Participative	Supporting
4. High	Laissez-faire	Delegating

Directing, coaching, supporting, and delegating each calls for a different mix of communication skills. The ways in which leaders communicate with the low-development employee or group should be different from the way leaders talk to a high-development employee or group.

The appropriate leadership style will probably be more autocratic with low-development workers. Managers will direct these workers more and will not expect much participation—at least not at first. The highly developed workgroup—the self-motivated, personally responsible, experienced team with a success record—may well thrive under a leader who lets the group do its own thing (so long as it continues to work toward organizational goals). As Kenneth Blanchard, Patricia Zigarmi, and Drea Zigarmi said, "In determining what style to use with what development level, just remember that leaders need to do what the people they supervise can't do for themselves at the present moment."[4] An objective of any manager should be to move the workgroup toward increasing development. The payoff includes more motivated, stimulated workers who work on their own without close supervision. Such workers tend to be productive even when their managers aren't monitoring them.

How Organizations Shift to Participative, Laissez-Faire Styles

Management consultant Ed Yeager explains that successful organizations must eventually grow into participative, self-directing units:

> Here is how the most successful organizations make the shift. The focus in the organization moves from vertical or hierarchical to horizontal. The emphasis shifts from accountability of "the boss" to accountability of the team. Empowerment, a currently popular but badly misunderstood term, becomes pervasive. The orientation of everyone is up- and downstream, working with coworkers, rather than up and down the channels and "chain of authority."

To be empowered, a person, or better, a team, must have the authority to make virtually any decision or initiate any action that comes to him or her with no escalation, no higher-order approvals, and no second-guessing. Teams of operators, professionals, and specialists are organized around responsibilities or outputs directed toward their internal or external customers. They are trained in the basic team skills, communication skills, problem solving, service improvement, quality management, performance measurement techniques, etc.[5]

Coaching, he says, becomes the primary focus as people master skills and become fully responsible for their own work and that of the team.

Becoming a Linking Pin

Boosting workers' development level allows the leader to take on a new role. The leader can become a liaison between workers and top management, acting as the workers' advocate to get resources and rewards. This is what management theorist Rensis Likert calls the **linking-pin function** of management. The manager becomes the link (or linking pin) that ties the group that he or she manages to the next higher group in the organization (see Figure 9.4). Likert describes this function as follows: "The capacity to exert influence upward is essential if a leader (or manager) is to perform his . . . functions successfully. To be effective in leading his own boss, that is, he needs to be skilled both as a supervisor and a subordinate."[6]

Every supervisor is a member of two workgroups: the one he or she is responsible *for* and the one he or she is responsible *to*. When workers become more mature, their supervisor need not supervise them closely and can spend more time in the linking-pin role.

As the workgroup evolves toward higher development levels over time, the leader must be ready to adjust his or her behaviors accordingly. As communication scholar Franklin Haiman said, "The man officially called leader performs only those tasks which the group itself is not yet mature enough, intellectually or emotionally, to handle for itself. The leader's goal is to work himself out of a job."[7]

FIGURE 9.4   The linking-pin role.

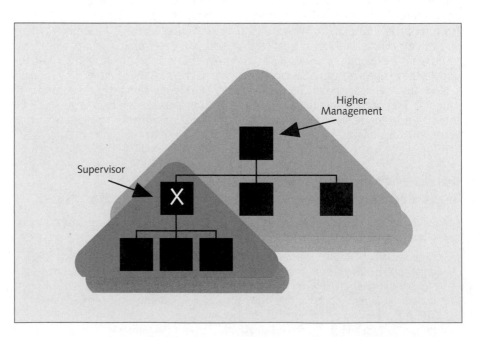

Leaders become representatives of their employees or peers to higher management.

The Importance of Feedback and Flexibility

As our discussion implies, leaders wear several hats. They serve and are served. They direct, coach, support, and delegate. To be effective in these many functions, leaders must be sensitive to feedback and willing to adjust as needed. To charge blindly ahead with an inappropriate leadership style is folly.

Leadership Styles: A Review

How does one develop a style that works? This chapter suggests that one can recognize different leadership styles by the mix between decisiveness and participation. Each of the four general styles—autocratic, consultative, participative, and laissez-faire—may be appropriate in certain cases. These styles come to life as leaders direct, coach, support, and delegate to followers.

The leader's situation is influenced by the tasks to be accomplished, the followers' needs for both task and relationship guidance, the personalities of both leader and followers, and the position power of the leader.

As leaders help followers achieve higher development levels, the boss's role becomes one of a linking pin—a representative of the workers to higher management instead of primarily a supervisor.

When group members grow under appropriate leadership, everybody wins.

Summary of Key Ideas

- The four general leadership styles are autocratic, consultative, participative, and laissez-faire.

- The two types of activities that are influenced by a leader are task and maintenance.

- Task behavior focuses on getting the job done, whereas maintenance behavior concentrates on making the work experience rewarding for the employee.

- The three key variables of Fiedler's contingency approach are leader-member relations, task structure, and position power.

- Fiedler suggests that when the leadership situation is highly favorable or highly unfavorable, the leader should emphasize task, and when the situation is mixed in favorability, the leader should focus on relationships.

- The curvilinear relationship among Hersey and Blanchard's four situational leadership styles flows from directing to coaching to supporting to delegating, depending on the follower's development level, which is based on competence and commitment.

- According to Likert, the successful manager serves as a linking pin between subordinates and superiors and has some degree of upward influence with superiors.

Key Terms, Concepts, and Names

Autocratic style
Kenneth Blanchard
Consultative style
Development level
Favorableness of the situation
Fred E. Fiedler
Paul Hersey
Laissez-faire style
Leader member relations
Leadership contingency model

Linking-pin function
Maintenance activities
Mixed situation
Participative style
Position power
Situational leadership theory (SLT)
Situational variables
Task activities
Task structure

Questions and Exercises

1. Observe a leader at work. How would you characterize this person's style? How does he or she adjust to situational variables?

2. List a series of activities you engage in on the job or in school. Now categorize these into either *task* or *relationship* activities. If your activities include leading others, study your task-relationship mix. Is it appropriate?

3. Describe in your own words the concept of *development level*. How does this concept help us determine appropriate leadership behaviors?

4. What are some implications of being a linking pin?

5. What does Fiedler mean by "favorableness of the situation"? How does the degree of favorableness affect the way a leader should lead?

6. Discuss the statement, "The leader's goal is to work himself or herself out of a job." What are the potential benefits of such a goal? Is this goal attainable?

7. Read the following articles and then answer the introductory questions at the beginning of this chapter.

Notes

1.   Fred E. Fiedler, *A Theory of Leadership Effectiveness* (New York: McGraw-Hill, 1967), p. 13.

2.   Situational leadership theory was articulated by Paul Hersey and Kenneth H. Blanchard in *Management of Organizational Behavior,* 3d ed. (Englewood Cliffs, NJ: Prentice-Hall, 1977). The term *development level* was originally called *task-relevant maturity.* A recent updating of the theory using simpler terms is found in Kenneth Blanchard, Patricia Zigarmi, and Drea Zigarmi, *Leadership and the One Minute Manager* (New York: William Morrow, 1985).

3.   Blanchard, Zigarmi, and Zigarmi, p. 68.

4.   Ibid., p. 69.

5.   Ed Yeager, "Organizations Embrace Power of Teamwork," Salt Lake City *Desert News,* March 17, 1991, p. B10.

6.   Rensis Likert, *New Patterns of Management* (New York: McGraw-Hill, 1961), p. 14.

7.   Franklin S. Haiman, *Group Leadership and Democratic Action* (Boston: Houghton Mifflin, 1951), pp. 38–39.

Another Look: Four Roles of a Leader: Wanted: Pathfinders with Principles

by Stephen R. Covey

A Whitewater World

The world has changed in a very profound way. This change continues to happen all around us, all the time. It is a whitewater world. The consumer revolution has accelerated enormously. People are so much more enlightened and aware. There are so many more dynamic, competitive forces operating. The quality standards have raised to the point, particularly in the global marketplace, that there is simply no way to fake it. You may be able to survive in a local marketplace without meeting these standards, perhaps even in a regional marketplace, but certainly not in a global marketplace.

In all sectors—business, government, healthcare, social, nonprofit, etc.—the marketplace is demanding that organizations transform themselves. They must be able to produce services and goods and deliver them in a fast, friendly and flexible way, and on a consistent basis that serves the needs of the customers (both internal and external). This requires a work force who is not only allowed, but is enabled, encouraged and rewarded to give of its full creativity and talent. Even though thousands of organizations are deeply involved in quality initiatives designed to produce those very results, transformation is still being demanded. The fundamental reason why most quality initiatives do not work is because there is a lack of trust in the culture—in the relationships between people. Just as you cannot fake world-class quality, so also is it impossible to fake high trust. It has to come out of trustworthiness.

Modeling

The most effective leaders are first models of what I call principle-centered leadership. They have come to realize that we're all subject to natural laws or governing principles and that these operate regardless of our awareness or our obedience to them. Our effectiveness is predicated upon alignment with these inviolate principles—natural laws in the human dimension that are just as real, just as unchanging, as laws such as gravity are in the physical dimension. These principles are woven into the fabric of every civilized society and constitute the roots of every organization that has endured.

To the degree that we recognize and live in harmony with such basic principles as fairness, service,

equity, justice, integrity, honesty and trust, we move toward either survival and stability on the one hand or disintegration and destruction on the other. Principles are self-evident, self-validating natural laws. In fact, the best way to know they are self-evident is by trying to imagine a world, or for that matter, any effective, enduring society, organization or family, based upon its opposite.

Correct principles are like compasses—they are always pointing the way. They don't change or shift. And if we know how to read them, we won't get lost, confused or fooled by conflicting voices and values. They provide "true north" direction to our lives when navigating the streams of our environments.

So the first role of the leaders is to be a model of principle-centered leadership. Whenever we're principle-centered or when an organization is principle-centered, the person or organization becomes a model to other people and organizations, an example. It is that kind of modeling, that kind of character, competence and action that produces the trust among the people so that they identify with the modeling and are influenced by it. Modeling, then, is a combination of character (who you are as a person) and competence (what you can do). That is your potential. But when you actually do it—when you put action together with character—you've got modeling.

What is it, then, that the principle-centered leader models? Essentially, I suggest you can break leadership into three basic functions or activities: Pathfinding, aligning, empowering. Let's explore each one in turn.

Pathfinding

The essence and power of pathfinding is found in a compelling vision and mission. It deals with the larger sense of the future. It is getting the culture imbued and excited about a tremendous, transcendent purpose. But in relation to what? To meeting the needs of your customers and other stakeholders. Pathfinding, then, is the tying together of your value system and vision with the needs of customers and other stakeholders through a strategic plan. I call this the strategic pathway.

Aligning

The second activity of a leader is aligning. It is assuring that your organizational structure, systems and

continued

Four Roles of a Leader, *continued*

operational processes all contribute toward achieving your mission and vision of meeting customer and other stakeholder needs. They don't interfere with it; they don't compete with it; they don't dominate it. They're only there for one purpose—to contribute to it. Far and away the greatest leverage of this principle of alignment comes when your people are in alignment with your mission, vision and strategy. When your people are filled with true understanding of the needs, when they share a powerful commitment to accomplishing the vision, when they are invited to create and continually improve the structures and systems that will meet the needs, then you've got alignment. Without these human conditions, you cannot have world-class quality. All you have is brittle programs. Ultimately, we must learn that programs and systems are vital, but that people are the programmers.

Empowering

The third activity of a leader is empowering. What does that mean? People have enormous talent, ingenuity, intelligence, creativity. Most of it lies dormant. When you get true alignment toward a common vision, a common mission, you begin to co-mission with those people. Individual purpose and mission is co-mingled with the mission of the organization. When these purposes overlap, great synergy is created. A fire is ignited within people that unleashes their latent talent, ingenuity and creativity. They then will do whatever is consistent with the principles agreed upon to accomplish their common values, vision and mission in serving customers and other stakeholders. This is what we mean by empowerment.

But then you have to study what happens. What are the results? Are we really meeting the needs of the customers and the other stakeholders? Information that indicates whether the needs are truly being met must be fed back to these empowered people inside the culture so that they can use it to make the necessary course corrections and continue to do whatever it takes to fulfill the mission and to serve the needs.

A New Paradigm of Leadership

These roles of modeling principle-centered leadership pathfinding, aligning and empowering represent a paradigm that is different in kind from traditional management thinking. There is a very significant difference between management and leadership. Both

are vital functions, and because they are, it's critical to understand how they are different so one isn't mistaken for the other. Leadership focuses on doing the right things; management focuses on doing things right. Leadership makes sure the ladders we are climbing are leaning against the right wall; management makes sure we are climbing the ladders in the most efficient ways possible. Most managers and executives operate within existing paradigms or ways of thinking, but leaders have the courage to surface those paradigms, identify the underlying assumptions and motivations, and challenge them by asking, "Does this still hold water?"

For Example

- In health care, new leaders might challenge the assumption that medicine should focus upon the diagnosis and treatment of disease. Some medical schools today don't even teach nutrition, even though one-third of all cancers are nutrition-related and two-thirds of all diseases are tied to lifestyle.

  Still, the medical community heads down the path of diagnosis and treatment of disease. They claim that they deal with the whole package—the health and welfare of people—but they have a treatment paradigm. Fortunately, new leaders are creating more preventive-medicine alternatives.

- In law, new leaders might challenge the assumption that law is best practiced in courtrooms using confrontational win lose litigation. They might move toward the use of synergy and win-win thinking to prevent and settle disputes. Alternative dispute resolution usually results in compromise. New leaders will seek "win-win or no deal" options that lead to synergy. Synergy is more than cooperation; it's creating better solutions. It requires empathic listening and courage in expressing views and opinions in ways that show respect for the other person's view. Out of genuine interaction come synergistic insights.

- In business, new leaders will challenge the assumption that "total customer satisfaction" represents the ultimate service ethic. They will move toward total stakeholder satisfaction, caring for all who have a stake in the success of the operation. They make decisions that benefit all stakeholders, all who have a stake in the success of the organization. To bring about this new mindset, leaders must develop a

continued

Four Roles of a Leader, *continued*

new skill set of synergy. Synergy comes naturally from the quality of the relationship—the friendship, trust and love that unites people.

If you can put the new skill set of synergy together with the new mindset of interdependency, you have the perfect one-two punch for achieving competitive advantage. When you have the mindset and skill set, you create effective structures, systems and processes, and you align these with your vision and mission. Every organization is perfectly designed and aligned to get the results it gets. If you want different results, you need a new mindset and a new skill set to create synergistic solutions. It's only enlightened self-interest to keep all stakeholders in mind when making decisions, because we are so interdependent.

Who Is the Leader of the Future?

In many cases, the "leader of the future" will be the same leader of the present. There will be no change in personnel, but rather an internal change within the person who becomes the leader of the future by an inside-out transformation. What drives leaders to change, to become more centered on principles?

I think the main source of personal change is pain—pain from disappointment, failure, death, troubled or broken relationships with family or friends, violated trust, personal weakness, discouragement, boredom, dissatisfactions, poor health, consequences of poor decisions, loneliness, mediocrity, fear, financial stress, job insecurity, life imbalance, etc. If you aren't feeling pain, there is rarely enough motivation or humility to change. Most often there just isn't a felt need. Without personal pain, people tend to be too deeply invested in themselves and their own world to rise above their own interests or the politics of running things—both at work and at home. When people are experiencing personal pain, they tend to be more open to a new model of living where the common elements of humility and personal sacrifice lead to inside-out, principle-centered change.

Again, the primary driving force of organizational change is the global economy. The standard of quality is now so high that unless you have an empowered work force and the spirit of partnership with all stakeholders, you can't compete, whether you work in the private, public or social sector.

When you're facing competitors who think more ecologically and interdependently, eventually the force of circumstances drives you to be humble. That's what's driving the quest for quality, learning, process reengineering and other initiatives. But many of these initiatives don't go far enough. The mind shift was not great enough. The interests of all stakeholders must be dealt with in an orchestrated way.

We're either forced by circumstance to be humble, or we can choose to be humble out of recognition that principles ultimately govern. To be humble is good, regardless of the reason. But it's better to be humbled by conscience rather than circumstance.

The Leader of the Future— A Family Within

The leader of the future has the humility to accept principles and the courage to align with principles, which takes great personal sacrifice. Out of the humility, courage and sacrifice comes the person of integrity. In fact, I like to think of these kinds of leaders as having an entire family within them: humility and courage the parents, and integrity the child.

Humility says, "I am not in control; principles ultimately govern and control." It understands that the key to long-term success is learning to align with "true north" principles. That takes humility, because the traditional mindset is: "I am in control; my destiny lies in my hands." This mindset is arrogance— the sort of pride that comes before the fall.

Leaders of the future will have courage to align with principles and go against the grain of old assumptions or paradigms. It takes tremendous courage and stamina to say, "I'm going to align my personal value system, my lifestyle, my direction, and my habits with timeless principles." Courage is the quality of every quality at its highest testing point. Every virtue gets tested ultimately at the maximum. That's where courage comes to play. When you confront an old approach directly, you experience the fear of ripping out an old habit and replacing it with something new.

Out of the marriage of humility and courage is born the child of integrity. We all want to be known and remembered as men and women of integrity. Integrity suggests integrating ourselves with principles. The leaders of the future must be men and women of integrity who internalize these principles. They grow in wisdom and cultivate an abundance mindset. If you have integrity, you are not caught up in a

continued

Four Roles of a Leader, *continued*

constant state of comparison with others. Nor do you feel the need to play political games, because your security comes from within. As soon as you change the source of your security, everything else flows from it. You have greater power, wisdom, security and guidance because you constantly draw upon the strength of these principles as you apply them.

A Final Note

We are becoming increasingly and painfully aware of the perilous weakening of our social structure. Drugs, gangs, illiteracy, poverty, crime, violence and the breakdown of the family all continue in a downward spiral. Leaders of the present are beginning to recognize that these social problems put at risk every aspect of society. The leaders of the future realize that the solutions to these problems are far beyond the ability of those sectors that have traditionally been looked toward to deal with such problems—namely government and social sectors. My intent is not to criticize these sectors. In fact, I believe that they would be the first to admit that they are bound to fail without a broader network of helping hands.

The problem is, on the whole, there has been a marked weakening of a sense of volunteer responsibility to our communities. Too often such hand washing is done in the name of government and working women. I believe it is a family responsibility and that everyone should have a sense of stewardship about the community—every man, every woman and child. There should be some real sense of stewardship around service on the part of young people and

particularly when they hit their most idealistic ages, seventeen through twenty.

The leader of the future will be a leader in every area of life—especially family life. The enormous needs and opportunities in society represent a great responsibility toward service. There is no place where this spirit of service can be cultivated like in the home. The spirit of the home and also of the school is that we are preparing you to go forth and serve. You are supposed to serve. Life is a mission, not a career. The whole spirit of this philosophy should pervade our society. I also think it is a source of happiness, because you don't get happiness directly. It only comes as a by-product of service. You can get pleasure directly, but it is so fleeting.

How, then, do we influence our children toward the spirit of service and meaningful contribution? First, we must look inward. Am I a model of this principle of service myself? Does my family see me dedicating my time and abilities to serving them and the community? Second, have I taken time to immerse myself and my family in the needs of others in the community and created a sense of vision about how our family and each of us as individuals can make unique and meaningful contributions to meet those needs (pathfinding)? Third, have I, as a leader in my home, aligned the priorities and structures of our life so that this desire to serve is supported, not undermined? Finally, have I created conditions and opportunities in the home that will empower my children to serve? Do I encourage and support the development of their minds and talents? Do I organize service opportunities for the entire family and do all I can to create a fun environment around those activities? Regardless of the answers to these questions—even if it is a unanimous "No," we all have the capacity to decide what our lives will be about from today on.

This inherent capacity to choose, to develop a new vision for ourselves, to re-script our life, to begin a new habit or let go of an old one, to forgive someone, to apologize, to make a promise and then keep it, in any area of life is, and always has and will be a moment of truth to every true leader.

Source: Reprinted from Stephen R. Covey, "Four Roles of a Leader: Wanted: Pathfinders with Principles." Article reprinted from *Priorities* magazine, Vol. 1, Issue 5, pp. 12–15. © Franklin Covey Co. All rights reserved.

PERSONAL COACH

1. **DEFINE YOUR MISSION**   Decide what you are trying to accomplish and what you are about. What are the results or consequences of the leadership that you desire?

2. **IDENTIFY RELATED PRINCIPLES**   Brainstorm natural laws or principles that will result in the consequences desired.

3. **CONNECT PRINCIPLES AND POWER**   What actions are you in a position to take that could result in the desired consequences?

4. **RALLY YOUR FAMILY**   Ask your family if they are ready to commit themselves as leaders in community service.

Another Look: The New Post-Heroic Leadership

"Ninety-five percent of American managers today say the right thing. Five percent actually do it." That's got to change.

"Of the best leader, when he is gone, they will say: We did it ourselves." —CHINESE PROVERB

Corporate leadership used to be so simple. You had it, or you didn't. It was in the cut of your jib. And if you had it, you certainly didn't share it. The surest way to tell if you had it was to look behind you to see if anyone was following. If no one was, you fell back to flogging the chain of command. Because the buck stopped with you. Your ass was on the line. Your job was to kick ass and take names. These were the immutable truths of leadership that you learned as you progressed from the Boy Scouts to officer candidate school to the Harvard B-school, and they worked. God was in his heaven, and the ruling class . . . ruled.

Then, of course, the world turned upside down. Global competition wrecked stable markets and whole industries. Information technology created ad hoc networks of power within corporations. Lightning-fast, innovative entrepreneurs blew past snoozing corporate giants. Middle managers disappeared, along with corporate loyalty. And one day you noticed that many of your employees, co-workers, and customers weren't exactly like you anymore, not English-speaking white males—not even close. Some time after restructuring, but before reengineering and reinvention, you accepted the new dizzying truth: that the only constant in today's world is exponentially increasing change.

The few corporate chiefs who saw all this coming declared themselves "transformational" and embraced such concepts as "empowerment," "workout," "quality," and "excellence." What they didn't do—deep down inside—was actually give up much control or abandon their fundamental beliefs about leadership. As James O'Toole, a professor and leadership expert, puts it, "Ninety-five percent of American managers today say the right thing. Five percent actually do it."

The pressure is building to walk the talk. Call it whatever you like: post-heroic leadership, servant leadership, distributed leadership, or, to suggest a tag, virtual leadership. But don't dismiss it as just another touchy-feely flavor of the month. It's real, it's radical, and it's challenging the very definition of corporate leadership for the 21st century.

"People realize now that they really must do it to survive," says management guru Tom Peters. Just ask the fired ex-heads of such companies as GM, IBM, Kodak, Digital Equipment, Westinghouse, and American Express, where the time-honored method of ordering up transformation—maybe even stamping your foot for emphasis—proved laughably ineffective. When companies derive their competitive advantage from creating intellectual capital, from attracting and developing knowledge workers, explains Warren Bennis, a widely read author on leadership, "whips and chains are no longer an alternative. Leaders must learn to change the nature of power and how it's employed."

If they don't, technology will. Business already is moving to organize itself into virtual corporations: fungible modules built around information networks, flexible work forces, outsourcing, and webs of strategic partnerships. Virtual leadership is about keeping everyone focused as old structures, including old hierarchies, crumble.

"The effect of information technology is just beginning to be felt," says Edward Lawler, director of the University of Southern California's Center for Effective Organizations. "It enables individuals to think of themselves as self-contained small businesses. So the challenge to corporate leadership becomes, 'make me a case for why I should get excited about working for this company.'"

As the power of position continues to erode, corporate leaders are going to resemble not so much captains of ships as candidates running for office. They will face two fundamental tasks: first, to develop and articulate exactly what the company is trying to accomplish, and second, to create an environment in which employees can figure out what needs to be done and then do it well.

Executives who rose in traditional systems often have trouble with both. The quantitative skills that got them to the heights don't help them communicate. And if their high intelligence, energy, ambition, and self-confidence are perceived as arrogance, it cuts them off from information which makes the challenge of empowering the work force even more vexing.

Post-heroic leaders don't expect to solve all the problems themselves. They realize no one person can deal with the emerging and colliding tyrannies of speed, quality, customer satisfaction, innovation,

continued

The New Post-Heroic Leadership, *continued*

- -

diversity, and technology. Virtual leaders just say no to their egos. They are confident enough in their vision to delegate true responsibility, both for the tedium of process and for the sweep of strategic planning. And they are careful to "model," or live by, the values they espouse. In a distinction that has been around for a while but is now taking on new meaning, they are leaders, not managers.

What's the difference? Management, says the Harvard business school's John Kotter, comprises activities that keep an organization running, and it tends to work well through hierarchy. Leadership involves getting things started and facilitating change. In the past, most corporations groomed and promoted managers into so-called positions of leadership, while they discouraged or ran off leaders. Back in the era of mass production, when companies could succeed merely by doing more of what they were already doing, hierarchy substituted adequately for leadership. A company could be just about leaderless but still very well run—by middle managers, who operated by the numbers and by the book. When technology rendered them obsolete and competitive pressure made them an unaffordable luxury, corporations "flattened" their structures, pushing traditional management tasks down to the workers. Then upper management—often to its surprise—suddenly faced real leadership issues.

Virtual leadership requires courage, confidence, and, well, a leader, or a bunch of them. But it works to great effect in a variety of businesses. It's working right now at Ortho Biotech, a biopharmaceutical company with a diverse work force. It's working for W. L. Gore & Associates, the maker of Gore-Tex, which proudly calls itself unmanaged. And it's working in the traditionally rough-and-tumble 19th-century garment industry at Levi Strauss & Co.

If you don't believe it, come to the little Appalachian town of Murphy, North Carolina. Turn right just past the new Wal-Mart, and head up the hill over the Valley River to the old red brick Levi sewing plant. Here you'll meet Tommye Jo Daves, a 58-year-old mountain-bred grandmother—and the living incarnation of virtual management. She's responsible for the plant, which employs 385 workers and turns out some three million pairs of Levi's jeans a year.

Not that she's forgotten the old way. In 1959, Daves hired on at Levi's Blue Ridge, Georgia, plant for 80 cents an hour because she needed a new washing machine. It was so cold inside the place that she wore gloves, and it was so leaky that buckets sat everywhere to catch rainwater. Her job was to top-stitch back pockets. Period. She became a supervisor and eventually a plant manager. One part of traditional management she still remembers is the night somebody unloaded both barrels of a shotgun into her car during a nasty labor dispute.

But Daves prefers to talk about the personal invitation she received in the mail a few years ago from Levi CEO Robert Haas, great-great-grandnephew of Levi Strauss himself. Haas politely requested her presence in Santa Cruz, California, to attend something called Leadership Week. She accepted, having no idea what to expect.

"It was the most eye opening experience of my life," she says. "I learned for the first time how I was perceived by others." What she recalls best was a videotaped exercise in which everyone was organized into teams, blindfolded, and asked to work as a group to shape some rope into a square. They failed, but two lessons stuck with Daves: "You can't lead a team by just barking orders, and you have to have a vision in your head of what you're trying to do." Many CEOs haven't learned either lesson yet.

She and her line supervisors have since been converting their plant, first to a gain-sharing system in which workers' pay is linked directly to the plant's performance. Then, later, from the old "check your brain at the door and sew pockets" system to team management, in which teams of workers are cross-trained for 36 tasks instead of one or two and thrust into running the plant, from organizing supplies to setting production goals to making personnel policy. Now Daves and her mostly female management crew get lots of direction from the ranks but much less from above: The Levi policy manual has shrunk to 50 pages from 700. In the language of deep thinkers on leadership, controls are "conceptual," not procedural.

Levi, which is rolling out leadership training and team management worldwide, cites in its support significant improvements in quality, manufacturing costs, and quick response to customers' requests for product. At the Blue Ridge plant, "seconds," or flawed jeans, have been reduced by a third, time between an order and shipment has fallen by ten days, and the time a pair of jeans spends in process at a plant has shrunk to one day from five.

...

continued

The New Post-Heroic Leadership, *continued*

For all the post-heroic inspiration to be found in the conversion of old industrial models like Levi, the most fascinating, radical examples of virtual leadership tend to appear at companies built from the start on fresh leadership ideas. Perhaps the most advanced, or extreme, among these is W. L. Gore & Associates of Newark, Delaware, famous for the Gore-Tex waterproof fabric found in spacesuits and expensive outdoor catalogues. In fact, the late Wilbert L. "Bill" Gore, who founded the company in 1958 at age 45, would be one of two leading candidates—neck and neck with Herman Miller Chairman Max DePree—to be the first inductee into the post-heroic hall of fame.

Before founding his company, Gore spent 17 years at DuPont, where his last assignment as an R&D chemist was to find new commercial uses for Teflon. Fiddling around in his basement one night, he discovered a method for making computer ribbon cable insulation. After failing to persuade DuPont to enter that business, he founded his company—in the same basement.

Bill Gore had a number of funny ideas, not least of which was letting almost a dozen of his company's first employees live in his house in lieu of wages. And like a number of executives back then, Gore became interested in Douglas McGregor's classic management book, *The Human Side of Enterprise,* which expounded Theory Y, very similar to what we now call empowerment. Gore founded his company on Theory Y, and it hasn't wavered since.

Why should it? In 31 straight years of profitability it has grown into an enterprise with 5,600 associates (never "employees"), 35 plants worldwide, and annual revenue just shy of a billion dollars. The company won't disclose its profit margins but notes that it has been able to finance its growth while maintaining a "very strong cash position." In addition to Gore-Tex and cable insulation, the company's other Teflon products include vascular grating material for surgical repair, industrial filters, and—a recent offering—a no-stick dental floss called Glide.

. . .

Source: John Huey, "The New Post-Heroic Leadership," p. 42. Reprinted from the February 21, 1994 issue of FORTUNE by special permission; copyright 1994, Time, Inc.

A Case in Point: Two Approaches

There are several different ways a leader can give instructions to a subordinate. Compare the difference in approach used by two office managers as they handed out the same assignment.

Office Manager 1 "Call the Wilson Office Equipment Store as well as Ajax Office Supply. Get them to quote you prices on all the office dictation equipment they carry. Ask them to arrange for a demonstration. Invite two managers to that demonstration—make it Cribbs and Giroux—and let them try out the equipment. Get them to put their reactions on paper. Then prepare me a report with the costs and specifications of each of the pieces of equipment. Oh, yes, be sure to ask for information on repair costs, too. . . ."

Office Manager 2 "I'd like to do something about our stenographic system. A lot of the managers who don't have secretaries of their own are complaining it takes them too long to get a secretary who can handle their dictation. The secretaries are also complaining because dictating to them eats up a lot of their time. Could you check up on some of the various kinds of dictating machines, find their prices, advantages, and disadvantages, and give me a recommendation as to what we should do? I think we can spend about $3,000. Possibly you could talk to some of the managers to get their ideas."

Questions

1. Compare the approaches of these two managers as they delegated this assignment. In terms of the situational leadership approach we've discussed in this chapter, how effective would these two styles be?

2. Assume that one of your subordinates has a low development level. Which of the approaches just described would likely be more appropriate when instructing this subordinate?

continued

Two Approaches, *continued*

- -

3. Assume that the employee to whom you are giving some instructions has a very high development level. Which of the approaches just described would be more appropriate for this individual?

4. Assume that you have been given the instructions by office manager 1. What are your reactions? How do you feel about the task assigned to you?

A Case in Point: The Truth Is, The Truth Hurts

- -

Think back to the last time someone in the office proposed a truly harebrained project. Your public response was probably something like, "That's interesting. We should look into it." Your private reaction was, "Yeah, we'll do it when pigs fly." The truth is, it's easier to speak truthfully to strangers than to colleagues. Which means you're more likely to get the straight story from someone you don't know than from someone you've worked with for years.

There are lots of good reasons why the truth hurts. A colleague may be a friend, and no one likes to disappoint a friend. Companies that embrace a "can do" spirit often frown upon even well-intentioned criticism. There are political calculations too: Vetoing someone else's project may invite retaliation against your project.

But the more you avoid the truth, the steeper the price that you are likely to pay in terms of wasted effort, frustration, and even cynicism. It's a vicious cycle. Here are a few ways to break it.

Face the truth about the truth. Be honest with yourself about how good (or, more likely, how bad) you are at having difficult conversations. That's the first step to getting better at them.

Have sympathy for the devil. Encourage people to play devil's advocate. Even good ideas can be improved through critical, truthful give-and-take.

Don't ask for what you don't want to hear. If you invite people to offer a "warts and all" version of events, then you'd better listen. If messengers of bad news wind up stacked like cordwood outside your door, survivors will learn to censor themselves.

Honesty requires subtlety. Speaking and hearing the truth are acquired skills. Blunt questions can force people into corners where they feel compelled to shade things—even to lie. Instead of asking, "Are you in favor of this project?" you should ask, "How can we improve it?"

Questions

1. What are your reactions to Wheeler's statements about why we avoid telling the truth?
2. Wheeler gives a few suggestions for breaking the vicious cycle of avoiding telling the truth. He suggests that "Honesty requires subtlety." What does he mean, and do you agree with him?
3. Part of the difficulty in avoiding telling the truth is that we hate to give or receive criticism. How can we help each other by giving effective, honest criticism?
4. In sum, telling the truth can really hurt. What does this have to do with being an effective leader?

Source: Reprinted with permission. *Fast Company*, Issue 14, April 1998 p. 94. Edited by Anna Muoio. Based on interview with Michael Wheeler, who teaches in the Harvard MBA Program. His corporate clients include 3M, Johnson & Johnson, and Nabisco.

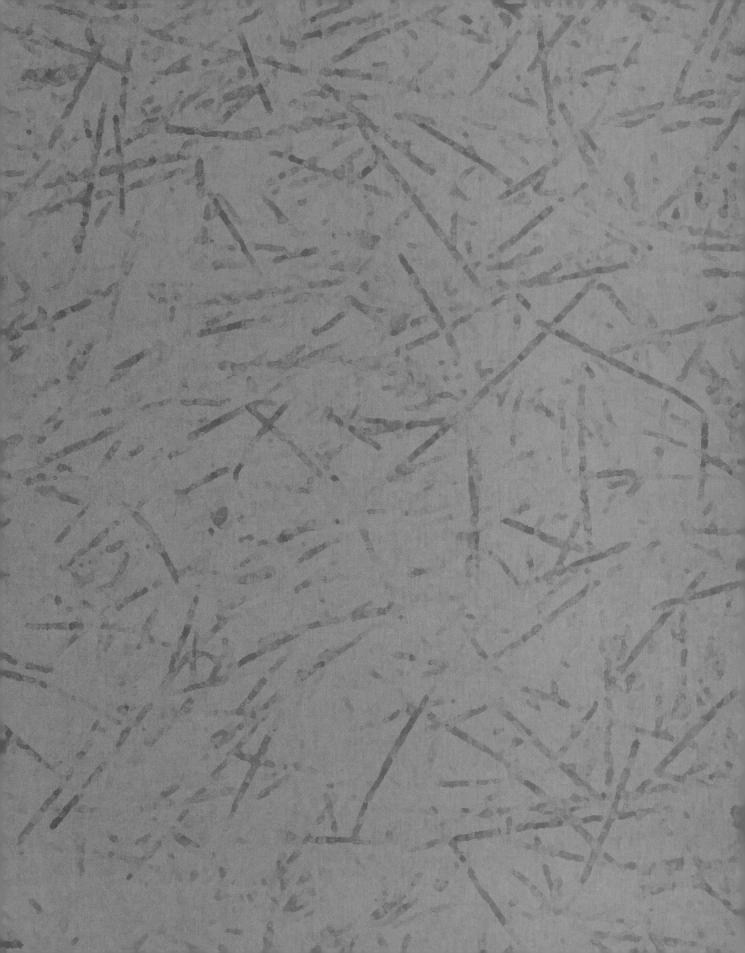

Motivating with Compensation and Other Rewards

- What options are available to a leader with regard to reward allocation?

- What is the challenge of "rewarding A while hoping for B"?

- What three options can organizations choose from to deal with the problem of misplaced rewards?

- What are the four types of external rewards managers can use to motivate employees?

- How and when does compensation really work as a motivator?

- What are some typical forms of deferred compensation, and what is their likely impact on employees?

- What is equity theory, and what can it teach us about rewards?

- How do people respond when they feel they have been unfairly rewarded?

- What does job design have to do with motivation and rewards?

- What are some important do's and don't's in giving praise and criticism?

- How does the outcome of a behavior affect future behaviors?

- How do different schedules of reinforcement serve to encourage continued behaviors?

The answers to these and other questions are coming up next in Chapter 10 . . .

Imagine that as you approach graduation, a rich uncle asks you to join his staff at the Italian Gourmet, a frozen-pizza manufacturing company that he just purchased. The plant has been operating fairly well, but your uncle believes the workers are not as motivated as they might be. Absenteeism is consistently 10 to 12 percent, and productivity as measured by output fluctuates by 15 to 20 percent each week, causing frequent delays in product delivery.

Your uncle asks you to design a rewards system that can be used to motivate workers in a positive way. What are some of the rewards and benefits that you might employ?

People are motivated by external and internal rewards. The things awarded to an employee by the boss (both tangible rewards like money and intangibles like compliments) are called external rewards. Intangible rewards that emerge from within the person such as a sense of personal satisfaction, feelings of accomplishment, and so on, are internal rewards unique to each individual.

Allocating Rewards: A Leadership Task

Use systematic strategies when rewarding others.

Leaders have a choice of either (1) distributing rewards haphazardly or (2) thinking through and developing *strategies* for reward allocation. If managers accept the first option, they risk rewarding the wrong behaviors and thus encouraging inappropriate actions from others. Furthermore, they risk the sin of omission: failure to reward that which is good.

Although organizations restrict what some levels of management can do to reward workers, some rewards are available to all supervisors.

In this chapter, we encourage you to consider the advantages of using the second option when rewarding others. Although systematic strategies apply equally to tangible rewards, such as money, office space, and other clearly recognized benefits, we will focus on the kinds of rewards that leaders at any level can realistically allocate: social rewards, such as recognition, opportunities for participation in organizational decisions, and opportunities to gain self-actualization through accomplishing objectives.

The Challenge: Rewarding the Right Behaviors

Using rewards to motivate the kinds of behaviors useful to the company can be tricky. A classic management article, "On the Folly of **Rewarding A, While Hoping for B**" by **Steven Kerr**[1] describes the dilemma of reward systems that reward one thing while hoping for another. For example:

- Universities hope professors will teach well, but they primarily reward them for publishing scholarly articles.

- The military hoped that soldiers in the Vietnam War would fight the enemy, but they rewarded them for avoiding danger by assigning a fixed one-year tour of duty. Contrast that with World War II, when soldiers got to go home only after the war was won.

- Society hopes that companies will not pollute the environment, but the punishment for doing so may be a simple fine—if they get caught at all.

- Companies hope employees will work efficiently but pay workers by the hour, essentially rewarding people for using up time.

Kerr's article concludes that in modern organizations, different things motivate different people. Using the same motivators for all employees will not produce the same results. Managers have three options to deal with the problem of Kerr's "folly":

1. *Selection.* Theoretically, an organization would employ only people whose goals and motives are wholly consonant with management's. Current selection processes, however, show scant grounds for hope that such an approach would be successful.

2. *Training.* Another theoretical alternative would be to focus on training to alter employee goals to make them consistent with the company's. Again, research on training effectiveness provides further grounds for pessimism that this approach would work.

3. *Altering the Reward System.* This option shows much more promise. Managers need to consider the possibility that their current reward system may just be motivating the wrong things and then make the necessary changes using a range of tangible and intangible rewards.

(An updated look at Steven Kerr's thinking appears later in this chapter.)

Categories of External Rewards

A leader can provide external rewards that may motivate workers toward organizational goals in at least four traditional ways. When appropriately used, these rewards can create conditions where motivation can result. Supervisors attempt to "motivate" through the following:

How do leaders create conditions for motivation?

- Compensation
- Job design
- Benevolence
- Communication

The word *motivate* is in quotes to remind you that we don't really motivate others; we can only motivate *ourselves.*

These methods are stimuli that attempt to help people be motivated; often we refer to them as *motivators.* That's okay so long as we keep in mind that there is no surefire cause-and-effect relationship between offering a stimulus and getting a specific outcome. The degree to which any of these may work depends on the individual and his or her needs.

Much of what motivates people comes from internal reinforcements, such as pride in a job well done, satisfaction in achieving something of significance, and so on.

Meanwhile, back to the external rewards that leaders can dispense to help employees be motivated. . . .

Compensation

When people speak of rewards, most listeners immediately think of money. But "pay" as we know it today is a comparatively recent invention, dating back only 200 years or so to the dawn of the Industrial Revolution. Throughout most of history, people generally lived, toiled, and died without pay, at least in a monetary form. Some unknown managerial genius, probably a mill superintendent in the midlands of England, invented the wage, and it has been with us ever since.[2]

How Pay Can Create Motivation: It's Not Just the Money, It's the Principle   Pay may well be overrated as a motivator. Although money is indispensable for survival in a cash economy, most advanced societies provide income even for those who do not work. Few people in modern industrial nations starve to death for lack of money. This has not been true historically, however.

Is pay overrated as a motivator?

Money motivates best at the survival or security levels.

The power of money to motivate is strongest when there isn't enough of it to ensure a decent standard of living. In this sense, money ties in with what Maslow called survival and security needs. Once these lower-order needs are met by money, the motivating power of cash decreases for most people.

When a person has enough money to survive, the importance of money as a motivator shifts in two ways, according to management theorist **Saul Gellerman.**[3]

First, for most (but not all) people, money loses a good deal of its power to compete against other needs. In very few cases does money become *unimportant;* for most people, it simply becomes *less* important. Other needs that previously might have been sacrificed for the sake of enhancing income now tend to take precedence over pay. For example, workers may no longer be willing to sacrifice leisure time to work overtime, even for double the normal wage. Likewise, employees may refuse to tolerate unpleasant or unsafe working conditions regardless of the money paid.

Once income rises above the "decent standard of living" level, money rewards have a less predictable effect on worker performance.

Second, money changes from a relatively simple motivator to a very complex one. This is because once survival seems assured, a whole host of needs, varying widely among individuals, surface. Thus, for one person newly raised to the rank of the affluent, money may mean security; for another, it may mean an opportunity to invest and grow richer; for still another, it may mean independence. Our ability to predict how any given individual or group will react to pay diminishes sharply as the pay rises above the subsistence level.

Pay as a Measure of Fairness   For many people, pay is regarded as a measure of *fairness.* The money received from an employer is regarded as a fair trade for the work one does. If an employee puts in more effort, accomplishes greater results, or helps the organization be more profitable, that employee expects more pay.

Sometimes a pay raise is appreciated as a sign of recognition more than for the actual cash increase.

Assuming that wages are sufficient to provide workers with their basic needs, an increase in pay may be seen as a sign of recognition—a way of "keeping score." Conversely, when workers see *inequities* in the way they are paid—when they feel they are being shortchanged—serious morale problems can arise.

Perceptions of fairness affect the ways people react to rewards.

Equity Theory and Pay: Research Findings   Social psychology helps managers understand how people react to what they see as unfair situations. Developed in the 1960s by J. Stacy Adams, **equity theory,**[4] seeks to predict how people will respond when they find themselves in "unjust relationships."

Suppose, for example, that you were hired by the Comatose Waterbed Corporation as a quality inspector. Your training in marine biology and your six years with another waterbed manufacturer made you a natural for this position.

After a few months on the job, you discover quite by accident (you were snooping through some old files) that Herm Talbutt, the other quality inspector, is earning eighty dollars a week more than you. He does exactly the same job you do, and he doesn't even have a marine biology degree!

You may suddenly perceive your employment as an unjust relationship, and you may be pretty upset. Equity theory predicts that you'll respond to the perceived unfairness in one of five ways. You might do any of the following;

1. Simply endure the distress: "It's a crummy deal, but I'll just have to live with it."

2. Demand compensation or restitution: "I'll go to the boss and demand a raise."

3. Retaliate against the perceived cause of the inequity: "I'll start letting defective waterbeds pass. That'll fix the company."

4. Psychologically justify or rationalize the inequity: "Herm has a bigger family than mine. He needs the money."

5. Withdraw from the inequitable relationship: "I'm gonna quit this lousy company."

Any response to perceived unfairness can be detrimental to an organization. Supervisors must be aware of the possible effects but at the same time be realistic about avoiding them. Because equity is in the eye of the beholder, there are wide differences among what people see as fair. Although managers should make every effort to be fair, inevitably someone will feel slighted.[5]

In many cases, pay is a potential motivator only in the sense of telling the employee, "You are of worth to the organization." In using compensation as a reward, the supervisor should be particularly sensitive to the issue of fairness.

Deferred Compensation   Not all compensation is disbursed each pay period. More companies are realizing the advantages of providing deferred compensation—additional rewards employees get as a bonus or at a later time. Several examples of deferred compensation are described below:

- *Bonuses.* A cash bonus may be paid at some predetermined interval if employees meet specific targets. These are widely used in sales organizations but can apply across other functions as well. Often the bonus is paid annually or at the point where a goal is achieved. Example: Employees receive a $500 bonus if the product error rate is reduced to .005%. Bonuses are easy to use and flexible to a wide range of operations.

- *Profit-sharing.* This approach distributes cash according to some predetermined formula tied to the company's profit. A certain percentage of the net profits are set aside and then distributed to employees.

- *Gain-sharing.* This is similar to profit-sharing, but here a percentage of the *gain* or *increase* in profits is distributed according to a formula.

- *Employee stock ownership plans (ESOP's).* Here, part of the employee's compensation is given as company stock or stock options. As the company grows, presumably, the stock value will also grow. This may motivate additional effort since the worker will eventually enjoy the fruits of his efforts when he sells his stock. Wal-Mart has more than 25 percent of its workers in an ESOP. At each store, a sign is prominently displayed that says: "Today's stock price is [$65 or whatever]. Tomorrow depends on you." Usually, employees buy this stock via a payroll deduction.

    ESOPs can motivate long-term commitment to the company. Employees who accumulate stock may be less likely to job-hop to another company for a slightly better salary. Reducing turnover can save the company a lot of money and effort.

"How much does it cost to replace departing workers? Plenty, according to a survey of 206 employers by New York-based consulting firm William M. Mercer, Inc. After factoring in lost productivity, search fees, management time to interview, and, finally, new-hire training costs, 45 percent of the responding firms said it cost them more than $10,000 to fill a vacated job."[6]

Job Design

In Chapter 5, various organization patterns and their effects on individual workers were discussed. One of the ways to motivate people is through **job design**—

Source: OVERBOARD reprinted by permission of United Features Syndicate, Inc.

Fitting employee abilities to the demands of the job helps motivate.

arranging their jobs so that they can gain a sense of satisfaction from the work. That is often easier said than done; some jobs necessary to the organization are unpleasant or boring to most people.

One attempt to reduce turnover in such jobs is to hire people who have mental limitations or perhaps lower expectations regarding work. Specifically, some companies have had considerable success in employing mentally disabled workers to do repetitive tasks generally found to be too boring for other workers.

Another approach, used especially in manufacturing, has been to automate—replace human labor with machines. Again, this is best when the task is repetitive and relatively simple. Don't assume that automation only involves sophisticated electronic robots. In many companies, countless tasks can be done by simple machines. The classic case is the collator, or sorting machine, attached to a photocopier. Many a secretary has complained loud and long about the time wasted sorting copies when a low-cost sorter could be purchased or rented.

Job enrichment—expanding the responsibilities associated with a job—is another viable alternative in job design.

Some organizations have tried to *distract* workers from dull work by using such things as music, frequent rest periods, or more attractive facilities. These are not likely to have long-term positive effects.

Today's workers tend to be better educated and are far less likely to put up with a dull or meaningless job. Reactions to such jobs (as perceived by the worker) include increased waste, low-quality work, inefficiency, absenteeism, and high employee turnover. Many workers will not tolerate a menial job as an alternative to collecting unemployment insurance. Collectively, these reactions to dullness produce a significant drag on organizational productivity.

Fitting the job to the individual and vice versa is no longer just a nice thing to do; it is an essential part of the reward system.

Benevolence

Is a happy worker always a more productive worker?

Another traditional motivator supervisors can use is **benevolence:** attempts to make the workers happy. The employer who gives workers turkeys at Christmas or sets up company athletic activities is using this motivational approach. The underlying belief is that happy workers are more productive than unhappy workers. This, however, is an oversimplification. The relationship between happiness and productivity works in complex ways and is subject to many exceptions. The same gesture of benevolence may be interpreted in widely different ways. In the 1950s, a company picnic may have been deeply appreciated. Today, the same picnic may be viewed as paternalism, or as an unwanted social obligation.

Again, the issue of fairness must be considered. Giving to one employee or to one group of employees some special benefit or gift may be resented by those who don't get the same reward. The results of giving gifts in an effort to distract, entertain, please, or placate employees have been mixed at best. Although such rewards may be regarded as nice gestures by the workers, their ability to develop long-term motivation is limited.

Management expert Saul Gellerman concludes that "there is little, if any, evidence that being nice to people, or providing them with enjoyable off-the-job experiences, has a significant or lasting effect on productivity. On the other hand, they don't hurt either; and when used in conjunction with more effective measures (such as appropriate job design and equitable pay), they no doubt help to ease some of the inevitable everyday strains of working in an organization."[7]

Communication

The quality of communication can itself be a motivator.

Communication with workers can in itself be regarded as a form of reward. A supervisor can use communication in at least three ways to motivate and encourage employees: (1) giving recognition through the use of praise and criticism, (2) being receptive to workers' ideas, and (3) providing timely information.

Praise and Criticism   Sometimes praise is embarrassing, and so-called constructive criticism can make one angry. Both praise and criticism can have either positive or negative impact on future behaviors.

Effective praise can have a positive impact on future behaviors because it is perceived as a reward. If improperly delivered or insensitively worded, however, praise may have no impact. Table 10.1 shows what kind of praise is likely to work and what is a waste of effort.

TABLE 10.1   *Ineffective Versus Effective Praising*

PRAISE THAT HAS LITTLE EFFECT ON EMPLOYEE PERFORMANCE	PRAISE THAT MAY HAVE POSITIVE EFFECT ON PERFORMANCE
1. Impersonal, generalized praise, such as "Good job, folks." This is meaningless and vague.	1. Specific, personalized praise for specific actions. "Charlie, you did a great job handling that upset customer."
2. Praise without explanation of just what is being commended.	2. Follow up of specific praise with "the reason I think you did such a good job is because you gathered all the information, took notes, and asked the customer what she thought would be a good solution." Attaching details like this reinforce the good actions and can teach others too.
3. Praise for expected performance, when it may be questioned. For example, Mabel, who is a prompt employee, is met one morning with, "Mabel, you're sure on time today. That's great," from her boss.	3. Praise for better than expected results, e.g., meeting a challenging goal, exceeding a quota, exerting extra effort.
4. "Sandwich" system praise where the positive comment is given only to soften up the employee for a criticism followed by more praise. (The real intent of the conversation is the criticism.)	4. Praise given alone, not diluted by mixing in criticism. No "left-handed compliments," e.g., "You dance really good for a fat guy."
5. Praise perceived as a blatant "carrot" given only to pressure the employee to do-more, do-better.	5. Praise aimed at recognition, not solely as a prod to further productivity.
6. Praise handed out lavishly only when the "brass" or higher-ups are present. The real intent seems to be to make the praiser appear to be a great boss.	6. Praise given when it is deserved, not deferred to special occasions or when it seems to build the image of the praiser or some other third party.

Source: Reprinted from James H. Morrison and John J. O'Hearne, *Practical Transactional Analysis in Management* (Reading, MA: Addison-Wesley, 1977), pp. 118–119. Used with permission.

Likewise, criticism can be useful (have a positive impact on future behavior) or destructive (create resentment or defensiveness in the employee). Table 10.2 shows examples of criticism that may be constructive versus that which will not improve performance.

TABLE 10.2 *Destructive Versus Constructive Criticism*

CRITICISM THAT TENDS TO PRODUCE A DEFENSIVE REACTION AND MAY WORSEN PERFORMANCE	CONSTRUCTIVE CRITICISM THAT MAY IMPROVE PERFORMANCE
1. Targeted criticism that accuses an individual when the problem may be more generalized. For example, "You are making way too many billing errors, Fred. What's the matter with you?"	1. Criticism as a situational description. For example, "Fred, we are getting an increasing number of billing errors. What do you think we ought to do?"
2. Criticism that is broadly generalized and opinion-based without factual support. For example, "This whole department stinks."	2. Discussion of possible causes and effects of certain conditions, avoiding emotion-laden words. For example, "What would you suggest we do to get our department productivity level up to quota?"
3. Criticism without any suggestion or coaching that could improve the situation.	3. Criticism followed by some tentative suggestions or tips. For example, "I used to have trouble with that process myself. One thing I tried seemed to help a lot. I . . . any chance that might work for you?"
4. Criticism in public which may be humiliating or embarrassing to the receiver and others around him.	4. Individual criticism given in private, allowing receiver to avoid embarrassment.
5. Criticism given only in the interest of getting recognition for the criticizer. For example, that which is given to show the boss how tough you can be.	5. Criticism given in the interest of helping the receiver improve performance and gain additional job satisfaction.
6. Criticism given as a one-way communication only—all telling, no listening.	6. Criticism given so that receiver can participate in the critique, even to the point of defining the unsatisfactory condition and suggesting his own corrective steps.
7. Criticism given as a calculated game to justify withholding raises or other incentives.	7. Game free criticism with candor and the desire to help.

Source: Reprinted from James H. Morrison and John J. O'Hearne, *Practical Transactional Analysis in Management* (Reading, MA: Addison-Wesley, 1977), pp. 120–121. Used with permission.

Receptiveness to Workers' Ideas

Another way to motivate employees is to be receptive to the ideas they offer. This requires the supervisor to have well-developed listening skills.

Receptive listening means being willing to receive, process, and deal with incoming information from workers. Receptiveness encourages creativity and involvement. To be genuinely receptive, the manager must recognize that employees can and do have worthwhile ideas, which they can creatively contribute to the organization. (Sounds a little like Theory Y, doesn't it?)

Receptiveness encourages creativity and employee involvement.

Being receptive to employees' ideas is an effective way to motivate them.

Timeliness of Information   Have you ever had the feeling that you are the last to know about some change or new procedure in the organization? It's an uncomfortable feeling. Most people want to be kept current on changes and organizational procedures, policies, goals, and the like—especially those that affect them on their jobs.

People want to be kept current with timely information.

One way a supervisor can motivate people is by providing them with **timely information.** Effective managers tell their workers what they *need* to know to do their job and what they *may* want to know to establish closer relationships and feelings of belongingness in the organization.

Again the concept of *equity* enters in here. When some people are consistently "in the know" and others are left without needed information, the situation is clearly inequitable. When people feel they are being treated unfairly, they will retaliate, withdraw, and respond in other detrimental ways.

Information is in itself a form of reward. Status arises from knowing key information. The classic example found in many organizations is the secretary to a top corporate leader. This person has little formal authority but enormous informal clout, which comes from having access to important information.

Information can be a form of status.

The effective leader will seek to see that followers have all the information they need, on a timely basis.

Rewards and Behavior Reinforcement

A basic premise: Future behavior is influenced by the outcomes of past behavior.

The key assumption underlying the use of any reward is that future behavior is influenced by the *outcome* from past behaviors. If we like what happened the last time we did something, we are likely to do it again, and vice versa. Phrased another way, if the outcome immediately following something one does is in some way, rewarding, one is likely to repeat the behavior. If the response is punishing, one is likely to not do the behavior again (unless one prefers punishment to other outcomes).

We can provide three types of responses to behaviors: positive reinforcement, negative reinforcement, or no observable reinforcement at all. The effects of each on the behavior it follows are shown in Table 10.3.

Some people question how far one can go with verbal approval as a motivator. Theoretically, it should work indefinitely so long as an appropriate *schedule of reinforcement* is used. The two main reinforcement schedules are *continuous* and *intermittent.*

Continuous reinforcement means the individual receives reinforcement (a compliment or supportive statement) *every time* he or she does the desired behavior. Continuous reinforcement is useful when the person is being taught a new behavior and needs to develop confidence in this new ability. People learn very quickly, at least initially, under continuous reinforcement. You'd see this when teaching a child how to catch a ball. Every time the ball is caught, you praise the child, and the child will usually develop the skill very quickly. The principle generally holds for employees working on unfamiliar tasks.

Different schedules of reinforcement produce different results.

TABLE 10.3   *Behavior Responses to Different Reinforcement*

TYPES OF RESPONSES TO EMPLOYEE BEHAVIOR	EFFECT ON THE RECURRENCE OF THE BEHAVIOR
Positive reinforcement	Tends to increase or strengthen the recurrence of such behavior
Negative reinforcement	Tends to decrease or weaken the recurrence of such behavior *unless* the employee is *seeking* negative reinforcement
Reinforcement withheld	Tends to decrease or weaken the recurrence of such behavior; can lead to extinction of the behavior

Source: Reprinted from Paul R. Timm, *Managerial Communication: A Finger on the Pulse,* 2d ed. (Englewood Cliffs, NJ: Prentice-Hall, 1986), p. 135. Used with permission.

Drawbacks to Continuous Reinforcement

Three main problems arise with continuous reinforcement. First, it takes too much time and effort. It is not feasible to always compliment each job done; you might as well do the task yourself!

Continuous reinforcement has drawbacks.

Second, there is a problem of "inflation." Just as dollars lose value when too many are in circulation, verbal approval is cheapened by overuse.

Third, once continuous reinforcement is expected, it can be hard to wean people away from it without certain risks. If a leader suddenly stops continuous reinforcement—that is, no longer expresses verbal approval for each good behavior—the message to workers may be that the behavior is no longer appropriate and should be stopped. This process is called **extinguishing behaviors.**

Overcome the Drawbacks with Intermittent Reinforcement

The drawbacks of continuous reinforcement can be overcome by using **intermittent reinforcement.** This means expressing approval not for every good action but at intervals, such as each time a unit of work—say a day's or week's quota—is completed.

Intermittent reinforcement can overcome drawbacks of continuous reinforcement.

Another intermittent reinforcement approach is to provide rewards at completely random times. Much of the lure of slot machine gambling comes from the anticipated random windfall. The anticipation keeps players engaged in the "desired behavior" (putting money in the slot).

When using random intermittent reinforcement in the workplace, the worker doesn't know exactly when he or she will be rewarded. So long as there remains any hope of eventually receiving a reward, extinguishing of the desired behavior is delayed. If the rewards are too far apart, the worker will not continue to produce unless he or she is particularly good at working hard today for some far-off but certain-to-be-worthwhile reward. Relatively few workers today are content to "get their reward in heaven."

The best approach is to use continuous reinforcement when new behaviors are being developed and then to gradually move to an intermittent schedule to maintain the desired performance.

Rewarding the Wrong Behavior

People too often reward one kind of behavior while hoping for another, often opposite, behavior.

We end this chapter with a point made at its beginning: Despite their best intentions, many leaders fall into the trap of rewarding the wrong kinds of behavior. They often do this without thinking. Most organizations offer innumerable examples of reward systems that pay off for one behavior, even though the management hopes for another, often the opposite, kind of behavior. For example, the common practice of paying people by the hour encourages filling up of time rather than productive use of effort. The mechanic who fixes a machine so well that it never breaks down again may soon be out of a job. The doctor who ostensibly is paid to make patients well can make much more money if patients stay sick and continue treatment. Few people take advantage of such situations, but the point remains that the reward system is not tied directly to the desired behavior. Instead, it rewards behaviors that are irrelevant or even counterproductive.

How many times has an ambitious junior executive suggested a remedy for a problem and been instructed to "write up a report on it"? For a potentially useful suggestion, the reward is to do more work! Or a clothing store owner constantly encourages the sales force to cooperate with each other—to share ideas with each other. Yet for a sales promotion, the boss offers an award only to *the* (one) top producer of *sales.* The result: salespeople tripping over each other to get to the customer, causing distrust and conflict among themselves. Or at a staff meeting, the member who suggests additional study of a problem is inevitably nominated to do the work.

It often makes sense to have the person who makes a suggestion "write up a report." But that person should be given assistance or at least time off from other responsibilities to avoid being burdened with additional work.

Here is another example. As a staff supervisor at a large corporation, one of your authors shared responsibility for evaluating employee suggestions. For each suggestion, he had three options:

1. Accept the suggestion (in which case he would then need to see that it was implemented).

2. Reject the suggestion (he would not have to do anything further).

3. Refer the suggestion to a higher organizational level where his counterpart would have the same options.

He had little or no real incentive to approve valuable suggestions because if he did accept a suggestion, his work had just begun—he was then responsible for implementing it. For instance, he would have to go to all the offices to teach a new procedure, or create needed forms if that was the nature of the suggestion, or arrange budget expenditures, and so on. A rejection avoided all that work. In fact, these suggestions were simply extra work piled on his "regular" duties.

Finally, his work evaluation was in no way affected by the number of employee suggestions he approved. No reward was provided for doing what the organization would *like* to have had done. The organization wanted to accept as many suggestions as would possibly work, yet the reward system discouraged it.

Summary of Key Ideas

- Four categories of rewards are available for managers seeking to motivate appropriate employee behaviors: compensation, job design, benevolence, and communication.

- These external rewards sometimes, but not always, motivate people to be productive. Other motivation comes from within the employee and are called internal motivators.

- Equity theory seeks to predict our response to an inequitable relationship; the five typical responses to an unjust situation are to endure, demand compensation or restitution, retaliate, rationalize, or withdraw.

- The three ways in which communication may be used to motivate and encourage employees are (1) giving recognition through the use of praise and criticism, (2) being receptive to workers' ideas, and (3) providing timely information.

- In spite of organizational financial restraints, supervisors can systematically allocate social rewards, such as recognition, and encourage participation in organization decisions.

- A recognition strategy is a plan for complimenting workers in order to encourage them to make continued improvements in reaching organizational goals. The strategy is based on the premise that the outcomes of past behavior influence future behavior.

- Reward systems can fail when the organization is rewarding the wrong behavior.

Key Terms, Concepts, and Names

Benevolence
Continuous reinforcement
Equity theory
Extinguishing behaviors
Saul Gellerman
Intermittent reinforcement

Job design
Steven Kerr
Receptiveness to workers' Ideas
Rewarding A while hoping for B
Timely information

Questions and Exercises

1. Why does company benevolence seem to be a less effective motivator than it may have been in years past? What social or personal factors affect benevolence as a motivator?

2. Do you agree with the thesis that managers often reward the wrong behaviors? Give some examples you have seen (within or outside the work environment), and suggest ways to rearrange the reward system to be more effective.

3. How would you respond to deferred compensation? Is this likely to motivate you to make a long-term commitment to a company? Which form(s) would you find the most attractive and why?

4. Do you generally agree with the idea that "it isn't just the money" that motivates people? Why or why not? What situational variables may cause you to give a different answer?

5. To what degree is it possible to design a job so that it motivates workers? What characteristics of job design would best motivate you?

6. Of the types of rewards described in this chapter, which would be *least* likely to motivate you?

7. In this chapter, we described examples of how a reward system can affect the employee suggestion process. Have you seen similar difficulties in your organizations? Give examples.

8. Answer the introductory questions at the beginning of this chapter.

Notes

1. Steven Kerr, "On the Folly of Rewarding A, While Hoping for B," *Academy of Management Journal* 18, 1975, pp. 769–783.

2. Saul W. Gellerman, *The Management of Human Resources* (Hinsdale, IL: Dryden Press, 1976), pp. 17–18.

3. Ibid., pp. 19–20.

4. The basic premises of equity theory can be found in J. Stacy Adams, "Toward an Understanding of Inequity," *Journal of Abnormal Social Psychology* 67, 1963, 422–436. Later studies are summarized in Leonard Berkowitz and Elaine Walster, eds., *Advances in Experimental Social Psychology,* vol. 9 (New York: Academic Press, 1976).

5. For some recent research dealing with equity theory in a managerial context, see Sherron B. Kenton, "The Role of Communication in Managing Perceived Inequity," *Management Communication Quarterly,* 1989, 536–543.

6. "Tallying Turnover's Cost," *Training* August 1998, p. 10.

7. Gellerman, *The Management of Human Resources,* p. 33.

Another Look: Risky Business: The New Pay Game

If you continue to link financial rewards with rank, you're likely to create an army of malcontents.

Pay—the subject's enough to make even the most macho manager cringe. No matter how you handle this sensitive issue, you wind up making some, if not most, of your employees angry and confused. Many managers unintentionally short-change their stars and overpay their sluggards. Or they design pay plans that send employees the wrong message or a mixed message or no message at all.

I know. I've spent two decades as a manager, a teacher, and a consultant. When it comes to pay, I've seen almost every mistake that can be made, and I've seen—and tried—a host of solutions. To find what works best, I looked at compensation practices at 75 companies. The good news is that I've found a few principles and practices that make sense. The even better news is that you can probably do most of these things at your firm without spending much money. Really.

Most of us know instinctively how to motivate and reward people. We do it with our kids or with the guy who mows our lawn or the gal who cuts our hair. When it comes to our jobs, though, we tend to get distracted by a blizzard of ideas with jargony names, offered by high-priced consultants. Does your daughter Jenny want to ride her bike with her new friend Claire? If you tell her she can, but only after she cleans her room, you've just put into place an "operationally defined, cost-neutral, performance-contingent reward system." Got it?

Where, then, to start. If your company's pay program is broken—and it probably is—don't fix it! Not yet. You've got two other issues to address before you even think about rewards: goals and measurements.

First, you need to tell people exactly what's expected of them. Not some vague mumbo jumbo about making the company or the division the best and biggest in the world, but what role you, Mr. Salesman or Ms. Engineer, are supposed to play in this great enterprise. Here's an exercise I used when I taught executive education classes at the University of Michigan. I asked all the students to write down their company's mission statements, as well as the amount of senior management time it took to develop them. I put all the notes in a shoebox, then picked one out at random. Whose finely crafted credo is this, I asked the class? Inevitably, five or six hands would go up, as managers from airlines, pharmaceutical companies, and plumbing-supply manufacturers all claimed the statement as their own.

Though it can take hundreds of hours to devise these declarations, many top managers can't distinguish their own slogans from those of their neighbors. If executives can't clearly articulate their company's reason for being, how can we expect line workers or supervisors to know their roles?

At General Electric's leadership development center in Crotonville, New York (where I work), we try to get managers to bring those lofty mission statements down to earth. Imagine you're at a party a year from now, we tell them. You're celebrating the successful completion of a big project in your division. How exactly did your leaders, peers, and subordinates change their behavior to reach this goal? We don't accept imprecise answers. What do you mean your people have become empowered? Do they participate more in meetings? Do they feel free to constructively criticize their superiors? Did they find a solution that boosted sales or improved quality or cut costs?

Once you know specifically what you want your employees to be doing in the future, then you need to measure it. Even seemingly fuzzy stuff, like how well a manager satisfies customers or delegates authority or gets along with colleagues can be measured through 360-degree evaluations—where an employee is rated by people above and below him in the organization—and through one-on-one interviews. The key is to ask not only the right questions but also the right people—customers, coworkers, and bosses.

People, though, aren't likely to change their behavior unless you reward them for it. Companies typically hand out bonuses or stock options as recognition for past performance. Great job landing that account, Judy, here's $2,000. But the real purpose of that award should be to induce Judy to perform even better in the future. Studies show that to truly motivate people, you have to offer them an award that's at least 10% to 12% above their base salary. In practice, companies pay out much less than that. Variable compensation—including bonuses, stock options, and profit sharing—accounts on average for only 7.5% of compensation.

So a key principle of compensation is to link more of it directly to performance. Sounds obvious, doesn't it? But consider the way we currently pay people. The two factors that usually carry the most weight are an employee's title and length of service.

continued

Risky Business: The New Pay Game, *continued*

When you reward employees according to seniority or you give everyone on the staff the same annual percentage increase, you've turned compensation into an entitlement, not an incentive. You're giving your weakest performers a free ride. And you're encouraging your best employees to polish their resumes and look elsewhere.

Okay, so you've defined exactly what people should do to make your company flourish; you've figured out how to measure their activities; and you've committed your company to actually paying for performance. Now, you have to execute. To make things easier, keep these guidelines in mind:

RULE 1 Don't tie pay to power. In the halcyon days of the 1950s and 1960s, when companies had umpteen layers of management, it was fine to tell every subaltern with a college degree and a starched white shirt that he could aspire to fatter paychecks and juicier perks as he climbed each rung on the ladder. But in these days of downsizing, we've got a bulging cohort of baby-boomers chasing a shrinking number of slots in the hierarchy. If you continue to link rewards to rank, you're likely to create an army of malcontents. Popos is what the experts call them: "passed over and pissed off."

At GE we've tried to get away from the idea that you have to move up to make more. We cut from 29 to six the number of different salary grades—a technique known as "broad banding." This gives people more opportunities to get a raise without a promotion. We've also sharply increased the number of employees eligible for stock options, and we're experimenting with programs that reward managers for what they know, not for how many workers they supervise or how long they've been on the job.

RULE 2 Make compensation comprehensible. A Detroit auto supplier I worked with a few years ago was stunned to learn that some of its best factory workers were taking jobs at a rival company offering inferior pay packages. The competitor paid higher hourly wages, but when you added in the fringes—like health, dental, and life insurance—there was no contest between the two companies. The trouble was that the auto supplier's benefits department communicated in such abstruse actuarial double talk that workers didn't have a clue what their total compensation was worth. The company solved the problem by creating a clearly

written booklet, complete with cartoon drawings, that explained all the perks.

RULE 3 Start spreading the news. When you give a deserving worker a reward, broadcast it! If you hand out a $1,000 spot bonus, but no one knows it except you and the recipient, the total number of people you've motivated is somewhere between zero and one.

Yes, paychecks are supposed to be private. That's ingrained in our corporate culture. Only the top guys disclose their comp packages, and that's only because the SEC requires them to. But when employees don't have real information, they spread rumors. And surveys invariably show that folks underestimate how well they're being paid in relation to their peers. If you posted everyone's salary and bonus on the bulletin board, the dominant reaction might well be a sigh of relief.

A couple of caveats: Don't talk about other people's money unless you're sure your measurement system works. If you aren't prepared to explain and defend your decisions—why Joe got only a $2,500 bonus while Sam in the next cubicle got $3,000—then it's better to be discreet. Also, not all workers like being singled out for praise. Some employees come from cultures like Japan that consider public commendation of an individual an affront to the harmony of the group.

RULE 4 Forget about the calendar. A reward delayed is almost as bad as a reward denied. If a rat in a cage pulls a lever and nine months later (on the anniversary of his arrival in the laboratory) you give him a cube of sugar, he's not likely to connect cause with effect. Time and again I run into companies that review people in May, then reward them the following January. Some firms require so many layers of managerial sign-offs that by the time an extra lump sum shows up in a worker's paycheck, she may be left scratching her head, trying to remember just what she did to deserve it.

At GE we invite employees to assess—and reward—their peers on the spot. A program called Quick Thanks!, used by GE Medical Systems, lets an employee nominate any colleague (even one in another department) to receive a $25 gift certificate from certain restaurants and stores in appreciation of an exemplary job done. (Over the last year GE has given out 10,000 such awards.) The employee himself often hands out the award to his deserving co-worker. And

continued

Risky Business: The New Pay Game, *continued*

guess what? Peers are often a whole lot tougher than bosses in dishing out praise. For the recipient, it's the approbation of a colleague, not the $25, that matters most.

That's not to say instant gratification should always prevail. I once saw a chief executive give only a perfunctory "thank you" after receiving a briefing from a midlevel manager. But the next day he telephoned to say, "I really appreciated your contribution yesterday." In this instance, the theatrical pause enhanced the value of the recognition.

RULE 5 Make rewards reversible. It's no good pretending you have perfect judgment. Some of the compensation decisions you make are going to be bad ones. Also, let's face it, business conditions can change. So give yourself an out. It's virtually impossible to take back a raise. You have to deal with mountains of paperwork and endless appeals. But if you give an employee a bonus, as opposed to an increase in base pay, you don't have to live with your decision forever. He knows he'll get another bonus next year only if he keeps performing.

But be careful. For variable compensation to work, it really has to be, well, variable. At some companies, bonuses have become so routine that employees look at them as wages by another name, as just another entitlement. And be mindful of what your competitors are doing. If your employees need to collect a bonus just to bring their compensation up to the going rate, chances are you're not paying enough base salary to begin with.

RULE 6 You can't always give what you want. But you can still, to paraphrase Mick Jagger, give what you need. I've seen companies with minuscule salary pools spend hundreds of management hours rating, ranking, and grading every single employee. But everyone gets such a small piece of the pie that virtually no one is happy. If you don't have enough cash in the kitty, try some nonfinancial incentives. Don't get me wrong. Money, when used properly, is a great motivator. But nonmonetary rewards pack potent advantages.

- They're reversible (see Rule 5). It's easier to cut back someone's authority or to stop giving some-

one opportunities to participate in plum projects than it is to reclaim a 6% raise.

- You can create your own supply. If you give $1,000 to Employee A, you have $1,000 less to give to Employee B. With nonmonetary awards there are fewer constraints. You can give Employee C more interesting assignments, a mention in the in-house newsletter, and a chance to make a presentation to the division head today, and then you can give the same things to Employee D tomorrow. Of course, if you create too much supply you end up debasing the currency. A nonmonetary reward quickly loses its value if it's overused.

RULE 7 Don't be a compensation chauvinist. If you're operating overseas, be aware that some cultures are not big on the idea of incentive pay. Once, after I lectured an executive education class on the need for more performance-based pay, a Japanese manager rose in protest: "You shouldn't bribe your children to do their homework, you shouldn't bribe your wife to prepare dinner, and you shouldn't bribe your employees to work for the company." In some countries, the objections to bonuses are more fiscal than philosophical. Instead of cash, employees would rather have more leisure time, access to vacation villages, or anything the tax man can't get his hands on. I'm not suggesting that you abandon your principles, but do modify them to account for cultural differences.

RULE 8 Cheer up! If your company is breaking most of rules 1 to 7, don't despair. Your competitors' compensation practices are probably at least as messed-up as your own. You've got a wonderful opportunity to gain an edge over your rivals without necessarily having to invest more cash. In how many aspects of business is that ever the case? When it comes to rewarding employees, the key is not how much more you have to give. It's how well you give what you already have.

Steven Kerr, chief learning officer at GE, runs the company's Crotonville, New York, leadership center.

Source: Steven Kerr, "Risky Business: The New Pay Game," p. 94. Reprinted from the July 22, 1996 issue of FORTUNE by special permission; copyright 1996, Time Inc.

Another Look: Incentives: Pay Purview

How one knowledge-intensive company has over-hauled its incentives

"If a person starts behaving oddly, saying things that don't make sense, or putting forth weird arguments, you can always trace it back to the compensation system, and a perverse incentive." That, in a nutshell, is how Jon Moynihan describes the approach of his firm, PA Consulting, to paying its employees. It is an approach that others might consider copying. For despite the spread of performance bonuses and share options during the past decade, many firms still fail to think carefully enough about how they reward their staff.

An assembly worker, salesman or chief executive can be motivated by a simple piece rate, sales commission or share-option scheme. But for the growing cadre of workers, call them "knowledge workers" if you must, whose basic task is to share ideas and to meet customers' needs, the gulf between their company's best interests and their own can be vast. As the executive chairman (and, until this year, chief executive) of PA Consulting, a management and technology consultancy based in Britain, Mr. Moynihan has spent the past five years tackling this problem. The result has been not only a change in the behaviour of PA's consultants, but also in the type of person who wants to work there.

For years PA's consultants were paid through a traditional partnership arrangement: every year the profits were carved up among the senior consultants in proportion to their salaries. This created three problems. It rewarded veterans for hanging on, even if they were no longer productive; it discouraged the best consultants from joining, since they could not immediately get a big share of the rewards; and it encouraged talented consultants to leave. During the 1980s, as other opportunities appeared, PA bled talent, and at one point in the early 1990s almost went bankrupt.

Mr. Moynihan goes out of his way to say that those who left were not money-grubbers. "But these people felt compelled to leave because the system was so bad." PA is not the only firm to find it difficult to attract and keep the best talent. But what managers miss, argues Mr. Moynihan, is that buying talent is a lot harder than simply writing bigger cheques.

As evidence, he cites the results of a survey that PA conducted of 400 big British firms. The firms that did worst were those that relied less on variable pay—that is, pay related to performance—and more on high fixed salaries. The main reason, argues Mr. Moynihan, is that high fixed salaries attract "mediocrity disguised as talent." In other words, more money attracts the best people only if it depends on performance. Another survey of 100 big American companies, completed earlier this month, showed the same thing.

PA began to overhaul its system in 1993. Like a legal partnership, the firm is entirely owned by its employees, and the most senior consultants, known as "partners," own most of the shares. As with many partnerships, the most awkward question PA faced was how to divide each year's profits between bonuses (which reward people for their contribution to that year's performance) and payments to owners (who have accumulated stakes based on longevity and past performance).

Selling shares to the public, Mr. Moynihan argues, is the worst solution to this dilemma, since fresh profits no longer go to either present or past performers, but to outsiders. So he condemns the decision of Goldman Sachs's partners to list the investment bank as "the worst, in business terms, of the 1990s." Yet partnerships still face the awkward balance between bonuses and payments to owners. Mr. Moynihan's first response has been to make the trade-off explicit: 58% of each year's profits are now paid to employees as performance-related bonuses; the rest, after taxes, is doled out according to ownership. Comparable figures are hard to come by, but Mr. Moynihan claims that the bonus share is higher than at any of PA's competitors.

Moreover, nearly half of that bonus pool goes to junior employees. So ambitious young consultants can expect to receive huge bonuses right away, rather than waiting for a decade. This has led to plaudits from newer recruits, as might be expected. One danger, however, was that valuable older partners would jump ship.

To prevent this, PA gives out some of its bonuses as options, rather than cash. This still allows consultants to accumulate large shareholdings over time. But the best performers acquire shares more rapidly than their peers. The idea is to give senior consultants an incentive to stay, but to target that incentive to those who are most profitable, rather than simply to those who are most senior. "If you are any good,"

continued

Incentives: Pay Purview, *continued*

says Mr. Moynihan, "those things are worth a small fortune. And if you leave, they go 'poof' right in front of your eyes." As a result, he says, PA consultants now feel little animosity towards colleagues who think they can do better with a competitor.

Besides solving the problem of mixing old and new, PA has also tried to promote co-operation. By allowing consultants to keep a bigger share of the profits from their own business units, it risked creating a less co-operative environment. To avoid this, it bases employees' bonuses on the clients they bring in, those they serve, and on subjective reviews by peers, subordinates, superiors and clients. If a consultant drums up business for another unit, it has as big an effect on his own bonus as on the consultant doing the work. Similarly, if a consultant thinks he can better serve a client by asking for help, he has strong incentives to do so: if it leads to better reviews by clients and colleagues it will increase his bonus.

All Together Now

There are signs that PA's scheme is working. Its consultants point to many examples of co-operation across business units. Moreover, now that business units can keep a share of the profits they contribute, they no longer spend so heavily on perquisites. Despite its obvious attractions for young consultants, the firm is drawing senior ones as well: it hired 84 top-level consultants in 1996 and 1997, compared with only 29 in the two previous years. And although it has stepped up its recruitment, the firm's attrition rate has fallen by half, to 15%, roughly the industry average. Finally, the people PA has found and retained appear to be good ones; over the past five years its "share price"—calculated by independent auditors—has increased 16-fold.

The system is working even by Mr. Moynihan's subjective test: when pressed about their motives and their performance, PA's consultants rarely behave oddly or put forth weird arguments. If even a consultant can undergo such a transformation, imagine what could happen at other companies.

Source: "Incentives: Pay Purview," *The Economist,* August 29, 1998, pp. 59–60. © 1998 The Economist Newspaper Group, Inc. Reprinted with permission. Further reproduction prohibited. *www.economist.com.*

A Case in Point: Setting Team Goals

Susan had called her entire team together to review goals and objectives for the coming year. She said, "We all know the importance of goal setting. We've heard that over and over again in this company. I trust that each of you are setting personal objectives that are tough to reach, goals that really will stretch your efforts. In fact, I think that is so important that I'm going to sit down with each of you individually in the next day or so and go through your personal goals."

Some of the members of the team turned and looked at each other and scowled. Susan picked up on that and said, "What's the problem back there? You guys do have goals set, don't you?"

"May I be perfectly frank with you?" asked Mark. "I've been selling for this outfit longer than you've been alive. I've been constantly producing good results. I've probably made millions of dollars for this organization. And you know what? I think goal setting is the pits, I'm so sick and tired of hearing about how important it is to set these stupid goals! Why don't you just get off our backs, let us go out and sell the best we can, and forget about all this nonsense."

Susan was flabbergasted. She had always known that goal setting was the only way to gain self-motivation. But here is one of her best salespeople saying he hates goal setting. Several of the other salespeople immediately chimed in. They too felt that goal setting had been carried to a ridiculous extreme, and that it really didn't make much difference to the results obtained.

"Don't you get sick of some of this 'rah-rah' stuff that the company gives us all of the time?" asked Mark. "I sure do. Why not just do this: Tell us to go out and do the best we can in selling. And you sit back and accept the results that we get. It would take a lot of anxiety off of everybody. The pressures of goal setting and trying to achieve these ridiculous goals simply aren't worth it to a lot of us who have been around selling for quite a while."

"Okay, okay. I'll try not to preach too much about goal setting," said Susan. "You guys go ahead and get

continued

Setting Team Goals, *continued*

the results any way you can. But I've prepared a list of our team goals, and I expect that we will reach these goals this year. In fact, I expect that we'll exceed them. I've spent a lot of time planning these out, and despite your objections, I'm going to give copies of them to each of you, and I expect each of you to do your share. Complain if you will, but we are going to achieve the objectives for this team that are listed on this sheet of paper."

With this, the team manager passed out a list of six key targets. The sales representatives in the team looked them over and said absolutely nothing about them. The meeting was adjourned.

Questions

1. Why do you think the experienced salesman had some complaints about the process of goal set-ting? What kinds of experiences might he have had that turned him off to the goal-setting process? How do you feel about goal setting?

2. What do you think of the way the sales manager handled the objections to the goal-setting process? Was she wise to pass out the list of team goals?

3. What alternatives to the team manager's approach might have been used? What do you think the results might have been?

4. Is it important for this team manager to convince all of the sales representatives of the value of goal setting? In trying to convince them, what arguments does she have going for her? What arguments might be working against her?

A Case in Point: Living Overtime: A Factory Workaholic

On Wall Street, deal makers toil long hours to lock in six- and seven-figure incomes. In Silicon Valley, programmers burn the midnight oil in the hopes of creating—and owning—the next big computer application. Here, in this small city [of Blacksburg, VA] in the heart of the Blue Ridge mountains, Joe Sizemore does it to make ends meet.

The 34-year-old factory worker has adopted many trappings of a middle-class life: a nice brick house on a hilltop in nearby Christiansburg, two cars, vacation trips to Walt Disney World, even a time-share at a Virginia ski resort.

Long hours pay the bills. And so for today, Mr. Sizemore is starting work at 6 P.M. and won't be done until 6:30 A.M. tomorrow morning—a normal shift in Corning Inc.'s small factory here, which operates around the clock churning out ceramic cores for catalytic converters.

"It's nice to have a job that pays halfway decent, if you've got to do it," says Mr. Sizemore. He is one of the plant's workaholics—a band of workers known for their eagerness to take on a large number of extra hours. Such workers make up about 10% of the factory's 250 unionized employees, though the vast majority do some amount of overtime. You can quickly identify the hard-core group simply by glancing at the big bulletin board near the entrance to the factory. This is where workers hang up yellow index cards seeking volunteers to sign up to cover for their coming absences.

Mr. Sizemore's name is penned on many of them, which explains why it isn't uncommon for him to work 60 hours or more in a week. Anything over 40 is considered overtime. Indeed, Mr. Sizemore isn't even the most prominent workaholic at the plant. That would be Michael Tucker, the undisputed king of overtime. Mr. Tucker, 48, usually works between 67 and 70 hours a week. "I've got five kids," explains Mr. Tucker, adding that his wife doesn't work.

Mark R. Cates, the plant manager, says the factory prefers paying overtime to hiring more workers for several reasons. For one, training new workers is a lengthy and costly process and existing workers are constantly being taught new skills, so it makes sense to cover the normal ebb and flow of orders with existing workers. Using overtime also fits the plant's philosophy, which is to stay as flexible as possible and offer workers a high degree of job security. Overtime is one thing that can get cut before management has to resort to layoffs.

Mr. Sizemore used to hunt and fish as well as collect Star Trek memorabilia, but doesn't do any of that anymore. He doesn't have time, he says. Many days, he only sees his wife for a few hours. Much of the free time he does have, he devotes to working on his

continued

Living Overtime: A Factory Workaholic, *continued*

house. "When we bought the house, we wanted to get something nice—but it's an older home, you know," he says. And so there always seems to be some repair project or remodeling job waiting for his attention. Next up: building a sunroom under the deck in the backyard.

Overtime helps pay for it, though Mr. Sizemore does have one rule: He only works extra shifts offered on days, never nights. He hates nights. "Nights just ain't kind to me," he says in his soft Virginia lilt.

But he can't avoid them completely. Rather than assigning workers to work only days or only nights, the factory requires everyone to take turns. Corning managers say having separate shifts would create a split within the work force that would, among other things, undermine team spirit.

Even so, Mr. Sizemore figures he could adjust more easily to working nights, if that was his regular schedule. Switching is a killer. He often doesn't sleep well when he is working nights, and that leaves him grumpy and silent. His stepdaughters and wife know to leave him alone. "I love him dearly," says Barbara Sizemore, whom he calls Bobbi, "but when he's on overnight, we just stay away from him."

In addition to varying shifts, workers at the plant learn a variety of tasks and move around frequently so they don't end up doing one job over and over.

Indeed, Corning, based in Corning, N.Y., considers Blacksburg one of its most cutting-edge plants in terms of the way workers are trained and organized. Workers are grouped in teams and take a big role in managing themselves. Mr. Sizemore says he likes not having a boss standing over him, but the main thing he likes about his job is the pay. As an "operations associate"—the job description for a majority of workers at the plant—Mr. Sizemore earns $13.66 an hour, and time-and-a-half for overtime.

Questions

1. To what extent do you agree with Joe Sizemore's willingness to work overtime? Would you do the same if given the opportunity?
2. What does this case say about the popular argument that pay isn't really a consistent motivator?
3. What else besides the money is likely to be motivating Mr. Sizemore?
4. What part of Joe's job is most likely to become a dis-satisfier? If night work were more required, do you think Joe would continue to work the long hours he does now?

Source: Timothy Aeppel, "Living Overtime: A Factory Workaholic," *The Wall Street Journal*, October 13, 1998, p. B1. Republished by permission of Dow Jones, Inc. via Copyright Clearance Center, Inc. © 1998 Dow Jones and Company, Inc. All rights reserved worldwide.

PART 5

COMMUNICATION

Understanding Communication at Work

- What are the essential principles of understanding communication?

- What is the role of a symbol in communication?

- What does the concept of transaction have to do with effective communication?

- What are the three major aspects of communication theory presented in this chapter?

- How do human values and human personality affect human communication?

- Why is it important to understand people if one wants to be a good communicator?

- It is often said that meanings exist only in people. What does this mean?

- What are the differences between verbal and nonverbal symbols?

- Why is it important to be aware of the environment in which communication takes place?

The answers to these and other questions are coming up next in Chapter 11 . . .

The ability to communicate effectively is based on one's understanding of how people communicate and why they fail to communicate. The Latin root word for communication is *communicare,* which means "to make common." So the degree to which a message sender and receiver have a *common understanding* of a message is the measure of how effective the communication process has been. Effective communication tends to produce success in understanding and influencing coworkers. By studying the principles of communication, we can learn to express concern, help others, get needed information, and develop good working relationships.

Through communication, people find, establish, and foster close relationships; corporations make decisions that affect millions of people; supervisors coordinate the efforts of employees to produce goods and services; employees are hurt and helped; and organizational success or failure is established. Clearly, communication—especially when effective—matters. Nevertheless, effective communication is not easy to achieve nor to maintain. "Communication breakdown" has just about taken the place of original sin as an explanation for the ills of the world—and perhaps with good cause. As our world becomes more complex and we spend more time in organized activities, the need for interpersonal understanding has never been greater. And just as important, the cost of failure has never been higher.

Communication and Making Sense

What essential principles can help us understand communication? What is the essence of communication? These questions have been considered by many different theorists in this field who generally agree that communication occurs when a person is able to make sense out of something, to see some connection among aspects of a situation. Communication is therefore a wholly human activity performed by people. When two people come together, each tries to make sense of the other and of their common environment. Making sense is aided by the use of symbols.

A symbol is something that stands for something else.

A **symbol** is something that represents something else. A word is a symbol that refers to something else. When we communicate we must be able to develop a mental picture of something, give it a name, and develop a feeling about it. Effective communication with another person requires that we create a mental picture, a name for the picture, and feelings that are similar to those held by the other person. Effective communication simply means that you and I refer to the same things when we talk. We share understanding.

If effective communication is taking place between us, and you say to me, "Meet me at my office at seven o'clock tomorrow," then I should visualize the same office as you do, the same time of day as you do, and about the same purpose for the meeting as you do.

How do we know what other people mean when they talk to us? How can we make certain that other people know what we mean when we talk to them? We might ask each other, "What do you mean?" If we can physically point to what we are talking about, we have a better chance of discovering what we mean. Many things that we talk about, however, are difficult to point to physically—for example, feelings, plans, and experiences. How can we determine what a message means when we cannot look at it directly? We must describe to each other the concepts we have inside each of us.

Communication is a process that is not very well controlled. As I speak to you, I am interpreting you and your behavior, while you are reacting to my nonverbal behavior and the things I am saying verbally. While you are reacting, you are also trying to determine what you will say when I finish speaking. You might even decide to interrupt me. At the same time, I might recall something of importance to me that sprang to prominence because of something you have said.

Source: DILBERT reprinted by permission of United Features Syndicate, Inc.

What I have recalled is likely unrelated to our immediate conversation. The times we actually respond to what each of us means are few and far between. Effective communication depends in part on our abilities to sense and respond to these fleeting occurrences of meaning.

Communication begins when a person has a purpose for communicating.

Three major aspects of communication must be understood for effectiveness: people, messages, and the environment.

Communication begins when a person has a purpose or a reason for communicating. Purpose is expressed through symbols—verbal or language symbols and nonverbal or behavioral symbols—that, when combined into units, become messages. A person's messages are interpreted by another person.

Three major aspects of communication must be understood for anyone to be an effective communicator: (1) people, (2) messages, and (3) the environment. First, in communication, the person, or both *people,* is the focus of understanding. Communication represents people in the act of transacting. Second, although the people are of primary importance in a study of communication, it is through the sending and receiving of messages that people make sense of one another. Third, communication takes place in a social environment. The workplace can be a primary environment in which one communicates.

When these components merge, they create a communication event. Effective communication occurs through a process of human transactions in which people share symbolic messages in social environments for the purpose of achieving effective human relationships. For example, a one-to-one communication event is a transaction in which both people are simultaneously engaged in producing messages and responding to each other's messages.

Understanding People and Ourselves

People are the keys that unlock the mysteries of communication.

People are the keys that unlock the mysteries of communication. To comprehend communication, we must discover some of the factors that affect the creation of meaning in people. Factors such as personality and values seem to be critical to understanding people. Other aspects of understanding could be studied, but we will focus on these two.

To be effective communicators, we each must know how others see us. Often someone asks: "How do the workers I supervise see me as a manager or as a leader?" Other questions that might be asked are "How do I see myself, how do I feel about myself as a person, and how do I feel about myself as a managing, communicating human being?"

It is essential to comprehend clearly one's own personality and to sense how one perceives and understands one's own values and the values of others. Self-understanding is the first step toward evaluating the quality of one's own contribution to a communication relationship. By better understanding people, one begins to develop understandings that make communication more beneficial to all concerned. Discovering your own communicating personality will help you understand human values.

Our thoughts and especially our feelings about ourselves influence our thoughts and feelings about, and our communication with, others. Self-evaluation is therefore important. We need to mentally look into a full-length mirror from time to time—to take a long look at ourselves and to consider how others see us. What kind of communicators are we? Do people see us as effective or ineffective in this role? Is the way others see us different from the way we see ourselves?

Objectivity is sometimes difficult for people when they analyze themselves. Therefore, we have included a questionnaire titled "Attitudes toward Interacting with People" that may help you learn how others might see you. Complete it and see how you do. However, remember that questionnaires may or may not be accurate. Keep your eyes open to see how others react to you.

ACTIVITIES

ATTITUDES TOWARD INTERACTING WITH PEOPLE

University of Connecticut psychologist Kenneth Ring and his associates have developed a test designed to show a person's attitudes about interacting with people. Here is an adaptation of Ring's test, with simplified scoring and analysis.

Consider each statement carefully. Then circle **T** or **F** to indicate whether you find it true or false. Each item is designed to bring out the presence of specific attitudes about working with people.

T F **1.** I often feel like telling people what I really think of them.

T F **2.** I would be uncomfortable in anything other than fairly conventional dress.

T F **3.** I enjoy being with people who are suave and sophisticated.

T F **4.** When in a new and unfamiliar situation, I am usually governed by the behavior of others present.

T F **5.** In social situations, I often feel tense and constrained.

T F **6.** At times I suspect myself of being too easily swayed by the opinions of others, and perhaps too open-minded and receptive to other people's ideas.

T F **7.** I usually have trouble making myself heard in an argument.

T F **8.** I don't like formality.

T F **9.** I feel I can handle myself pretty well in most social situations.

T F **10.** I like to meet new people.

T F **11.** I don't mind playing a role or pretending to like something I really don't like if it serves some good purpose.

T F **12.** I enjoy "putting people on" sometimes, and playing conversational games.

T F **13.** I usually find it difficult to change someone else's opinion.

T F **14.** I like to do things that other people regard as unconventional.

T F **15.** I enjoy being the host (or hostess) of a party.

T F **16.** I think a person should adapt his or her behavior to the group that he or she is with at the time.

T F **17.** I often find it difficult to get people to do me favors, even when I have the right to expect them to.

T F **18.** I would like to belong to several clubs or lodges.

T F **19.** I think it is important to learn obedience.

T F **20.** I like to avoid situations that do not permit me to do things in an original way.

T F **21.** Just the thought of giving a talk in public scares me.

T F **22.** I can fit in pretty easily with any group of people.

T F **23.** In general, I find that I dislike nonconformists.

T F **24.** It is usually easy for me to persuade others to my own point of view.

continued

ACTIVITIES

ATTITUDES TOWARD INTERACTING WITH PEOPLE, CONTINUED

T F **25.** I like to go to parties.

T F **26.** I prefer to listen to other people's opinions before I take a stand.

T F **27.** When in a group of people, I have trouble thinking of the right things to talk about.

T F **28.** If I am with someone I do not like, I am usually diplomatic and do not express my real feelings.

T F **29.** I have the knack of recognizing people's talents and abilities and putting them to the best purpose.

T F **30.** I like to follow instructions and do what is expected of me.

	SCORING AND ANALYSIS							
Item	If Your Answer Was	Letter	Item	If Your Answer Was	Letter	Item	If Your Answer Was	Letter
1	False	C	11	False	A	21	False	B
2	False	B	12	True	B	22	False	A
3	False	A	13	False	B	23	True	C
4	True	C	14	False	C	24	True	B
5	True	A	15	True	B	25	False	A
6	True	C	16	True	C	26	True	C
7	False	B	17	False	B	27	True	A
8	False	C	18	False	A	28	False	A
9	False	A	19	True	C	29	True	B
10	True	B	20	True	A	30	True	C

Now total the number of A's, B's, and C's that you scored. If you have more A's than anything else, you are predominantly a Type A in your attitudes toward management. A score of mostly B's indicates strong Type B tendencies, and a majority of C's indicates you are basically a Type C. Of course, few people fit wholly and completely into only one of these categories, but most people are predominantly one or the other. The more one letter outnumbers the other, the more completely your tendencies lie in the direction of that type. The number of eggs you have in all three baskets indicates the extent to which you share characteristics of all three types.

continued

ACTIVITIES

ATTITUDES TOWARD INTERACTING WITH PEOPLE, CONTINUED

Type A Attitudes

Type A people are highly individualistic, strongly opinionated, and have little patience with sham or pretense. People in this category are by nature frank and outspoken; they believe in saying exactly what they think. They are not socially adept or skilled in the subtleties of diplomacy. The round-about approach is completely foreign to them. They are uncomfortable in situations where they cannot be forthright and direct. They want to be "themselves" at all times, and they expect others to do the same. Their tendency to be independent minded may alienate people. Type A people would think nothing of telling off an irate client.

Type A people are happiest and most successful in situations where they can be their own bosses or where they can be selective about their clientele and do not have to meet the public at large. Such people may have many talents, and they possess strength of character, but they tend to lack skill in interpersonal relations and the ability to get along harmoniously with all types of people in various situations. Type A people would be least happy in public contact situations.

Type B Attitudes

Typically, Type B people are highly skilled in inter-personal relations. They get along well socially. They have an innate understanding of people. They are quick to grasp the underlying motivations of other people. This insight serves them in excellent stead when they wish to gain the support of others who may have conflicting views. They not only understand people but also enjoy them. They rarely feel at a loss in any circumstance where people are involved.

Type B people have ability as strategists, which makes them highly effective in influencing others. Type B people are happiest and function most effectively in public contact situations. A Type B person could easily and happily manipulate an irate client.

Type C Attitudes

One secret of getting along in this world is the ability to adjust to conditions, roll with the punches, make allowances for other people's faults, and appreciate their virtues. Type C people can get along with almost anybody, in any setting, and can exhibit admirable patience even with difficult people under trying circumstances. They "pour oil on troubled waters rather than make waves." They are often found saying to clients, "I'm sorry, I only work here."

They are respectful of the rights of others and go out of their way to avoid antagonizing others. They are interested in what other people think, their concepts and ideas. A Type C person would exhibit great understanding and empathy in dealing with an irate customer. Type C people can work quietly, efficiently, and competently in practically any field that does not require them to be aggressive, impose their will on others, or mold others' opinions. They tend to be uncomfortable in jobs that require them to order people around, enforce discipline, and become involved in conflicts of will.

Now that you have scored and analyzed your test, you might say to yourself, "I'm an excellent communicator. The way I scored on this test is simply wonderful." Others might say, "The way I scored on this test stinks, I feel terrible." And some may say, "It's just a dumb test. We ought to get rid of it. It should never have been put in the book." It's okay for you to think any way you wish. The important thing is for you to say to yourself, "Whether the test is good or bad, let me watch the people with whom I work and see how they treat me and see if I can determine how other people see me in terms of my communication personality. Do I enhance situations with my personality, or do I cause problems because of the way I communicate?"

Messages

The term **message** is often used in a popular sense to refer to the form in which language symbols are used. Technically, a message represents the meanings that people assign to things, but it can also be used in a nontechnical sense to refer to the form in which the symbols are presented. The materials presented in this section deal with the way people assign meanings to verbal and nonverbal symbols.

Words alone have no meaning; people assign meaning to them.

We assign meaning to events in our lives, the people we work for, the things we see on television, and so on. When we listen to another person talk, the meanings we assign to what that person says make up the messages we are creating. Messages develop inside of us. It is often said that *meanings exist only in people.* This can also be said about messages. A message is simply a group of meanings assigned to some experience.

The creation of a message depends on a person's ability to use symbols. The two most common types of symbols are verbal and nonverbal. The term *verbal* refers to language symbols. The study of how people use language is a study of verbal symbols. *Nonverbal* symbols are nonlanguage behaviors, appearances, emblems, sounds, silence, and time-space relationships that stand for, represent, or refer to something else. When a person assigns meaning to a nonverbal activity, communication through nonverbal means is taking place.

Verbal Symbols

Simply stated, a **verbal symbol** is a word or arrangement of words that we use to convey our thoughts and experiences to others. We each have developed our own unique way of processing and arranging words, which we do in our *language structure.* The number and variety of verbal symbols that we understand and have at our command constitutes our *vocabulary.* Our ability to communicate effectively is mainly determined by our perceptions of reality, our vocabulary, our language structure, and our use of nonverbal symbols.

Nonverbal Symbols

The extent to which people control and understand nonverbal symbols determines their effectiveness as communicators.

Nonverbal symbols have tremendous impact on communication. The extent to which people are able to control them, or at least take them into account as they speak and listen, determines their success as communicators.

The common expression that a person "cannot not communicate" is derived from the recognition that behavior is the open display of a person's thoughts. Your appearance, for example, is a symbol to others. Approximately 35 percent of the social meaning in a normal conversation is conveyed by the verbal components and approximately 65 percent by the nonverbal components—and these figures are probably conservative. Consider the communication that takes place in the way you style your hair, the type of clothes you wear, the condition of your body, the way you stand, the expression on your face, the eye contact you maintain, the gestures and body movements you use, the way you position yourself in relationship to those with whom you communicate, the tone of voice you use, and so on. Nonverbal communication is taking place constantly.

Physical distance between people communicates meaning.

Personal Space and Territoriality   The concept of **personal space** can be defined as the distance you allow between yourself and others. According to **Edward Hall's** landmark research, people carry their personal space with them and allow it to expand and contract according to the type of communicative encounter in which they are participating.[1] Hall classified personal space in four subcategories related to distance and situation: (1) *intimate,* ranging from actual physical contact to a distance of about 18 inches; (2) *casual personal,* from about 1.5 feet to 4 feet; (3) *social consultative,* from 4 to 12 feet; and (4) *public,* from 12 feet to the limits of visibility.

We all seem to adjust to the proper distance for various communicative situations. If you have just been introduced to the president of a corporation for a job interview, you most likely use the casual personal distance. On the other hand, if you are with your best friend or sweetheart after a very rough day at school or at work and you need love and sympathy, you will probably use the intimate distance.

Problems of communication can occur when someone invades another's personal space. People do this by not using the proper distance demanded by the other person and the situation. For example, it's probably not a good idea to slap the back of a supervisor or manager on the day you go to work for him or her. However, after you have worked well together for some time and established a positive relationship, he or she might welcome the warmth you show by this gesture.

Communication problems can arise from invading another person's space.

We all take our personal space with us wherever we go. In certain situations, people identify so clearly with a given location or space that they act as if it were their *territory.* Reflect on your territory. Where do you sit in class? Have you stayed in approximately the same place throughout the semester? Do you get upset when someone else sits in your seat? Do you have your own personal study chair in the library? Is there a specific place you sit at the dinner table? Territorial behavior seems to be a standard part of our everyday contact with other people.

How do you feel when someone invades your personal space or territory? How do you protect your favorite seat in the cafeteria? Some common techniques used to defend territory are as follows:

People protect and defend their personal space.

1. *Markers.* These can include books, coats, briefcases, or backpacks.

2. *Tenure.* For example, if you continue to come to the same seat or territory over a period of time, everyone finally realizes that the territory is yours and leaves it alone.

3. *Friends.* For example, you may say, "Marsha, will you watch my place until I get back with the hamburgers?"

We all define our personal space and territory according to the situation in which we are communicating. The proximity between two individuals who want to establish a friendship can have a major effect on the outcome of their relationship. And we know that some behavior can be explained by the need to stake out and defend territory. The key is to learn as much as possible about these issues, so that we can use them to help us obtain desired responses in others. Understanding personal space and territory can help us be better communicators.

Appearance   Every morning when we pull ourselves out of bed, we make a series of decisions that affect our **appearance** and the messages we wish to convey by the way we look. If we are in a hurry and are not concerned about impressing anyone, we might not spend much time with our appearance. If we have a job interview, we might spend considerable time preparing ourselves to look the way we feel the interviewer would want us to look.

People strive to send appearance messages that meet their own expectations and the expectations of others.

In essence, people strive to send appearance messages that correspond with others' expectations. Americans spend millions of dollars on weight-reduction programs, makeup and beauty aids, hair spray, mouthwash, soap, clothes, hair stylists, acne creams, jogging outfits, and many other items just to improve the way they look. Advertisers have a heyday with statements such as "The dry look

We communicate through our
grooming and the way we dress.

is in, the wet head is dead," and "Lipstick is not to be seen, it is to be used to
make women appear natural."

Attractiveness, body shape, hair, clothing, and other artifacts people place
on their bodies all have an impact on behavior. Physical attractiveness influences
the types of messages people send and receive in a variety of encounters. This
is particularly true in persuasive situations. Perceived attractiveness increases the
credibility of the speaker and possibly gives that person a persuasive advantage
over a less attractive person. What messages do the physical attractiveness and
body shapes of others send to you? Study your own physical appearance and
body shape, and analyze what you might be saying to others.

**What can we learn from
nonverbal cues?**

What can we learn about a person by the clothes he or she wears? Do
clothes give us helpful nonverbal cues for understanding others? Personal apparel
includes a wide variety of items other than clothing. Nonclothing apparel, or
artifacts, include eyeglasses, cosmetics, and wigs. Most theorists agree that clothing and artifacts contain much information about people.

R. Hoult's research suggests that the clothes we wear have a greater influence on people we do not know than they do on our friends.[2] Hoult found that
when subjects knew each other well, changes in clothing did not significantly
alter the way they rated each other. However, when subjects rated pictures of
unknown attractive faces paired with unattractive clothing, the attractive faces'
ratings went down. When unattractive faces were paired with attractive clothing, the unattractive faces' ratings went up. According to Hoult, clothing is not
a highly influential factor in nonverbal communication when individuals are well
acquainted.

Attractiveness, body shape, hair, clothing, and artifacts together create personal appearance. Appearance has a major impact on how others see us and
what we think and feel about them.

Body Language   Another aspect of nonverbal communication, **body language,** created excitement as a result of the best-selling books *Body Language,*
by Julius Fast, and *How to Read a Person Like a Book,* by Gerald Nierenberg

and Henry H. Calero. People wanted to be able to detect subtle body movements and stances in others and to determine what they meant. These popular books seemed to be saying, "Read us and learn what your employer really thinks, or read us and know what your date really has in mind for the evening."

However, the study of body language is not that precise. Most body movements in themselves have little meaning. We must be aware of other aspects of nonverbal communication if we are to be effective symbol readers. Body movements must be studied in concert with other nonverbal cues. We generally respond to nonverbal symbols that are a combination of more than one isolated cue.

Body movements need to be studied in concert with other aspects of nonverbal communication.

Touch Behavior   Touching is an effective means of communicating. By hugging your parents and sincerely telling them you love them, you strengthen the bonds that hold your family together. Touching seems to work best in combination with other stimuli. The combination of a hug and supporting words creates a message that is probably more effective than giving the hug alone or just saying the words.

While touching is an effective means of communicating in many circumstances, it can cause innumerable problems if done in an improper way. It is quite acceptable for a quarterback to slap a tackle on the fanny for making a good block. However, this gesture is quite inappropriate for most other people or in most other settings. Many companies are now providing specific guidelines as to what type of contact can be considered "sexual harassment" in order to avoid potential lawsuits.

Even though touching is usually used with other types of messages and can often be used inappropriately, it is one of the best methods for creating relationships. The handshake and pat on the back enhance communication.

Facial Expressions and Eye Contact   The face is a major source of messages about how people feel. It reveals much about internal emotional states. The face can show whether a friend is happy or upset. It may be the primary source of messages outside of human speech.

Our faces tell the rest of the world how we feel.

The mouth has received a great deal of research attention, because it is used to frown and smile. As a rule, smiles communicate friendliness and a desire to get along. People smile when seeking approval or in communicating acceptance of others. The smile can be used in a sarcastic way as well. Looking at other cues from other parts of the face and body can help determine the sincerity of the smile. A smile can be "heard" in an individual's voice; so smiling while you are on the phone can also communicate acceptance and openness.

The eyes are a major message sender of the face. **Eye contact** has a great impact on determining who receives and does not receive messages. However, customs and mores surrounding eye contact differ among cultural groups and nationalities.

Facial expressions are complex and therefore difficult to deal with. But of all the areas of the body, the face can give the best external feedback of internal feelings. Looking a person in the eyes creates a linkage—a sense of communication—not available without such contact.

Vocal Cues (Paralanguage)   **Paralanguage** is the study of *how* something is said (not *what* is said) by the words that are used. Sarcasm is an example of paralanguage. The young quarterback who has tossed a pass that resulted in an interception and a touchdown for the other team could hear from his coach words such as "Way to go, Bill. That was the most beautiful pass I've ever seen anyone throw!" If Bill were to listen only to the words of the coach, he would interpret them as a positive reaction. But Bill will probably realize from the

Smiles communicate friendliness and a desire to get along, and can even be "heard" over the telephone.

coach's tone of voice that he was displeased. Studies of conflicting messages on the vocal and verbal levels indicate that most of the time people read vocal cues accurately.

Nonverbal symbols can have a great impact on communication. Keep verbal and nonverbal symbols working together.

Nonverbal symbols have a great impact on communication. We have presented six groups of nonverbal communication variables. These are perhaps the most common variables. If you wish to be an accurate reader of nonverbal communication, you must be sensitive to the entire context in which the nonverbal symbols are being sent. You must read as many cues as possible and then make a composite judgment of their meaning. Therefore, to be effective, you must minimally evaluate the personal space and territory, the appearance, the body movements, the touching behavior, the facial expressions and eye contacts, and the vocal cues as they are used in the communication context. Along with these nonverbal messages, be awake to the words that are being spoken. If you take the entire communication context and all of its variables into account, you will be a much more effective receiver and sender of symbols.

Organization Environment

The environmental aspect of human communication concerns the conditions in which communication occurs. The environment is the social context: the physical surrounds, setting, and location. For three employees in a room, the immediate environment might be the room (its shape, size, and furnishings), the air (its circulation, temperature, and humidity), and the sounds (their tone, frequency, and quality). The extended environment can be the entire organization in which you find yourself. This environment consists of many aspects.

People are constantly interacting with a variety of changing cultures and situations. The broad organization is constantly changing and is often in a state of unrest. We will not cover or discuss the impact of the organizational environment here because it has been presented in previous chapters.

Summary of Key Ideas

- Communication is the process of making sense of (assigning meaning to) symbols. Effective communication occurs when two or more people share a similar understanding of a symbol.

- People, messages, and the environment combine to form a communication event.

- Since communication is a wholly human activity and people are the key to understanding communication, self-evaluation of our personalities helps us be effective in this area.

- The successful communicator is able to control and understand nonverbal symbols.

- Hall's four classifications of personal space based on distance and situation are intimate, casual personal, social consultative, and public.

- The major appearance factors are attractiveness, body shape, clothing, and artifacts.

- Along with appearance, nonverbal cues include body language, touch, facial expressions and eye contact, and vocal cues.

Key Terms, Concepts, and Names

Appearance
Body language
Communication
Environment
Eye contact
Facial expressions
Edward Hall
Message

Nonverbal symbols
Paralanguage
Personal space
Symbol
Touch behavior
Verbal symbols
Vocal cues

Questions and Exercises

1. List all the new information you have learned about yourself from completing the "Attitudes toward Interacting with People" activity.

2. List the way people behave toward you throughout one day. At the end of the day, look at your list. What have you learned about how people see you?

3. Analyze your nonverbal symbols. How do others see you?

4 Answer the introductory questions at the beginning of the chapter.

5. How can value differences complicate communication?

6. Rank the following values according to their importance to you, with 1 being the most important and 18 the least important. Then compare your rankings with the general American sample on the next page.

_____ Ambitious (hardworking, aspiring)

_____ Broad-minded (open-minded)

_____ Capable (competent, effective)

_____ Cheerful (lighthearted, joyful)

_____ Clean (neat, tidy)

_____ Courageous (willing to stand up for one's beliefs)

_____ Forgiving (willing to pardon others)

_____ Helpful (willing to work for the welfare of others)

_____ Honest (sincere, truthful)

_____ Imaginative (daring, creative)

_____ Independent (self-sufficient, self-reliant)

_____ Intellectual (intelligent, reflective)

_____ Logical (consistent, rational)

_____ Loving (affectionate, tender)

_____ Obedient (dutiful, respectful)

_____ Polite (courteous, well mannered)

_____ Responsible (dependable, reliable)

_____ Self-controlled (restrained, self-disciplined)

Instrumental Values	General American Sample	Instrumental Values	General American Sample
Ambitious	2	Imaginative	18
Broad-minded	5	Independent	14
Capable	10	Intellectual	17
Cheerful	12	Logical	15
Clean	8	Loving	11
Courageous	6	Obedient	16
Forgiving	4	Polite	13
Helpful	7	Responsible	3
Honest	1	Self-controlled	9

Notes

1. Edward T. Hall, *The Hidden Dimension* (New York: Doubleday, 1966).

2. R. Hoult, "Experimental Measurement of Clothing as a Factor in Some Social Ratings of Selected American Men," *American Sociological Review* 19, 1954, pp. 324–328.

Another Look: Sure-fire Success Secrets for the Leader in Each of Us

One summer I worked in the shipping department of a steel mill. My job was to be sure the structural steel had been inspected and then arrange to have it put on railroad cars and sent to the customers. It was totally different from anything I had ever encountered and the training I got was way too brief. One day one of the old hands in the office handed me a shipping order form and said, "Send this order out." On top of the form there was a company name to which we'd sent some previous orders, so I proceeded to verify that the steel had been inspected and then shipped out several tons of structural steel just as I'd done before.

Two days later, my supervisor inquired about the order. I said I'd already shipped it out and happened to name the city where it was going. A look of horror came over his face. "Oh, no, that's the wrong location," he groaned. This customer had two major facilities and the order was for a destination I didn't know existed. The goof was compounded by the fact that the right destination was east and the train with the steel on it was headed west. It was an expensive mistake.

So what happened? Everything my co-worker said to me was correct. He just didn't go far enough. And I should have known that big corporations have more than one location. I should have confirmed the destination. This was one of those classic communication foul-ups that well-intentioned people commit every day. The trouble was that both the company and the customer paid the price for our communication snarl.

Work has changed a great deal in the past 20 years. It used to be that people could do their jobs and keep pretty much to themselves. They got by with a John Wayne "yup" or "nope" style of interacting with others, because their work was done in isolation. Farmers, artisans, and factory workers didn't need to communicate all that much with others. Then everything changed. Now we're living on an information superhighway. One person's work is highly intertwined with many other people's. The communication that used to be a luxury has now become a necessity. The problem is, many people haven't yet gotten the message about the need to act differently.

If you're like most of us, you think that, although you communicate enough, *other* people need to communicate more.

Why don't we communicate more? Because we assume other people already know what we know. Because we think communicating something once is enough. Because communicating takes time away from our "real work." Because we don't stop to think about how important it is for others to know what we know. Because we prefer to communicate only good news and hide problems under the rug.

All of the above reasons (or excuses) for not communicating more are understandable, but they throw sand in the gears of the best organizations. Today's organization demands that people keep each other well informed.

Highly successful people make a point of keeping other people informed every step of the way.

- They let others know of current problems or potential problems down the road.
- They give periodic progress updates even if they have no progress to report.
- Sometimes they check in simply to review what's going on.

To some people, all this communicating can seem like overkill. To the highly successful, it's barely enough. That's because in today's organizations people work on many different projects with many different people, frequently in different locations. With such busy schedules, people need constant updating about what's happening and what needs to be done, when, and by whom.

Many people have a hard time grasping the fact that communicating to others about important issues—the status of a project, a call from an unhappy customer, a machine that's not working properly—is as much part of their job as finishing a drawing, completing a report, or shipping out the materials.

Highly successful people are straightforward about communicating their mistakes. They know that disclosing their mistakes saves others from unpleasant surprises and sets the stage for doing it right the next time. Telling others about mistakes also builds credibility. People will believe what you tell them when they see that you're an absolutely straight shooter.

What You Can Do

Almost all of us could communicate more in virtually every area of our work.

continued

Sure-fire Success Secrets for the Leader in Each of Us, *continued*

1. If you're involved in carrying out a change of some kind—an improvement in how you do your work, for example—let others know. Tell them what you're doing, why it's important, and how they'll be affected. Afterward, check in frequently to see how they're doing.

2. When you're working on a project, prepare a project update. List key developments since your last communication. Don't forget to communicate lack of progress as well.

3. If there's a rumor floating around that you think could stir up trouble, try to get to the bottom of it. Ask your manager about it. Do your part to clarify what's truth and what's error.

4. Communicate your whereabouts. If you have voice mail, update your announcement every day. "I'm sorry I can't take your call right now, please leave a message," isn't very informative. Have you stepped away for a minute? Are you on a three-day business trip? Get more specific: "Hello, today is April 12, and I'll be in meetings all morning. I'll listen to your message this afternoon." Announcements like this let callers know what to expect.

5. If someone leaves you a message asking for information (or some other request), and you're working on it, don't wait until you've finished to respond. Let the person know you got the message. Say, "I'm working on it," and state when you expect to get back to them with an answer.

Tips from the Highly Successful

- *Value mistakes, but don't repeat them.* A mistake-free life is a good indication you're not trying any-

thing new. At the same time, learn from your mistakes. Never make the same mistake twice.

- *Select the right medium.* Should you communicate orally or in writing? If your message contains a lot of complicated information, put it in writing. If it's short, or if you want to get immediate feedback, have a discussion. Also, what would the recipient prefer: A conversation? Memo? Voice mail?

  Incidentally, even if you plan to deliver spoken information, consider writing it down first. The process of writing is clarifying. Some people don't know what they want to say until they write it down.

- *Communicate up, down, and all around.* In the old days employees had to communicate through official channels: up to the boss and then down to employees. Today those channels are breaking down. So if you need to communicate to someone in another department, send the message straight to him or her.

  If your message is positive, put it in writing and copy the world. If it's corrective, negative, or a mistake that must be put in writing, limit distribution to protect the self-esteem of those involved.

- *Outline complex requests.* If you're the recipient of a complex or complicated message, outline the request as you understand it and ask the sender to confirm that you've got it right.

Source: Reprinted from John H. Zenger, *Not Just For CEOs: Sure-Fire Success Secrets for the Leader in Each of Us,* (Chicago, IL: Irwin Professional Publishing, 1996), pp. 85–90. Reprinted with permission of The McGraw-Hill Companies.

Another Look: Five Ways to Stop Costly Misunderstandings

Office communications can be like a game of telephone. You know, the game in which you whisper a message to someone who relays it to someone else. And by the time the message reaches the last person in line, it barely makes any sense.

The game shows how even relatively simple remarks can get distorted. In an office, these distortions can lead to misunderstandings, hurt feelings and worse.

"Most disagreements are really misunderstandings," said Michael Bryant, principal of Career Transition Services in Baltimore, a career and management consulting firm. "What often happens is that human beings tend not to communicate exactly what they want, and then they get mad when they don't get it."

If you want to avoid communication breakdowns with co-workers, customers and others, follow these five guidelines from mediators and other communication experts.

continued

Five Ways to Stop Costly Misunderstandings, *continued*

----

1. *Speak out and be specific.* If you don't, you may allow preconceived notions to interfere.

   Charles Forer, chairman of the alternative dispute-resolution practice group at the Philadelphia law firm of Connolly Epstein Chicco Foxman Engelmyer & Ewing, said preconceived notions are the basis for many misunderstandings that end up in court.

   Forer recalled a multimillion-dollar lawsuit that recently resulted from a simple case of two people viewing the same conversation from different perspectives: "A buyer cornered a seller about a piece of equipment and asked, 'It does do this, right?' The seller responded by essentially saying, 'Check it out for yourself.' But all the buyer heard was 'Yes,' because that's what he wanted to hear. The seller could have replied, 'No, it can't do that,' but the seller wanted to make a sale. So the buyer left thinking the seller agreed this equipment could do certain things, while the seller thought he gave full disclosure."

2. *Don't be shy.* If you're nervous about having to criticize an employee, you might be tempted to take the easy way out by dropping indirect hints or simply keeping quiet. But that strategy can lead to communication snafus.

   "Supervisors usually say that they don't want to discourage the employee, so they'll emphasize the positive and minimize the negative," said Jane Juliano, an Arlington, Va.-based lawyer and president of the Virginia Mediation Network. "But miscommunication is bound to result if you don't level with the individual in a straightforward manner about both the good and the bad."

   As a mediator, Juliano said she has observed many workplace disputes in which warring parties wind up at each other's throats based on faulty assumptions or incomplete information. "In mediation," she said, "I try to engender trust so that they can calm down and say what needs to be said."

3. *Use "I" statements.* If you want a staffer to change his or her behavior, begin by explaining your point of view.

   A boss can say to an employee, "I need to count on you to get the job done." That's more effective than, "You're not making it here." By the same token, a worker is better off saying, "I need

more flexibility to do the job" than "You're not managing this situation well."

   "You have to communicate your needs to prevent conflicts," said Douglas Harbit, director of external affairs for the National Institute for Dispute Resolution, a nonprofit group in Washington, D.C., that supports mediation in the workplace. "In a conflict, say what you need the other person to do rather than accusing them of doing something wrong."

4. *Watch your words.* If you let slip just one phrase that rubs a listener the wrong way, you may lose a chance to make yourself understood.

   "People often home in on negative words," said John McCammon, president of Richmond, Va.-based McCammon Mediation Group. "What you say might get processed very differently by people when they hear something that they don't like."

   He gives the example of a performance review in which the boss says, "You're great in eight areas and crummy in two others." "What word does the subordinate hear? 'Crummy,'" McCammon said. Replacing "crummy" with "less effective" or another less loaded word can foster clear communication.

5. *Listen actively.* A common culprit in communication breakdowns is that people assume that they know what someone is trying to say and then act accordingly.

   "Sometimes what we see is an individual who communicates what he or she thinks is a directive, but the other person doesn't pick it up that way," said Peter Maida, director of the Key Bridge Therapy & Mediation Center in Arlington, Va.

   The solution is to listen attentively and summarize what you hear before drawing a conclusion or moving on to another point. Use phrases such as, "It seems what you're saying is . . ."or "As I understand it, you want me to . . . . "

   "We teach active listening, in which people work to understand what a speaker meant by the words used," Maida said.

Source: Morey Stettner, "5 Ways to Stop Costly Misunderstandings," *Investor's Business Daily,* July 16, 1997, pp. A1, A5. Reprinted by permission of *Investor's Business Daily,* for people who chose to succeed.

A Case in Point: Schultz and Peterson: A Dispute

In an effort to control costs of servicing customer accounts, Jim Schultz, manager of systems at Washburn National Bank, was charged with making a study and subsequent recommendations to reduce the operating expense of the department.

Thirty days later, Schultz's recommendations were put into operation; six months later, costs for operating the department were reviewed against costs for the preceding six-month period. It was found that costs had decreased by $2,715. This decrease was due primarily to savings in salaries charged against the customer service department. During the preceding six-month period, 9,037 customers had been provided service. Under the new system, 4,812 customers had been provided service.

The vice-president of the bank reported the savings to the president, Mr. Peterson. Peterson expressed surprise that the vice-president thought a savings had taken place. "In the first place," the president said, "you moved the customer service department from the main floor to the sixth floor so that fewer customers would take the trouble to check their balances and review their statements; furthermore, you require each customer to show positive identification before they can obtain any information about their accounts; on top of this, you have instructed the personnel in customer service absolutely to refuse to give out any banking information to anyone requesting it over the telephone. It's my opinion that you should revert to the old system and give our customers the kind of service they deserve."

Questions

1. What should Schultz say?
2. What, if any, communication problems are occurring between Schultz and the vice-president? between the vice-president and Peterson? between the bank and its customers?
3. What effects might be occurring inside each of the parties involved in this incident?
4. What should be done now?

A Case in Point: Speaking the Same Language

As director of communications I was asked to prepare a memo reviewing our company's training programs and materials. In the body of the memo one of the sentences mentioned the "pedagogical approach" used by one of the training manuals. The day after I routed the memo to the executive committee, I was called into the HR director's office, and told that the executive vice-president wanted me out of the building by lunch.

When I asked why, I was told that she wouldn't stand for "perverts" working in her company. Finally, he showed me her copy of the memo, with her demand that I be fired—and the word "pedagogical" circled in red.

The HR manager was fairly reasonable, and once he looked the word up in his dictionary, and made a copy of the definition to send back to her, he told me not to worry. He would take care of it.

Two days later a memo to the entire staff came out, directing us that no words that could not be found in the local Sunday newspaper could be used in company memos. A month later, I resigned. In accordance with company policy, I created my resignation memo by pasting words together from the Sunday paper.

Questions

1. What caused this rather crazy communication problem?
2. Is this type of miscommunication typical in organizations? Present to a friend at least two similar types of miscommunication that you have heard about.
3. What do you think caused the director of communications to resign?
4. How could this situation have been avoided?

Source: Taken from the Internet: http://www1.iastate.edu/ bshoemak/stories/stories.htm.

Interpersonal Communication: Being Effective with People

- What does support listening do?

- How do the open-question, "uh-huh," and content reflection techniques work to create support listening?

- How does retention listening differ from support listening?

- What are the eight points for effective retention listening?

- When is it appropriate to use the skill of accurate understanding?

- How does accurate understanding work?

- What three approaches constitute the conflict-managing technique?

- What do you do to manage each of the following types of conflict: simple conflict, pseudoconflict, and ego conflict?

- What are some circumstances in which the communication conflict approach should be used?

The answers to these and other questions are coming up next in Chapter 12 . . .

Some problems are associated with communication in organizations. Employees are forced to communicate through other employees who may or may not get the message. Feelings are often crushed. Trust can be lost. Production might fall off. Life can be miserable.

Managers need good interpersonal communication skills.

People engaged in managing, supervising, selling, and providing services depend on good interpersonal communication to accomplish their objectives. In this chapter, we deal with skills to help managers more effectively attain their objectives through efficient interpersonal communication. What kinds of objectives tend to be associated with interpersonal communication? Among other things, a manager should be able to:

1. maintain close relationships without developing feelings of uncertainty or rejection;

2. help others understand themselves and achieve a degree of personal growth;

3. interpret and pass on information to another person with minimal distortion and misunderstanding; and

4. listen so as to create a supportive atmosphere in which another person can talk without being defensive.

During the past 20 or 30 years, many helpful approaches to the study of interpersonal communication have been proposed. The study of transactional analysis (TA), especially, has done much to foster effective interpersonal relationships. TA has been successful because it suggests that people evaluate their communication effectiveness. Furthermore, and most important, it helps individuals step out of the communication situation, to evaluate how the messages of both the speaker and the listener influence the effectiveness of communication. For communication to be effective, people must stand back and be aware of what they are doing. A casual, unthinking approach results in ineffective communication.

Effective communicators are aware of what they do to influence others.

Besides being aware, you must be concerned about the other person. If you are not, the skills that we are about to present may seem phony and manipulative. However, they do work if you are aware and concerned and practice them. We will discuss skills of effective listening, accurate understanding, and managing communication conflict.

Effective Listening

As the quiz in the following activity indicates, **effective listening** can be a challenging process. A starting point for improvement lies in recognizing that we engage in two types of listening:

1. listening to show support for the other person *(support listening),* and

2. listening to retain and evaluate information *(retention listening).*

These two types of listening are generally discussed and studied independently by communication theorists. The nondirective counseling approach of psychologists like Carl Rogers exemplifies support listening, while education specialists and communication scholars like Ralph Nichols focus on retention. All approaches assume that people spend a large portion of their lives listening, and that is true. The next section of this chapter presents important ideas and aids dealing with both support and retention listening.

ACTIVITIES

SUPPORT LISTENING QUIZ

Test your listening skills. Select the one best answer among the three given, even though you may feel that all answers may be correct to some degree. See the next page for comments.

1. A person is a good listener only if he/she
   a. Does not think while the other person is talking
   b. Hears everything the other person has to say
   c. Seeks information as she/he listens about his/her own and the other person's assumptions, viewpoints, and feelings

2. To get a clear picture of the other person as we listen
   a. We have to "tune in" on some things that are never actually voiced
   b. We must concentrate on everything she/he says
   c. We must clear our minds of any prejudices or evaluations we may have made in advance

3. The biggest block to interpersonal communications is
   a. One's inability to listen intelligently, understandingly, and skillfully to another person
   b. One's inability to be logical, lucid, and clear in what one says
   c. The fact that any statement may have several meanings

4. It is necessary for everyone who must deal with other people on important matters to know how to listen with understanding because
   a. In a crucial conversation, false ideas of other people can lead to misunderstanding and disagreement
   b. There will be less argument
   c. People usually try to conceal their real feelings

5. You can determine whether you have communicated with the other person by
   a. Asking him/her questions
   b. Watching her/his facial expressions
   c. Knowing whether he/she should be interested in what you are talking about

6. When we talk to another person, we can assume
   a. That the other person is listening to what we say
   b. That what is important to us may not be important to her/him
   c. That he/she knows and shares our unspoken feelings

7. Three factors enter into our daily person-to-person listening. Which is most important?
   a. Assumptions
   b. Viewpoints
   c. Feelings

ACTIVITIES

"SUPPORT LISTENING QUIZ" COMMENTS

Compare your responses with the following comments about each question:

1. It is not enough to be just a blotter or photographic negative that soaks up everything that is said. Good listening requires active participation on the part of the listener. The correct answer is *c*.

2. It is not enough to concentrate on everything that is said; we have to be actively thinking as we listen. It is actually impossible to cleanse our minds of our prejudices and evaluations, but it helps to "know thyself." The correct answer is *a*.

3. No matter how logical, lucid, or clear the transmitter is, unless the receiver is "tuned in," there can be no communication. The fact that one statement may have several meanings complicates the process of interpersonal communication, but good listening habits can overcome this obstacle. The correct answer is *a*.

4. [Answer] *b* is wrong because elimination of arguments in itself does not mean good commu-

nication. [Answer] c is also wrong because the purpose of listening with understanding is not just to get at hidden feelings, but to be able to communicate with others. The correct answer is *a*.

5. Many times facial expressions can be very deceiving. Just because a person appears interested in a subject does not mean he/she actually understands. The correct answer is *a*.

6. People often think of something else when someone else is speaking, and these unspoken feelings vary with each individual. It is safest to assume that the other person probably has a different set of values from your own. The correct answer is *b*.

7. Feelings are deeply imbedded in people and are not subject to logical argument. Viewpoints and assumptions are more easily changed by new facts and perspectives. The correct answer is *c*.

Source: Quiz and comments reprinted from *American Business* © Geyer-McAllister Publications. Permission to reprint granted by Elliott Service Company, Mount Vernon, New York.

Conversation

i have just wandered back
into our conversation and find
    that you are still rattling on
about something or other
i think i must have been gone
    at least
twenty minutes
and you never missed me

now this might say something
about my acting ability
or it might say something about
    your sensitivity
one thing troubles me though
when it is my turn to rattle on
    for twenty minutes
which i have been known to do
have you been missing too?

Ric Masten

Support Listening

Support listening consists of hearing and remembering what others say with a minimum of emotion or observable reaction. The idea is to focus on listening to another to learn what that person thinks and feels. Avoid speaking except to encourage or cause the other person to speak.

Support listening consists of three responses:

- Open questions

- "Uh-huh"

- Content reflection

Open questions cannot be answered with a simple yes or no. The **"uh-huh" technique,** the simplest kind of oral response, consists of saying "uh-huh" or "hmmm" as the other person talks. Content reflection involves repeating, mirroring, or echoing the content of a statement made by another person in the form of a question. Each reaction is designed to cause the speaker to keep speaking and the listener to keep listening.

Support listening places the responsibility for continuing a conversation, dialogue, or interview on the other person. If you ask the question "What do you think about our firm?" and then look intently and inquiringly at the person you addressed, the responsibility for continuing the dialogue is placed firmly on the other person. The commitment is equally strong when you simply say "uh-huh" or "hmmm" when the other person makes a comment. The effect is essentially the same when you echo the idea just stated. Support listening establishes that you want the other person to either begin or continue talking. When you respond this way, you create an expectation that can be fulfilled only when the other person talks and when you listen.

Each skill of support listening encourages the other to talk. The following dialogue illustrates support listening:

RITA: Doris, how do you feel about the department? (Open question)

DORIS: Working in this department is extremely difficult.

RITA: Uh-huh. ("Uh-huh")

DORIS: What I mean is that I have problems getting along with Dan.

RITA: Hmmm. ("Uh-huh")

DORIS: He just can't accept the fact that I'm his boss.

RITA: Dan can't accept you as his boss? (Content reflection)

DORIS: That's right! He's always making snide comments about women bosses.

RITA: What kinds of things does he say? (Open question)

Support listening is grounded in the theory of positive reinforcement. People like to talk to others who support them or at least do not deny or reject them. Reinforcement theory suggests that a person's behavior is influenced by its consequences. Thus, if you react or respond in a supportive manner to something the other person said, he or she will feel that the comments have been reinforced and will continue to talk. If you begin talking and get positive reactions in return, you will tend to continue talking. Each support listening skill provides positive reinforcement by indicating that you have an interest in what is being said and care enough to listen.

> Support listening places the responsibility for continuing a conversation on the other person.

> Support listening is grounded in the theory of positive reinforcement.

What You Must Do

To listen supportively, you need to have concern for the other person and an interest in listening to what he or she has to say.

Although each type of response can be used individually and independently, the techniques of support listening are most effective when they are used together. The open question is often used to open the conversation, after which a content reflection or an "uh-huh" response is given. Thereafter, as the conversation runs through a sequence of interactions involving reflections and "uh-huh" responses, another open question can be asked.

Begin the conversation or interview with an open question:

ARLENE: How have you been getting along with George?

Then look at the other person and lean slightly toward him or her. Indicate that you are listening by nodding your head occasionally as the other talks. Vocalize your support by giving an "uh-huh" response:

SALLY: I really appreciate all that he does for me.

ARLENE: Uh-huh.

SALLY: He really seems to care about me.

ARLENE: Uh-huh.

The "uh-huh" response provides support and indicates that you are following the conversation.

Or you might want to secure more information about a topic. In that case, content reflection and additional open questions are appropriate:

SALLY: But I simply can't stand this place any longer.

ARLENE: You can't stand being here any longer!

SALLY: You said it! If I have to work with George any longer, I'm going to go out of my mind.

ARLENE: Well, how do you feel about the board of directors?

Support listening is a basic technique that shows support and encourages the other person to continue talking. Support listening is nonevaluative—it avoids expressing approval or disapproval—and requires careful hearing of the other.

In using the "uh-huh" response, focus on the other person and verbalize your support by saying "uh-huh," "hmmm," "I see," or some equivalent nonjudgmental comment.

Content reflection responses are provided by echoing or mirroring back the content of what the other person said. Avoid using a questioning tone of voice that makes the reflected question sound like a challenge to and an evaluation of what the other said.

The open question involves asking a free-response inquiry that requires a statement or explanation rather than a simple yes or no answer.

Although the evidence is quite strong in support of the efficacy of the technique of support listening, it depends on the sincere interest of the user to truly hear and remember what the speaker is saying. If the listener is not sincerely interested in what the speaker has to say, then the technique is merely a gimmick. In those instances, the speaker usually recognizes what is happening, refuses to cooperate, and focuses on the technique rather than on communicating. Used wrongly, the technique fails to help the other person communicate. If this happens, just let the other party take full control of the content of the conversation. Then gradually reinforce the other's comments by using the

Source: By permission of Johnny Hart and Creators Syndicate, Inc.

"uh-huh" response. Introduce new topical areas through an open question, but refrain from content reflections until they can be worked into the conversation unobtrusively. Keep in mind that the combination of facial expressions, tone of voice, and body language plays a vital role in support listening.

Retention Listening

Lyman K. Steil makes the following points about listening for retention:[1]

1. Because of the listening mistakes of workers (and most make several mistakes each week), letters have to be retyped, appointments rescheduled, and shipments rerouted. Productivity and profits decline.

2. A simple $10 mistake by each of the 100 million workers in the United States would add up to a cost of $1 billion.

3. "Good" or effective listening is more than merely "hearing." Effective listening involves:

   a. hearing;

   b. interpreting (which leads to understanding or misunderstanding);

   c. evaluating (weighing the information and deciding how to use it); and

   d. responding (based on what we heard, understood, and evaluated).

4. When all four stages (hearing, interpreting, evaluating, and responding) are considered, people on average listen at an effective rate of 25 percent.

5. The ability to listen is not an inherent trait; it is learned behavior that has to be taught. Unlike reading, writing, speaking, and many other subjects, however, it is not systematically taught in our schools.

6. People have not been taught to listen well. We spend 80 percent of our waking hours communicating and 45 percent of our communication time listening (with speaking, reading, and writing taking up the other 55 percent). Ironically, our schools devote the greatest amount of time to teaching what we do least: writing. The least amount of teaching time is devoted to what we do most: listening.

7. Listening is more complex than reading. If we misread something or are distracted, we can go back and read it again. But listening is transient: "The message is written on the wind. If we don't get it the first time, there usually is no going back."

8. According to a recent study, managers rate listening as the most important competency among the abilities they considered critical for their managerial success. "The higher one advances in management, the more critical listening ability and skill become." Most problems in business arise because management fails to listen.

9. Most people recognize the lack of listening skills in others but consider themselves good listeners. Listening exercises usually demonstrate that people are not as good at listening as they thought they were.

I hear   I forget
I see   I remember
I do   I understand

Chinese proverb

What You Must Do

Steil makes eight points that he feels are extremely important for a manager, or anyone, to operate effectively as a retentive listener.[2]

1. *Resist distractions.* This point emphasizes the importance of concentration. Force yourself to keep your mind on what is being said.

2. *Be an opportunist.* Do your best to find areas of interest between you and the speaker. Ask yourself, "What's in this for me? What can I get out of what is being said?"

3. *Stay alert.* It is easy to daydream if the speaker is a bit boring. Force yourself to stay alert even if the speaker is slow and boring. If your thoughts run ahead of the speaker, use the extra time to evaluate, anticipate, and review.

4. *Identify the speaker's purpose and adapt to it.* What is the speaker trying to do? Is the speaker informing, persuading, or entertaining? Whatever the speaker's purpose, identify it and adjust to it.

5. *Listen for central themes rather than isolated facts.* Too often, people get hopelessly lost as listeners because they focus on unimportant facts and details and miss the speaker's main point.

6. *Plan to report the content of a message to someone within eight hours.* This forces the listener to concentrate and to remember. It is a good practice technique.

7. *Develop note-taking skills.* There are many approaches to note taking. Whichever approach you use, the simple process of writing things down as you hear them helps you retain what you hear even if you do not read the notes later.

8. *As a listener, take primary responsibility for the success of two-way communication.* Don't blame the other person for your listening inadequacies. Listening is your responsibility, not the speaker's.

The effective communicator can listen both supportively and retentively. Be aware of both types of listening, and practice the skills presented in this section of this chapter.

After people have developed the skills of effective listening, they must determine if they understand what they have heard. The skill of accurate understanding helps make certain that people understand one another.

"I lift, you grab....Was that concept just a little too complex, Carl?"

Source: The Far Side © Gary Larson. Reprinted by permission of United Features Syndicate, Inc.

Accurate Understanding

Accurate understanding consists of restating in your own words what the other person's statement means to you. With this sort of restatement, the other person can determine whether the message getting through to you is the one intended.

With understanding, you provide the other person with an indication of how you have interpreted his or her statements and feelings. This technique involves more than just repeating what a person says or restating the other person's ideas in some other way. For example, the following conversation between Sue and Bill demonstrates what happens when you repeat or rephrase without repeating what it means to you:

SUE: Business management is really a different program.

BILL: You mean business management is not like other programs?

SUE: Yeah. It sure is an awfully different program.

Bill may feel that he understands about a program in business management, but the understanding is illusory because little if anything was expressed. Instead of merely rephrasing Sue's statement, Bill could have asked himself, "What does Sue's statement mean?" Bill could then restate Sue's comment to reveal his understanding of what it means to him. For example, he could have said, "You mean business management is a lot more exciting than other programs?" Sue would then verify whether or not Bill had actually understood her comment as she intended it. If the restatement was not an accurate reflection of what Sue meant, she would probably restate the comment in other terms in an effort to communicate more clearly.

Listening is important, but if you do not understand, who cares?

Here is a detailed example of how understanding might proceed:

BOB: Majoring in management is fantastic!

RHEA: You mean that the professors in the management department make their courses exciting?

BOB: Yes, partly at least. But studying about how to get people to better complete their jobs is fun.

RHEA: Then you think that a major in management can prepare people to make a difference in their own lives as well as to help others be more successful on the job?

Accurate understanding is not a gimmick or trick. The technique translates the desire to know what the other person means into a simple procedure for checking the meaning of the other's comment. It is done by a simple restatement of what you understood.

The accurate understanding technique is based on the premise that when an individual expresses an idea, that idea is restated in another way by the listener. The initiator of the statement then clarifies, expands on, or further explores the ideas and feelings embodied in the statement. Often the individual moves on to express a new idea or feeling that is now more meaningful to him or her.

What You Must Do

To convey understanding you must focus on the other person; listen carefully (use the support listening responses) to what the person is saying, and how it is being said, to catch both verbal and nonverbal cues to what the other person probably means. Ask yourself, "What does the statement mean to me?"

If the other's statement was general, it might suggest something specific to you:

LES: Mahogany office furniture is the best kind.

DELLA: You mean that mahogany wood takes a more brilliant polish than other kinds.

LES: No, mahogany furniture lasts longer.

On the other hand, if the other person's comment was specific, it may elicit a more general interpretation from you.

JILL: I've got to have 30 sheets of lined notepaper right away.

DAN: Do you mean you need something to write on? I have some plain copier paper.

JILL: That will be fine. Anything on which I can write some notes will do.

Use these guidelines to state your accurate understanding of the other person:

1. Restate the other person's expressed ideas and feelings in your own words.

2. Preface your statements with a tentative introductory phrase, such as one of the following:
    - "Are you saying . . ."
    - "You mean that . . ."
    - "You feel that . . ."
    - "You think that . . ."
    - "It seems to you that . . ."
    - "It appears to you that , ,"

Listening is considered by managers to be a competency critical to success.

3. Avoid any indication of disapproval or approval: refrain from blaming, or expressing rejection or strong support; avoid giving advice or persuading.

4. Wait for the other person's response.

5. Where necessary, paraphrase the other's response to secure the most accurate understanding possible.

After you have listened and are certain that you understand, then in many cases the communication process is complete. However, you often must go beyond listening and understanding. One difficult aspect of communicating is knowing how to deal with conflict situations. The next section deals with skills for effectively managing communication conflict.

Interpersonal Communication Conflict

Conflict (a state of disharmony or disagreement between two or more persons) is a normal part of our daily lives, at home, at school, or on the job. According to researchers Gerald R. Miller and Mark Steinberg, the three major types of **interpersonal conflict** are simple conflict, pseudoconflict, and ego conflict.

What is interpersonal conflict?

Conflict is almost always **communication conflict** and is usually prevented, resolved, or alleviated through the use of some type of communication technique. **Managing conflict** effectively requires responses that reduce the frequency and likelihood of caustic, angry, defensive, and sarcastic reactions that lead to or aggravate conflict. It allows people to see all sides of a conflict situation and to integrate what they see into their perceptions. This technique involves three response approaches that specifically address the three major types of conflict.[3]

Simple conflict arises when two people or two groups of people know each other's goals but neither side can attain its personal desires without blocking the goal of the other person or group. The *communication conflict-managing* *approach* is a method of controlling and possibly overcoming simple conflict by using response approaches that keep the conflict simple, delay the interaction, and cast the conflict in a mutual noncompetitive frame.

Pseudoconflict may result from ineffective communication. People who agree on an issue but are unable to communicate their agreement assume they disagree. Your boss wants you to complete the Harper report tomorrow, and you also want to do this; however, from your boss's attitude, you believe she wants you to spend the day tomorrow doing research. Thus, pseudoconflict takes place. The *pseudoconflict-managing approach* is a method of eliminating distortions in communications.

Ego conflict occurs when people become emotionally involved to the point that there is some threat to their egos. Ego conflicts bring people to the point of saving face at any cost by putting others down in order to protect themselves. The *ego conflict-managing approach* is to (1) focus on relevant and factual matters (as opposed to extraneous matters and conclusions), (2) encourage the other person to focus on relevant and factual matters, and then (3) quit talking and let the other person describe the conflict and the reasons for its occurrence.

The communication conflict-managing technique is intended to help people manage their defensive responses so that they build relationships rather than hinder them. For example, suppose that you want to go to Disneyworld for a vacation, but your spouse wants to visit his or her mother in Oklahoma. You cannot afford to do both, so you may be in a simple conflict situation. Depending on your relationship, you may or may not get involved in conflict, but the potential exists. The simple conflict-managing approach would work well in this situation because it allows you to keep the conflict from escalating to the ego conflict stage and it provides you with responses that can keep the conflict from ever occurring. A possible response might be "It is obvious that we cannot go to both places. Why don't we take a day or so and try to see each other's point of view and then try to make a decision?"

If the conflict escalates beyond the simple conflict stage and in fact becomes a pseudoconflict, the pseudoconflict-managing approach helps the two people realize that they do not have a conflict. A possible response might be "We both want to see your mother, and we both want to take the kids to Disneyworld. Why don't we invite her to go with us?" Conflicts often escalate as people become ego-involved with the topics at hand. The ego conflict-managing approach can help cool off this kind of situation.

The technique of managing communication conflict is based on the notion that conflict is inevitable and that no relationship can expect to be totally free of it. To completely eliminate conflict is impossible. Therefore, it must be managed so that relationships can be continued.

Through conflict, we sometimes learn important things about ourselves, significant others, and how we relate to one another. Conflict is not necessarily destructive as long as we treat people with respect and honestly try to control the conflict. This technique does not offer specific solutions to specific conflicts, but it does suggest some general approaches to problems of conflict. The technique will work when you treat people as they should be treated.

In the simple conflict-managing approach, you treat people well by speaking openly and frankly, by not letting your perceptions get in the way of how you relate to others, and by treating both the person and the idea as being equal to you and your ideas.

In the pseudoconflict-managing approach, you treat people well by eliminating the distortions that have occurred between you and the others. This can be done by asking for clarification and by presenting your understanding of the other.

In the ego conflict-managing approach, you treat people well by not letting your own ego push you to respond in negative terms, by letting the other speak his or her piece, and by helping describe the conflict that exists between the two of you.

What You Must Do

The technique of managing communication conflict includes (1) understanding the three major assumptions about interpersonal conflict, (2) being aware of the possible outcomes of conflict management, (3) determining the form of interpersonal conflict in which you are involved, and (4) using the proper conflict-managing approach to keep the conflict from causing problems or escalating.

To be able to minimize problems associated with conflict and to maximize the value associated with conflict, be aware of the following three assumptions. These will guide you in effectively using any of the three approaches to managing conflict.

Three assumptions are made regarding conflict.

1. *Conflict is inevitable.* Keep in mind that people cannot be together without experiencing conflict situations. It is natural for conflict to occur.

2. *Conflict is not a dirty word.* When conflict occurs, it is not a sign that those involved are bad people or that they are less worthwhile as members of our society. On the other hand, conflict can be extremely important and beneficial to relationships.

3. *Conflict arises for many reasons and takes many forms.* Although three approaches to handling conflict are suggested, there are many reasons for people getting involved in conflict and many ways that this conflict can manifest itself. The key is your ability to recognize differences in situations and to adjust your conflict-management approach to the specific conflict.

Conflict has many possible outcomes, and they all require different approaches for effective management. To this end, be aware of at least the following five possible outcomes:

Conflict has at least five possible outcomes.

1. *Discontinuing the relationship.* If any given conflict gets too severe and the participants cannot manage it effectively, there is a tendency to give up on the relationship.

2. *Suffering through the relationship.* Because some people are unable to discontinue a relationship, they simply suffer through, hoping it will get better without managing it.

3. *Dampening the conflict.* This is a type of conflict managing. Those in conflict reduce the pain by avoiding it temporarily, but the conflict still exists.

4. *Resolving the conflict.* In simple conflict situations, people are usually able to resolve their problems. They do this by communicating effectively using listening and understanding skills.

5. *Managing the conflict.* Occasionally people can manage and handle conflict in a very effective manner. The three approaches presented next identify the skills necessary to do this.

Managing Simple Conflict The three approaches to communication conflict are linked to the three forms of conflict discussed previously.

1. **Keep the conflict simple.** Do not let the conflict become pseudoconflict or ego conflict. Try your best to prevent misunderstandings, and do not attack the other's pride or ego. Try to state the misunderstanding as clearly as possible. For example, say, "Is the issue here to determine which color of carpet we want? I want dark brown and you want light brown." Try not to use emotional language or attack the other person.

For example, do *not* say, "Let's get this clear! The issue seems to be to determine which crummy color of carpet you want. I want a rich dark brown, and for some stupid reason you want an ugly light brown!" Keep the conflict simple by using nonthreatening language and stating the problems as clearly as possible.

2. *Wait a while.* If tensions are beginning to build and you can put off making a decision, let the issue drop for a while. While waiting, analyze your reasons for your point of view. Perhaps a solution that neither of you thought of will materialize. You might say, at a later time, "I'm glad we selected pink carpet."

3. *Face the problems together.* Do not compete with one another but try to work together as a team. Mutually agree that the outcome of the situation will affect both of you. Try to work together to solve your problem. Nothing stifles problem solving more than a dictatorial approach from one or both sides of a conflict. Work together.

Managing Pseudoconflict

1. *Verify that the pseudoconflict exists.* The problem in dealing with pseudoconflict is that you do not know it exists. Check the other's perceptions of what is going on, and review in your own mind if something is wrong. Have you done anything to alienate the other? This leads to the second step.

2. *Ask for clarification.* The second step is simple. Ask the other person to help you by telling you what has happened. You might ask, "What do you mean by that?" or "What is on your mind?" The idea is to get the other to talk and to explain what the pseudoconflict is. This allows for the correction of both sets of perceptions concerning the conflict.

Managing Ego Conflict

1. *Never miss an opportunity to keep your mouth shut.* When people let their egos get involved in an interaction, they put up barriers to cooperative communication. To manage ego conflicts, lower those barriers. You can bring down barriers by allowing people to express their relevant concerns. However, be careful not to allow these expressions of concern to escalate or cause further problems of conflict. Therefore, let the person speak, but then restrict him or her from saying more than necessary.

2. *Do not explain the conflict, describe it.* When the people in conflict are able to talk to each other, have them describe the conflict as best they can. Try not to explain what happened from any point of view; simply describe what happened. Do not allow competition to enter into the descriptions of the conflict.

3. *Determine the sources of conflict.* After you have agreed about what caused the conflict by describing it, then you can begin to determine what its sources were. If you can get to this point, you will most likely be able to manage ego conflict. However, getting to this point is extremely difficult in ego conflict situations.

Summary of Key Ideas

- Effective listening is a two-part process requiring support listening and retention listening.

- Steil's eight points that aid the retentive listener are: resist distractions, be an opportunist, stay alert, identify and adapt to the speaker's purpose, listen for central themes, plan to report the content of a message within eight hours, develop note-taking skills, and take the primary responsibility for the success of two-way communication.

- When stating your understanding of a communication, use the following guidelines: restate in your own words, use an introductory phrase, avoid indication of approval or disapproval, wait for the other person's response, and paraphrase when appropriate.

- The three approaches that constitute the communication conflict technique are: simple conflict, pseudoconflict, and ego conflict. The management techniques used to deal with each of them will differ.

- The three assumptions one should remember concerning conflict are that conflict is inevitable, is not necessarily harmful, and arises for many reasons and takes many forms.

- The five possible outcomes of conflict are: discontinuing the relationship, suffering through the relationship, dampening the conflict, resolving the conflict, and managing the conflict.

Key Terms, Concepts, and Names

Accurate understanding	Pseudoconflict
Communication conflict	Retention listening
Content reflection	Simple conflict
Effective listening	Lyman K. Steil
Ego conflict	Support listening
Interpersonal communication	"Uh-huh" technique
Managing conflict	
Open questions	

Questions and Exercises

1. Give an example of where and when you might use support listening, and explain how it can help you communicate more effectively.

2. Answer the introductory questions at the beginning of the chapter.

3. Read each of the following statements, and then write a content reflection and an open question for each. Check your answers with a friend to make certain you are responding appropriately.
   a. "Look, we have been having considerable success with this method. Why should we gamble and make a change in critical times like these?"
   b. "Gosh, I think your ideas are terrific. But to tell you the truth, my boss just can't see something new like this. I just don't think she would buy it."

4. In the following dialogues, identify the type of conflict and then structure an appropriate way to manage it:

a. JOHN: I think this organization stinks. You are a poor manager. In fact, I have an eight-year-old sister who can handle people better than you can.

BILL: This is a good organization. I can't for the life of me understand why you feel this way. No one else feels this way. Several feel this is the best organization they have worked for.

b. JOHN: I think you should give me a raise for each good idea I have given this firm.

BILL: I never give raises for doing your normal job. You were hired to give good ideas.

Notes

1. Lyman K. Steil, interview with *U.S. News and World Report* May 26, 1980.

2. Ibid.

3. Gerald R. Miller and Mark Steinberg, *Between People: A New Analysis of Interpersonal Communication* (Chicago: Science Research Associates, 1975), pp. 260–270.

Another Look: Turning Listening into a Powerful Presence

Those of us who specialize in training and human resource development know the importance of perfecting listening skills—our own and others'. But often-powerful, unconscious factors combine to keep us from becoming good listeners.

You probably don't have any trouble listening and responding to a subject you like or can relate to. But if you're like most people, you lose focus after a presenter says something that doesn't make sense. You lose patience when someone takes too long to get to the point. And you may lose interest when you find the speaker is boring and the message is irrelevant.

Why is it so hard to control our concentration? How can we stay focused longer? What can be done to strengthen our retention? In short, what does it take to be a great listener?

Let's begin by defining the average listener so that we can better distinguish the excellent listener. A merely adequate listener is someone who slips in and out of focus in a conversation, gets only the gist of what is said, and provides only minimal feedback or response.

Present issues

The better-than-average listener is keenly aware of these important issues:

- **p**artnership
- **r**eviewing systematically
- **e**ffort
- **s**tar events
- **e**mpathy
- **n**eutralizing snap judgments
- **t**enacity

The first letters of those issues spell out "present" (as in, being fully present). Let's look at each one.

PARTNERSHIP Listening in conversation is typically viewed as a thought process only. Too many of us are quick to accept, albeit unconsciously, the popular wisdom that a listener's first—and—only priority is to receive a speaker's information accurately. But is listening really only a lonely stroll down a one-way street? What about matters of rapport and relationship in conversation? of feedback and perceived commitment? Surely,

conversations succeed best as dialogues not as parallel monologues that may only occasionally intersect.

Everyone has a need to be fully understood, fully received. That's why appropriate reaction or response is a credential of the committed listener. Remember that feeling you had as a speaker the last time someone affirmed or acknowledged what you said? You felt great! But we tend to be frugal with our feedback, often displaying detached attention with scant involvement. (We may be "in," but not "come to the door.") Eye contact often serves as the only evidence of connection. Is the conventional thinking wrong? No, it has just always been incomplete.

In today's more team-oriented work environments, a wider perspective is needed to help us collaborate with others for mutual benefit. Conversations take time to pull themselves together (sometimes a connection isn't even made). Withholding our feedback (problem solving?) may leave a trainee feeling uncertain (wondering whether communication took place), a customer deprived interpersonally (missing an expected reaction or response), or a staff member feeling devalued (not worthy of attention).

Connect better by letting more of your listening show. The other person is more likely to open up and offer more useful information. Think of the ramifications of that in training classes, team meetings, and sales interviews.

REVIEWING SYSTEMATICALLY As listeners, our job is to understand. But it is also to be understanding. In your efforts to understand another person's reality, know the wisdom of taking stock. Now and then, check with the speaker to make sure you both agree on the intended meaning. Too many listeners get caught up in fact-finding and fail to take advantage of that quality-assurance measure. Besides, taking a moment to paraphrase what you heard can give you welcome relief from having to constantly process information.

Consider, for example, the benefits of such summarizing statements in the following dialogue:

A: "I'm thinking about . . . but I don't know if it's the best thing for the department right now."

B: "So you're sort of 'on the fence' and unsure which way to turn . . .?"

continued

Turning Listening into a Powerful Presence, *continued*

A: "Exactly. I think the idea is good, but getting others to buy in may be a problem."

B: "In other words, you see some merit, but selling others on the idea may be tough."

A: "Yeah. They tend to be bottom-line thinkers and a pretty skeptical bunch."

Restatement takes little time and can even save you some time in the long run. Actively testing your assumptions—on a selective basis—can be a surge forward even when seemingly backtracking. Note, too, that it lets others know that you understand (or are trying to) and that you care.

EFFORT   Are you a reactive listener? Do you place most of the responsibility for your listening on the shoulders of the speaker? Many people do. They say they will listen, but only if the speaker and message are sufficiently concise, clear, interesting, and relevant. Alas, far too few speakers measure up: there simply may not be enough happening on the verbal level to anchor our ears. Instead, take the initiative and be a proactive listener. Don't count on the speaker. Make a conscious commitment to develop your own skills to cope with distraction and to compensate for speakers' shortfalls.

For starters, recognize the demons of distraction, distortion, and defensiveness. Savvy listeners keep them at bay by grounding themselves in astute observation and response. Pledge to be more observant of, say, team members, and increase both your level and range of responsiveness.

For example, how many of us in conversation notice an expectant face, a surprised or happy look, or a sardonic smile? Try to react and respond more often to what the speaker is expressing. That keeps you in the moment and also helps speakers focus their message. Also work to enlarge your repertoire of appropriate responses, which can make you a more interesting listener.

Guard against hearing what you expect or want to hear (a challenge for us all). Use paraphrasing and questioning to avoid distorting understanding. Conscientiously clarify meaning to prevent defensive reactions that can block your perception.

Realize that your feedback is crucial for the success of a conversation. Don't hide behind a silent, deadpan demeanor; intake on its own holds little interest for either listeners or speakers. Adopting a more open, inclusive listening style shows your involvement, and keeps you focused externally and not driven by your own internal conversation.

Bear in mind, too, that when speech enters our ears, the words are only a part of the process. The full meaning of the message is found not only in the spoken words, but also in the actions taken to deliver them: voice tone, gesture, and posture. With practice, you will become more attuned to those elements.

STAR EVENTS   We are all allergic, interpersonally speaking. That is, there is often something in a speaker's behavior—a word or phrase, gesture, facial expression, or style of speaking—that causes us to overreact. If we're not careful, such emotional triggers, or star events, can sidetrack our thinking, and cause us to "lose" the speaker. Star events can stop concentration in its tracks, before it can get past the roadblock and back on course.

Get to know your own personal star events. Discovering what tends to stall your mind and ruffle your emotional feathers will help you take such turbulence in stride. For example, how do you react when someone says to you, "You're not listening!"? What does it do to your mental serenity to hear, "That's a good idea, but . . ." or "We've always done it that way"? Do you become defensive? Do you feel put down? Do you bristle with irritation?

Strong disagreement, a speech impediment, a racial slur, a mispronounced word, and poor grammar are just a few things that can cause us to lose focus. Don't let them; at those moments when concentration slips, act! Ask an open-ended, clarifying question (such as, "Why do you say that?"). Restate what you think the speaker said: "So you feel if it's not broken, why fix it?" A neutral response can help you cope with swerves of thought and keep the connection. As in basketball when the referee blows the whistle, you have to "reset."

EMPATHY   People think and they feel. You know that your feelings are real. On some level, you also know that other people's feelings are just as real to them. It's one thing to think along with a speaker and another to feel along. Too often, we approach listening as an intellectual exercise. For all its sophistication, our cerebral style has its off-putting aspects. We need to work with emotion as well. Otherwise, co-workers and key contacts may play it

continued

Turning Listening into a Powerful Presence, *continued*

close to the vest because they feel they are inhabiting an emotionless landscape.

How many of us in conversation might think to say something like, "That must be hard" or "That must really make you feel good"? Such responses show sensitivity, and the speaker responds in kind.

Don't think you have to always agree with the expressed feelings to acknowledge that they are registering on your personal Richter scale. But to do that takes both will and skill. We are neither accustomed nor attuned to picking up on the emotions of others; we resonate more readily to the realm of ideas. We all need practice at that. Watch what other listeners do and observe what they say. That can greatly expand your listening-response repertoire, making you a better listener.

NEUTRALIZING SNAP JUDGMENTS   Have you noticed how quick we are to judge others? How much pride we take in being able to size up people in an instant? No, it's not easy to keep an open mind. But it is necessary, and it marks a true leader.

Perhaps the most common—and self-defeating—mistake we make as listeners is to give short shrift to people and their viewpoints. This person speaks with a lisp. That one has a sizable space between two upper-front teeth. To our judgmental eyes and ears, it is doubtful that they will repay us with listening that has value.

It is normal, too, to react negatively or defensively when presented with a different or "wrong" point of view. More than we like to admit any challenge to our own pet beliefs or ideas may elicit strong resistance on our part.

Qualities like good, bad, right, and wrong are important categories, but they should be permeable. Make no mistake: Too hasty an assessment undermines our efforts to get needed information from others to accomplish strategic goals.

But we can override our reflexes. We can develop a higher threshold for tolerating differences. That takes discipline and mental toughness. But the payback—in terms of saved time, enhanced productivity, and greater satisfaction—is worth it.

TENACITY   Most listeners keep a safely detached distance from a speaker. That makes tracking difficult. Excellent listeners are proactive participants in a conversation. Not willing to leave responsibility for understanding to a speaker, they strategically pursue meaning by design. They seek to take the full measure of the spoken message and to let that show. That means relating to both cognitive and emotional aspects of the message. They try to connect all of the dots of a speaker's experience. That includes exploring beneath the surface to excavate the deeper meaning (reading between the lines).

The average listener is ambivalent about intervening, often preferring to wait until the other person asks a question or finishes a complete thought. But excellent listeners know that response does not have to be invasive or interruptive. For misplaced etiquette, they substitute a closer reading of the situation and then seize opportunities to bring a speaker closer, engender trust, and achieve a greater flow of information.

Plan to be a more tenacious listener. Recognize the following facts about feedback:

- The fortunes of conversation fluctuate with that of feedback.
- Responsive feedback is a solution to navigating mental potholes and detours (star events) along the road to listening.
- Feedback helps speakers manage their speaking.

As a manager of training, human resources, or sales, you have an important stake in improving the conversation process.

Keep your listening sharp by exercising it. With practice—in doing and observing—those elements will soon become a natural part of you. You can then take pride in knowing that you have elevated yourself from being an average listener to becoming a truly excellent one.

Source: Richard M. Harris, "Turning Listening Into a Powerful Presence," *Training & Development*, July 1997, pp. 9–10. Reprinted from *Training & Development*. © July 1997 the American Society for Training & Development. Reprinted with permission. All rights reserved.

Another Look: Six Ways to Be a Better Listener

What is the best way to get employees, friends, customers, and significant others to feel that you care about what they say? Listen to them! Though that should hardly be surprising, listening is a skill that every one of us could improve.

So, what can you do to improve your listening effectiveness? Here are six ways.

1. *Let the other person finish speaking, and encourage him or her to go on.* The very best listeners are people who will wait to hear all that you have to say before they respond. They wait, and they let you finish. They don't cut you off. They don't interject. They don't go off on their own tangent. And they don't assume that they know what you are going to say before you say it. Instead, they show you that they want to hear what you have to say—by letting you say it. In addition:

- Give the person verbal messages that you are following what is being said. For example, use expressions such as, "umm-hmm," "I see," and "Is that right?"

- Don't get in someone's way by asking excessive questions, giving advice, or diverting the communication to a topic that you want to talk about.

- Be silent after the person has finished talking. Don't assume there's nothing more to be said. Being silent encourages the speaker to continue.

2. *Use your body language to demonstrate that you are listening.* According to Steven R. Covey in *The Seven Habits of Highly Effective People,* communication experts estimate that our words represent only 10 percent of our communication. Our sounds represent another 30 percent, and our body language represents 60 percent. Use all of those modes to help people open up to you. Specifically:

- Face them, look at them, and give them your full, undivided attention. Remember how it feels if someone you are talking to isn't paying attention to you.

- Maintain comfortable eye contact. Look into their eyes, but don't stare. Look away when it seems natural to do so.

- Mirror body language. You don't want the other person to have to talk up or down to you. So, if he or she is already sitting, you should sit too.

- Use your body movements to encourage communication. For example, nod for understanding, move your arms for enthusiasm, and avoid playing with anything (such as your keys, ears, or watch) with your hands.

- Encourage communication through the sound of your voice. For example, vary the pitch of your voice so the person can hear your concern, support, and interest in hearing more.

3. *Focus on what the person is saying, not on your response.* If you really want to hear and understand what someone is saying, you need to pay attention to what they are saying. Though that may sound simple, it is often hard because we allow ourselves to think about other things while we are listening. And what we often pay attention to is our response. Here's how to do better:

- Mentally paraphrase what people are saying.

- Consider what is new to you. What are you learning? What is interesting?

- Don't assume you know what people are going to say next.

- Check your understanding. Are people saying what you assume they are, or are they really saying something else?

4. *Put your tendency to evaluate on hold.* When we judge and approve or disapprove of what people are saying, we close the door to really hearing them. We often make assumptions, jump to conclusions, and quit listening mentally. Instead, do the following:

- When listening, try not to judge or evaluate what the other person is saying. The more you evaluate, the more you become blinded by your own point of view and the less you really listen. For example, if you conclude that an idea is ridiculous even before you finish hearing it, you are less apt to hear everything that a speaker has to say because your mind is already coming up with reasons the idea won't work.

- Try to understand what a person is saying from his or her point of view. Try to keep an open mind about what is being said. There are as many points of view as there are people.

- Understand that our tendency to evaluate becomes worse when we become involved emotionally. So, be aware of your feelings and emotions.

continued

Six Ways to Be a Better Listener, *continued*

Make an extra effort not to let your emotions impair your ability to listen. Know that one of the quickest ways to ruin effective communication—by shutting it down or provoking a defensive response—is to make a negative, judgmental statement about the person who is speaking.

5. *Try to see things from the speaker's perspective.* Go beyond the content of the words. A good listener will do more than listen to the words; he or she will also try to understand "where the speaker is coming from." A good listener knows that the words we use, even when carefully chosen, often represent little more than a rough attempt to communicate what we really mean. To guard against that:

- Recognize that the speaker is coming from a different perspective than yours; try to understand it.

- Ask yourself what the person is feeling. Is he or she afraid, hurt, angry, or upset?

- Ask yourself what the person really means to say.

- Ask yourself how the person perceives things. Remember that people see many things different from the way you do.

6. *Let a speaker know you hear and understand.* But to be a really good listener, you need to do more than just hear and understand. You need to make the person feel heard and understood. Paraphrasing, clarifying, and summarizing what is said are ways to accomplish that. Don't take over the conversation; just try to confirm that you understand. For example, try repeating one of the person's key words. Notice the difference that makes in helping him or her feel heard and understood. The following tips are adapted from People Skills, a book on interpersonal communication by Robert Bolton:

- Reflect some of the content of what a speaker says. To reflect means to paraphrase back to a speaker the essence of what was said, felt, or meant. For example, "So, you had to start over from scratch."

- Reflect a speaker's meaning. Can you restate more concisely the essence of what he or she meant to say? For example, "They ruined it, didn't they?"

- Reflect a speaker's feelings. What do you think a speaker feels or felt about what he or she is telling you? For example, "That must have been agonizing."

- Ask necessary clarification and follow-up questions. For example, "What did that involve?"

- Consider summarizing the overall message. For example, "What a pain!"

If you practice those six ways, you will demonstrate that you hear, care, and understand. And who knows? You just may have saved an employee's day, a friendship, a customer, or a marriage.

Source: Paul C. Blodgett, "Six Ways to Be a Better Listener," *Training & Development,* July 1997, pp. 11–12. Reprinted from *Training & Development.* © July 1997 the American Society for Training & Development. Reprinted with permission. All rights reserved.

Another Look: In Any Field, People Skills Are Valued
Above All in Managers

Top salesmen do not necessarily make good sales managers. Top production workers do not necessarily make good foremen. Top teachers do not necessarily make good principals. And the list goes on.

In any line of work, the ability to be an outstanding performer does not always translate into the ability to be a good manager.

Many skills are transferable, of course. Skill in getting along with others is perhaps the No. 1 management credential, just as it is a top asset for the rank and file.

The work ethic that helps someone prosper in an entry-level job will continue to be a valuable tool in management. But there's a big change when a first-time supervisor is thrown a larger net of responsibility.

A manager becomes responsible for motivating others, for conveying or setting policies, and for being the relay point between those above and those below on the organizational ladder.

One of the biggest differences between management and nonmanagement is that the workday becomes consumed with meetings, budget-making, and, perhaps most unsettling of all, conflict resolutions. In general, the management paperwork is a piece of cake compared with the people part.

Suddenly, a worker's success no longer is measured by how well he or she performs individually. It is tied into how well the new manager encourages and enables others to perform.

Woe to the star performer who always paddled a skilled but solo route through the company. There is a new, unfamiliar standard for performance evaluations. Managers are rated as much on people skills as on measurable output.

Some workplaces do a good job training and preparing workers for management roles. Others don't. In fact, most don't. Most organizations see good people in the ranks, tap them for promotions, then trust them to do well.

Many adapt and prosper. They find that management is a day-to-day learning experience. Their individual experience expands geometrically. They become more valuable to their employer.

But neophyte managers must know this: You won't believe how often you will be called upon to manage or resolve conflicts.

A survey of executives by Accountemps asked, "In general, what percentage of management time is wasted on resolving personality conflicts?" While I question the use of the word "wasted," it does indicate that most managers would prefer doing something other than adjudicating spats.

The average response of those polled was 18 percent—not quite double what the average response was to the same question a decade earlier.

Source: Reprinted from Diane Stafford, "In Any Field, People Skills Are Valued Above All in Managers," Provo, UT, *The Daily Herald*, September 20, 1998, p. C3. Reprinted with permission of Knight-Ridder/Tribune Information Services.

A Case in Point: A Hot Traveler and a Hot Motel Manager

The Motel Manager's Story

A fellow from a city several hundred miles away has just checked into your motel. He gives the impression that he is a big-shot government worker. After a short visit to his room, he storms into your office, claiming his air conditioner is faulty. You have recently spent $75 to repair the unit in his room. You are certain that he must have banged it with his fist and that he is responsible for the trouble with the unit. You are not about to let him push you around.

The Traveler's Story

You have just settled into a rather dumpy motel. It is mid-August, and the temperature is 109 degrees. You flip on the switch to the air conditioner; there is a buzz, a hum, and smoke starts to pour out of the vents of the air conditioner. After several bangs with your fist, the smoke vanishes, but the air conditioner will not work. You are hot and tired, and wish you had selected a better motel. At that point, you storm into the motel manager's office, inform him that he runs a cheap, dumpy, and poorly cared-for motel. You demand that he rush immediately to your room and repair your air conditioner.

Questions

1. What would you recommend be done by the traveler and the motel manager using the skills and techniques presented in this chapter?
2. What could the traveler do to solve his problem and also be a good communicator?
3. What could the motel manager do to reduce the conflict?

A Case in Point: Sears: In with the New, Out with the Old

Ed Brennan chose Arthur Martinez to succeed him as CEO of Sears, partly, says Brennan, because the two men think so much alike. In fact, they couldn't be more different.

FORTUNE: *What is Sears?*

Brennan: Sears is a great American retailer providing merchandise and merchandise-related services to the consumer at competitive prices with excellent quality.

Martinez: Sears is a moderate-price department store. This resolves a fairly major identity crisis. When I came in, we didn't know if we were a discounter or a specialty store or a department store.

FORTUNE: *Have Sears' competitors changed?*

Brennan: As we improved our merchandise mix, we had to expand the competitive base. At the low end, you're competing with the discounter. At the high end, with the department store. And in the middle, you're competing by product line.

Martinez: Sure. Because we're in multiple lines of business, we have multiple sets of competitors. But you can't keep the universe on your radar screen. We said, "We're not going to compete against Wal-Mart and Kmart in apparel. We're going to compete against mall-based department stores and specialty stores. We'll be the price leader." You could drive yourself crazy worrying about everybody else.

FORTUNE: *Has Sears' target customer changed?*

Brennan: No. Not really. The customer who buys appliances or lawnmowers from us covers a very broad economic spectrum.

Martinez: Yes. Strange as it may sound, nobody in the company really understood who was shopping in the departments, who was making the purchase decisions. In almost every case, it was the woman in the family. And we didn't seem to care very much about her. The businesses we seemed to care most about were male oriented: hardware, tools, automotive. There was a mistaken belief that these purchases were predominantly male driven.

continued

Sears: In with the New, Out with the Old, *continued*

FORTUNE: *What is the most important characteristic of a good manager?*

Brennan: Conviction.

Martinez: I can only tell you what has served me well. And that is a very open attitude. A willingness to try things, to let people try things. To be a sort of loose type. And not treating mistakes as fatal.

Questions

1. Now that you have read this case, describe to a friend what it has to do with interpersonal communication. What did you learn from this case?

2. How did Ed Brennan and Arthur Martinez differ?
3. Did their communication styles have anything to do with their effectiveness at Sears?
4. Which person would you prefer to work for? Why?

Source: Patricia Sellers, "Sears: In with the New . . . , Out with the Old," p. 98. Excerpted from the October 16, 1995 issue of FORTUNE by special permission; copyright 1995, Time Inc.

Effective Teamwork in Organizations

- What makes a good leader in a small group?

- Why is involvement of all group members so important for the success of a group?

- Why are cohesiveness and conformity important for a group to function effectively?

- What are the five steps of problem solving?

- How does one structure a group?

- What is the brainstorming approach, and when is it used?

- What are the four rules of brainstorming?

- What is the nominal group process?

- How can criteria help in the decision-making process?

- How does one state a criterion?

The answers to these and other questions are coming up next in Chapter 13 . . .

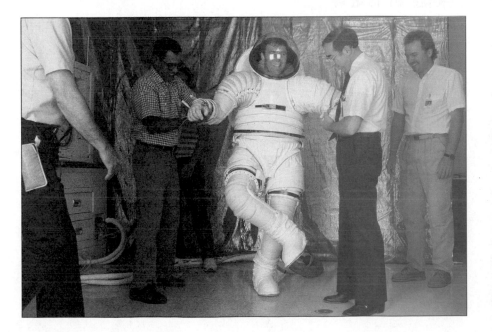

The use of groups to solve problems is so widespread that most people have questions about how to make group processes more effective. They want to know how to improve group action, how to make leadership more meaningful, and how to get people to work together.

The first characteristic of problem-solving groups is that they focus on tasks—they want to find a solution to a problem. The individuals involved come together to work toward the accomplishment of a task. A typical problem-solving group is a work team in an organization.

The second characteristic of problem-solving groups is that the individual members communicate face-to-face.

The combination of these characteristics yields a definition of a small problem-solving group: "Several people, but in small enough numbers to permit communication with all other members, who are assembled face-to-face for the purpose of solving a problem."[1] **Small-group problem solving** requires a variety of forms of communication, which are known by different names—for example, committees, teams, panels, conferences, boards, and councils. At the university, committees are appointed; in a government agency, teams are created; in a research foundation, panels are appointed; in a union organization, conferences are called. In all these settings, these small groups are assigned to work at solving a problem.

In this chapter, we focus on how to make group teamwork effective by discussing some general characteristics of groups and by presenting procedures for effective problem solving by groups.

General Characteristics of Groups

Because principles of communication discussed in the previous two chapters apply equally well to interpersonal communication in small groups, we focus attention in this chapter on five basic characteristics of **small groups** that help explain the behavior of people in them. Those characteristics are group leader attitudes, leader behaviors, communication patterns, communication climate, and cohesiveness. Regardless of the group's agenda, or content issues, all small groups have universal process issues.

Leader Attitudes

Leadership in groups or work teams is not always a formally delegated authority. Nevertheless, for groups to excel, especially in problem-solving tasks, the leaders must have seven characteristics:

1. *Trust* in the other group members, regardless of their rank or position. You can't expect others to go all out for you if they think you don't believe in them.

2. *A vision of what is possible.* Generally, the most profitable vision is the long-term view. Sometimes a quick fix is needed, but the long-term ramifications of a group's efforts must be anticipated by the leader.

3. *A cool head* to deal with difficult, often exasperating pressures and conflicts of opinion in a rational, objective manner.

4. *A willingness to encourage risk.* Nothing discourages group members like the feeling that if they fail in any way, disaster will result. People need the latitude to fail and learn from their mistakes.

5. *Expertise.* Leaders need to know what they are talking about or be willing to learn. Such learning can come from often unpredictable sources.

Each team member plays an important role in the success of the team.

6. *An openness to dissent.* Group members cannot contribute fully if they cannot speak up. Encourage differing points of view, even when they may be unpopular or poorly expressed.

7. *An ability to simplify* all that has been said into a concise plan of action. You need to see the big picture in order to set a course, communicate it, and maintain it. Don't get tangled in details; keep it simple.[2]

Leader Behaviors

Leadership consists of behaviors that keep a group together and working to solve a problem. Group members' behaviors can be grouped into **roles.** A *role* is the pattern that characterizes an individual's contributions to the group. In other words, what an individual does and says in a group can be thought of as either a contribution to or distraction from the functioning of the group.

Effective group leaders are people who act like leaders

People often talk about the role a person is playing in a group. Leadership consists of performing roles that keep a group together and working on a task. So leadership is a combination of roles that are taken by members of a group. Kenneth D. Benne and Paul Sheats compiled a list of *functional roles* of group members that help the group accomplish its task, that promote and maintain group member relationships, and that help meet individuals' needs, although they may on occasion distract from either the task or the maintenance goals or both.[3] Some of the major roles that group members may perform are listed here. Keep in mind that leadership behaviors should contribute to task and maintenance goals.

Task Roles: To Solve the Problem and Perform the Task

1. *Initiator.* Suggests methods, goals, and procedures; starts the group moving in a positive direction by proposing a plan.

2. *Information seeker.* Solicits ideas, data, personal experiences, and reports.

3. *Information giver.* Offers ideas, data, personal experiences, and factual statements.

4. *Opinion seeker.* Asks for statements of belief, convictions, values, or expressions of feeling.

5. *Opinion giver.* States own beliefs, convictions, values, and feelings.

6. *Clarifier.* Interprets issues, elaborating on ideas expressed by others, giving examples or illustrations.

7. *Coordinator.* Demonstrates relationships between ideas, restating them, summarizing, and offering integrated statements for consideration.

8. *Energizer.* Prods group to greater activity, stimulating others to action.

9. *Procedure developer.* Handles such tasks as making seating arrangements, running the projector, passing out papers.

10. *Recorder.* Keeps written record of meeting on paper, recording ideas on chart or chalkboard.

Maintenance Roles: To Foster Member Satisfaction

1. *Supporter.* Praises, expressing warmth, indicating solidarity.

2. *Harmonizer.* Mediates differences among others, conciliating.

3. *Follower.* Listens to others, accepting group decisions.

4. *Tension reliever.* Introduces humor, joking, relaxing others, diverting attention from tense situations.

5. *Gatekeeper.* Facilitates participation of everyone in group, bringing in members who might not speak, preventing dominance by one or two members, maintaining permissive atmosphere.

Personal Roles: Behaviors to Meet Individual Needs at the Expense of the Group

1. *Blocking.* Constantly raising objections, insisting nothing can be done, introducing irrelevant digression.

2. *Aggressing.* Deflating status of others, expressing disapproval and ill will.

3. *Recognition seeking.* Boasting, calling attention to self, seeking sympathy or pity, claiming credit for ideas.

4. *Confessing.* Engaging in personal catharsis and using group as audience for mistakes.

5. *Clowning.* Diverting attention of group to tangents, engaging in horseplay and ridicule, disrupting with cynical comments.

6. *Dominating.* Giving directions, ordering people, interrupting, and insisting on own way.

7. *Special-interest pleading.* Supporting personal projects and interests, pressing others for support, acting as representative or advocate for other groups.

A leader performs more leadership roles than do other members of the group. An organization or formal group often designates a person as its leader or head to represent the group or carry out some of the organizing and mechanical chores needed for the group to complete its work. Groups are sometimes categorized according to the pattern of leadership roles taken in the group. For example, a democratic group is one in which the leadership roles are shared somewhat equally by all members of the group. An autocratic group is one in which the leadership roles are performed almost exclusively by one person. A laissez-faire group is one in which the leadership roles are not performed or are only used minimally. Most problem-solving groups need someone to serve as a designated leader or as a chairperson who can take the initiative in getting the group organized and functioning.

A leader is a person who performs the most leadership roles in a group.

Communication Patterns

In problem-solving groups, greater efficiency is likely to be achieved in completing the task if agreement is reached on the communication patterns to be used. In small groups, each member cannot speak whenever he or she wishes. Out of courtesy and to hear what others have to say, members of the group take turns talking. Nevertheless, some members tend to contribute more, while others contribute less.

For example, a person with status in the group may find that he or she has become the center of **interaction,** so that other members of the group speak to this person and then he or she talks to the group as a whole. The result is a *hierarchical* communication pattern (see Figure 13.1). In this pattern, the high-status person is in the center and all communications appear to flow to and from her or him; little, if any, communication takes place directly between other group members. Although this is not the preferred pattern from a communication point of view, it is sometimes used by authoritarian leaders with varying degrees of success.

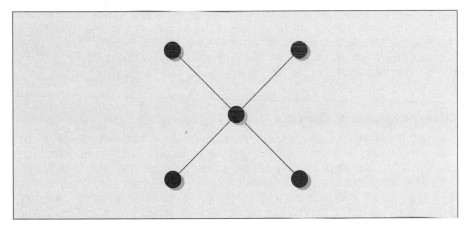

FIGURE 13.1 Hierarchical communication pattern.

On other occasions, especially with newly formed groups, people speak only to those members nearest them. There is little group interaction, and messages are passed along, creating a chain pattern (see Figure 13.2).

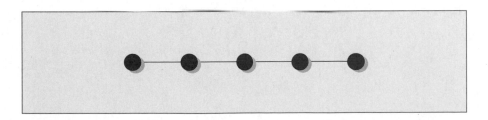

FIGURE 13.2 Chain communication pattern.

FIGURE 13.3   Isolate communication pattern.

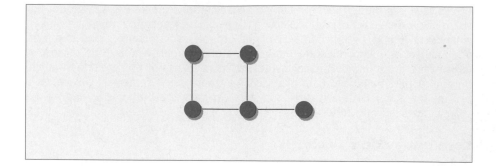

The chain communication pattern is inefficient and is quickly replaced by a pattern of scattered communications. For example, if one group member is reticent (speaking only when drawn into the conversation) while the other members openly communicate with one another, an *isolate* pattern develops (see Figure 13.3). The isolate communication pattern is also inefficient and may result in some other pattern of communication. In some instances, the group may achieve efficiency by having two or three of its more communicative or outgoing members assigned the task of communicating with the isolates as well as with one another.

Many other possible communication patterns exist, but the one that is usually most desirable for small groups is the *completely connected (com-con)* pattern (see Figure 13.4). This pattern results when every member of the group makes a significant contribution to the accomplishment of the task and interacts regularly with every other member of the group. Although the com-con pattern may require more time than other patterns, the cohesiveness and flexibility of the group increases because members feel they have influenced the group as often as they want to. In general, discrepancies of status, power, influence, and control are minimized, and members feel a sense of belonging. Teamwork seems to be heightened.

Communication Climate

The **communication climate** of the group is the prevailing atmosphere or conditions regarding the exchange of information, ideas, and feelings within the group setting. The climate is revealed most clearly by the often subtle verbal and nonverbal interactions between group members. The leader has, depending on his or her power and style, a more or less significant influence on the communication climate of the group. The communication style of each member of the group also contributes to the overall climate.

FIGURE 13.4   Completely connected, or com-con, communication pattern.

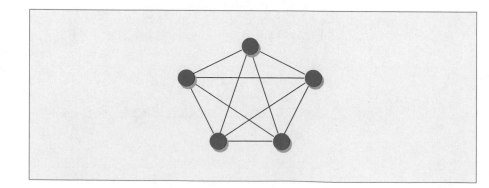

Jack R. Gibb identified individual behaviors that created two different general climates in groups: a defensive climate and a supportive climate.[4] A **defensive climate** often leads to hostility and destructive group relations. A **supportive climate** creates helpful, cooperative, positive relationships.

Defensive When attitudes, assumptions, and subtle behaviors are perceived by other members of the group as threatening and potentially punishing, especially to a person's sense of self-respect, then the climate is defensive. Behaviors that may be interpreted as threatening include the following:

- *Evaluative.* A tone of voice, a physical reaction, the content of a statement, or judgments that indicate that a person is less competent, inferior, or out of line.

- *Controlling.* Behaviors and verbal messages that seem intended to limit, block, alter, or impose attitudes, feelings, or behaviors on a person that he or she does not want.

- *Deceptive.* Devices, tricks, and ploys that are interpreted as having some hidden or unstated intention or that appear to involve the withholding of information.

- *Noncaring.* Communicative behaviors that indicate a lack of concern for the plight of others, that seem cold, detached, and impersonal.

- *Superior.* Ways of interacting that imply inequality and superiority, especially when tinged with an attitude of arrogance, tending to demean the other.

- *Dogmatic.* Statements, vocal tones, and postures that imply an attitude of absolute certainty or that suggest that no other alternatives are available or none will be considered.

- *Hostile.* Negative evaluations, limitations on and blocks to the accomplishment of goals, deceptiveness and withholding of information, lack of concern about what happens to others, arrogance and demeaning attitudes, and an unwillingness to compromise.

When threats are posed to such an extent that hostility and destructive drives are excited, physical attacks are not uncommon. If a person chooses not to engage in physical violence, he or she might react in one of the following ways:

- Complete avoidance of interaction

- Suppression of topics in the areas of hostility

- Pretense that no threat exists

- Verbal aggression as a substitute for physical violence

None of these avoidance and adjustive reactions is conducive to a positive interpersonal climate; each tends to produce a negative spiral, resulting in distortion and misunderstanding.

Supportive A supportive climate exists when parties in the interaction feel that they have a sense of worth and importance. Supportiveness involves helping others attain goals that are important to them. Such help is provided by understanding what others want to accomplish and by encouraging them to try new approaches without fear of reprisal. Supportiveness is communicated most clearly by the following types of responses:

A supportive climate is effective in a group because all the members feel they can say what they think.

- *Descriptive.* Statements that are nonevaluative and that provide reports of information.

- *Problem-oriented.* Ways of reacting that focus on problems to be solved, rather than on what can and cannot be done.

- *Open and honest.* Reactions that communicate to others a willingness and ability to express positive interests and helpfulness as well as reservations about what is happening.

- *Warm and caring.* Expressions and behaviors that indicate understanding and empathy with the goals of the other; listening to understand what the other means so that help can be provided.

- *Egalitarian.* Comments and reactions that suggest attitudes of equality and a willingness to participate in a shared relationship, rather than in a superior/demanding, subordinate/complying one.

- *Provisional.* Communicative behavior that allows for potential error, indicating that both parties are involved in working out ways of helping one another where both can make contributions and be right some of the time.

Cohesiveness

If group members feel like a team and genuinely care about each other, the group is more productive.

Productivity is usually highest when the group is cohesive. Teamwork, group morale, and team spirit also contribute to **cohesiveness.** For example, when the spirit of a basketball team is high, members are dedicated to the entire team, they place great value on working hard for the team, and they have a deep sense of belonging to the team. Because of this commitment, members have a concern for one another and are willing to exert great effort to accomplish the goals of the group. Such concern and effort usually result in increased productivity.

Although cohesiveness tends to produce higher levels of group accomplishment, it also places demands on members of the group. When membership in a group is attractive and important to an individual, the norms or expected and acceptable behaviors exert a strong influence on the individual. The stronger the influence of norms on behavior, the greater the likelihood of a person conforming to group expectations.

As a person comes to feel that a group provides satisfaction and benefits, the group more readily exerts influence over the person. Individuals who deviate from what is expected by the group often find themselves denied some of the benefits they expect through membership in the group. But adherence to norms and expectations tends to increase acceptance and cohesiveness. Feelings of warmth and confidence increase as acceptance and cohesiveness increase. Finally, membership in highly cohesive groups tends to reduce personal anxieties and increase a sense of personal value. Thus attractiveness leads to cohesion, cohesion leads to productivity, and adherence to norms leads to **conformity.** Conformity often leads to satisfaction and increased personal value.

In contrast, feelings of cohesiveness may be undermined by conflicts, divisive attitudes, emotional reactions, hostilities toward others, and defensiveness. When these feelings are held privately by group members and influence how individuals work in a group, they constitute a *hidden agenda.* That is, any desires, aspirations, feelings, and motives of group members that cannot be brought into the open and recognized directly operate in the group as hidden objectives. Like the formal or public agenda of a group, the hidden agenda is a schedule of desires to be achieved. In a highly cohesive group, members feel free to express their feelings rather than suppress them. In an uncohesive group, much time and energy may be wasted on a hidden agenda.

Groups can accomplish tasks that an individual would not attempt.

Understanding these four concepts of group interaction is crucial if you wish to be an effective group member. The next section of this chapter deals with procedures for group problem solving.

Steps of the Group Problem-Solving Process

The quality of any decision is a function of the process used in arriving at the decision. That is why so much time and effort is put into designing systems and procedures for doing things. For example, law enforcement agencies have been obligated, over the years, to adopt procedures for ensuring that the rights of defendants are protected. How defendants are handled, what is said to them, and when they are to be advised have been specified because the sequence has been found to influence the way in which decisions are made and how human rights are protected.

The quality of a good decision is often a function of the process used in making the decision.

Problem solving is based on a similar philosophy. The process that a group follows in solving problems affects the quality of the solutions. Group problem solving is at least a five-step process: (1) getting the group together and working, (2) stating and analyzing problem questions, (3) generating ideas for solving the problems, (4) selecting the most useful ideas for a solution, and (5) deciding which ideas will be used. The rest of this chapter systematically reviews these five steps.

1. Successfully Launching a Group

Getting a group together to work requires effective **group structuring.** A technique developed by R. Wayne Pace, Brent D. Peterson, and M. Dallas Burnett lists three specific skills or activities that organize a group and get it functioning properly: (1) planning for the group, (2) acquainting the group members with each other, and (3) orienting the group members.[5]

To *plan* for the group, do the following:

- Prepare a list of important ideas and topics for the group to discuss.

- Prepare an agenda that stimulates the group to act on the important ideas and topics. Include such items as the call to order, roll call, reading and approval of minutes of previous meeting, and introduction of guests. Order items of business according to importance, and be willing to skip low-priority items as necessary to stay on schedule. Allocate time for each item of business, and note times on agenda.

- Prepare the physical setting for the expected interaction of the group. Consider such things as seating arrangements, chalkboards, projectors, and handouts.

To *acquaint* group members, do the following:

- Introduce members to one another. This may be done formally, or informally with each member introducing himself or herself to the group.

- Ask each group member to share experiences and feelings with other group members. This opens the door for the development of genuine relationships.

To *orient* the group, do the following:

- Present the topic, objectives, and work to be completed by the group.

- Present the format to be followed, informing group members of the roles, hows, and whens of expected participation. If the group is to be unstructured, tell members this so they can act accordingly.

- Discuss whether or not the group is to make decisions and, if so, the decision-making process that will be employed.

- Assign specific roles or duties to each group member, as appropriate.

- Answer questions before the beginning of group interaction.

This approach takes time initially but saves time ultimately in that it helps groups quickly organize and begin functioning productively and efficiently. It applies to all types of groups but is vitally important for problem-solving groups. Once the group is together and ready to work, it can state the problem.

2. Articulating the Problem to Analyze It

What are the key features of precisely articulating a problem in the form of a question?

The second step in group problem solving involves analyzing a problem at hand and then articulating it in the form of a precise question to focus on how best to solve it. For example, if a labor union is concerned about its image, it might ask, "In what ways might we improve our image?" Let's examine this question to recognize the key features of an apt question.

First, a creative question asks, "Precisely what is to be changed?" In the sample question, the image is to be changed. Second, an effective question indicates what type of change is to occur. The sample question indicates that the image is to be improved—although it could be changed in other ways; for example, it could be reduced, lowered, or made less visible. Third, a creative problem question allows for many alternatives in solving the problem. In the sample question, the phrase "In what ways might" suggests that many alternatives are sought. Fourth, a creative problem question specifies who is expected to solve the problem. In the sample question, the who is "we," referring to the problem-solving group. After the problem has been stated and accepted by all members of the group, then it is time to move to the third step, generating ideas for solving the problems.

3. Generating Ideas for Solving the Problems

We shall present two approaches for generating ideas in groups: (1) brainstorming and (2) the nominal group process. Brainstorming is used when you have an interactive group that can talk, work, and get along together. The nominal group process is best used when you can expect only a limited amount of group interaction.

Brainstorming **Brainstorming** is used to identify and list—without the interference of critical and judgmental reactions—as many ideas as possible that could help solve a problem. Brainstorming can generate ideas on any kind of problem that has a wide range of potential solutions. It can answer questions such as these:

- "What information do we need?"

- "How might we get the information?"

- "What guidelines might be used to evaluate the ideas?"

- "What might we do?"

- "How might we put our ideas into effect?"

- "What might be the advantages and disadvantages of what we do?"

Brainstorming can produce large numbers of ideas for use in solving problems. It can also develop attitudes that improve individual idea finding.

The four basic rules governing brainstorming allow each individual in the group to contribute facts and experiences that other group members may not possess. Thus an atmosphere is created in which individual contributors may freely offer unusual ideas without fear of contradiction or evaluation. This enables a large number of possibilities to be produced in a short period of time. The four rules of brainstorming may be summarized as follows:

1. *Criticism is ruled out.* Judgmental thinking inhibits the entire process. Killer phrases—such as "We've never done it that way. It won't work. It's too expensive. That's too hard to administer. It needs more study. Let's be practical. It's not good enough."—should be banished from the session.

2. *Freewheeling is wanted.* The wilder the ideas, the better. Even impractical ideas may trigger practical suggestions from others. Let imagination soar and then bring it down to earth later.

3. *Quantity is wanted.* The larger the number of ideas, the greater the likelihood of usable ideas. Paring down a long list of ideas is easier than expanding a short list. Most likely the best ideas will be far down the list, because the routine ones will tend to be offered easily and quickly.

4. *Combination and improvement are sought.* Be constantly on the alert to piggyback onto the ideas of another person. In addition to contributing ideas of your own, make suggestions concerning how others' ideas can be bettered or how two or more ideas can be combined into a still better one.

When conducting a brainstorming session, follow these steps:

1. Review the problem question that has been previously determined by the group. No questions should be asked once the brainstorming session begins. All questions should be answered before the session begins.

2. Set a specific amount of time for the session to last. Stick with the time limits.

3. Follow all brainstorming rules faithfully. No one should criticize, belittle, or degrade the ideas of anyone else.

4. Throw the floor open to unrestricted presentation of ideas. As recognized by the leader—and leaders, do this quickly—participants should shout out all ideas, from crackpot to crackerjack.

5. Record the ideas through a tape recorder or a secretary, and prepare a copy of the list to be given to each participant following the session.

The brainstorming technique is generally used in groups to help them develop new ideas. Whenever a group faces a situation that requires creative problem solving, this technique can be effective. Brainstorming leads to better understanding of problems.

The Nominal Group Process   The **nominal group** process refers to "a structured group meeting in which participants alternate among silently thinking up ideas, listing ideas on a flip chart, and voting on ideas. The decision of the group is secured through ranking or rating of ideas."[6]

The nominal group process is used most effectively where the emphasis is on getting ideas for making decisions. When you want to get information and suggestions from a number of people, the nominal group process is especially appropriate if there are differences in power, rates of interaction, and status. This process tends to equalize such differences and allows group members to contribute their best ideas.

This technique requires preparation and involves approximately four steps.

1. Select and arrange a meeting room large enough to accommodate participants in groups of five to nine members at tables. Seat participants along each side and at one end of a rectangular table so as to create an open U-shape: put a flip chart at the open end of the table.

2. Provide the following supplies:

   a. Worksheets for each participant with question printed on top

   b. A flip chart for each table

   c. A roll of masking tape

   d. A pack of 3" × 5" cards for each table

   e. Felt pens for each table

   f. Paper and pencil for each participant

   Note: Since NGP meetings rely heavily on the posting of ideas in front of each small group, it is essential to have a flip chart or some other device for posting ideas for continuous viewing by the group. A chalkboard is undesirable for this purpose; however, sheets of newsprint, butcher paper, or other kinds of large sheets of paper can be used after they are attached to the wall or to a chalkboard.

3. Welcome participants and explain how the NGP works; stress the importance of the task and each member's contribution.

4. Place an NGP question on the flip chart to elicit ideas or information. Avoid questions that can be answered with a simple yes or no. Avoid questions that ask for decisions, such as whether something should be

Whether a meeting is formal or informal will vary based on the problem to be solved, the individual participants, and the company culture.

done. Phrase the question or questions to provide for the largest number of answers possible with such wording as:

a. What kinds of difficulties are being experienced?

b. In what ways might we reduce waste?

c. What are the ways in which we can increase production?

Some guidelines for conducting an NGP session follow:

1. **Silent generation of ideas in writing**

   a. Distribute sheets with question; read the question aloud and illustrate how specifically ideas should be listed.

   b. Indicate that each member should write ideas in short phrases or statements, working silently and independently.

   c. Give the group five minutes to write ideas without interruption; maintain the rule of silence firmly; discourage any attempts to work together.

   d. Call group up for movement to Step 2.

2. **Public portrayal of ideas in writing**

   a. A recorder asks for one idea from each member, going one at a time around the table. The recorder writes the idea on a flip chart at the head of the table and proceeds to the next group member in turn.

   b. Each idea is written in a short phrase of three or four words. Continue to record ideas until all ideas are publicly portrayed before the group, omitting duplicate items but listing variations of ideas.

   c. Restrain the group from making any comments about ideas until all suggestions are posted. Make the entire list visible to the group by tearing off sheets as they are filled and taping them to the wall or chalkboard.

3. Serial clarification of each idea

a. Serial clarification means taking each idea in the order listed on the sheets and talking about each one in that order.

b. The purpose of this stage is to clarify the meaning of each of the suggestions, *not* to argue its merits.

c. During the discussion period, team members should be making notes and recording their judgments of each item.

d. During the discussion period, participants are encouraged to provide brief analyses of the logic underlying each suggestion and the relative importance of the item in solving the problem.

e. Individuals should feel free to express agreement or disagreement with the analysis and the relative importance of the items.

f. The leader should keep the discussion moving so that all items are clarified and some expression of importance is attached.

4. Rank-ordering of priority items

a. Have the group identify, from the entire list of suggestions on the flip chart, a specific number of most important items. Anywhere from four to eight items might be indicated.

b. Have each group member write his or her priority items on separate 3" × 5" cards and rank-order the cards from one to seven by placing an appropriate number and drawing a circle around it in the upper left-hand corner of each card. For identification purposes, place the item numbers in the lower right-hand corner of each card.

c. Collect all the cards and shuffle them, recording each idea and its rank-order on a flip chart.

d. Study the rank-ordering and eliminate all items that did not receive any votes.

5. Discussion of initial rank-ordering

a. Since some items may be ranked differently by members of the group, it is advisable to increase the likelihood of making the most accurate decisions by reducing misinformation, by increasing clarification, and by allowing for the interpretation of items. Following the discussion, a final ranking will take place. Members need not change their original ranking, but they should vote differently if they have a new perspective on the items as a result of the discussion.

b. The discussion should take no longer than ten minutes and should consist of clarifying statements. Avoid focusing too much attention on the items discussed so you won't distort perceptions of items not commented upon.

6. Final ranking

a. In order to refine judgments of participants, the final ranking may also include a rating of each of the final-ranked items.

b. Instruct the group to choose the five most important items from the flip chart and list them in rank order on a sheet of paper as shown below in Table 13.1.

c. Collect all sheets. Post rankings and ratings on the flip chart for studying the group decisions.

d. Make plans for devising ways to implement ideas.

After ideas have been generated, using either the brainstorming approach or the nominal group process, the group can select the most useful ideas for a solution.

TABLE 13.1 *Ranking Priorities to Focus Decision Making*

LIST ITEM IN RANK ORDER (NUMBER)	PHRASE DESCRIBING ITEM ON FLIP CHART	RATING OF ITEM IN TERMS OF RELATIVE IMPORTANCE						
		UNIMPORTANT						IMPORTANT
_____	_____	1	2	3	4	5	6	7
_____	_____	1	2	3	4	5	6	7
_____	_____	1	2	3	4	5	6	7
_____	_____	1	2	3	4	5	6	7
_____	_____	1	2	3	4	5	6	7
_____	_____	1	2	3	4	5	6	7
_____	_____	1	2	3	4	5	6	7
_____	_____	1	2	3	4	5	6	7

---

4. Selecting the Most Useful Ideas for a Solution

The fourth step in group problem solving is to select from the ideas generated in Step 3 those that could be combined into a workable solution for the stated problem. One critical task is to develop a list of requirements that indicate the difference between an idea that is desirable and workable and one that is less satisfactory.

Criteria are standards by which one can determine which ideas are the most acceptable for solving a problem. Criteria represent guidelines for mentally testing the acceptability of a proposal or plan. They are phrased as statements that indicate the minimal requirements that any suggestion, idea, plan, or proposal must meet in order to be acceptable.

Criteria should be phrased in the following manner: "Anything that is done (idea or course of action) must meet the following requirements." They consist of declarative statements that specify what must and must not happen for a course of action to be considered acceptable:

- "The idea must . . ."

- "The idea must not . . ."

Decision-making standards or criteria are keys to effective decision making.

The clear and explicit statements of criteria bring both so-called logical and emotional reasons for making decisions to the surface for close scrutiny by all group members. In group problem solving, one major difficulty lies in getting all group members to reveal the criteria that they hold. In many cases, you may not even realize that you have a restriction you would like to impose on an idea until the idea is outlined in some detail. Therefore, listing as many criteria as possible may help in locating key restrictions that you and others may have overlooked.

In group problem solving and communication, it is often helpful to rank the criteria after a long list has been compiled. Criteria of high importance can be considered seriously, allowing less important ones to be modified or set aside as part of the process of arriving at agreement. After the ideas and criteria have been established, the group can finally decide which idea or ideas best solve the problem by meeting the established criteria.

5. Deciding Which Ideas Will Be Used

The fifth step in group problem solving is to decide which one of the potentially desirable and workable ideas will be used and how it will be put into practice. The group should make certain that all members are satisfied with the idea chosen because its implementation usually requires full support from the problem-solving group.

In large organizations with professional planners or a "plans" section or department, the task of preparing plans, developing operational procedures, and securing equipment is normally handled by planning professionals. Even with such staff available, however, selecting ideas and a general plan of implementation usually remains the work of the problem-solving group.

Ways of Making a Decision   In determining which problem-solving ideas should be used, one must understand the different ways of making decisions so that an appropriate approach can be selected. Occasionally, the issue and the cause unify the group so that each person fully subordinates personal differences to the interest of the group. The recommended action so captivates the group members that it transcends all differences and impels a *unanimous* decision.

Unanimity occurs only rarely. However, most of the time **consensus** can be achieved—provided a reasonably high level of open discussion has prevailed. Consensus is achieved by having the group members talk out their differences. Each member of the group must be given a full and uninhibited opportunity to express differences of opinion, to contribute to and influence the form of the action to be taken. Although making decisions by consensus may take more time than do other modes of decision making, it provides for the widest possible base of support and the resolution of as many differences as possible. Group members ideally should have at least some areas of strong agreement with the choice to be made, even though they may have some reservations.

"Majority rules" is the most common decision method, although it is not always appropriate.

Majority decision making is probably the most common method used in most areas of human endeavor, at least in democratic countries. Deliberative bodies usually accept the will of the majority. Decisions are made by identifying members of the majority and the minority points of view. This is accomplished by taking some type of vote or poll. Individuals are asked to indicate their preferences in one of the following ways: by saying aloud "aye" or "nay"; by raising their hands; by writing their preferences on slips of paper; or by a "division of the house," in which the individuals move to either side of the room to indicate their preference.

Decisions made on the basis of a **plurality** represent majority decision making except that the acceptable decision is the one supported by the largest number of individuals. The tally of those who approve and those who disapprove may be taken following the pattern of majority decision making. Decisions made by a *minority coalition,* by *unilateral action,* and by *inaction* are usually considered to be less desirable than are decisions arrived at through any of the other modes. Nevertheless, occasionally groups can be difficult to move to make a decision, even though a procedure is provided. Under those conditions, an informed minority or a single individual may proceed to make the choice, seeking the concurrence and sustaining vote of the entire group in the process.

Selecting an Appropriate Way   Each group must be encouraged to identify and adopt a specific decision-making procedure that is appropriate for the issue under discussion and the climate of the group. When a group is functioning at a high level of involvement and with mutual concern and enthusiasm, seeking unanimity or consensus may be appropriate. When agreement may be more difficult to achieve, majority and plurality procedures may be more appropriate. When the group is indecisive, inhibited, or unable to proceed with majority decisions, it may have to accept the alternatives favored by a strong minority or a well-informed individual. Inaction may be used strategically in making decisions, because it allows a choice to be made without requiring anyone to assume responsibility or blame for the action.

The quality of almost any decision is a function of the procedures one uses in arriving at the decision. For individuals to be committed to a course of action, they must feel that the choice of alternatives was arrived at in an acceptable way.

How can we select the best decision-making procedure?

Summary of Key Ideas

- The five characteristics of a small group are: group leader attitudes, leader behaviors, communication patterns, communication climate, and cohesiveness.

- The three primary types of roles that a group member may assume are: task, maintenance, and personal. A person may be involved in a variety of activities that are subsumed under each role.

- Group communication patterns, which are determined by the direction of communication interaction, may be arranged into four general types: hierarchical, chain, isolate, and com-con.

- The group communication climate may be either defensive or supportive.

- Cohesiveness tends to produce higher levels of productivity but demands that group members adhere to norms in order to achieve a level of conformity.

- The five-step process for group problem solving involves assembling the group, stating and analyzing the problem, generating possible solutions, selecting the most useful solutions, and deciding which solution will be implemented.

Key Terms, Concepts, and Names

Brainstorming	Leadership
Cohesiveness	Majority
Communication climate	Nominal group
Conformity	Plurality
Consensus	Roles
Criteria	Small group
Defensive climate	Small-group problem solving
Jack R. Gibb	Supportive climate
Group structuring	Unanimity
Interaction	

Questions and Exercises

1. Rank the following statements that might describe the characteristics of a good group. Place a 1 in front of the statement that you feel is the most important characteristic of a good group, a 2 in front of the next most important characteristic, and so on. Place a 12 in front of the statement least descriptive of a good group. When you have ranked all of the statements, discuss with a classmate why you both ranked them the way you each did.

   _____ A healthy competitiveness exists among members.

   _____ Everyone sticks closely to the point.

   _____ The group avoids conflict situations.

   _____ Members perform leadership functions.

   _____ Each member gives and receives feeling feedback.

   _____ The leader suggests a plan for each group meeting.

   _____ Aggression is openly expressed.

   _____ Informal subgroups develop spontaneously.

   _____ Members freely express negative feelings.

   _____ The goals of the group are clearly stated.

   _____ Information is freely shared among members.

   _____ Members' feelings are considered when tasks are performed.

2. Form a group with some friends and practice brainstorming using the following problems:

   a. How can an egg be packaged so that it will not break when dropped from a ladder?

   b. What adjustments would our society have to make if there were three sexes instead of two?

   c. Select one or two of the following diagrams. What might they be?

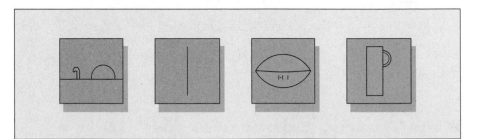

3. Criteria come into play in every situation in which a choice must be made between competing proposals, products, ideas, and even people. One way to learn how to identify and state criteria is to take a problem and make a list of criteria that might be used in judging from among possible ways of solving the problem. For example, suppose you feel that you want a new job. You have several alternatives, such as going to school, changing to a new job, and moving to a new location. What should you do?

   On a blank sheet of paper, list all the criteria you can think of that should govern the kind of decision you make. Now look over the list and assign a rank to each criterion. This will give you an opportunity to think about each criterion and to consider the importance of each one in evaluating your plan.

4. Answer the introductory questions at the beginning of the chapter.

Notes

1. R. Wayne Pace, Brent D. Peterson, and M. Dallas Burnett, *Techniques for Effective Communication* (Reading, MA: Addison-Wesley, 1979), p. 137.

2. Adapted from Kenneth Labich, "The Seven Keys to Business Leadership," *Fortune Education Program,* © 1989 Time, Inc.

3. Kenneth D. Benne and Paul Sheats, "Functional Roles of Group Members," *Journal of Social Issues* 4, 2, pp. 41–49.

4. Jack R. Gibb, "Defensive Communication," *Journal of Communication* 11 September 1961, pp. 141–148.

5. Pace, Peterson, and Burnett, pp. 148–154.

6. Ibid., pp. 194–200.

Another Look: Wasteful Meetings

There's an ancient idea in legal circles that a group is more likely to solve a problem or discover the truth than a single person working alone. "Twelve honest" jurors is one of the precepts of the Anglo-Saxon jury system.

It's a very valid idea: Good minds—better yet, great minds—can do extraordinary work when focused on the right problem. That's what makes research universities so special. But in internal company meetings, just the opposite appears to happen: Most waste valuable time that could be better spent on real problems. These time-wasters come in different forms: Here's how to identify them.

PROGRESS REPORTS: Reviews of numbers no one wants to hear or may have heard already. Dubbed "operations meetings," they are uniformly never held until it's too late to do anything about last month's performance.

BEAUTY PAGEANTS: Presentations intended to please managers. Little is accomplished because there's never a customer in sight.

INFORMATIONAL MEETINGS: Held to get approval for work under way. In reality they stop progress as political issues—implicitly or explicitly—are put on the table.

FOREIGN POLICY MEETINGS: People from large, fragmented companies come together to enact business rituals. One manager told me these sessions are like "foreign countries negotiating treaties."

PLANNING MEETINGS: The problem here is that the planning never stops. Often such meetings are heavily populated by well-intended staff people who don't have the power to act. Or maybe it's because managers see less risk in planning than in action.

We are now at the risk of technology, such as videoconferencing and groupware, automating these wasteful management processes. I'm inclined to advise clients to ban internal meetings involving more than two people. Time has become a manager's most critical asset. I suggest that multiperson meetings should only be held when they do one of the following:

- **Resolve a customer problem or need.** Remember, these people pay for what we do.

- **Create a new way for an organization to do its work.** Corporate change and renewal require the effort of collective thought and the alignment of senior management.

- **Solve a systemic business problem.** Meetings often recur because something in the business remains broken. Be sure that you are working on the real problem, not just the symptoms.

It's useful for people to spend time in meetings to get to know each other, to understand each other's style, values, beliefs and even prejudices. Technologies like E-mail and videoconferencing can be most effective when the people using them know each other.

But the ultimate test of the value of any multiperson company meeting lies in the answer to two questions.

First: Was there enough open debate to get to the truth of what's happening in the markets, the business and our minds? Second, and most important: Did the meeting result in real actions?

Perhaps the most dramatic meeting in modern times was held in a room in England in the early morning of June 5, 1944. Outside, a driving rain and howling wind rattled the French windows. The Allies' top generals and admirals debated a go/no-go for D day, an undertaking already delayed a day because of bad weather. One hundred seventy-five thousand British, French, Canadian and American troops waited anxiously on transports in the English Channel, as did paratroopers at British airfields.

Dwight Eisenhower listened to the chief meteorologist, a dour Scotsman named J.M. Stagg, who predicted clearing weather—even though the storm seemed to be getting worse. Eisenhower then polled all the ranking officers. There were serious differences of opinion. Air Vice Marshal Sir Trafford Leigh-Mallory urged postponement until June 19. But when all had spoken, Eisenhower ended the meeting with his final decision.

"Okay," Ike said, "let's go."

Source: James Champy, "Wasteful Meetings," *FORBES*, November 2, 1998, p. 173. Reprinted by permission of FORBES Magazine © Forbes Inc., 1998.

Another Look: Team Communication: It's in the Cards

In making the transition to a team environment, team members need many new skills in group decision making, leadership, conflict resolution, and performance feedback.

One area in which skills are also required is communications, which affects all of these areas. A team leader develops both intra- and inter-team communications. Members within the team need to learn how to communicate with each other, other teams, and the rest of the company.

There are several different types of communications networks in most organizations. In a typical hierarchy, a manager tells a staff member what to do and how to do it. That form of communications network is called a star, an inverted Y, or a chain. The flow of communications is usually one way—from upper management down. Company policies and directives follow that information flow.

Those kinds of networks support centralization and the emergence of leaders, but they tend to rate low in areas of satisfaction. A team environment cannot function efficiently under such networks. What works better are the circle or all-channel networks in which each team member can communicate with his or her peers. That way, information is passed to all members, and everyone is kept up-to-date on changes and procedures. Communications in that form helps increase levels of satisfaction within the team and with individual team members.

Communications within a team environment still invoke unique challenges. During team meetings, how long do you discuss an issue before trying to reach an answer? Some members are ready quickly, while others are still deciding. A long discussion can create long meetings. Additionally, how do you get everyone to participate in the discussion and the voting? Some people are content to sit quietly on the side and let others dictate the action. For teams in which members are separated physically or work in different shifts, how do they communicate operationally or administratively with their peers? With teams working in different shifts, how do they get information about company policies or talk with off-shift managers? Let's explore how such issues are handled at two different facilities.

Rockwell Card System

The Test and Metrology Services department of the Collins Commercial Avionics division of Rockwell International in Cedar Rapids, Iowa, operates as a self-directed team. The team primarily provides test-equipment calibration and repair support to try out equipment users according to calibration-system requirements and customer demands for the various electronic systems manufactured at the facility.

Team technicians have a high technical expertise that enables them to support their customers. The team is composed of 20 members with a lab manager as the linchpin to upper management. An early issue the team had to overcome was its long weekly meetings. Even with a set agenda, the meetings exceeded the allotted time. Many members had to leave early to satisfy customer demands.

Based on input from the team members, a card system was devised to help speed up discussions. Two 8-by-10-inch cards are passed out to each member at the beginning of a meeting. Each side is color-coded and inscribed with words. (See Card Method illustration.) The colors red and green are on one card; white and yellow are on the other. When an issue is brought before the team, it is explained by the team facilitator. During his or her initial explanation, all team members display the red "needs discussion" card.

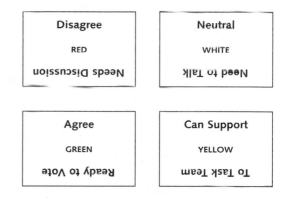

If someone wants to talk about the issue, he or she shows a white "need to talk" card to the facilitator, who recognizes the card holder. As the discussion progresses and team members make a decision on the issue, they change their cards to a green "ready to vote" card or one of the other options. The cards provide feedback to the facilitator and to team members as to who needs additional information on the issue. The facilitator terminates the discussion only when no more red "needs discussion" cards are displayed.

continued

Team Communication: It's in the Cards, *continued*

Based on the cards presented, the facilitator then formulates a voting action for the issue. When voting, team members can agree (green card), can be neutral (white card), can support (yellow card)—even if they do not like it, or can disagree (red card). The first three responses allow consensus on any issue. The team members also can hold up a yellow "to task team" card that indicates more information is required. (See Example of Card Usage.)

"The card system has increased dramatically team members' discussion and participation," says George Fluharty, lab manager. "The cards have cut down on the length of meetings and provided each team member with a chance to voice his or her opinion."

Another advantage to the system is that everyone votes. No issue is dropped until the facilitator views each member's card. Additionally, the cards have helped reduce side discussions and disruptive noise during meetings.

The cards have also reduced the time team members spend discussing issues, because they show when they are ready to move ahead. The cards are also an easy way to see which team members desire to talk, instead of everyone talking simultaneously.

The card system does have some disadvantages. On some issues, team members form an opinion quickly and show their answers before a discussion is completed. The system also lends itself to subtle, nonverbal communications.

For instance, laying the cards on a table may signal nonverbally a member's opinion on a certain subject. To stop that from happening, team members have suggested that the cards remain in their laps until an action is requested. And during meetings, side discussions can be conducted only with the cards.

Source: Jeff Pettit, "Team Communication: It's in the Cards," *Training & Development*, January 1997, pp. 12–13. Reprinted from Training & Development. © January 1997 the American Society for Training and Development. Reprinted with permission. All rights reserved.

Example of Card Usage

Team member 1:   Show (white) Need To Talk

Facilitator: Yes, team member 1?

Team member 1:   Our current printer can't handle the types of forms now required by customer A. We need to upgrade or purchase a new printer. I have investigated several printers that would be adequate, and have the prices and technical data with me.

Team member 2:   Showing (white) Need To Talk

Facilitator: Yes, team member 2?

Team member 2:   What is our budget to date and was any provision made for new equipment?

Lab manager: Showing (white) Need To Talk

Facilitator: Yes, lab manager?

Lab manager: The budget is $XYZ and no provision was set for new equipment.

Team member 3:   Showing (yellow) To Task Team

Facilitator: Yes, team member 3?

Team member 3:   I think we should send this to our software task team for resolution.

Facilitator: Is there any other discussion (no white Need To Talk or Needs Discussion cards)? Let's vote on team member 3's proposal to forward the issue of a new printer to our task team.

All team members: Showing (green) Agree.

Facilitator: Next item!

Another Look: The Great Conundrum—You vs. the Team

You're supposed to be a team player. You're also supposed to look out for No. 1. How can you do both?

Squatting between the lines of the "new contract" between employer and employee is an ugly and befuddling contradiction. You know what the new contract says: We, your employer, no longer offer or even imply a guarantee of employment—you're here only as long as we need you. Instead, we offer you employability—stick with us, kid, and we'll reward you well, and when we dissolve the bonds, no hard feelings, no stigma, no problem. Plenty of people will want you because you picked up valuable skills here. Two birds in the bush are worth one in the hand.

That's the deal; here's the contradiction. On the one hand, you're on your own. You're responsible for your career. You're the CEO of "You Inc." in an every-man-for-himself universe of individual initiative and reward; whatever color your parachute is, you sew it and pack it yourself. Ah, but on the other hand, folks here at ol' Amalgamated don't cotton to self-aggrandizement. We want team players, all for one and one for all, because we're a team and we work in teams. Teams may hire their own members, manage their own work, receive rewards as a group, and parcel them out to members according to their collective view of each person's contribution to the group's enterprise. Of the skills you learn here, the most valuable is teamwork.

So it's You Inc. vs. the Team. Says David Witte, CEO of Ward Howell International, an executive search firm: "Do we have a problem here? Oh, yeah, we got a big problem. Talk about individual responsibility—it's absolutely important. But you're part of a team—that's absolutely important. But has anybody married that?" The short answer: No, and maybe the marriage can't be made. But maybe we can find ways to help You Inc. get along in a world of teams.

Mind you, this taffy pull—toward the self, toward the team—is ancient; it's probably as old as the use of sports images in business. Under the old dispensation, however, obeisance paid. When Organization Man subordinated his ego to the group, he got safety in return. Now you can do that and still be on the street when this project is done.

Today's teams are, well, *teamier*—less a metaphor and more a reality. Gone is the phony "team" where the leader tells the finance guru to run some numbers, the marketing wiz to do some research, the manufacturing maven to come up with cost and capacity data, and everyone to report back two weeks hence. These days team members are likely to work together many hours a day, mucking about in one another's specialties and jointly hammering out the final product rather than slotting together individually made components.

Why does teamwork matter more? First, the content and culture of knowledge work require it. Simple-minded work—may I offer pinmaking as an example?—permits a division of labor in which people don't have to work together so long as the pieces of the system fit. But knowledge work—designing a product, writing an ad, reengineering a process—rarely moves systematically forward. It's an open-ended series of to-and-fro collaborations, iterations, and reiterations. Says Fran Engoran, senior partner for intellectual capital at Price Waterhouse Consulting: "Complex, cross functional business problems demand a diverse set of skills. 'It takes a team,' Mrs. Clinton might say."

Fly solo on these teams, and you'll be ostracized so fast one would think you'd been caught wiping your nose on the tablecloth at Lutèce. The ethos is to make your teammates look good, not to make sure the boss knows how much you contributed. Him you can fool, but your teammates value only substance. "Shark skills are not appreciated," says George Bailey, a Price Waterhouse consultant who is an expert on teams. "Dolphins beat up on sharks." The cult(ure) of teamwork helps explain why people give themselves self-effacing titles like "facilitator" and "coach" instead of "boss" or "leader."

If knowledge work depends on teams, it makes sense to reward them, not individuals. People who move from project to project cannot be paid according to the number of direct reports they have any more than a road warrior can flaunt her status by the number of windows her office has. Top industrial-design firm Ideo Product Development (it designed the mouse for both Apple and Microsoft, and the snazzy housing for Silicon Graphics computers) is a good example. It has several "vice presidents" who

continued

The Great Conundrum—You vs. the Team, *continued*

awarded themselves the title to get the free subscriptions some magazines give VPs. Ideo's performance reviews used to be done by a person's boss and two peers of the employee's own choosing, but that system, offbeat though it was, had to be scrapped a couple of years ago when the company realized that for many employees (more than one in ten) it was impossible to identify a boss. Now people pick two peers plus one from a slate of six "management types." According to Tom Kelley, people tend to pick demanding evaluators: "The culture says don't pick softies, because this is about improving performance, not about getting ahead."

This kind of teamwork can be very seductive to the individual. At work or on the playing fields of Eton, everyone has experienced transcendental teamwork, a sweet spot of accomplishment and fellow-feeling. When it's working, says Ward Howell's Witte, "the more you contribute, the more other people promote you. It is inspiring." Out at Boeing, people on the teams that make the 777 jetliner weep when one of those babies rolls out of the hangar. "Hot groups," emeritus Stanford business professor Harold L. Leavitt calls them. While they last they can make you think, if your mind inclines this way, that Rousseau was right: In the state of nature we were noble savages, none better than any other, free adherents to a social contract, and if we could only extirpate hierarchy we could return to that paradisiacal place of mutual and reciprocal fraternity.

Teams can do extraordinary work, but it's a dicey proposition to put You Inc.'s fate in collectivist hands. Teams are often inhospitable to oddballs and to some forms of ambition. Says Ideo's Kelley: "I warn recruits, if your needs are to climb the ladder, don't come here. Ambition is getting on the coolest projects." Peer-oriented meritocracy flourishes at Ideo, says Robert Sutton, a professor at Stanford's engineering school who is writing a book about the company. But, he cautions, it succeeds partly because the work is so complex that the hottest hotshots know they can't go it alone, and also because Ideo sits smack in the middle of Silicon Valley, where a reputation as a great teammate is the ticket to new ventures.

But there are limits. From a company's point of view, teams are of doubtful value as nurseries of executive talent, because no one knows why great teams come together or how to replicate their magic. The experience might happen once in a lifetime. By contrast, Douglas Smith, a consultant and author of *Taking Charge of Change,* says that with the old machinery of promotion and rewards, "when superiors made a judgment to move you up a grade, they could be pretty comfortable that you'd live up to their expectations." As for money, companies can rarely offer significant incentives—the kind that change your life—to reward teamwork. A smallish company of 1,000 people might have a couple of hundred teams, with many people serving on more than one. "How in the world can you ever keep track of it all?" Smith asks.

Companies always say they plump for the pack over the wolf—there's a reason it's called corporate life—but they're really looking for leadership. When Laurie Siegel, director of compensation policy at AlliedSignal, sees a great team, "I will ask, 'Was leadership what made it great?' The answer is always yes. Then I ask, 'Who were the leaders?' and it is always easy to name them." Those are the people AlliedSignal is determined to keep and to create careers for. To be sure, leaders need team skills—as Siegel puts it, "Lone Rangers or political types don't survive at this company"—but they're a means to what AlliedSignal sees as the greater end. Siegel calls it "a culture of individualism that drives team performance," a paradoxical phrase that brings us back to our problem, You Inc. vs. the Team.

So what's to do? First, Smith says, "get a life: You need team skills to succeed." You can find an argument about whether team players are products of nature or nurture, but people compete for status in any group. The "status auction" is more polite in a team culture like Ideo's, says Sutton—it might reward sharing and punish dissers or swaggerers—but it still goes on. Even a natural-born egoist can be a valued teammate and adapt to local rules.

But—second—don't believe everything you hear about teams. Take team-play rhetoric to its limits, and you'd think capitalism had spawned New Soviet Man. Look at the business plan instead. Says Witte: "If you've got a company with a 9% net profit and it needs to get to 11% or 12%, and a couple of divisions are way below average, you want someone to shake up that organization but good. A team player? Not necessarily. But if the strategy is niche acquisitions, improved customer focus, a new service organization—then you need a team builder."

continued

The Great Conundrum—You vs. the Team, *continued*

Third, whatever you do, put yourself on what George Bailey calls "the shareholder value team." You ought to be able to tell a convincing story—that is, an honest one—about how your work or your team's work has increased the value of the company.

If that story's true, You Inc. will be fine. If it's not, no team can help you.

Source: Thomas A. Stewart, "The Great Conundrum: You vs. the Team," pp. 165–166. Reprinted from the November 25, 1996 issue of FORTUNE by special permission; copyright 1996, Time Inc.

A Case in Point: A New Approach to Final Examinations at State University

State University is in the midst of a major discussion concerning how to handle the final examination period. The students have brainstormed and given many suggestions to the administration about how to deal with it. The basic problem facing the administration is, "What type of final examination period is best for a college or university?"

The examination period might be handled in a number of different ways, including: set aside a week or more at the end of the semester devoted exclusively to giving exams; or give exams at the final class meeting or during the last two or three weeks of class without formally designating an exam week.

Questions

1. To practice brainstorming, list three other solutions.
2. Which of these suggestions would be most acceptable to you? Why? The answer depends on the criteria used to evaluate the proposals. Some potential criteria would require any final exam period to do the following:

- Provide opportunity for an overall evaluation of what students have learned (this may come from a desire or value held about examinations).

- Allow instructors time to meet grading deadlines (to many, this represents a practical consideration).

- Avoid creating a financial burden on the university, staff, and students (this seems to come from the desire to avoid introducing disadvantages).

- Avoid creating scheduling problems (this may come from practical considerations of administering a school).

3. Develop at least six more criteria that could be used to make the best decision about the type of final examination period.

A Case in Point: Cutback at Commercial Air

Chuck Stewart's small commuter airline had flourished during the early days of deregulation. When the government lifted many of the restrictions on the cities the airlines could serve, the rates they could charge, and the like, Chuck saw a golden opportunity to set up a business. Commercial Air was born.

Because of its fuel-efficient, short-range jets, Commercial Air soon found itself to be very profitable serving a network of smaller cities in the Midwest. Business travelers used Commercial to link up with the major airlines in Chicago, St. Louis, and Mem-

phis. Stewart had a fast-growing and very lucrative business.

Problems began to arise when a labor union organizer convinced about 25 percent of Commercial's employees that only through unionization could they strengthen their job security and improve benefits. Stewart bitterly fought unionization but eventually realized that some of his workers were dead set on joining the Brotherhood of Airline Workers.

The company's financial position started to deteriorate about eighteen months ago. Higher interest

continued

Cutback at Commercial Air, *continued*

rates on newly purchased equipment and a decline in passengers hurt. Chuck Stewart realizes now that it's time for belt-tightening, or the company could go under. The thought is depressing to Chuck.

Bill Baker, the company's general manager and a close friend of Chuck, was talking with Chuck over a few beers last Thursday after work:

Chuck: I'm not sure exactly what it's going to take, Bill, but I'm going to save this company any way I can. Obviously, we need to trim the work force.

Bill: You're right, Chuck. But I can't see just making blanket cuts. We need a scalpel, not a meat ax.

Chuck: I'm with you. Say, you're the big believer in participative decision making. Why don't we just get the people together, explain our problem, and let them figure out how to reduce the work force?

Bill: I'm not sure that'll work. We're looking at 20 percent of those people being terminated. How would you feel if you were asked to decide your own fate that way?

Chuck: I'd feel lousy. But isn't the big advantage of participation supposed to be less resistance to change? Our people are adults. They know the reali-

ties of the business world. Let's give them some general guidelines and see what they come up with.

Bill: I suppose it's possible. I could get each work group together—there are sixteen to twenty people in each group—and see if they can draw straws or something.

Chuck: That sure would take some heat off me. I hate letting people go. Oh yes, and Bill—off the record—I'd sure appreciate if the groups would decide to ax mostly union people.

Questions
1. What do you think of Chuck's and Bill's approach to decision making?
2. Is participative decision making a good option in this case? Explain your response.
3. What motivations lie behind the decision to use participation?
4. What problems do you foresee in Chuck and Bill's approach?
5. We discussed a hidden agenda in this chapter. Describe Chuck's.

Source: Reprinted from Paul R. Timm, *Supervision* (St. Paul, MN: West Publishing, 1992), p. 149. Used with permission.

PART 6

WORKFORCE
ISSUES

Workforce Issues: Diversity, Socialization, and Stress

- How do efforts to employ culturally diverse workers reflect the value system of a free society?

- Why do some employers resist hiring a culturally diverse workforce?

- How does the unemployment rate among African American workers compare with that of other workers?

- Why is racial discrimination potentially wasteful?

- What is being done to overcome discrimination against various racial/ethnic groups?

- What is affirmative action, and what does it seek to accomplish?

- What are the four major minority groups in the United States and Canada?

- What special pressures are experienced by many African Americans, Hispanic Americans, Asian and Pacific Island Americans, and Native Americans in our North American culture?

- How does the plight of Native Americans differ from that of other racial/ethnic groups?

- What can we do to reduce cultural misunderstanding and the waste of human energy?

The answers to these and other questions are coming up next in Chapter 14 . . .

Every morning at seven o'clock
There's twenty tarriers aworking
    on the rock
And the boss comes along and
    he says "Keep still,
And come down heavy on the
    cast iron drill."
And drill, ye tarriers, drill. Drill,
    ye tarriers, drill.
For it's work all day for sugar in
    your tay,
Down beyond the railway,
And drill, ye tarriers, drill!
And blast!
And fire!

Irish Railroad Song by
Thomas Casey, 1888

**The door to opportunity in the
workforce has not always been
open to all people.**

From its early days, the United States has depended on the inexpensive labor of newly arrived people to build its businesses. Black slaves worked on southern plantations; Irish and Chinese workers built the railroads; Polish, Italian, and other groups filled factory, domestic, and other unskilled jobs.

Yet the door to better opportunities was often posted with signs such as "Whites Only" and "No Irish Need Apply." While the past century has seen many European immigrants assimilated into the American "melting pot," some ethnic and cultural groups are still struggling for economic equality. In addition, economic and political conditions abroad have brought new groups of immigrants from Mexico, Southeast Asia, and other areas. Many Hispanic Americans, African Americans, Asian and Pacific Island Americans, Arab Americans, Native Americans, and other ethnic and cultural groups face significant pressures in the workplace.

In this chapter, we focus on issues that minorities face and suggest ways that human-relations-smart managers can deal with these issues.

Managers Must Deal with Diversity Issues

Organizations are expected to reflect the values of the societies in which they function. In the United States and Canada, a key value is the notion of equal opportunity for all people. These countries have long been regarded as the lands of opportunity: with hard work, anyone might make his or her fortune; a son or daughter might even become the nation's leader. Indeed, in the 1988 U.S. presidential race, the two major contenders for the Democratic Party nomination were Michael Dukakis, son of Greek immigrants, and Jesse Jackson, son of an African American South Carolina mill worker.

The possibility of upward social mobility has attracted group after group of immigrants from different countries to the United States and Canada. Once they arrived, however, many found obstacles to enjoying real economic opportunity. Each wave of immigrants faced resentment and hostility from those already here.

Economic opportunities in the
United States continue to attract
immigrants.

Established citizens—including earlier immigrants—feared that the economic pie could not be cut into ever-smaller pieces, that soon their nation would run out of jobs. In addition, they were often suspicious of those who looked, talked, and acted differently.

Through subsequent generations, Europeans and some other immigrant groups have blended into their new culture and entered the mainstream of U.S. and Canadian business, moving up to white-collar and eventually management and executive positions. But for others, especially visible ethnic and racial groups such as African Americans, Hispanic Americans, and Asian and Pacific Island Americans, the problems of exclusion from opportunity persist.

Groups that blend into the mainstream culture have more upward mobility than those that do not.

U.S. society has taken two approaches to increasing minority employees' opportunities: voluntary action of organizations and government legislation. As discussed later in this chapter, the results have been mixed.

Assisting the Culturally Diverse Begins with Helping Them Get Jobs

While unemployment rates in the United States dropped and remained low during most of the 1980s and 1990s, some groups were left out of the economic boom. In particular, the unemployment rate among African American youths has remained exceptionally high. It is a chronic problem with no easy solutions.

High unemployment is a chronic problem for African American youths.

The unemployment problem affects just about every aspect of Black life in the United States: high youth unemployment is widely seen as an early link to the chain that shackles Blacks to higher crime rates than whites, a higher incidence of family breakups, and a lifelong economic disadvantage.

While lack of education is a major barrier to getting and keeping a job for some groups, other issues compound the problem. A lack of role models, particularly in professional positions, can discourage youths from seeking job training or a college education. Inadequate basic job skills can also limit opportunities.

Many factors limit opportunities for minorities.

Prejudice Begets Discrimination

At the root of many problems faced by culturally diverse workers are prejudgment and discrimination. **Prejudice**—an opinion formed without all the facts—often is rooted in misunderstanding or lack of exposure to different types of people. When we prejudge others, we often are led into acts of **discrimination**—into giving unequal and unfair treatment to people different from ourselves.

Robert Hayles, vice president of cultural diversity for Grand Metropolitan's North American Food Sector in Minneapolis (which includes Pillsbury), is certain that **diversity** is a noble goal. The more diverse the workgroup, he maintains, the more different points of view, the higher the creativity of the group, and hence the more effective the organization. Hayles's experience in workshops indicates that diverse groups are more creative.

Robert Hayles's experience in workshops shows diverse groups are more creative.

It is interesting to note that of the Fortune 1000 companies, 70 percent recognize diversity as an important issue that they must address. However, currently only a third of them have begun programs to deal with this. The third that has taken the leap lists the following reasons for doing so:

1. *Demographics.* Today, the workforce is 43 percent white men, 35 percent white women, and 22 percent racial and ethnic groups. In the year 2005, the workforce will be 32 percent white men, 33 percent white women, and 35 percent racial and ethnic groups.

2. *Results.* Many have seen higher profitability by enacting long-range affirmative action programs. Hayles's work is cited frequently as a reason for enacting diversity programs.

3. *Lawsuits.* The average cost of a discrimination suit against a company in the United States is $475,000.[1]

Discrimination Can Be Overcome

Since the Civil War, many people have worked to break down the barriers of discrimination against racial and ethnic groups. Beginning in the 1950s, the modern **civil rights movement,** led by such activists as Martin Luther King, Jr., brought the problem of discrimination, especially against African Americans, into the public consciousness. This movement was instrumental in establishing several approaches to reducing discrimination, including legislation and affirmative action programs.

Legal Responses

Federal laws seek to overcome discrimination.

Congress passed several significant laws during the 1960s to deal with discrimination. The Manpower Development and Training Act of 1962 permitted many individuals to gain occupational training for the first time. The **Civil Rights Act of 1964** presented strong support for equal employment opportunities. It "prohibited employers, labor unions, and employment agencies from discriminating against persons on the basis of color, religion, sex or national origin." Smaller organizations, however, were not affected by this legislation, as it applied only to companies with 15 or more employees.

The **Civil Rights Act of 1991** amended the 1964 Act to strengthen and improve federal civil rights laws and to provide damages in cases of intentional employment discrimination.

Civil rights legislation has done much to reduce or eliminate the visible, outward acts of discrimination against racial and ethnic groups in jobs and other areas. There are limits, however, to what legislation can accomplish. Laws do not automatically change people's behavior, attitudes, or values. Some people still harbor feelings of hatred toward other groups of people, as can be seen in the rise of various hate groups in the United States during the 1980s.

Can society legislate morality?

Many people argue that society cannot legislate morality. Some people resist laws that require them to do what is right and fair. After Congress passed the Civil Rights Act of 1964, for example, many companies obeyed the new law only on a token basis. They hired one or two African Americans and put them in highly visible positions to demonstrate compliance with the law. In more recent years, however, many major organizations have responded to additional government pressure by initiating legitimate programs with a sincere desire to provide more opportunities for minority members. The Civil Rights Act of 1991 is a further testament of how seriously the government and our society regard civil rights.

Government Pressures

To supplement the new laws, over the past 25 years the federal government has started many programs to pressure organizations to alleviate racial discrimination. Many of these programs came to be known under the umbrella term **affirmative action.** The implication of affirmative action was that companies would aggressively seek to hire and promote more culturally diverse workers by such methods as special recruitment and training programs. Companies were urged to do something *affirmative* to compensate for past discrimination.

The intent of affirmative action programs is to alleviate racial discrimination and provide educational and career opportunities for members of ethnic and racial groups.

The federal government established the **Equal Employment Opportunity Commission (EEOC)** to help carry out affirmative action programs. Although there are critics of the EEOC's effectiveness, the agency's efforts to change hiring policies have had positive results. Many more racial and ethnic groups now enjoy opportunities for good jobs—jobs with growth potential.

On the other hand, affirmative action has also produced some negative reactions. Some employees have balked at what they see as preferential hiring treatment and arbitrary quotas for racial and ethnic groups, a situation often called **reverse discrimination.**

The 1976 case of Allan Bakke established that discrimination against whites is just as illegal as discrimination against racial and ethnic groups. Bakke, a white male, sued the state of California when his application to a state university medical school was turned down. His suit contended that minorities less qualified than he had been admitted through a special admissions program at the school. The U.S. Supreme Court ruled in his favor, and he was admitted to medical school. In handing down this decision, the Supreme Court pointed out that affirmative action is okay as long as rigid preferential systems are not used. The goal of affirmative action is fine, but quotas are not. In fact, the goal of affirmative action is not quotas.

However, as a result of the *Bakke* **decision,** business leaders face the challenge of creating affirmative action opportunities for racial and ethnic groups while avoiding reverse discrimination. As businesses now face a shrinking labor pool, however, some labor experts say that affirmative action programs will become increasingly important to maintaining a sufficient qualified workforce.[2]

What is the EEOC?

The Bakke decision puts business leaders in a bind.

When John Henry was a little baby,
Sitting on his daddy's knee,
He took up a hammer and a little piece of steel
And said, "This hammer's gonna be the death of me,
Lord, Lord, this hammer's gonna be the death of me."

—Ballad about an African American railroad worker killed during construction of a West Virginia tunnel about 1873

Challenges and Progress of Racial and Ethnic Groups

Members of ethnic and racial groups traditionally have had to start out in the most dangerous, difficult, and unpleasant jobs. The pay, like the skill level, was low. Through years of hard work and education, with the assistance of civil rights legislation, some ethnic and racial groups attained the American dream of successful careers. However, success stories remain more the exception than the rule.

The 1988 Commission on Minority Participation in American Life was a 40-member panel of business, education, and civic leaders including former presidents Gerald R. Ford and Jimmy Carter. It reported that the four major minority groups—African Americans, Hispanic Americans, Native Americans and Alaskan Natives, and Asian and Pacific Island Americans—potentially will constitute one-third of the United States population just after the year 2000. "In education, employment, income, health, longevity, and other basic measures of individual and social well-being, gaps persist and, in some cases, are widening between members of minority groups and the majority population," said the commission.[3]

The above four segments of the American population were the only ethnic and racial groups listed by the 1988 commission; nonetheless there are many more diverse ethnic groups in the United States, each with its own specific problems. However, all share common concerns about education, discrimination, and other matters.

In many measures of well-being, gaps persist and are widening between members of nondominant cultural groups and the dominant population.

African Americans

Civil rights legislation and affirmative action programs have helped increase opportunities for African Americans.

The civil rights legislation and affirmative action programs originally aimed at African Americans, historically the largest racial and ethnic group, have helped provide increased job opportunities for that group. Once, working as a Pullman porter was once the best job many African Americans could gain; today young African American people can aspire to management and professional positions.

Yet special pressures are placed on African American workers, especially those in predominantly white businesses. There is some evidence that African American professionals are leaving large corporations to work at smaller African American-owned companies. One African American bank officer who made the move said some African Americans believe that to succeed in a mostly white business, they must "compromise their identity as Blacks." An attorney who took a pay cut to join a smaller African American law firm said he saw more chance for advancement there than at a large white firm.

Discrimination does not end for African Americans who achieve executive status.

African Americans who work their way into management in largely white organizations often find new challenges. Some white workers may resent having an African American supervisor. Others may constantly second-guess an African American manager and question his or her authority. Some African American executives find white clients reluctant to do business with them.[4]

Hispanic Americans

New Hispanic immigrants face more challenges than do more established ethnic groups.

Hispanics are the latest large wave of immigrants to the United States. Most have settled either in Sun Belt states or in large northern cities. Hispanic American groups now in the United States who were originally from Puerto Rico or Cuba are more established than these more recent immigrants because they have lived here longer. Most recent Hispanic immigrants are refugees from economic and political problems in Mexico and Central America. According to the U.S. Census Bureau, by the middle of the next century the nation's Hispanic population is expected to reach 96.5 million—representing 24.5 percent of the population (up from the current 10.9 percent) and the largest ethnic segment in the United States[5] (see Figure 14.1).

The newest Hispanic immigrants, many penniless, face more challenges in the workplace than did the more established groups. Unskilled Hispanic Americans, like immigrants before them, have done some of the most difficult and least desirable work, such as domestic, farm labor, and sweatshop-type factory jobs. Some have opened small service businesses in Hispanic American communities.

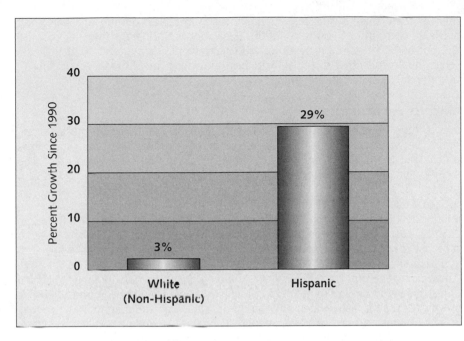

FIGURE 14.1 The Hispanic population is the fastest growing in the U.S.

Source: U.S. Census Bureau, 1998.

In addition to educational and language barriers, Hispanic American workers, especially illegal ones, face other pressures. The Immigration Reform Law of 1986, aimed at reducing the number of illegal aliens in the United States, requires them to register for temporary residency status. It also makes employers responsible for keeping records on employees' work authorization papers.

Many employers dislike having to be the enforcers of the new law. Intentional or accidental paperwork violations can bring civil fines of up to $10,000 per employee. Such fines are especially hard on owners of small Hispanic American businesses. Some employers acknowledge they will avoid hiring Hispanic Americans rather than risk fines.

Employers dislike being responsible for enforcing immigration laws.

At the time it was enacted, the law provided an 18-month residency status to workers who could prove they had lived in the United States since 1982. They then had one year to become permanent residents by passing English and U.S. civics tests. But getting together the necessary documents to prove residency, plus the $185 application fee, were major obstacles for many immigrants.[6]

Asian and Pacific Island Americans

Waves of immigrants from various Asian countries have been coming to the United States and Canada for more than one hundred years. Many have faced harsh racial prejudice. Over the years, many Asians have become assimilated into the American mainstream while others have chosen to remain in Asian enclaves in large cities. Recent Asian immigrants, sometimes fleeing economic or political hardships, have come mainly from Korea and Southeast Asia.

Like other racial and ethnic groups, Asians and Pacific Islanders have seen education as one step to becoming successful in their new country. Even though many immigrant parents have often been forced to take blue-collar jobs, many have encouraged their children to enter professional fields. In addition, Asian and Pacific Island American communities have provided social and financial support for newcomers. The Korean custom of the **kye,** for example, has helped

Many immigrants see education as the ladder to success.

finance many small businesses. Friends meet monthly for dinners and pool their available cash, from $100 to $40,000. Each month a different member receives the pot and pays for dinner. Along with hard work, saving, and good business sense, such collective financial help has allowed many Korean Americans to become successful entrepreneurs.

Native Americans

Native Americans have a unique legal and political status.

Native Americans have a unique legal and political status based on special agreements between them and the U.S. government. Unfortunately, this status has not helped them gain access to the American dream and may even help keep these original Americans largely outside the mainstream of U.S. society and economic life.

To understand the plight of Native Americans, one must know something about their background and history. As the United States developed from the Atlantic coast westward, many Indian tribes were removed from their lands in the East to *reservations* in the West. These reservations were often wild, arid, and rich in natural resources that increase in value over time. Today, Native Americans generally have a very low economic standing despite living on tribal lands that often contain potentially valuable oil, gas, coal, and uranium deposits as well as timber, fish, water, and highly desirable recreational areas.

To understand the relative isolation of Native Americans, one must examine their cultural heritage and their historical relationship with the U.S. government. Unlike other ethnic and racial groups, the Native Americans did not leave their cultural homelands to come to the New World. They have largely stayed together as tribes and have sought to maintain their cultural heritage, which is vastly different from that of mainstream America.

Relations between the U.S. government and Indian tribes have ranged from open warfare to a situation in which the tribes are captive nations. The term **captive nation** conveys the limited political autonomy of tribal governments as well as the isolation of the people from mainstream society. It has often been used to describe the condition of Eastern European countries under the Soviet Union.[7]

One of the ways Native Americans have gotten into business is by creating and selling their art.

Tribal leaders, aware of past exploitation from outsiders as well as the pressure to avoid development that might disrupt the traditional lifestyle of the tribe, are generally not eager to make major changes rapidly. Nonetheless, some development is taking place. At the same time, some Native Americans are entering the world of business. Among other developments, the Native American Chamber of Commerce of Mid America, an organization to support American Indian businesses, was established in Kansas City, Missouri, in 1986. Forums and workshops allow successful Native American businesspeople to share their experiences with other Native Americans.[8] Predictions are that as the twentieth century draws to a close, Native Americans will establish a place of prominence for themselves in U.S. society while maintaining their distinctive culture.

Native Americans are entering the world of business at an increasing rate.

What Does All This Mean for Human Relations?

We need powerful beliefs to impel us to accept, respect, and work with others successfully. Some of us have inherited or embraced religious or philosophical beliefs that make this task easier. We learned that we should "Love our neighbor as ourselves," or that "All are created equal," or to "Have compassion on all sentient beings," or "Live and let live." Such values are often stated in creeds of faith or in the constitutions and anthems of nations. We recite them or sing them on public occasions to remind ourselves of our basic commitments to each other.[9]

The human-relations-smart person knows the value of understanding and appreciating differences. We can learn about the cultures of other people in many ways, including books and films. But knowledge about others is not a substitute for getting to know them personally.

Human-relations-smart people know the value of understanding and appreciating differences in others.

The way to get to know people is no mystery. You talk with them. You seek to gain common understanding (our definition of communication discussed earlier). Author George Simons suggests using friendly curiosity, in a respectful, nonjudgmental way. You can use questions such as these:

What does it mean to you when . . .?

What do you say to yourself about . . .?

What's it like for you when . . .?

What do you imagine when you say . . .?

How do you picture it?

Tell me what is important to you.

Remember that we each come from only one of many cultures. Racial and ethnic cultures are different, but the solar system does not revolve around the ways of the dominant culture. When you encounter something in another's culture that is unacceptable to you, don't reject or blame the person, even though you need to deal with the things that frustrate you. By blaming, you risk creating hostility, prejudice, and social injustice.

By becoming culture conscious, you not only can communicate and collaborate better, but you can learn new and interesting ways to do things and look at things. People who are different can bring out the best in us if we allow them to.

ACTIVITIES

BEYOND DIVERSITY

Everyone agrees that from time to time a conversation between a man and a woman may as well be in two different languages for all the miscues that occur. Truth is, the miscuing can happen anytime there is communication between people who are different from you—in looks, beliefs, language or customs. These differences are delicately packaged under the moniker "diversity." The growing diversity of the workforce has caused many migraines for those managers who must encourage interaction and tolerance, which commonly requires reshaping attitudes and behaviors previously set by a more uniform group.

Most of us are not born with the multicultural awareness now needed in the workplace. We have to acquire it along the way. How well are you doing at it?

Your Diversity Awareness

Check the box next to the phrase that best describes your approach or attitude most of the time. This is an attitude inventory, not a test, so just go with your first inclination, and enjoy yourself!

1. ❑ Follow orders and don't make waves, do as you're told.
   ❑ It's fun to find ways around the rules, to question authority.

2. ❑ Time is a river.
   ❑ Time is money.

3. ❑ Watch what I do; learn by modeling or demonstration.
   ❑ Do as I say; learn by explicit instructions.

4. ❑ Get closer so we can talk.
   ❑ Can we have a little breathing room between us?

5. ❑ The more things change, the more they stay the same.
   ❑ Things are getting better all the time.

6. ❑ I need to take risks.
   ❑ I need to feel secure.

7. ❑ We're all in this together.
   ❑ It's every man for himself.

8. ❑ Doing your duty is most important.
   ❑ Expressing yourself or having fun is most important.

9. ❑ A case-by-case application of rules works best.
   ❑ A uniform application of rules works best.

10. ❑ Relationships are important.
    ❑ Knowing things is important.

Ethnic orientation, racial identification, learning styles, sexual preference, age/life-stage, male/female perceptions—all breed differences in the perspectives and values we bring to shared human problems and goals. While there are no "right" answers to the quiz here, it is important that you compare your attitude with that of your boss and your employees. If an employee has one attitude and you have another, chances are you've been experiencing conflict. Perhaps a different method of motivation will get the results you've been looking for.

In or Out?

Following are some exercises to help you understand your own diversity awareness as well as that within your company. Characterize the dominant group within your company. What are the predominant attitudes? How were they shaped? What are

continued

ACTIVITIES

BEYOND DIVERSITY, CONTINUED

the consequences of such attitudes? Do you fall inside or outside the dominant group?

Rate your ability to perform the following:

1 = Cannot do
2 = Can do with difficulty
3 = Can do reliably
4 = Am truly excellent at this
5 = Could teach others how to do this

When I Am in the Dominant Culture

_____ I am aware that I am part of a dominant culture and know how its dynamics work.

_____ I realize that people of other cultures have fresh ideas and different perspectives to bring to my life and my organization.

_____ I work to make sure that members of other cultures get heard and are respected for their differences.

_____ I coach others on how to succeed in my culture. I tell them the unwritten rules and show them what they need to do in order to function better.

_____ I give others my personal support and loyalty even if they are rejected or criticized by members of my culture.

_____ I recognize how stress causes individuals to revert to older and narrower beliefs and to make oneself and one's culture right and others wrong.

_____ I apologize when I have done something inappropriate that attacks or offends someone of a different background.

_____ I go out of my way to recruit, select, train and promote people from outside the dominant culture, despite feeling less comfortable with them. I see this as one of my responsibilities as a manager.

_____ I listen to people of other cultures when they tell me how my culture affects them.

When I Am Not in the Dominant Culture

_____ I realize that, because of my background, I have something distinctive to contribute to the organization in which I find myself.

_____ While I know that I do not have to lose my cultural distinctiveness to fit in, I realize that I may have to learn new information and skills that will enable me to succeed in the dominant culture.

_____ I look for members of the dominant culture who will help me "read between the lines" to understand the unwritten rules about "how the system works."

_____ When I succeed in the dominant culture I am careful not to make myself an exception and separate myself from others of my background.

_____ I share what I learn about the dominant culture with others like myself.

_____ I recognize that when the pressure is on I tend to revert to older and narrower beliefs and want to make myself and my culture right and others wrong.

_____ I resist the inclination to cluster exclusively with my own kind of people or exclusively with people from the dominant culture when I am in mixed company.

_____ I resist blaming the dominant group for everything that goes wrong.

_____ I know how to present distinctive features of my culture and its points of view in ways that others can hear and understand.

_____ I can respect individuals of other cultures and treat them fairly even though I may be fiercely committed to conflicting political goals.

continued

ACTIVITIES

BEYOND DIVERSITY, CONTINUED

Critical Issues

Below is a list of issues that may be diversity-related. Next to each issue, indicate whether it is a critical issue within your company by writing C for Critical, O for Occasional, or N for Nonexistent.

_____ Offensive slurs, jokes, stereotyped remarks

_____ Insensitive or exclusionary language (sexist, racist, etc.)

_____ "We" versus "they" distinctions

_____ Sabotage or harassment of minorities

_____ Different senses of time and urgency about dealing with diversity

_____ Communication, delegation problems

_____ Inequities in pay scale, promotion, or job definition

_____ Dead-end jobs; people forced into narrow, specialized niches

_____ Lack of training opportunities

_____ Lack of role models or mentors

_____ Double standards

_____ Understanding how to use different strengths

_____ Lack of management skills

_____ Violations of work rules, policies, procedures

_____ Lack of motivation/participation

_____ Lack of training or resources to deal with diversity

_____ Sexual harassment

Look at the issues that you marked C. Do others in your office agree over what is critical? What beliefs and values seem to be at the root of these issues?

Source: Reprinted from "Beyond Diversity," _Executive Female_ May/June 1991, pp. 49–50. Used with permission.

Summary of Key Ideas

- The issues of cultural diversity require special attention by organizational leaders in order to (1) avail the organization of the talents and capabilities of racial and ethnic workers, (2) comply with the law, and (3) provide fair opportunities to workers.

- Prejudice based on what we've been taught and experienced is natural but often poses barriers to effectively working together.

- When we put ourselves at the center of a cultural solar system, we tend to see those who are different as wrong, bad, ugly, incompetent—as adversaries instead of potential friends.

- Although results are mixed, voluntary action and legislation serve as the two primary approaches for increasing opportunities for racial and ethnic groups.

- The Civil Rights Act of 1964 made it illegal for an organization to discriminate on the basis of color, religion, sex, or national origin.

- The Civil Rights Act of 1964 was strengthened with the advent of the Equal Employment Opportunity Commission, which enforces equal employment opportunity laws.

- The Civil Rights Act of 1991 amended the Civil Rights Act of 1964 to strengthen and improve federal civil rights laws and to provide damages in cases of intentional employment discrimination.

- African Americans, Hispanic Americans, Asian and Pacific Island Americans, and Native Americans often face difficult social pressures. Sensitivity to these pressures enables a manager to better work with those of different cultural backgrounds.

- The most effective thing the human-relations-smart person can do is get to know *individuals* with different backgrounds. This can be done by asking questions and seeking understanding.

Key Terms, Concepts, and Names

Affirmative action
Bakke decision
Captive nation
Civil Rights Acts of 1964 and 1991
Civil rights movement
Discrimination
Diversity

Equal Employment Opportunity
    Commission (EEOC)
Robert Hayles
Kye
Prejudice
Reverse discrimination

Questions and Exercises

1. *How to deal with the dominant culture:* Depending on where we find ourselves, we may sometimes be part of a dominant culture and at other times be an outsider. Use the two checklists below to find out how well you do things that enhance multicultural harmony and collaboration. The first is for those who are in the dominant culture; the second is for those in a different culture.

    Check the items that are true of you. *Hint: The more true, the better! However, don't kid yourself about how well you see yourself perform in these areas. Get feedback from others as well as rating yourself.*

    A. When I belong to the dominant culture:

    ❏ I am aware that I am part of a dominant culture and know how its dynamics work. I listen to people of other cultures when they tell me how my culture affects them.

    ❏ I have a philosophy of fairness and I let others in my culture know about my commitment.

    ❏ I realize that people of other cultures have fresh ideas and different perspectives to bring to my life and my organization.

    ❏ I ensure that members of other cultures are heard and respected for their differences.

    ❏ I coach others on how to succeed in my culture. I tell them the unwritten rules and show them what they need to know to function better.

    ❏ I ensure that my subordinates and colleagues from other cultures are prepared for what they have to do to meet the demands of my culture.

❑ When I train or coach others I do not put them down or undermine the value of their differences.

❑ I give others my personal support and loyalty even if they are rejected or criticized by members of my culture.

❑ I am aware that outsiders to my culture recognize my cultural peculiarities better than I do and I go to them for information about the effect of things that I do and say.

❑ I recognize that when under pressure I tend to revert to narrower beliefs to make myself and my culture right and others wrong.

❑ I apologize when I have done something inappropriate that offends someone of a different background.

❑ When answerable to someone of a different culture, I avoid the tendency to "go over his or her head" to a person of my own culture.

❑ I make others aware of unfair traditions, rules and ways of behaving in my culture or organization that keep them out.

❑ I resist the temptation to make another group the scapegoat when something goes wrong.

❑ I give those from other cultures honest yet sensitive feedback about how they perform on the job.

❑ I distribute information, copies, results, etc., to whomever should get them regardless of cultural differences.

❑ I go out of my way to recruit, select, train, and promote people from outside the dominant culture.

B. When I Don't Belong to the Dominant Culture:

❑ I realize that, because of my background, I have something distinctive to contribute to my organization.

❑ Even when rejected, I take pride in my culture. I take steps to build my self-esteem and the self-esteem of others who, like me, do not belong to the dominant culture.

❑ While I know that I do not have to lose my cultural distinctiveness to fit in, I realize that I may have to learn new information and skills to succeed in the dominant culture.

❑ I look for and cultivate members of the dominant culture who will help me "read between the lines" to understand the unwritten rules about "how the system works."

❑ When I succeed in the dominant culture, I am careful not to make myself an exception or separate myself from others of my background.

❑ I share what I learn about the dominant culture with others like myself.

❑ I recognize that when under pressure, I tend to revert to narrower beliefs to make myself and my culture right and others wrong.

❑ I sympathize and collaborate with other nondominant groups to achieve common objectives in the dominant culture.

❑ I resist the inclination to cluster *only* with my own kind of people or *only* with people from the dominant culture when I am in mixed company.

❑ I resist blaming the dominant group for everything that goes wrong.

❑ I share with members of the dominant culture the distinctive qualities and accomplishments of my own culture.

❑ I know how to present distinctive points of view in ways that others can hear and understand.

❏ I can respect individuals of other cultures and treat them fairly even though I may be fiercely committed to conflicting political goals.

❏ I know how to refresh myself from the wellsprings of my own culture when I am exhausted by trying to understand and work in the dominant culture.[10]

2. What can you do as a manager to reduce problems of minority discrimination?

3. Write a brief article describing what it is like (or what you think it would be like) to work (or study) in an organization in which you are a nondominant culture member.

4. Commit yourself to improving your vision of greater cultural diversity. Pick two people with whom you share your vision during the next week. Make a commitment to do this now. Report your experience.

5. Interview an ethnic and racial group businessperson to gain insights into her or his experiences in the workplace.

6. Answer the introductory questions at the beginning of the chapter.

Notes

1. Julia Lawlor, "Diversity Provides Rewards," *USA Today* April 24, 1992, p. 2B.

2. "Labor Letter," *Wall Street Journal* November 1, 1988, p. A1.

3. Wiley M. Woodward, "Study Rules Plight of One-Third of a Nation," *Black Enterprise* August 1988, p. 24.

4. "When the Boss Is Black," *Time* March 13, 1989, pp. 60–61.

5. "Diversity: the Bottom Line," *Forbes* September 7, 1998, Special advertising section, p. 4.

6. Diana Solis, "Amnesty's Next Steps, toward U.S. Citizenship, May Be Long Ones for New Hispanic Immigrants," *Wall Street Journal* May 2, 1988, p. 52; "Illegal Aliens' Amnesty Program Ends on a Note of Desperation in Some Cities," *Wall Street Journal* May 4, 1988, p. 15.

7. C. Matthew Snipp, "The Changing Political and Economic Status of the American Indians: From Captive Nations to Internal Colonies," *American Journal of Economics and Sociology* 45, April 1986, p. 145.

8. Victoria S. Long, "Indian Support Group to Be Based in KC," *Kansas City Times* April 30, 1986, p. 1.

9. George Simons, *Working Together: How to Become More Effective in a Multicultural Organization* (Los Altos, CA: Crisp Publications, 1989), p. 71.

10. Ibid., pp. 67–68.

Another Look: Diversity—Strengthening the Business Cases

Companies that have been successful in making diversity a business priority share a common characteristic: They have strong leaders who know how to value diversity as a competitive advantage. Effectively capitalizing on the talents of a diverse workforce, these leaders not only bring out the best in their employees, they also bring results to their customers, business partners and shareholders.

As the 21st century approaches, business leaders are experiencing the tightest labor market and the toughest competition—both here and abroad—that they've seen in decades. At the same time, senior executives are faced with a workforce and a marketplace that are more diverse than ever before. Add to this mix shareholders who are increasingly more vocal about how companies treat their employees and customers, and the importance of addressing diversity becomes crystal clear.

Today, CEOs are the most effective champions of diversity. The vision they apply to business issues, such as expanding abroad, improving quality or launching a new product, is also being applied to diversity strategies. Senior management leadership means diversity is treated just as any other business initiative, with clearly measurable goals, accountability and detailed marketing plans. Often, CEOs themselves head up corporate diversity councils or task forces, thereby ensuring that this work will be viewed as a top-level priority.

Corporate Champions

At Xerox Corporation, CEO Paul A. Allaire "clearly sets the tone" for the company's focus on diversity, according to Corporate Diversity Manager Julie Baskin Brooks. Allaire considers workforce diversity a business *opportunity* rather than a business necessity or a moral imperative. "For us, diversity goes beyond numbers and targets," explains Allaire. "It is the acceptance of people of all ages with globally diverse backgrounds whose fresh ideas, opinions, perspectives and borderless creativity enrich the lives of others."

Allaire and other senior managers are personally involved in several of Xerox's diversity initiatives. Both Allaire and Chief Operating Officer G. Richard Thoman host periodic CEO roundtables with groups of employees from all of Xerox's business units to hear about the status of ongoing corporate diversity efforts firsthand. Managers who report directly to the CEO also serve as senior-level "champions" to Xerox's several employee caucus/employee advocacy groups. The champions, says Brooks, serve as a voice at the corporate officer level to focus, represent and educate senior management on the unique diversity issues within a particular constituency. The caucus groups, which are initiated and funded by employees, serve as self-development forums for groups such as women, African Americans, Hispanics, African American women, and gay and lesbian employees.

Xerox employees will be required to attend up to eight modules of diversity training and may elect to attend eight additional recommended modules. Each course runs two to four hours in length; they may be taught separately or "bundled" with other Xerox training programs. "The modules target key junctures in an employee's career," notes Brooks, adding that training courses are categorized as either awareness training, skill building or leadership. Required modules include "Interviewing for a Diverse Workforce," "Creating and Supporting an Inclusive Work Environment" and "Multicultural Teams and Work Environments."

Xerox used to consider its Balanced Workforce Strategy—a system that resembles affirmative action reporting by focusing on race/gender representation by grade level—as the key to measuring managers' success in achieving their diversity goals. Now, "given the broader definition of diversity," says Brooks, "we are beginning to focus on a broader range of measurements." These include managers' results on the Employee Motivation and Satisfaction Survey (an annual employee attitude survey), as well as ensuring pay equity and achievement of both internal and external awards that relate to diversity.

Spreading the Message

Strong senior management commitment to diversity at The Dun & Bradstreet Corporation begins with Chairman and CEO Volney Taylor, who initiated the company's inclusion initiative in 1997. "If you want to have a winning organization," says Taylor, "you have to attract the best people. You can't say there is a monopoly on talent based on race, religion, gender or anything else. That defies my experience. And if that is the case, you have to create an environment

continued

Diversity—Strengthening the Business Cases, *continued*

that appeals to all people. Otherwise, you won't succeed. That is what motivated me to launch an inclusion program at D&B."

Along with communication of Taylor's firm commitment, Dun & Bradstreet also takes a person-to-person approach through Inclusion Leadership Councils in each of the company's business units. According to Dory Gasorek, vice president of organizational performance and inclusion, these groups advise their business-unit heads and work with D&B's Advisory Group for Inclusion to develop specific strategies for each unit. In addition, Site Leadership Teams at select office locations provide an opportunity for managers to gain feedback from employees on such issues as the need for disability access, child-care and enhanced communications.

Andre Dahan, president of Dun & Bradstreet U.S., says the site teams focus on "how we make inclusion a key contributor to the business and link it to the return on shareholder value." Some senior executives have "adopted" specific corporate sites and are spending time with local site teams at these locations. Dahan has personally visited most of Dun & Bradstreet's more than 50 U.S. offices to spread the word of the strategic importance of the inclusion initiative to each associate and the company's bottom line.

Accountability: Managers Take Ownership

When diversity is considered a corporate business goal, it is essential not only that senior management champions the efforts, but also that operating managers are held accountable for carrying out diversity plans. At Merrill Lynch, the corporate goal is to build "One World-Class Company," requiring a diverse and multicultural workforce. As Merrill Lynch has expanded into new markets around the world and has attracted an increasingly diverse customer base, it has become a business imperative to address diversity. "In the past, we have compared ourselves with other financial services companies," observes David H. Komansky, chairman and chief executive officer. "Now we're raising the bar. We're going to compare ourselves with world-class companies in every industry whose success can be attributed to principled leadership—and the fact that their workforces reflect the diversity of the population."

Komansky and Merrill Lynch President and Chief Operating Officer Herbert Allison this year sent a letter to each Executive Management Committee member, who represent every business unit and support group, asking them to submit, within 30 days, a Diversity Business Plan with steps to increase diversity through specific recruiting efforts, strategic goals for promotions and succession planning. Implementing this plan is a determining factor in senior executives' compensation. In addition, these diversity plans are part of the annual "critical few objectives" of these executives, says Westina Matthews, first vice president and senior director of corporate responsibility.

To facilitate the achievement of these plans, Merrill Lynch senior executives conduct annual Management Review meetings with senior managers to ensure that candidates for key management positions are as diverse as possible. The meetings provide a forum for discussing developmental plans at every level of the company. Plans include executive coaching, training courses, rotational assignments and high-level task force assignments. "This process increases the visibility of women and minorities with senior management, thereby increasing the likelihood of promotional opportunities," says Matthews.

Another key element of Merrill Lynch's diversity strategy is community involvement. "Women and people of color value the company's presence in the communities where they live and work. In order to attract and retain valued employees, we need to be involved in our communities," says Matthews, adding that clients, too, are interested in outreach efforts. "This is a competitive business. People want to do business where they think their values will be valued."

Prepared for Opportunity

As the line between insurance and banking begins to blur, and as consumers can choose from a growing number of financial products, the ability to respond rapidly to emerging opportunities becomes key to market leadership. In response to this changing environment, The Hartford has made leveraging diversity and building inclusion key strategic initiatives. "We are all different, all diverse," says Chairman and CEO Ramani Ayer. "Building inclusiveness will allow all of us to bring our differences to work in a way that can enhance our workplace and our capacity to achieve. I believe there is incredible power in our people."

continued

Diversity—Strengthening the Business Cases, *continued*

At the corporate level, The Hartford's Corporate Diversity Roundtable dates back to 1992. According to Karen Harshaw, chairperson of the Roundtable, the group consists of 29 self-nominated individuals from each business segment of the company who communicate with their business units quarterly on diversity activities. The group also encourages the establishment of networks where employees sharing a commonality can communicate and support each other.

Source: © 1998, Hemisphere Inc. *www.diversityinc.com*

Another Look: Where the Rubber Meets the Road: Automakers Embrace Diversity

The auto industry—the largest manufacturing employer in the U.S.—is addressing workforce diversity as a major priority and a way to achieve a competitive edge.

As the industry's workforce becomes more diverse, so does the population of buyers. According to the National Association of Minority Automobile Dealers (NAMAD), minorities spend over $40 billion every year on new and used cars and related purchases. Women account for over 50% of all new vehicle purchases; that number will rise to 60% by the year 2000. Automakers are looking for ways in which to tap into this growing market and are approaching diversity not only by addressing workforce issues, but also by implementing targeted marketing strategies and striving to increase the diversity of their suppliers and dealerships.

Sheila Vaden-Williams, executive director of NAMAD, explains, "Without a doubt, the day when corporations can count on finding employee talent from and selling to a homogenous group of white males has passed. Astute corporations are making the sound business decision to understand how a comprehensive diversity initiative creates a competitive advantage."

An Innovative Approach

In deciding to address diversity, Jaguar Cars has taken a unique step by forming an Advisory Council on Diversity made up of industry experts as well as Jaguar executives. Council members include senior management leaders from private industry, government, community service organizations and the automotive sector. "To my knowledge, Jaguar is the first company that has pulled together an outside advisory board to provide it with suggestions on how to implement a comprehensive diversity initiative," says Vaden-Williams, who sits on Jaguar's Council. She is conducting nine sessions of diversity training for every Jaguar employee throughout the U.S. and Canada.

To effectively address key diversity issues, the Advisory Council has established several subcommittees. For example, the Marketing/Advertising subcommittee is working with Jaguar and its advertising agency, Ogilvy & Mather, to determine how to most effectively reach ethnic markets. The human resources subcommittee will be studying internal diversity issues as well as recruiting and hiring policies and procedures. The final subcommittee focuses on dealer franchise development and other dealer diversity issues. This group also identifies minority dealer candidates, and recently helped Jaguar identify its first African American dealer.

Jaguar President Mike Dale initiated the council in 1997 and has taken a strong leadership role in tying diversity to the company's business mission. Dale and Jaguar's vice presidents meet at least once a quarter with the Council. As a result, Dale has committed to appoint minorities to at least one-third of new dealerships planned through the year 2003.

To encourage diversity in Jaguar's future workforce, the company has initiated cooperative education programs to introduce minority students to the automotive industry. For example, a one-year apprentice program for graduates of the Youth Automotive Center in Newark, N.J., provides graduates with full-time employment either with Jaguar Cars or with a local dealership.

Workforce Strategies Drive Change

"The key driver in our diversity work has been our senior management involvement," according to Romero McNairy, director of corporate diversity and work-life planning, Ford Motor Company. Ford's

continued

Where the Rubber Meets the Road, *continued*

Chairman and CEO Alex Trotman and his direct reports make up the Executive committee, which last year identified 12 initiatives the committee would champion to fast-forward diversity at the automaker.

For example, Executive Committee members last year conducted 90-minute diversity focus groups, each member working with different demographic groups. Trotman and his direct reports heard employees' experiences, concerns and recommendations. "This creates an emotional connection that may not result from reading about someone's experience," says McNairy.

The commitment that comes from Trotman, from President of Ford Automotive operations Jacques Nasser and from other senior managers clearly springs from their belief that diversity is good for business. "All of the changes we're making are focused on making us the best automotive company in the world, as defined by our employees, our customers and our stockholders," says Trotman. "The only truly sustainable advantage that any company has is the quality, commitment, energy and competitiveness of all its people. We have to use the best talent and experience we can find, regardless of race, gender, sexual orientation, cultural or national differences."

A Winning Team

In the late 1980s, Chrysler Corporation moved to a system of car and truck "platform teams"—cross-functional teams for each vehicle were organized across the company and suppliers. The reason? Management thought that a diversity of skills and viewpoints contributing to car and truck development would yield stronger results and bring vehicles to market faster. This, in fact, proved to be the case. The value of diverse ways of thinking and diverse skills that go into platform teams illustrates why Chrysler is so committed to workforce diversity as a means of strengthening the company's bottom line. "We believe in diversity, and we are paying attention to diversity work because of the value it brings to our shareholders," explains Monica Emerson, Chrysler's director, diversity and work/family.

Chrysler's senior-level Diversity Committee, made up of 10 officers and other senior executives, meets monthly and conducts an annual review with each corporate officer in the company. At these Officer Diversity Reviews, vice presidents present progress reports on goals and diversity initiatives intended to create a more balanced and inclusive workforce. "By openly sharing accomplishments and challenges before the committee," says Emerson, "the commitment to diversity and best practices is strengthened."

The Diversity Committee is currently co-chaired by Dennis Pawley, executive vice president, manufacturing (one of the co-chairs rotates annually). "Diversity doesn't take anyone out of the picture, it just widens the picture," says Pawley. "We need to go after the best people with the same vigor that we address our quality problems." To help managers more effectively conduct diversity planning, the committee last year implemented a diversity measurement system to determine how each Chrysler organization performs on certain business processes.

"The key," says Kathy Oswald, vice president, human resources and the other co-chair of the diversity committee, "is that top management took the targets seriously, recognizing that a diverse workforce provides a business edge."

Market Opportunity Drives Diversity

For Pontiac-GMC and its parent company, General Motors, valuing diversity presents an opportunity to be a market leader. "With the globalization of industry and business, it's become abundantly clear that those companies that maximize their human resources are going to be the winners," says Roy S. Roberts, GM vice president and general manager, Pontiac-GMC.

"If you put diversity around a table," adds Roberts, "diversity of thought, diversity of people— you will get a much stronger answer in terms of how you run the business. When you think of whom we are trying to reach as consumers, it is a very fragmented marketplace. To the degree that I have people around me, challenging me, thinking differently than I do, but thinking about that marketplace, we will benefit."

General Motors Chairman and CEO Jack Smith and Vice Chair Harry Pearce as well as Roberts have been strong champions of diversity and have gone through diversity training along with all of GM's senior managers. The company recently held its first annual Diversity Day, an event designed to provide diversity partners, champions and organizational

continued

Where the Rubber Meets the Road, *continued*

leaders with tools to educate their divisions on GM's commitment to diversity.

At Diversity Day, Roberts outlined GM's target marketing efforts for populations such as women, African Americans, Hispanics and Asian Americans. He notes that building a diverse workforce is one of the most critical steps in reaching new markets. "There are hundreds of different cars for sale out there. People can buy anything they want to," he says. "To the degree that we build the best product and provide the best value, we will get the best returns for our shareholders. I don't think we can do that without maximizing on the diversity of our employees. Nothing is more important than our people. When we talk about technology, product design, marketing—people make all of that happen."

Source: © 1998, Hemisphere Inc. *www.diversityinc.com*

Another Look: The Diversity Trap

Expanded diversity training at Texaco is prescribed as the remedy for a problem that diversity training seems to have produced.

Texaco's chief executive, Peter Bijur, has committed his company to racially targeted hiring, promotion and contracting. He gave all black employees a 10% raise and claimed that such measures were "good business for Texaco, and essential for our future success."

Who can blame the poor man for saying such things with a gun to his head? He was faced with the threat of a boycott in a highly competitive market. Yet Bijur must have recognized the irony of the situation, even as he fell into the diversity trap.

The most inflammatory statement on the infamous Texaco tapes is where an executive compares African-Americans to jellybeans at the bottom of a jar. Far from being a racist remark, this was a direct reference to language used in a diversity workshop at Texaco. What a travesty. Expanded diversity training at Texaco is prescribed as the remedy for a problem that diversity training produced.

Recent surveys suggest that at least half of all major American companies have signed up for such "diversity workshops." If the Texaco example is at all typical, these efforts may be causing more harm than the good they do. Instead of minimizing the differences among ethnic groups and striving to find common ground, these workshops usually tend to sharpen the differences and heighten tensions.

The Institute for Managing Diversity, based in Atlanta, urges companies to "aggressively recruit" women, African-Americans, Latinos and Native Americans "at all levels." An excellent idea. But the institute's head, Roosevelt Thomas, calls for the development of new standards based on an affirmation of ethnic and cultural differences. His premise is that women and minority groups embody distinct ethnic and cultural "perspectives" that are business assets in themselves because they contribute to creativity and productivity. In other words, the new recruits needn't be integrated into the business. The business should change its way to fit the new recruits.

If Avon Products wants to expand its cosmetics marketing in San Antonio, it probably makes sense to recruit Hispanics for its sales staff and to include Hispanic media outlets for advertising. But there is no Hispanic, Black or Asian perspective on computer programming. And this is true in most businesses. Most scholarly research throws serious doubt on the assumption that "managing diversity" leads to a more innovative or productive work force. It may broaden the pool of potential recruits, help marketing and be good public relations. It does not in itself improve productivity. It may even lessen it.

Indeed, Taylor Cox, a strong advocate of diversity training, admits in his recent book, *Cultural Diversity in Organizations,* that "highly cohesive groups have higher member morale and better communication" and that "too much diversity in problem-solving groups can be dysfunctional."

Bradford Cornell, who teaches at UCLA's graduate school of management, goes further, contending that homogenous groups organize more efficiently. This is because the people in such groups can relate to each other better and minimize confused signals that are the product of different languages and

continued

The Diversity Trap, *continued*

cultures. He concludes that some companies may realize important gains by maintaining a relatively homogenous work force.

To deliberately strive for a homogenous workforce would, of course, bring down the wrath of the Washington enforcers and the whole diversity establishment. It would be bad public relations, too. Some form of diversity management is inevitable, and may even promote a social good.

But in order to pay off at the bottom line, diversity has to be approached pragmatically, not ideologically. This means recognizing that managing diversity

is part of the cost of doing business. It means cutting out the hypocrisy about enhancing productivity. It means helping recruited minorities enter the mainstream.

Can anyone believe that paying black workers more than white and Asian workers for the same job improves employee morale and racial harmony? That it will make Texaco a stronger and more profitable company? Do you really believe that, Peter Bijur?

Source: Dinesh D'Souza, "The Diversity Trap," *FORBES,* January 27, 1997, p. 83. Reprinted by permission of FORBES Magazine © Forbes Inc., 1997.

A Case in Point: The Downsizing of ABC Learning, Inc.

The ten persons listed below are coworkers at ABC Learning, Inc. Due to general financial problems in the economy, ABC has experienced a drastic reduction in the attendance at its public seminars. Consequently, to be able to keep functioning during what it believes to be a temporary turndown in the economy, it has decided that it must reduce its staff by 30 percent. Your task (given the information below) is to select the three employees to be cut.

After you have selected your three, get together with several other students to see if they selected the same ones. If not, why not? After talking with others, would you change any of your selections?

List of ABC Employees:

Sue Winder, president of ABC, raised in Kansas City, Missouri, and a human resource management graduate of the University of Iowa. Started ABC with her brother John in 1990. The company, although small, has been very successful in the public seminar business. Occasionally she must downsize, and occasionally she must increase the size of her firm, depending primarily on the state of the economy.

Bill Jonas, vice-president of marketing, a Navajo from Tuba City, Arizona. Bill graduated from Northern Arizona State University in Flagstaff with a degree in marketing. His studies emphasized direct-mail marketing. He worked with three large direct-mail, public seminar companies prior to coming to work for ABC. He has ten years of experience.

Paul Singh, vice president of finance, is a graduate of Madras University in accounting who emigrated to the United States in 1980. He has taken a few special finance courses from the University of Phoenix. He is fiscally conservative and is constantly concerned about cash flow.

Jose Gonzales, legal counsel, received his law degree from Pepperdine University. Born and raised in Los Angeles, he has focused his career on small start-up companies such as ABC. He has been with the company two months and is very concerned about the cutback and the legal problems associated with laying people off.

Chick Sanderson works as the key salesperson for ABC and is responsible for making the plans of Bill Jonas work. Chick's dad owned a used car lot and taught him the tricks of the sales trade. Chick knows that if ABC would let him sell his way, he could sell thousands of seminars. Chick went to work for his dad after he graduated from high school. He has been with ABC for two years.

Sally Kozlowski is the secretary. She spent one year at secretarial school and can operate all the company's computer programs. She is especially proficient in WordPerfect and Lotus. Everyone in the company comes to her for any secretarial work.

Roberta Johnson is the receptionist. She graduated from City College of Pomona. She is African American and an excellent employee. Many of those who call the company for a seminar or for help

continued

The Downsizing of ABC Learning, Inc., *continued*

comment on the wonderful treatment they get from the receptionist. Roberta has been with ABC for a month.

Jake Waters graduated from the University of California-Los Angeles in speech communication and has become the best-rated trainer at ABC. He is handsome and intelligent. His blond hair and muscular build attract many interesting comments in his teacher evaluations. He has been considering asking for a raise because he is the most productive trainer at ABC.

Sheldon Brown graduated from the University of Washington with a degree in human resource development. He is an African American with a strong feeling about the importance of education and training. His seminars get good ratings because he spends so much time dealing with the content of the seminars. His delivery is OK, and he comes across as someone who is in the know.

Lola Pongi was born and raised in Samoa, moving with her family to Oakland, California, when she was ten. Lola attended the University of California-Berkeley for two years and then went to work selling makeup for a local firm, during which time she discovered that she was an excellent presenter. She

auditioned with ABC to teach its professional appearance seminar and has been a successful trainer in this area for ten years.

List the three individuals that you would cut from the company. Give at least one reason for each decision.

Person One   _____

Reason   _____

              _____

              _____

Person Two   _____

Reason   _____

              _____

              _____

Person Three _____

Reason   _____

              _____

              _____

A Case in Point: Frank's Choice

Frank Santiago was the first Hispanic to be promoted to supervisor at fast-growing Ridgeway Telecommunications. He had always felt that management treated him fairly, but he also recognized that many minority workers seemed to fare less well. At times he wondered if he was a "token" Hispanic promoted to illustrate that the company was fair to minorities. But overall he could find no evidence to support that suspicion. Indeed, Frank was generally seen as a "fast-track" manager destined for higher leadership possibilities.

But now the shoe was on the other foot. Jeff Buchanan, a black worker who had lost his left arm below the elbow while serving in Vietnam, was discouraged about his career opportunities. He wanted the new foreman's position that had opened up, and he had talked for almost an hour to Frank without getting much reassurance. The conversation weighed

heavily on Frank's mind as he called Marsha Mason, the personnel manager, for some advice.

"Marsha, I'm confused. I'm well aware that Ridgeway claims to have an affirmative action program, but I'm not sure how I should handle Jeff," he began. "He wants the second shift foreman's job, but frankly he's not the most qualified. But at the same time, every other candidate for the job is white, and he may be pretty upset if he's not selected. How serious are we about this affirmative action stuff, Marsha?"

"You are well aware of our AA plan, Frank, but we also have to be realistic about who we promote," said Marsha. "We're not a giant corporation where a few less-effective people can be absorbed without much damage. Who is best qualified?"

"If that's the only question, I'd recommend Billy Joe Hammond. He has more seniority than Jeff and I think he's more conscientious," Frank replies.

continued

Frank's Choice, *continued*

"Well, you do what you think is best," Marsha responded. "But you probably should be aware that the EEOC people have been in here counting noses and have made it pretty clear to me that they'd like to see a few more dark ones. And with Jeff being handicapped, we'd make a few more points. So if your recommendation of Billy Joe gets overruled, don't take it personally."

Questions

1. What potential problems would Frank face if he recommended Jeff Buchanan for the promotion?

2. What problems might Frank face if he recommended Billy Joe Hammond?

3. What longterm benefits might Ridgeway Telecommunications gain from promoting Jeff?

4. If you were Frank, what would you do?

Source: Reprinted from Paul Timm, *Supervision* (St. Paul, MN: West Publishing, 1992), p. 364. Reprinted by permission from *Supervision* by Paul R. Timm © 1992 by West Publishing Company. All Rights Reserved.

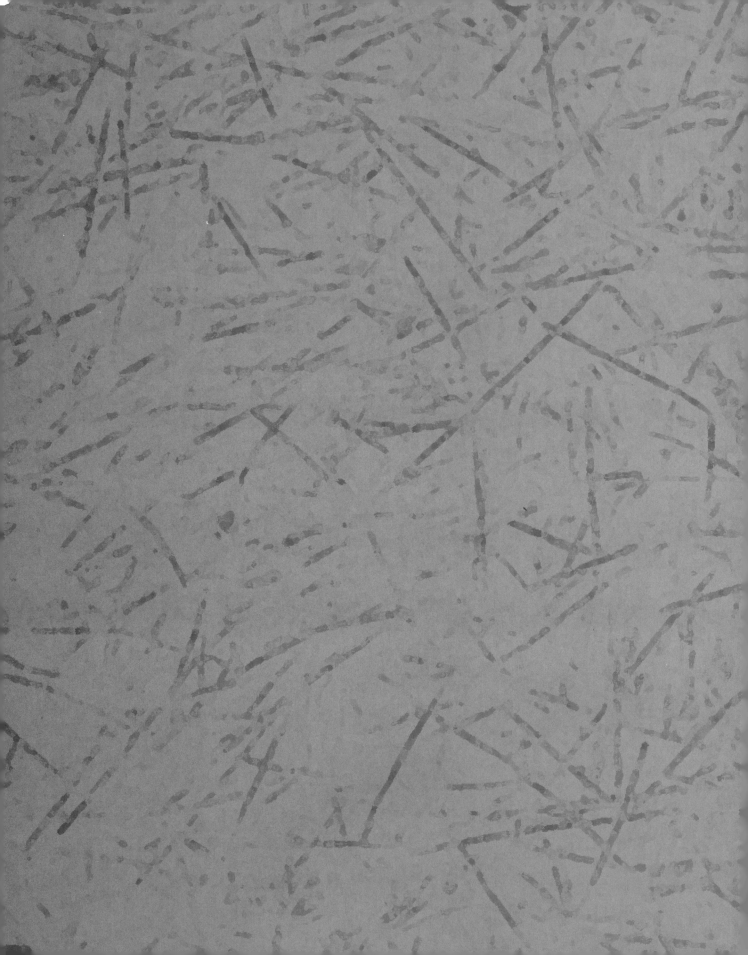

Perspectives on Cultural Socialization

- How has the role of women in the workplace changed over the last 50 years?

- Why should women seek line-management positions in a company?

- Why are mentor relationships important?

- What are some effective ways of dealing with sexual harassment?

- What can managers do to support and encourage female employees?

- What is affirmative action for workers with disabilities?

- What are some of the problems alcoholism presents at work?

- What special pressures do many old and young people and persons with disabilities face at work?

- What stereotypes do many people hold about the old, the young, or persons with disabilities in the workplace?

- How might a manager best react to people who are differently abled?

The answers to these and other questions are coming up next in Chapter 15 . . .

Women

The changes in the demographics of the workforce during the past 50 years have been dramatic. While most women were once full-time homemakers, today 48 percent of the U.S. labor force is female. The number of mothers with part-time jobs has increased, too.

The reasons women work are as numerous and varied as the reasons men work. Some are economic; women who would like to stay home with their children often find that two incomes are needed to make house and car payments. But many women are seeking levels of self-fulfillment they cannot attain by staying at home. Broader educational opportunities for women beginning in the 1950s and 1960s allowed greater numbers of women to enter traditionally male fields such as medicine, law, and engineering. Assisted by the feminist movement, women no longer have to give up a satisfying career for marriage and children but can combine all three.

As with any change, there was considerable resistance to the women's movement; changing roles for women in the workplace confused and angered some men, and women had difficulties seeing themselves and other women as executives, managers, laborers, and so forth.

Nevertheless, it appears that women have won the initial battle in the fight for equal rights. Society has largely accepted the idea that they have a legitimate place in the economic structure and a right to any job for which they are qualified.

Recruiting and Promoting Female Workers

Modern organizations generally value an effective strategy to recruit, employ, promote, and develop female employees. In recent years, there have been enormous social and governmental pressures to include women as potential employees. The Civil Rights Acts of 1964 and 1991 help protect women against discrimination in hiring and promotion. Affirmative action programs have helped women gain a more equitable proportion of jobs.

Many traditionally male positions are now being filled by females; likewise, men are taking jobs traditionally filled by women, such as nursing, secretarial, and flight attendant positions. Human-relations-smart companies aggressively seek competent women outside the organization and provide greater opportunities for potential female managers already within the firm. In the spirit of affirmative action, a business might set a goal of hiring or promoting a certain number of qualified women into management positions during the coming year.

Organizations should be careful, however, to avoid setting quotas. The *Bakke* case, discussed in Chapter 14, indicates the importance of avoiding quotas. To announce a rigid preferential system in which, say, 20 percent of all employees must be female is exclusionary; it is also illegal as well as bad business. Recent Supreme Court decisions have allowed challenges to some affirmative action agreements set up by companies or local governments.

To effectively move women into positions of authority in organizations requires a dual responsibility: companies must actively develop women's management skills, and female employees must learn how to advance their careers.

Promotion Opportunities in Line Management

Why are promotions to line-management jobs preferable to many women?

For women to genuinely participate in organizational power, they must be encouraged to seek **line-management positions.** In many organizations, women are more likely to be offered management-level jobs in *staff* roles such as public relations, personnel, accounting, and data processing. Yet responsibility for making more substantive decisions that affect a company's bottom-line often lies in sales, finance, and production departments. In these more fiscally responsible areas, decisions can affect corporate profitability and growth. Titles, nice offices, and less important assignments are only cosmetic in nature and will do little to respond to the demand for power. Women can use a number of strategies to advance their careers. *Working Woman* magazine suggests that when making career decisions, at the least the following should be done:

1. *Develop a step-by-step career plan.* A well-conceived plan gives an outline for success.

2. *Get as much education as possible.* Investing in education can be the single smartest move a career-oriented woman can make.

3. *Be flexible.* Be willing to relocate for a new job or switch to a new career.

4. *Select a predominantly male field.* Salaries are usually higher in male-dominated fields.[1]

Mentor Relationships

Several studies of women who have been highly successful in management positions indicate that supportive bosses often assisted them in their rise through **mentor relationships.** As a mentor, such a boss acts as a wise and trusted counselor and supporter of his or her subordinates.

What is a mentor?

The female employee who is interested in advancement can benefit from an older, more experienced employee who shows her the ropes. Women who have worked their way into middle- and upper-management positions serve as mentors to younger women. Many women who have been successful in management positions want to be supportive of younger female employees as **role models.** These successful women want to mentor and help other females in any way they can.

Organizations should attempt to break down **sex-based roles** to ensure that women—especially those new in management positions—receive opportunities to develop mentor relationships.

Organizational Support

In addition to fostering mentor relationships, successful organizations can provide female employees with a manager who performs four essential functions:

1. Provides an effective role model for women to emulate.

2. Helps female subordinates identify alternative ladders to success and helps them design career development programs.

3. Knows the importance of identifying concrete goals and facilitates plans for achieving them.

4. Evaluates and provides systematic, valid, ongoing feedback on the employees' efforts.[2]

Working Mothers

In 1978, Title VII of the Civil Rights Act of 1964 was amended to prohibit sex discrimination on the basis of pregnancy. Women affected by pregnancy, child birth, or related medical conditions must be treated the same for all employment-related purposes, including receipt of benefits under fringe benefit programs, as other persons not so affected but similar in their ability or inability to work. This Act has been a great help to women during pregnancy. However, as more women continue to work after having children, they face the challenge of providing proper care for their children. A number of companies realize that worried parents are not productive workers. Hoping to retain trained

On-site day care continues to increase in popularity as a benefit for working parents.

employees, they are looking for ways to help parents cope with the stresses on the single-parent family or the family in which both parents work.

Parental Leave   **Parental leave** is one benefit that some companies are now providing. It allows parents to take a certain amount of time off to care for a newborn or newly adopted child or for very ill children or elderly parents. Legislation to make parental leave a mandatory benefit nationally was introduced in Congress every year since 1985 but died without a vote until 1991. In that year, the Family and Medical Leave Act (FMLA), which would have required businesses with 50 or more employees to provide up to ten weeks of unpaid family leave, was passed by Congress but vetoed by President George Bush.

However, in 1993 the FMLA was passed, requiring companies with more than 25 employees to allow parents up to 12 weeks of uncompensated time off to care for their children. In addition to this national legislation, some states are taking the initiative to ensure that families can survive in the face of demanding work schedules. California's Family School Partnership Act prohibits companies employing 25 or more from discriminating against workers who take 40 hours or less of annual leave to participate in school activities. Minnesota has a similar program, and guarantees 16 hours a year to attend scholastic events that cannot be scheduled outside working hours.

What is flextime?

Child Care   Single parents or caretaker parents who decide to work face the difficult task of finding quality care for their children at an affordable price. In recent years, some companies have begun working with employees to find solutions to the childcare dilemma. Concepts such as in-house day care, job sharing, and **flextime** (where parents arrange their own hours) are helping both two-worker families and single parents.

The Campbell Soup Company has had on-site day care for several years. The company also has a flextime policy in which flexible work hours compensate for child-care demands; for example, one parent might work from 7 A.M. to 3:30 P.M., to arrive home when the children are out of school. Campbell also provides a one-month paid maternity leave and a three-month unpaid leave for any worker to care for a new child or sick relative.

To help its employees across the country, IBM began Child Care Referral Service in 1984, which now offers information on child-care providers in more than 200 communities. IBM has also provided money to improve facilities and recruit additional childcare providers for its employees. In 1988, the company began a program to help with care of elderly relatives as well.

In addition to these benefits, some companies are trying out other family policies. Some allow two or more employees to share a job, each working part-time; this is called *job sharing*. Others allow employees to work a reduced schedule to care for children or sick relatives while staying on a career track. Still others provide group insurance covering nursing-home costs for elderly parents. Many managers believe that a family policy attracts good employees and reduces turnover.

What is job sharing?

Sexual Harassment

A pat on the rear end. Unwanted flirtation. Obscene jokes or comments about appearance. Public display of nude photos or calendars. Pressure to trade sexual favors for a promotion. These are forms of **sexual harassment.** As more women have entered the workforce, sexual harassment on the job has become a growing problem—primarily for women, but occasionally for men as well.

What is sexual harassment?

The Civil Rights Acts of 1964 and 1991 made sexual harassment illegal, as a form of sexual discrimination. But this provision has been difficult to enforce, even after 1980, when the Equal Employment Opportunity Commission published guidelines to help corporations follow the law.

The EEOC defined sexual harassment as follows:

> Unwelcome sexual advances, requests for sexual favors, and other verbal or physical contact of a sexual nature constitutes sexual harassment when:
>
> 1. Submission to such conduct is made either explicitly or implicitly a term or condition of an individual's employment.
>
> 2. Submission to or rejection of such conduct by an individual is used as the basis for employment decisions affecting such individuals.
>
> 3. Such conduct has the purpose or effect of unreasonably interfering with an individual's work performance or creating an intimidating, hostile, or offensive working environment.

The 1986 Supreme Court decision in the case of *Meritor Savings Bank v. Vinson* expanded the definition of sexual harassment to include a hostile work environment created by unwelcome flirtation, lewd comments, or obscene jokes.

Based on this case, to make a claim of hostile-environment sexual harassment, a claimant must show that not only was he or she affected and offended by the sexual conduct but that an objective third party—a "reasonable person"—would also have been offended. Prior to this case, companies had to deal with a notion of sexual harassment that was pretty much subjective.

What Companies Can Do   One article estimates that sexual harassment costs a typical Fortune 500 company $6.7 million per year in low morale and productivity, absenteeism, and employee turnover. Many corporate leaders therefore "have come to realize that companies that tolerate sexual harassment in the workplace pay a price, in the form of lost productivity, the exit of valuable employees, and expensive and damaging lawsuits."[3]

Companies that tolerate sexual harassment pay a price.

A worker who is unable to stop sexual harassment alone should have a way to lodge a formal complaint with the company. Generally, companies handle sexual harassment in the same way they handle racism or other forms of discrimination.

The tone and attitude of the company can go a long way in preventing sexual harassment as well. The company should have a clear written policy outlining sexual harassment and the appropriate disciplinary measures. In addition, many companies are now providing training programs on handling this problem. And company officials must make it clear that managers are accountable for dealing effectively with sexual harassment complaints among their workers.

Women face some unique and difficult pressures at work. Supervisors need to be responsive to these special problems. Susan L. Webb in her book *Sexual Harassment in the Workplace: What You Need to Know!* presents six necessary factors for controlling sexual harassment:

1. *Top management's support*—Leaders of organizations must view harassment as a legal and a business problem—one that interferes with productivity. By adopting a serious attitude, top management influences the way people approach the problem.

2. *A written, posted policy*—The written policy should include:

    a. Statement of purpose: to set out the organization's position on sexual harassment.

    b. Legal definition of harassment.

    c. Descriptions of behaviors that constitute harassment.

    d. Importance of the problem.

    e. How employees should handle harassment: how they should confront the harasser and report incidents.

    f. How the organization handles complaints.

    g. Disciplinary action.

    h. Names and numbers of individuals to call to make a complaint.

3. *A procedure for handling complaints*—Give employees an option of going to any of several people with their complaints.

4. *A timetable for handling complaints*—Act quickly and fairly.

5. *Training programs*—Short training programs regarding harassment, assertiveness, and gender-awareness have proved helpful.

6. *Follow-up*—Keep the concept of harassment on the minds of the employees by occasional memos and other follow-ups.[4]

What Individuals Can Do   The first thing to keep in mind is that the longer sexual advances are allowed to go on, the harder they are to stop. Initially, advances may not be in earnest; the aggressor may make them because he or she thinks it's expected. But if they continue, personal feelings become involved and an enormous amount of organizational energy can be wasted.

If you are a victim, speak out early—tell the aggressor in a direct, businesslike way that what is going on isn't acceptable. Unfortunately, this is often difficult, especially when the aggressor is your boss. If the problem continues, keep a written record of the advances and your response. Ask other men or women in the office if they have experienced sexual harassment as well.

Differently Abled Workers

A recent college graduate who was remarkably intelligent was unable to get employment. She had completed a law degree and passed the bar examination in her state. She had also completed her M.B.A. degree with honors. However, since she was barely four feet tall, most people saw her as a child. She had a very real physical disability. We believe her size caused many organizations to pass over her for employment.

Organizations are made up of all sorts of people, including: people with disabilities that are mental and/or physical, older people, younger people, people with drug- and alcohol-dependency problems, and people who are seriously ill with diseases such as AIDS. All of these people in organizations and those who are trying to get into organizations deserve to be treated equally. They deserve to be respected. They deserve to receive equal wages. Like our law student with great qualifications, they should be given a chance.

Workers with Disabilities

Individuals suffer a wide variety of disabilities both physical and mental. Fortunately, public awareness of the difficulties and the courage of people with disabilities is increasing. A few years ago, for example, a disabled athlete ran from Boston to Los Angeles, despite having lost one leg to bone cancer. Upon completion of this grueling run, he told news reporters: "I'm not physically disabled. I'm physically *challenged.*"

Physical or mental impairments, when severe enough to affect the job, typically involve one or more of the following:

1. Physical appearance

2. Physical functioning (especially motor skills)

3. Mental functioning

Many disabilities can be corrected to the extent that an individual can function as well as a person without a disability. Crutches, artificial limbs, wheelchairs, and many other modern technological developments have helped people with physical disabilities function effectively in many jobs.

Changes and Adjustments Faced by Workers with Disabilities

Employees who have physical or mental disabilities face considerable frustration when they are not hired for work that they can do. The problem, in this sense, is similar to that of racial or sex discrimination, and likewise can result in lowered self-esteem and psychological adjustment problems.

Should we have affirmative action for the disabled?

Many organizations have **affirmative action programs for workers with disabilities.** Legislation has placed considerable emphasis on encouraging companies to hire people with disabilities. This is not a new idea; workers with disabilities have been hired for many years, and most organizations regard such hiring as good business.

Congress passed the **Americans with Disabilities Act** in 1990 to provide people with disabilities equal opportunity in employment, public accommodations, transportation, government services, and telecommunications. This act was a direct result of statistics showing that a large number of the nation's employable persons with disabilities simply were not getting job offers.

Federal law calls for businesses to have affirmative action programs that include the following types of activities:

- Outreach and positive recruitment of people with disabilities.

- Internal communication of the obligation to employ and advance persons with disabilities. Such communication should foster acceptance and understanding of workers with disabilities among other employees and management.

- Development of internal procedures ensuring fair treatment of workers with disabilities.

- Use of all available recruiting sources—state employment and vocational, rehabilitation agencies, workshops, and other institutions that train persons with disabilities.

- Review of employment records to determine the availability of promotable workers with disabilities.

- Accommodation of the physical and mental limitations of qualified employees with disabilities.[5]

Changing the physical environment of an organization to accommodate an individual with disabilities is quite different from creating a corporate culture that openly welcomes such employees. It is also the responsibility of organizations to debunk many of the myths held about the differently abled.

Stereotypes and Misconceptions about Workers with Disabilities

A **stereotype** is a generalization about the nature of people that is often incorrect. Many people have misconceptions and stereotypes about workers with physical or mental disabilities. Among these are:

 - *"They are accident-prone."* Not true. Little evidence exists to indicate that people with physical or mental disabilities have any more accidents than do other people. Some people with disabilities do not have the physical agility to do certain things, but they are often more aware of their own limitations than others may be.

   Studies of accident-proneness indicate that it has little or nothing to do with physical disabilities. Most people who suffer frequent accidents do so because of attitudinal problems, specifically, people find themselves in accidents because they make wrong assumptions about what is about to happen. Similarly, they fail to consider potential hazards.

   People with disabilities are thus no more accident-prone than other individuals. In fact, in many cases they have to be more careful.

- *"They are distressing to look at."* Not true. Probably the single greatest difficulty that disabled people have is that they make "normal people" feel uncomfortable when they are around us. Can you recall as a child, staring at a physically disabled person? Most young people do.

   Many people are uncomfortable around those with disabilities because they don't know what to say or expect or how to respond. People feel sympathy for someone who has lost a limb or who is otherwise physically or mentally impaired—in part, perhaps, due to a fear of being similarly challenged. At any rate, such discomfort is rooted in fear and a lack of understanding.

   Getting to know others on a personal basis is one effective way of reducing racial or gender prejudices. The same can be said about the

People are uncertain about how people with disabilities will react to questions or comments.

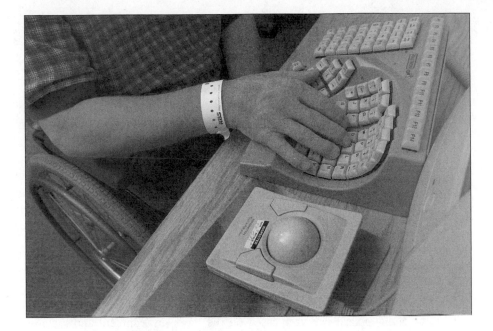

Technological advances can help to break down stereotypes about disabled workers.

person with disabilities. Getting to know such a person often reveals many more similarities than differences—"they" are really very much like "us."

- *"They can't pull their own weight in the organization."* Not true. This criticism is similar to that leveled against the older employee—that these employees cannot do a fair amount of work. Again, due to modern technological devices and assistance, this idea is false. With certain assistance devices people with disabilities can and do complete a productive day's work. In addition, the awareness of the extra effort that an employer may be making to hire and keep the disabled is often highly appreciated. The result is reliable, loyal workers.

Workers with Alcohol- and Drug-Dependency Problems

The excessive use of alcohol and drugs continues to be a prevalent and costly problem to many organizations. Estimates show that approximately 18 million people in the United States have serious drinking problems, with the lives of double that number adversely affected by alcohol. Drug abuse affects the lives of still more millions of people. How widespread and serious are these problems in industry?

Alcoholism in the Workplace

Alcoholism is a problem of epidemic proportions in the United States, Canada, and many other countries. Although considerable debate exists over where social drinking ends and alcoholism begins, there is little doubt that alcoholism is a serious problem in the workplace.

The problem is not limited to the workplace, however. The excessive use and abuse of alcohol occurs in colleges, secondary schools, and in some cases, even elementary schools. It appears in governmental bodies, in churches, and in the home. Although our focus is on the workplace, most of the material presented here is applicable in a much wider arena.

Studies of alcoholism among workers conclude that:

1. Workers who suffer from job stress and organizational frustration frequently turn to alcohol as a tool for unwinding.

2. While depression, lack of close personal relationships, guilt feelings, social rejection, and genetic, chemical, mental, and other disorders are associated with excessive drinking, there is also a clear correlation between job stress and high alcohol consumption.

3. Even though it is widely recognized that excessive drinking can lead to physical or psychological dependence on alcohol, many organizations encourage social drinking. Company activities often revolve around cocktail parties or other events that involve drinking. Most companies show little concern for the heavy drinker until his or her work is adversely affected.[6]

Alcoholic employees often remain on the job for years after the onset of alcoholism because they are able to camouflage the symptoms of their illness. Symptoms of alcoholism will vary based on the work environment and include those on the following list. Supervisors will be better able to help afflicted employees if they recognize these symptoms early on.

- Avoidance of boss and associates

- Uncharacteristically outgoing or pushy

- Pronounced and frequent changes in work pace

- Elaborate or bizarre excuses for work deficiencies

- Severe financial difficulties

- Increased nervousness, hand tremors, gastric upsets, and insomnia

- Sloppy personal appearance with signs of hangover

- Frequent lapses of efficiency, occasionally causing damage to equipment or creating safety hazards

- Frequent trips to water cooler and break area

- Marked increase in medical claims for accidents and illnesses both on and off the job

Drug Abuse in the Workplace

Drug problems involve both addiction and illegal actions.

Drug-dependent workers face many of the same problems as those who abuse alcohol. **Drug abuse** is a problem of great concern in the workplace. Most estimates place the number of drug users as slightly less than the number of abusers of alcohol. Statistics regarding the use of drugs vary greatly. Further, drug users are harder to identify than alcohol abusers. However, when all drugs—including over-the-counter preparations—cocaine, crack, marijuana, LSD, PCP, peyote, mescaline, "ecstasy," and heroin are considered together, drug abuse obviously becomes a large problem both in and out of our major organizations. Statistics regarding drug abuse are difficult to obtain because drugs, unlike alcohol, are illegal and many users are unwilling to admit or discuss their use. The costs of drug abuse in the workplace are not as well documented as the costs of alcoholism, but it is believed that they are huge—and growing. The symptoms of drug abuse are similar to those of alcoholism and also include the following:

- Slurred or incoherent speech

- Dilated eyes

- Uncontrollable laughter or crying

- Sloppy appearance without the smell of alcohol

- Unsteady walk or impaired dexterity

- Wide mood fluctuations

There are many other symptoms depending on the type of drug used. The end result is that the abuser is normally unfit for work.

Policies for Dealing with Alcoholism, Drug Abuse, and Privacy

Many companies have written policies for dealing with alcoholism and drug abuse. Those policies include the following ideas:

- Alcoholism and drug abuse are diseases that can be successfully treated.

- Workers will be treated confidentially.

- Workers will not be forced to accept treatment under the company treatment program if they can show that they are actively engaged in solving the problem through other means.

Workers with AIDS

A newcomer to the list of human relations concerns is **Acquired Immunodeficiency Syndrome (AIDS).** The likelihood that a company will have people with AIDS among its employees is ever-increasing. Some businesses are especially vulnerable to fears about the disease. For example, a restaurant's business could be devastated if word got out that a person with AIDS was an employee.[7]

Companies must be careful to avoid taking actions against employees with AIDS that could be ruled discriminatory, lest they be subject to legal action. In many places, employers are forbidden by law to fire or to refuse to hire a person with AIDS unless it can be shown that employment alone or the duties of a specific job will intensify the person's risk of illness and death. Most laws provide for discharge action when the person with AIDS cannot adequately perform the job. However, more important than the legal ramifications of dealing with employees with AIDS should be the simple desire on the part of the organization and its employees to understand, accept, and assist fellow employees with this illness.

Many companies have written policies stating that AIDS and other serious diseases are confidential matters. These require AIDS to be treated discreetly and withheld from public knowledge.

By developing simple yet inexpensive AIDS training programs, U.S. companies can take positive action toward reducing direct costs, limiting and possibly eliminating indirect costs, and increasing social responsibility. The best training programs emphasize sensitivity and provide information to dispel myths and preconceptions about AIDS.

Companies avoid actions against the seriously ill (especially employees with AIDS) for fear of being accused of illegal discrimination.

Older Workers

What is an older worker? Age is highly relative. A recent radio commentary was phrased as a "good-news/bad-news" story. The reporter told the good news: "A recent survey at a major southern university showed that female college students

How old is old?

found middle-aged men very attractive." The bad news: "They defined 'middle-aged' as 'about 32.'"

A corporate president, Supreme Court justice, or high-ranking political figure in his or her early forties is considered very young. A professional athlete can be washed up at 33, whereas a medical doctor is just starting a career at that age. So age is indeed relative.

Age has different values in different cultures, too. In Western nations, people tend to pride themselves on being young and vigorous. Enormous amounts of money are spent by people trying to regain their youth and keep a young appearance. In other cultures, notably in Asia, great value is placed on the "wisdom of age."

Tragically, some highly productive workers are forced to retire when they reach a particular numerical age—usually age 65. A lot of talent is wasted when able employees are no longer given opportunities for productive work. Yet this too seems to be changing. An increasing activity and even militancy among older people has begun to develop, as illustrated by such movements as the Gray Panthers and the increasing power of such organizations as the American Association for Retired Persons (AARP). Many older Americans are enjoying unprecedented good health and vigor, and they want to continue being productive members of society.

Changes and Adjustments Faced by Older Employees

The U.S. population has grown older since 1950: life expectancies have increased by more than seven years while the birth rate has dropped by a third. This will greatly alter the labor force between now and 2005 as the 55 years and older segment of our population grows 2.5 percent per year.

As workers reach the age of senior citizenship, they face some potentially dramatic adjustments. They experience, for example, changes in their family and social needs and responsibilities. Over the years, they have been responsible for being breadwinners and for raising families. Suddenly they are likely to be more alone, perhaps with only their spouses. Sometimes they feel they are not needed. For some, this can lower self-esteem.

In addition, with age comes a heightened awareness of the implication of one's own death. Older employees have usually lost many of their peers and associates. Inevitably, workers in their sixties or seventies face this greatest of all changes with apprehension.

Other changes too must be faced. Frequently, the older worker considers the possibility of retirement. Although retirement may pose a very pleasant change for many workers, it nevertheless calls for significant adjustments in daily activity. Psychologists tell us that major changes in daily activity are very stressful. Some organizations hold preretirement training sessions with older employees to help prepare them for this process.

Finally, the older worker usually experiences some physical infirmities. A natural decline in strength and a rise in physical impairments come naturally with age. For example, loss of hearing, changing sleep patterns, chronic illness, hypertension, arthritis, lack of energy, and loss of sight are common difficulties. As workers age, they encounter more physical problems.

Although such changes and adjustments are normal among older workers, their supervisors need to be sensitive to these changes and also need to be aware of stereotypes about the older worker, which are often misconceptions. Let's take a look at some of these.

Stereotypes and Misconceptions about Older Workers

Stereotypes applied to older workers, especially those in their sixties or beyond, include the following:

"There is only one thing age can give you, and that is wisdom."

S. I. Hayakawa

Does mandatory retirement waste organizational resources?

Changing family responsibilities can lower older people's sense of self-worth.

Older workers generally have more physical problems.

Most stereotypes of older workers are without foundation.

Older workers' maturity and experience often make them valuable employees.

- *"They cannot pull their own weight on the job."* Not true. What is meant by "pulling their own weight" differs among various organizations. Does it mean having physical stamina and the ability to handle heavy work? Or keeping up with clerical or nonphysical activities? Either way, the generalization does not hold up.

    Although older employees do tend to have increasing physical infirmities and often decline in strength, this tends to have little effect on their work. Mature workers develop a clear understanding of their physical limits and work within them. Furthermore, they are generally more stable and less likely to "job hop" than their younger coworkers.

    From a physical perspective, older people can almost always lift as much as the upper limit set by law. When laws were demanded requiring machines for many lifting jobs, they were initiated by younger people who felt they were having to work too hard—not by older people.

- *"They resist changes."* Not true. The old adage "You can't teach an old dog new tricks" seems to have been taken too literally. Many people assume that older people cannot learn new tasks quickly, that they tend to be in a rut. The fact is that people of all ages resist changes. There is no evidence that this is limited to older workers.

- *"They are costly to the organization."* Not true. Some assume that older employees cost the organization more money. Again, there is virtually no support for this statement.

Some older employees have developed expertise and skills that make them extremely efficient on the job. In addition, turnover rates among older employees are significantly lower. As workers face imminent retirement, they have little motivation to change jobs. Older employees tend to stick with current positions and thus eliminate for their organizations the cost of hiring and training workers to replace them.

Older people, in fact, have better attendance records than younger employees. Most studies of worker absenteeism, tardiness, and attendance show that older people create fewer problems for their employers than do other workers.

> **"Old age is when you know all the answers but nobody asks you the questions."**
> Laurence J. Peter

> **"When your friends begin to flatter you on how young you look, it's a sure sign you're getting older."**
> Mark Twain

Although inevitable health problems or physical difficulties may cause them to miss work occasionally, most absenteeism in organizations is not a result of sickness. Employees of all ages take time off for personal or family reasons, or simply because they want to go to a baseball game or some other activity, more often than because of illness. In summary, most stereotypes of older employees are without foundation. Mature workers experience some changes and adjustments in their lives, but no more so than do other people.

Antidiscrimination Legislation

In 1967, Congress enacted the Age Discrimination in Employment Act (ADEA) which stated that no employee aged 40 to 65 could be discriminated against in employment practices due to his or her age. In 1986, an amendment to the Act protected all workers over 40, and in 1990 a Supreme Court ruling initiated another amendment that detailed the terms under which employee benefits may be provided to older workers.

Younger Workers

Younger workers (those under age 25) are also subject to certain changes and adjustments in their lives as well as to stereotypes and misconceptions held by others.

Changes and Adjustments Faced by Young Workers

The awareness that one is not a kid anymore can call for major adjustments.

The young, full-time employee may suddenly realize that he or she is "not a kid anymore." This can be quite an adjustment. As people leave the school environment and enter the workforce full-time, they experience some serious changes in their lifestyles. They suddenly have responsibilities—to get up and be someplace at a particular time, and to produce useful effort on behalf of an organization. These responsibilities frequently cause a dramatic change in the life pattern of the young person.

The process of adjusting and conforming to a work routine is further complicated when we consider the uncertainties associated with new work expectations. Many young people begin jobs without fully understanding what is expected by their employers. Expectations can be clarified by the sensitive supervisor, but inevitably young employees will make some mistakes or misjudgments early in their work careers.

"Nobody can be so amusingly arrogant as a young man who has just discovered an old idea and thinks it is his own."
Sydney Harris

Finally, some special adjustments are faced by young people who suddenly find that they have a degree of financial independence. They now face more new decisions and problems as they earn and spend their own income—perhaps for the first time.

Stereotypes and Misconceptions about Young Workers

As with older employees, certain stereotypes exist about young workers, among them the following:

• *"They are reckless and irresponsible."* Not true. Many people think that young workers are cocky and don't consider the consequences of their actions. Some truth may be found in this, but these traits are not limited to young employees.

The air of recklessness and irresponsibility associated with some young adults may arise from inexperience, a lack of social graces, or ignorance of organizational protocol. The oft-mentioned statistic that younger people have more automobile accidents (and are therefore more reckless) than older people is a classic example of a stereotype.

Analysis of the ratio of miles driven—that is, the number of accidents compared against the exposure to accidents—disproves that younger people are more reckless, irresponsible, or careless. There is a tendency in our society to remember and talk about the few young people who get in automobile wrecks, belong to gangs, are arrested for disorderly conduct during spring break, and so on. Unfortunately, little is heard or said about the vast majority of young people who act responsibly.

- *"They are less committed to the organization."* Not true. The assumption is that young people are concerned only with their own interests and care little for organizational accomplishment. No basis exists for assuming that this is a general condition among young people, many of whom are in fact very committed to certain causes. Such commitment can often be effectively used in a business organization.

The supervisor who is aware of these common misconceptions will be more likely to deal effectively with, and reduce many of the pressures on, the young worker.

Young people often come to the work environment with a great amount of energy and a desire to put to work what they have learned at school. All too often companies are rigid and provide few opportunities for young people to expend their energy in positive ways or to employ their knowledge. The supervisor who is able to positively challenge young workers is likely to achieve considerable success with them.

Generation X

It's become very popular in the last few years to analyze and even "bash" those individuals born 1968 to 1978 who belong to **Generation X.** "Gen Xers" have been called lazy, whiny, and irresponsible. They have been accused of believing they are entitled professionally to personal time, raises, promotions, and titles, and have been maligned by the media with labels such as "slackers," "baby-busters," "twenty-somethings," and the "Instant Gratification Generation."

True, there are philosophical differences between baby boomer managers and their Gen X employees: younger workers believe in taking career risks, switching jobs, and balancing their careers with personal pursuits. However, a savvy manager employs and benefits from the post–baby-boomers' ease and adaptability with computer technology, and willingness to stand up for what is "fair" and meaningful for them.

Manager Reactions to People with Challenges

A manager is often defined as "a person who achieves organizational goals through the efforts of other people." To achieve their purposes, managers must be able to work with a variety of people with a wide range of special characteristics or problems.

We have discussed several such special human relations challenges in this chapter: old age, youth, disabilities, drug or alcohol abuse, and AIDS. The wise manager or supervisor realizes that he or she has a responsibility for helping employees deal effectively with special pressures or problems that may interfere with work. He or she also realizes that the costs of not dealing with these pressures effectively are prohibitive, whereas the ability to deal with them effectively is both professionally and personally rewarding.

The bottom line is that several special workgroups have special pressures on them. Managers can recognize some of these problems, including the stereotypes and misconceptions that others hold toward these people, and can help ensure fairness and equality of opportunity for all people. In addition, supervisors can help provide counseling services, when feasible, to help people with special challenges reach maximum satisfaction in their jobs.

Summary of Key Ideas

- The role of women in the workplace (and in the home) has changed dramatically over the past 50 years.

- Women are now moving into previously male-dominated fields such as law, trucking, and engineering, and men are taking jobs that were previously dominated by women.

- Mentor relationships can play a vital role in the upward mobility of both female and male workers.

- Sexual harassment is a serious, costly problem in many organizations.

- The overall lot of women in the workplace has improved significantly in recent years, and the future looks bright for women at work.

- The three misconceptions about persons with disabilities are that they are accident-prone, are distressing to look at, and cannot do their share of work.

- Alcoholism and drug abuse are major problems in the modern workplace; their resolution depends on the coordinated and cooperative efforts of management, labor leaders, and the affected workers.

- Alcoholism costs business enormous amounts of money and typically results in higher absenteeism, more on-the-job accidents, and additional health care costs.

- The three misconceptions about older workers are that they cannot pull their own weight on the job, they resist change, and they are costly to the organization.

- Two common misconceptions about young workers assert that they are reckless and irresponsible and that they are less committed to the organization than their more mature counterparts.

Key Terms, Concepts, and Names

Acquired Immunodeficiency Syndrome (AIDS)
Affirmative action for persons with disabilities
Alcoholism
Americans with Disabilities Act
Drug abuse
Flextime

Generation X
Line-management positions
Mentor relationships
Parental leave
Role models
Sex-based roles
Sexual harassment
Stereotype

Questions and Exercises

1. What four essential activities should managers perform to ensure that female employees are provided with the necessary organizational support to be successful? How important are these activities? How do they differ from supports that might be provided for male employees? What *specific* actions should a manager take to create these supports?

2. Describe what actions you would take as a manager to reduce problems of sexual harassment.

3. What stereotypes do you hold about old, young, and disabled people? Make a list. Then use this list as a basis for a class discussion. How realistic are these stereotypes?

4. In general, how can a manager best cope with the employment of workers with disabilities? What approach is likely to be most sensitive to the person with disabilities? Describe a general strategy for dealing with people with disabilities.

5. Review the discussion of affirmative action for persons with disabilities. How could you as a manager implement such a program? Be specific.

6. What are some symptoms of alcohol and drug abuse?

7. How should a manager deal with an obvious case of drug abuse or extreme alcoholism?

8. Make a case for or against the statement that "younger workers are more careless, impulsive, and irresponsible than older workers."

9. Answer the introductory questions at the beginning of this chapter.

Notes

1. Steve Guarnaccia, "The 25 Hottest Careers," *Working Woman* July 1995, pp. 45–51.

2. Margaret and Warner Woodworth, "Women Working," *Exchange* Spring/Summer 1978, p. 31.

3. Ronni Sandroff, "Sexual Harassment: The Inside Story," *Working Woman* June 1992, pp. 70–72.

4. Susan L. Webb, *Sexual Harassment in the Workplace: What You Need to Know!* (Seattle: Pacific Resource, 1991).

5. Larry Steinmetz, *Human Relations* (New York: Harper & Row, 1979), p. 295.

6. Gene Milbourn, Jr., "Alcohol and Drugs," *Supervisory Management* March 1981.

7. "How Business Owners Deal with AIDS in the Workplace," *Profit-Building Strategies for Business Owners* 18, (March 1998) pp. 11–12.

Another Look: Unwanted Advances, Unheeded Declines

The number of sexual harassment complaints in the United States has more than doubled since 1991. Researchers at Ohio University are studying the message these numbers send and their impact on society.

In 1990, the nomination of Clarence Thomas to the nation's highest court was clouded by allegations of sexual harassment that nearly killed his candidacy. Anita Hill's claims of workplace harassment fell on the disbelieving ears of a majority of senators who ultimately confirmed Thomas as a U.S. Supreme Court justice. Eight years later, the subject of sexual harassment remains on the social agenda.

Companies have been sued: In August, Mitsubishi Motor Manufacturing of America agreed to pay $9.5 million to settle a sexual harassment lawsuit brought by 27 female employees.

Legal precedents have been set: In March, the U.S. Supreme Court ruled that same-sex harassment violates the Civil Rights Act of 1964.

News stories have been filed: Early 1998 headlines told of sexual harassment allegations against the nation's president and the Army's former highest-ranking enlisted soldier.

The lines of news ink and hours of videotape have emphasized what many believe is a very important message: No office, not even the Oval Office, is immune to allegations of sexual harassment.

"It may be the most important issue affecting employers in the 1990s and the coming years," says Arthur Marinelli, one of several researchers at Ohio University who has studied sexual harassment and related issues over the last decade.

With the increased media attention came a nationwide increase in awareness of the sexual harassment concept and a dramatic rise in complaints of sexual harassment in the workplace, says Marinelli, a professor of law and management systems. In 1997, there were 15,889 sexual harassment complaints filed with the U.S. Equal Employment Opportunity Commission, more than double the number filed in 1991.

But what hasn't changed, Marinelli adds, is a fundamental lack of understanding of what behavior constitutes sexual harassment.

"We need more definition on pervasive, severe, and unwelcome advances and what the legal standard is for the employer," Marinelli says, referring to Supreme Court rulings defining sexual harassment. "What is severe to one person is not severe to another."

Based on Supreme Court rulings, most lawyers and researchers divide sexual harassment into two categories, "quid pro quo" and "hostile environment," says Rebecca Thacker, an associate professor of human resource management at Ohio University.

The quid pro quo, or "one thing in return for another," involves the stereotypical superior-subordinate harassment: "Sleep with me or date me or you are fired, demoted, or transferred," Thacker says. The harassment is more obvious and easier to document and prove, she adds, than the more vague "hostile environment" form of harassment. The latter involves behavior that interferes with an individual's work performance by creating an intimidating, hostile, or offensive working environment.

"Hostile environment is individually defined," Thacker says. "Behaviors such as sexual joking and commentary, touching, or requests for dates will not be viewed by some individuals as sexually harassing, and some will go along, simply because they are not bothered. Others who find the behavior distasteful, but not necessarily sexually harassing, will simply avoid individuals and situations that might produce such behaviors.

"I think a man putting his arm on a woman or patting her on the shoulder is normal male-female behavior. In my definition, it's not sexual harassment. If a woman doesn't like the behavior, she should tell the man she doesn't like it. Does that really justify a lawsuit?"

A Case of Perception

A 1996 American Management Association survey of 456 mid-sized to large businesses found that the majority of sexual harassment complaints reported were cases of coworker to coworker harassment, a finding that doesn't surprise Paula Popovich, an associate professor of psychology at Ohio University.

"Until recently, this was a topic confined to the rhetoric of feminists or the abstract discussion of academics," Popovich says. "However, recent, well-publicized events have shown sexual harassment has real implications—legal, financial, and emotional—for both the victim and the alleged harasser."

And regardless of who is charged in a complaint—a worker's peer or supervisor—the root cause is the

continued

Unwanted Advances, Unheeded Declines, *continued*

same, Popovich says. Sexual harassment is a reaction to a perceived power of one person over another.

"Because coworker to coworker sexual harassment is so prevalent, some people dismiss power as a factor," she says. "But there are different bases of power—expertise power, power of attraction, or physical power."

Perception is a key issue in hostile environment forms of harassment, according to Popovich, whose studies have found there were "definite differences in perceptions of men and women, as well as a tendency for subjects to identify more with the same gender."

And it's not only gender that influences these perceptions. Popovich has found that physical attractiveness also plays a role. In one study, Popovich had college students review a description of a sexual harassment complaint and then provided photographs of alleged harassers and victims with varying physical traits.

"We found that men and women were more likely to give a guilty verdict to an unattractive defendant accused by an attractive plaintiff," Popovich says. "Subjects were less likely to give a guilty verdict to an attractive defendant accused by an unattractive plaintiff."

Attractiveness and gender aside, Popovich found that perception is an important issue. "What we find of concern," she says, "is there is no absolute agreement, and that's why these cases must be reviewed on a case-by-case basis."

Courting a Definition

Despite the media attention and prominence of the issue in the public conscience, defining hostile environment sexual harassment remains difficult.

The Supreme Court has cited a "reasonable woman" standard in which a reasonable woman "would perceive that an abusive working environment has been created."

Two U.S. Supreme Court cases may result in rulings that clarify the law, and researchers such as Marinelli are regarding the suits carefully. In the case of *Joseph Oncale v. Sundowner Offshore Services,* an offshore oil rig worker alleged he was abused by his male coworkers and repeatedly threatened with rape by his boss and two colleagues. Lower courts rejected his allegations of harassment, saying same-sex harassment was not covered by federal laws

forbidding sex discrimination in the workplace. In March, that decision was overturned by the U.S. Supreme Court, which ruled unanimously that same-sex harassment is covered by the law.

A case still pending, *Faragher v. Boca Raton,* may extend the liability for hostile environment sexual harassment to the employer, even if the employer is unaware an employee is being harassed. The case involves a former lifeguard, Beth Ann Faragher, who sued the city of Boca Raton, Florida, and lost. Faragher argued that two male supervisors had harassed her, patted her thighs, slapped her on the buttocks, and made offensive comments. She alleged the city, while having an official policy forbidding harassment, had no mechanism in place to file a complaint.

The 11th U.S. Circuit Court of Appeals in Atlanta rejected Faragher's claim, ruling an employer is liable only if he or she knew or should have known about the hostile environment and failed to act promptly. On appeal to the U.S. Supreme Court, Faragher's attorneys argued she had no contact with city officials because of the remote location of her lifeguard post. The court is expected to render a decision in June.

"The ruling in the Joseph Oncale case shows the court is trying to be consistent in their application of our discrimination laws. It's the conduct and the social context itself that counts," says Marinelli, referring to comments by the court that a coach who pats his football players' buttocks is not guilty of sexual harassment, but a coach who pats his secretary's buttocks might be.

Despite this ruling and those that may follow, sexual harassment's roots in individual perception may not make the courts the best venue to resolve such issues, Marinelli says.

"There is a murky area when power and affection converge in the workplace, and it's questionable if the courts are the best place to resolve sexual harassment issues," Marinelli says.

The best place to work through these problems, Marinelli and Thacker say, may be the workplace in which they occurred in the first place.

Addressing the Problem

Regardless of the outcome of these legal battles, researchers say employers need to have a mechanism in place to deal with sexual harassment in the

continued

Unwanted Advances, Unheeded Declines, *continued*

workplace. Thacker has written about the issue, advocating that companies develop sexual-harassment policies that educate and allow employees to get mediation for their complaints.

Companies need to protect themselves and their employees by having both an informal and formal way to deal with the problem, says Thacker, who recommends that companies conduct sexual harassment prevention training for employees and implement a formal system for filing complaints. As a first step, she also recommends a less formal system of mediation in which both or all parties involved in a complaint meet with a mediator—perhaps someone outside the company—before a formal complaint is filed. The mediator makes suggestions on how to resolve the conflict, but the suggestions are not binding for those involved in the mediation.

"The voluntary, confidential nature of mediation may be the only framework in which some accused harassers become aware of the consequences of their actions and find the motivation to change their

behavior," Thacker says. "Using mediation can result in substantial dollar savings in both litigation and employee time, and offers employers a positive middle option between inaction and termination."

"My other suggestion is that we change the law so that before someone can file a lawsuit, the organization has the opportunity to deal with the problem internally. Employees would be required to go through an internal complaint system before going to the courts," she says.

A Place for Office Romance?

Twenty years ago, most U.S. companies frowned on employees being romantically involved. But just as sexual harassment court cases have dramatically increased, so has employers' willingness to allow employees to date and even marry.

In a survey four years ago, about 30 percent of managers who responded to an American

continued

Harassment by the Numbers

Sexual Harassment Complaints Filed with the Equal Employment Opportunity Commission
The rising number of complaints filed with the EEOC has been linked to increased social awareness of the harassment issue and passage of the Civil Rights Act of 1991, which allows for compensatory and punitive awards in sexual harassment lawsuits. Previously, only back pay could be awarded.

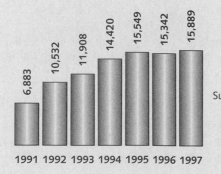

1991: 6,883
1992: 10,532
1993: 11,908
1994: 14,420
1995: 15,549
1996: 15,342
1997: 15,889

Profile of Alleged Harassers
A 1996 survey of 456 firms by the American Management Association revealed more sexual harassment complaints are filed against coworkers than superiors.

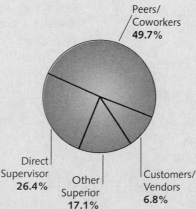

Peers/Coworkers 49.7%
Direct Supervisor 26.4%
Other Superior 17.1%
Customers/Vendors 6.8%

Taking Action
Company responses to complaints of sexual harassment as reported in the American Management Association's survey of 456 firms.

Offender reprimanded	**35.1%**
Mediation for parties	**35.0%**
Accuser dismissed	**16.0%**
Allegation dismissed	**15.0%**
Accuser transferred	**3.9%**
Offender transferred	**3.0%**

Unwanted Advances, Unheeded Declines, *continued*

Management Association survey said they had one or more office romances during their careers. A recent *Wall Street Journal* report says AT&T has 8,000 employees married to each other.

But what happens when an office romance goes sour and allegations of sexual harassment arise?

"I don't think companies can do much about office romances," Thacker says. "Males and females are attracted to one another and I don't think you can put an end to it. I think we've gone overboard in the hostile environment category. There is virtually nothing of a romantic or sexual nature that could not be considered sexual harassment by somebody. That is an onerous burden for companies."

Popovich has consulted with companies on sexual harassment policies and, while agreeing that office romances cannot be stopped, she advises supervisors to be very careful in their relationships.

"I caution men in supervisory positions about the potential for a mutual relationship going sour and turning into sexual harassment," Popovich says. "I try to point out the nature of the male-female and supervisory-subordinate roles and the responsibility that comes with each role."

With more than 3,500 employees, Ohio University receives one or two sexual harassment complaints a year and they generally are resolved internally, according to Professor of Geography Nancy Bain, who served as university ombud from 1991 to 1997.

"Some people don't understand what it is and that can be a problem," Bain says. "But I've seen women accused of harassment, men accused of harassment, and same-sex harassment allegations. In all cases, the offender was in a position of power."

Internal mediation programs and training courses for people in supervisory positions could prevent sexual harassment in the workplace, or at the very least, provide guidance for resolving complaints without involving the courts. But in the end, Popovich says, there is one message that must be clear: "With power," she says, "comes responsibility."

Source: Dwight Woodward, "Unwanted Advances, Unheeded Declines," *Perspectives*, Spring/Summer 1998 , Vol. 11, No. 1, pp. 10–13.

Another Look: Eight Steps to a Sexual-Harassment-Free Workplace

Katherine, an experienced compensation manager, had started her presentation about compensation and variable pay programs as executives Jay, Lance, and Hal listened. But she stopped abruptly in mid sentence upon feeling a foot under the table inching its way up her calf toward her thigh. Jay, executive vice president of sales, sat across the table smirking. Katherine was horrified but remained calm.

Jay pushed his foot a little farther up her leg, as he grinned mischievously and made minor counterpoints to Katherine's presentation. She steadied herself, grabbed Jay's foot, and yanked it upward for everyone to see. He nearly fell out of his chair. "OK, Kathy! Uncle, uncle! You win," he said howling with laughter.

How would you handle a similar situation? What would your managers do? The opening scenario is one of 36 authentic sexual harassment situations documented by N. Elizabeth Fried in her book, *Sex, Laws, and Stereotypes* (Intermediaries Press, 1994). In that particular case, the employee relations manager told Katherine: "Look, you've got to ignore those jerks. They're just testing you to see how tough you are. You've passed the test and from now on the rest is Easy Street."

For most working women and men, though, there is no Easy Street when it comes to sexual harassment. There can be embarrassment and lost productivity in organization without sound harassment policies.

Consider these questions:

- Would that incident have occurred if Jay's colleagues modeled strong anti-harassment practices?

- Did Jay and his peers get sufficient training on the impact on victims and the liability?

- If there were solid sexual harassment policies, were they clear and fully understood by Jay and his colleagues?

- If Katherine had pressed a formal claim, would Jay's colleagues have backed him or her?

continued

Eight Steps to a Sexual-Harassment-Free Workplace, *continued*

- What can make sexual harassment policies and training more effective?

Eight Strategies

We surveyed 2,200 experienced training and human resource practitioners from a cross-section of industries to find training, policies, procedures, and practices for making the workplace sexual-harassment-free. There were 663 respondents.

According to the survey, sexual harassment incidents had declined in 500 of the organizations. They had created effective training and modeled behavior to try to prevent unwelcome situations like Katherine's. Based on survey results, here are eight strategies for combating sexual harassment in the workplace.

1. *Enforce zero tolerance.*   Employers have a duty to prevent workplace sexual harassment. When the employee relations manager told Katherine to ignore Jay's behavior, upper management was, in effect, condoning offensive behavior. That can send the wrong message and cost a company resources and good will. Employers who become aware of sexual harassment are responsible for getting rid of it. In cases in which a manager or supervisor is aware of sexual harassment and fails to investigate or take action, the employer may be held liable.

2. *Set an example from the top.*   Rena Weeks sued her former boss, Martin Greenstein, a senior partner of 22 years in a large law firm. Greenstein allegedly touched her inappropriately, made suggestive remarks, and groped her for candy he poured down her blouse pocket. Colleagues tried to cover up those and other incidents reported by female employees. Nevertheless, the firm incurred punitive damages of $7.1 million in 1994 and a $50,000 fine for insufficient sexual harassment prevention practices.

    Employees (and customers) tend to focus on sexual conduct by highly paid executives, managers, and supervisors. Consequently, business leaders should practice lawful behavior. Policies should state that an organization doesn't tolerate offensive touching or sexually oriented materials at work. Also taboo are stares, innuendoes, comments about anatomy, and other behavior that tends to make people uncomfortable.

3. *Investigate complaints promptly and thoroughly.* Failure to respond to a sexual harassment complaint cost Domino's Pizza dearly. A store manager, David Papa, alleged that his area manager, Beth Carrier, made repeated unwelcome sexual advances. Papa failed in attempts to discuss the issue with upper management. When he threatened to file a formal complaint, Domino's fired him, only two weeks after he had been selected manager of the month. A Florida judge required Domino's to pay Papa more than $237,000. The judge also ordered the pizza chain to post its sexual harassment policy in each store and hold annual sexual harassment training for managers.

    Organizations that are successful in eliminating sexual harassment circulate guidelines widely and apply them equally to all employees. Because a supervisor is often the subject of a complaint, procedures should include provisions for employees to complain to someone other than the alleged harasser. Claims involving management or a pattern of pervasive social-sexual behavior require objective, thorough, and timely investigation.

4. *Conduct investigations confidentially.*   During a sexual harassment investigation, activity on the grapevine usually intensifies. Keeping an investigation within the sphere of the people with an absolute need to know is crucial. In one EEOC case, Astra USA fired CEO Lars Bildman when he reportedly tried to intimidate female complainants.

    An investigator may choose to remove any of the accused and accusers from the workplace temporarily. The investigator should tell everyone involved that it doesn't imply a prejudgment but is simply a way to minimize unnecessary interaction during the investigation. Such actions show that an employer takes sexual harassment seriously. They also help ensure greater cooperation by victims, witnesses, and perpetrators.

5. *Follow up on complaints.*   The measure of appropriate remedial action is whether it prevents recurrence. In our first example, Jay had often made unwelcome advances and comments to female coworkers. When there were no consequences for his behavior, he probably repeated it. Jay continued to undermine his firm's credibility, while Katherine's career suffered.

    It's also important to eliminate victim retribution. Many HR professionals meet with

continued

Eight Steps to a Sexual-Harassment-Free Workplace, *continued*

complainants personally. They document claims, all related meetings, and any disciplinary action.

In Jay's case, his company might have eliminated his sexual advances by investigating the claim and administering appropriate discipline, instead of the employee relations manager dismissing Jay's behavior. Progressive discipline and effective training help employees understand and accept the consequences outlined in organizational policies.

6. *Train to sensitize employees.*   Have participants take turns playing the roles of supervisor, victim, upper-level manager, and perpetrator of both genders. The practitioners in our study advocate defining what lawful social-sexual behavior is and is not. They suggest using case studies, videos, and role play to promote discussion and understanding.

Trainers can use coaching to help clarify procedures and policies. They can illustrate and encourage appropriate behavior, while preparing employees to confront alleged perpetrators. That helps reduce the liability from unlawful workplace behavior, overcome the negative influence on productivity and morale, and enhance an organization's image.

7. *Check people's understanding.*   Labor attorneys strongly recommend asking trainees written questions to evaluate their grasp of appropriate conduct, policies, investigations, organizational climate, and guideline enforcement. Many organizations require workers found guilty of sexual harassment to attend remedial classes and sign a statement saying that they understood the information.

You can check employees' comprehension by using pretests, posttests, performance records, surveys, interviews, observations, focus groups, and managers' perceptions. It's best to conduct workplace surveys six to 12 months after formal training to help assess policy implementation. Follow up to ensure that managers and supervisors know how to identify, handle, and investigate sexual harassment situations properly. Employers who record participation and document training outcomes can provide tangible evidence of good-faith efforts to eliminate sexual harassment. Such records can be especially valuable if litigation arises.

8. *Provide periodic refresher sessions.*   Most of the executives in our study recommended refresher sessions. We suggest one mandatory sexual harassment training session per year for each employee, regardless of job level.

Seventy percent of the respondents agreed with the need for formal sexual harassment training and saw related organizational benefits. Interest in such training has been increasing, especially in organizations with more than 100 employees.

Employers have the burden of proving that they're working to eliminate workplace harassment. With strong policy enforcement, effective training, and appropriate behavior models, your organization can come closer to being a safe, sexual-harassment-free workplace.

Another Look: Life Lessons in Disability Law

I was feeling awkward in my new wheelchair, borrowed from my college. In the next three months, I would become quite familiar with my new method of transportation. In fact, I would even find myself bragging that, along with the occasional "wheeze," I could roll along at up to 35 miles an hour on a straight hallway in our academic building!

While on vacation from my position as president of Onondaga Community College in Syracuse, New York, I had broken my heel. Now, I faced the prospect of three months without any weight-bearing activity, as well as a directive to keep my foot elevated for two weeks—usually considered rude in polite company.

At a meeting with staff from the college's Office of Students With Special Needs, I learned what people with disabilities call the rest of us: "TAB," for temporarily able-bodied. Over the next few months,

continued

Life Lessons in Disability Law, *continued*

----

with my no-longer-fully abled body, I realized that TAB is an accurate term. But the concept is not respected among those of us who take for granted our full abilities.

First Lesson: Accommodations as Barriers

Many people asked if my injury was painful. The actual pain soon faded. What endured much longer was the humiliation of having a disability.

As a manager, I learned from my experience that meeting the requirements of the Americans With Disabilities Act is not enough. Onondaga Community College is proud to have a fully accessible campus; it has the second largest number of students with disabilities in the state's community-college system. But fulfilling the letter of the law does not even come close to meeting the human need for addressing the humiliating conditions people with disabilities face—even those who anticipate returning to full health.

The first experience occurred on my first day back on campus. I was unable to drive, so the trustees assigned an employee as a temporary driver.

The driver dropped me off at the front entrance to our academic building just after the last snowfall of the season. As I exited the car, I realized that the snow had covered the cut-curb entrance at the front of the building. I stood suspended on my crutches, waiting for the wheelchair to be unpacked from the car. Suddenly, I found myself sliding backwards—out of control and frightened that I was about to fall into the street. The snow had made the curb cut slippery and dangerous.

This was my first lesson about accessibility and about what our students with disabilities must undergo during the long winters in Syracuse: Even mechanisms designed to help can become barriers.

Fortunately, spring arrived the next day, and I did not have to develop the winter skills of wheeling myself through slush, snow, and ice. I did learn to be cautious of the following accommodations that can become serious barriers:

- curb cuts that are not flush and that cause the wheelchair user to catch an edge, stop short, and be thrown forward

- sidewalk surfaces, including brick and stonework, which, if hit the wrong way, can send a chair into a spin, throwing its occupant

- wheelchair ramps that are difficult to ascend when wet, because they become slippery and make the wheelchair impossible to control

- long ramps, because they are physically exhausting to ascend, and because any speed gained on long, descending ramps can cause the chair to shake, reducing its braking powers.

Second Lesson: Common Traps

Surfaces and devices that seem perfectly appropriate to an able-bodied person can present serious challenges to a person who is in a wheelchair or dependent on crutches.

Of particular difficulty for me were thick carpets. Hotels usually provide wheelchairs, so I didn't have to bring my own. But I quickly discovered that trying to move through expansive hotel lobbies and hallways was nearly impossible unless the chair was motorized. That meant I had to use crutches in hotels much of the time. But crutches can be terribly exhausting when you're trying to move around a large facility.

My most memorable hotel experience while on crutches happened once when I was attempting to board an elevator to go upstairs. The elevator doors opened, and several people walked out. No one bothered to hold the door open for me to enter. By the time everyone had exited, the elevator was closing. I thrust my crutch between the doors, expecting them to rebound. Instead, they closed tightly on my crutch!

So there I was, standing in the lobby on one foot, with one crutch on the floor and the other stuck in the elevator. There was absolutely no way for me to get the doors to reopen or to remove the crutch from their grasp. I didn't know if I should crawl or hop away. Finally, after several minutes, a member of the hotel staff helped me extract the crutch. We tugged hard, and the crutch came loose. But the rubber stopper on the crutch got stuck in the door! Then we had to pry the doors open so that we could remove the rubber tip—which, of course, is necessary to ensure that the crutch doesn't slide away as you're using it.

Third Lesson: Helping Hands

Of course, I blamed that incident on the lack of courtesy on the part of the other elevator passengers.

continued

Life Lessons in Disability Law, *continued*

MAKING YOUR WORKPLACE WORK FOR PEOPLE WITH DISABILITIES

Here are some tips for increasing your understanding of the needs of workers with disabilities.

- Spend time—at least a week, or even a month—in a wheelchair.

- Have wheelchair users or people with other disabilities show you the problem spots in your work environment.

- Know which kinds of help will be appreciated by people with disabilities.

- Do more than meet the codes.

- Get to know your staff members who have disabilities.

That became my third awareness: Most people with disabilities don't want special help from other people all the time. But they do appreciate some common courtesy.

Think about how difficult it could be to transport a cup of hot coffee or tea in your lap while you're pushing your wheelchair. When I was recovering from my injury, I was grateful to colleagues who offered to help me carry such things. Some people would hold a door, but many others did not. Instead, they would simply let a door slam behind them, right into my chair—or into my face, if I was using crutches.

I also learned that the wheelchairs provided by hotels, airports, and other institutions aren't always as useful as they could be for the people who need them. The chair I borrowed from the college tended to veer to the right, so I always had to give extra pushes on the right side to compensate, cramping my right arm. Chairs I borrowed while traveling had similar problems.

In one case, a hotel lent me a wheelchair for a one-day group visit to Ottawa. The chair fitted nicely on the tour bus and was easy to set up when we arrived at our destination. But it seemed to drag and thump when I used it, making it difficult to wheel around. As it turned out, the wheels were flat. The

hotel hadn't bothered to check the tire inflation! I had to spend most of the trip trying to find a bicyclist who had a pump. By the time we finally got the chair tires inflated, we were all back on the bus.

Fourth Lesson: Humiliation

The same trip afforded me some important insights into something that people with disabilities face every day. This was the experience I found to be the most profound, troubling, and difficult to accept. It's called humiliation.

College presidents are used to being looked at. I'm frequently in front of groups, both large and small. But rarely am I stared at. Being in a wheelchair was a different story. Sometimes, the accommodation itself created a reason to stare.

For example, I had to use a stage lift in order to reach the dais in the auditorium during commencement exercises. But the noise and slowness of the lift grabbed everyone's attention. I had timed my use of the lift so that the pomp of the processional and the playing of bagpipes would distract people from the sound and motion of the lift.

Instead, my rise of about four feet stole the show. Everyone watched me rather than the academic parade. I seemed to take on the aura of Dracula rising out of the crypt. And on the reverse trip, I was descending into hell a la "Don Giovanni." Again, every eye was on me. It seemed to take hours to reach the floor.

That was a common problem. Every time I got out of or into a car, moved around an airport, or rolled my way across campus, anyone nearby seemed to stop and watch. Their interest was especially apparent when I used doors or maneuvered the chair through entrances. It's easy to feel paranoid when you're a college president. But a person in a wheelchair or on crutches feels not only watched, but *different.*

Another variable in the formula of humiliation relates to who you are with, what you are doing, and where you are. For example, a person with disabilities who is with a group of able-bodied people often cannot go where the rest of the group can go.

On a trip to Ottawa with a group, I quickly realized that I was different—that I could not share in the enjoyment of the moment. The shops in the old part of Ottawa tend to have steps, with no ramps. So a person in a wheelchair just can't get in.

continued

Life Lessons in Disability Law, *continued*

Even the one store that did have an accessible entrance (around back, of course) turned out to be a problem. When the proprietor opened the door, I saw that the aisles were so filled with merchandise that a wheelchair simply could not fit. I was forced to wait outside, alone, while my colleagues shopped and socialized.

One of my more cynical colleagues placed his hat in my lap and threw in a quarter, joking about the perception that a person in a wheelchair sitting in front of a store is there for the purpose of begging. I did not revel in the humor. In fact, after 20 minutes of waiting for my associates and feeling awkward as passersby stared at me, I decided I would prefer to be inside the store knocking down all the merchandise that blocked the aisles!

Throughout my recovery period, there were plenty of instances in which people showed small courtesies or shared their own stories of injuries and recuperation difficulties.

I can't tell you how often I was asked: "Did you do that playing basketball?" In fact, there seems to be quite a camaraderie—especially among men over 40—of people who have broken their Achilles' tendons or ankles while on the basketball court.

One trustee told me that she had heard a hundred different stories of how I received my injury. To each one, she responded, "That's exactly how he broke his heel!"

Humor is quite evident among people with disabilities. But something else lies behind the humor. It may be a technique for short-circuiting anger over people's attitudes and over the system's failure to take into consideration the needs of people who are living with disabilities.

I experienced some of that anger myself. On my own campus, I quickly learned that we had electric door openers on outer doors—but not on inner doors. I learned that we had sinks, paper-towel holders, and soap dispensers that all met appropriate codes—but that they weren't located next to each other, so a person in a chair had to wheel all over the bathroom, just to wash his or her hands.

In an Ottawa restaurant, I had to be carried up three steps in order to get to the elevator. In the bathroom, I found myself unable to turn around and open the door. It took me 15 minutes to get up the nerve to be aggressive and fight the bathroom itself, rather than embarrass myself by sitting in the men's room yelling for help! I finally broke a built-in towel receptacle and gouged a hole in the wall in order to get out.

Fifth Lesson: Additional Burdens

I was in the wheelchair when I went to the county courthouse to present my school's budget to the legislature. I attempted to use the restroom adjacent to the legislative chambers on the fourth floor. But a large step made the facility inaccessible to me.

My choice was to go all the way down to the basement to the only accessible men's room in the building—or to exit my chair and hop up the step and across the restroom in order to utilize the facilities. It was humiliating to have to hop all over the place before reestablishing myself in the chair and going forward with my very critical presentation in the next room.

This brings me to my fifth awareness. The code requires accessibility to a restroom—but not necessarily on every floor. I used to believe that one accessible restroom in a building was enough, even if the room was several floors away. My own experiences have taught me differently. To require people with disabilities to go out of their way in order to use a facility is more than discourteous; it places an additional burden on their lives.

Clearly, it is not enough to simply meet the codes for accessibility.

On a college campus, the typical student has the burden of carrying around a 40-pound book bag, a coat, an umbrella, and all sorts of other items necessary for classes and projects. Try placing them in a chair, along with a person who has to maneuver around all sorts of obstacles. Then ask that person to go out of his or her way in order to get into a building, ride in an elevator, or use the restroom.

While I was in the chair, people who were thinking positively about my situation commented that I would strengthen my arms. They had no idea that a person in a wheelchair is forced to go farther, fight harder, and battle bathroom walls and other obstacles, simply to accomplish the normal activities of the day. It is frustrating. And it is tiring. I found myself exhausted well before the end of the day, simply from trying to get around.

I had to become an efficiency expert. No matter where I went, I had to plan it out carefully. I had to be sure to take certain actions or bring along certain items, just because getting around required so much

continued

Life Lessons in Disability Law, *continued*

work. Traveling from one place to another required long routes around campus or the community in order to find the accessible entrances, useful elevators, or ramps that would allow me to take care of my business.

I had the good fortune of not having to drive. People who do have to drive have the additional burden of battling to get into the parking spaces that are set aside for people with disabilities—which are often filled by able-bodied people. I used to feel annoyed at what I thought was a waste of parking spaces that could have been available for everyone. But now I can see how important those spaces are to the people who really need them.

Rolling Along in Their Moccasins

I've spoken with people who have been pleased with themselves after spending perhaps an hour or even a day in a wheelchair or blindfolded, in order to experience what a person with disabilities feels. But so much can be avoided or missed in a one-day experience, especially when it is part of an organized function.

If you are able-bodied, and if part of your job is to be responsive to the needs of people with disabilities (which is the case if you are a college president, like me, or a corporate human resource specialist), consider the following suggestions for increasing your understanding of those needs.

DON'T SPEND A DAY in a wheelchair; spend a week or a month. Don't go just around campus or through the halls of your workplace, go elsewhere in the community. Try to get into shops and restaurants; utilize airports. See how people respond when they don't know you're doing this as part of an exercise.

GO WITH OTHERS who are wheelchair users or who have other disabilities. They can give you a great deal of insight into places on your campus or in your workplace where specific problems exist. You'll also learn about the routes they must use in order to get around, the problems of carrying books and other items needed at school or on the job, and the difficulties they have with restrooms—even if your institution is meeting all the codes.

For example, I learned something I hadn't noticed about a crosswalk that leads to our main building from the parking spaces reserved for people with disabilities, across the street. The crosswalk placed our wheelchair-using students in two difficulties:

- The traffic moves very quickly. And, because of a rise in the road, a blind spot places a person with disabilities in great danger of being hit by a car.

- During the winter, high snow banks obscure the sides of the road. At such times, a person entering the road from the parking lot can be invisible to drivers, until that person is well into the crosswalk.

We've now added stop signs to the area, which I hope will protect all people who use that crosswalk.

LEARN THE COURTESIES that will help people with disabilities, and know to avoid doing things that could humiliate them or interfere with their ability to proceed with what they're doing. Most able-bodied people don't know how to deal with issues that affect people with disabilities. And that can create embarrassment, confusion, and awkwardness.

The more you interact with people who are different from yourself in any way, the better you understand them and their needs—and the more you respect their differences.

DON'T JUST MEET THE CODES. Learn what they are and see how they affect the ability of a person with disabilities to carry out tasks that an able-bodied person would think of as normal routines.

GET TO KNOW YOUR STAFF or community members who have disabilities. Talk with them. What you will learn, of course, is that you're merely a "TAB," a temporarily able-bodied person. At any moment, you could find yourself learning firsthand—temporarily or permanently—that your office has to be rearranged, that you really don't want your staff to push you around in your wheelchair, that you are tired of doors closing on your hands, and that you're fed up with having to go around the back of buildings, as if you weren't worthy of going in the front door.

Above all, experience the humiliation of being stared at and excluded —and then do something about it. Make the changes in your workplace and in your life. Someday, you may be the one who will benefit from a more accessible and reassuring environment.

Source: H. Bruce Leslie, "Life Lessons in Disability Law," *Training & Development,* July 1995, pp. 41–44. Reprinted from Training & Development. © July 1995 the American Society for Training and Development. Reprinted with permission. All rights reserved.

A Case in Point: Is It Sexual Harassment?

The recent attention given to sexual harassment in the press may trigger complaints in your workplace. Do you know what is sexual harassment? To test yourself, see how you do with the situations presented below. Which ones are sexual harassment? How should your company respond in each instance?

Twelve Scenarios

CASE #1. For monthly staff meetings, Barry, the department head, always asks Jane to set up the meeting room, arrange for refreshments, and take the minutes. The work group is made up of engineers: Jane, John, Jorge, and Kumar.

CASE #2. Jerry is a supervisor. He has been having an affair with Mary, an engineering aide in another department. Jerry has an opening in his department that Mary qualifies for, and he chooses her over another qualified person even though Mary has significantly less experience.

CASE #3. Sam is a plant manager at a waste treatment plant. At the facility, calendars with pictures of naked women are posted everywhere. In the lunchroom, there is also a picture of a naked man and woman embracing pasted on a picture of the plant's instrumentation room. The caption on the picture reads, "There is more to life than sludge." The only female employee at the plant, a lab technician, has never complained.

CASE #4. When Harriet walks over to the department's computers, she has to pass Larry's door. Larry frequently wheels his chair to the opening, and as he watches her he often says things like, "Hey, sweetie, let me know when you finish so I don't miss the show on your way back."

CASE #5. Sylvia is a manager. Tom, a biologist, reports to her. While she and Tom are on a business trip, she tells Tom that she hopes he doesn't snore; they are going to share a room "to keep overhead costs down." Also, he should be aware that she doesn't wear pajamas so he doesn't have to bring any either. Tom refuses to share a room and complains when he goes back to work.

CASE #6. George is an accountant. When there are new female employees, he welcomes them by hugging them and kissing them "lightly" on the mouth. He tells them that he is the "social director" for the department and "to fit in, all new single women have to date him at least once, ha, ha."

CASE #7. Jose, a project manager, is quite "smitten" by Janice, the new department secretary. He sends her notes telling her that she is beautiful, and that he wants to date her. He continues to do so even after she tells him she doesn't want to go out with him. Nothing else happens.

CASE #8. Betty is a very shy and quiet person. Some of the jokesters in her department have decided to have fun at her expense and have left "girlie" magazines on her desk to see how she will react.

CASE #9. Marty is a new, recently relocated manager. He asks his secretary, Louise, to rent him an apartment because he's too busy with his new job. While Louise is at the apartment checking that everything has been done as requested, Marty shows up and suggests they try out the bed. She refuses. Nothing else happens. Two months later there is a reduction in force and Louise is laid off. The official reason is her undocumented inability to get along with coworkers (which is quite true—she is continually arguing with her coworkers).

CASE #10. Harold is a financial analyst. He is a good worker who always gets the job done even if he has to work long hours. One night while working late he went to the employee exercise area to use the equipment. Only he and Jennifer were there. Jennifer was using the treadmill. When she was finished, he cornered her, and ran his hands all over her body. She slapped him. He stopped. He still goes to the exercise room at night. When Jennifer is there, he stares at her. He has never touched or spoken to her again. When Jennifer complained to the human resources department, she discovered that he had been accused of doing the same thing (also without witnesses) a few months earlier. At that time he had been warned not to do anything like it again.

CASE #11. Jim, a vice-president, and Jane, a project manager, are at a professional conference. Jim shows up at Jane's room after the day's session is over and says he's lonely. He insists that she is the woman he's been looking for all his life. She invites him to spend the night. Back on the job, they decide it was a bad idea and do not see each other again.

CASE #12. Richard is a marketing manager. Ted is a technical writer in his department. Ted is homosexual. Richard continually asks Ted if he wants to date different women in the office. Richard tells Ted there should be a company policy to test people like Ted "because he could have AIDS." When Ted gets

continued

Is It Sexual Harassment?, *continued*

angry at statements like these, Richard says, "Careful Ted, don't bite me; you'll give me AIDS."

Is It Harassment?

Let's look at the 12 cases to see if they are examples of sexual harassment and what action is likely to be taken.

CASE #1. The answer to the first case is "No," but it is discriminatory to select women to do these "menial" tasks at each meeting. Barry should be told to rotate the tasks. Some might think this is a small matter, but Barry's behavior could be the basis of a discrimination suit if Jane receives lower raises than the others (or some other treatment).

CASE #2. Yes. Jerry said to his manager that he believed Mary had the right attitude for the new assignment and the other job candidate didn't. This other person (whether male or female) could claim that Jerry was guilty of showing favoritism because of his relationship with Mary and Jerry would not be able to show it was not the basis for the decision.

CASE #3. Yes. It's a hostile environment, whether the female employee complains or not. All the calendars and pictures should be taken down.

CASE #4. Yes, again, it is a hostile environment. Larry should be warned to stop. If he doesn't, he should receive discipline—for instance, a suspension without pay.

CASE #5. Yes. Women can be harassers Sylvia should receive a written warning.

CASE #6. Yes. It's not a joke. George should receive a written warning.

CASE #7. Yes. It's a hostile or intimidating environment. Jose should receive a written warning.

CASE #8. Yes. It is not a joke. The supervisor should verbally warn the jokesters and, if it happens again, there should be discipline.

CASE #9. Yes. It's harassment and even without the "try out the bed" part, it would be an abuse of power. Employees are not required to do personal tasks the manager should do for himself or herself. Even though it happened just once, and Louise did have difficulty getting along with co-workers, the layoff will be assumed by any investigating agency to be the result of her refusal. Therefore, if she complains about the termination, the company would probably have to rehire her or provide a monetary settlement.

CASE #10. Yes. Harold admitted it and, since it had happened before, he should be terminated.

CASE #11.
No. The behavior was not unwelcome and nothing else happened at work.

CASE #12. Yes. While it is not specifically mentioned in the law, harassment based on sexual orientation is frequently found in courts to be sexual harassment. Richard should receive a written warning for a first offense.

Bottom Line

Remember, sexual harassment is not limited to unwelcome sexual advances. Sexual harassment is also verbal or physical conduct of a sexual nature that creates an intimidating or offensive work environment.

Source: Reprinted from *Sexual Harassment in the Workplace* by Ellen J. Wagner. Copyright © 1992 Creative Solutions, Inc. Reprinted by permission of AMACOM, a division of American Management Association International, New York. All rights reserved. http://www.amanet.org.

A Case in Point: Kevin's Concern

Kevin was asked to leave a small family-owned company after an accident left him with both physical and mental impairments. Although the severity of Kevin's disability could in no way prevent him from leading a normal and useful life, his employer felt insurance premiums would increase, Kevin's work performance would decrease, and Kevin would cause embarrassment not only to the organization but to his peers. Kevin was let go, even though none of these concerns was justified. In fact, this manager's loss would prove to be another's gain.

Following are seven myths about workers with disabilities:

1. *They have a higher turnover.* Perhaps the most frequent reason employers cite for not hiring the person with disabilities is their belief that such people have poor attendance records and a high rate of job turnover. Nothing could be further from the truth.

2. *They are less productive.* Some managers argue that workers with disabilities are not as productive as similarly salaried employees and that their efficiency has to be lower due to their physical and mental limitations. Again, current research does not support these assertions.

3. *They are a greater safety risk.* A misinformed manager might assume that the company's safety records will become jeopardized, resulting in increased insurance costs. This is not the case.

4. *They are too costly.* Some managers insist that the firm will have to incur a great deal of extra expense in making adjustments to the work environment. Due to their loyalty and high motivation, workers with disabilities are often more cost-effective in the long run.

5. *They are too demanding.* A significant number of managers, when pressed, suggest that special privileges and working arrangements given to employees with disabilities will result in hostility and resentment from coworkers.

   In reality, workers with disabilities make no more demands than their counterparts and often are close friends of their coworkers.

6. *They would be an embarrassment to the organization.* Systematic examinations in the last several years have clearly indicated that most individuals having direct contact with people with disabilities have favorable perceptions of them.

7. *They won't fit in the organization's workgroups.* On the contrary, due to their often higher educational levels, realistic job expectations, and ability to work independently and longer hours, many companies view employees with disabilities as a needed addition to the workgroup.

Questions
1. What can be learned about workers with disabilities from Kevin's case?
2. What could you do to help integrate workers with disabilities into your organization?
3. Think of those you know who have disabilities. Do any of these myths describe them?

Coping with Personal Stress

- What is stress?

- Are we all slowly going crazy because of the stress in our lives?

- What are the major causes of stress?

- Why are jobs ruining workers' health?

- What is technostress?

- What impact does violence in the workplace have on business?

- How can good relationships with others help reduce personal stress?

- What is a midlife crisis?

- How can the knowledge of techniques for reducing stress make our lives more enjoyable?

- What are some techniques of stress reduction that can help you be a more effective employee?

- What are some management approaches to reduce stress among organizational employees?

- What role does your personality play in how you deal with stress?

- What is burnout and how can you avoid or relieve it?

The answers to these and other questions are coming up next in Chapter 16 . . .

John rushes to the plant. There he has several fights with an obstinate union leader and two disenchanted employees who claim that top management isn't concerned about anyone but itself.

After lunch, John returns to his office to dive into his stack of work, when the phone rings. On the other end, his wife says, "Hi, John—you're not going to believe this, but Suzy fell down roller-skating and broke her leg. Could you come quickly and help me take her to the hospital?"

After getting Suzy to the hospital, John rushes back to his office to complete his work, when he realizes that he doesn't have time. Besides, everyone is heading for home. He gives up, tosses his work in a briefcase, and goes to his car.

When John arrives home, his wife greets him with "good" news: The insurance policy will cover only one-half of Suzy's cast, and the doctor and cast will total $1,000. At this time John sighs to himself, walks into the family room, turns on the TV, and hopes to forget what is happening to him.

Although few of us have days that include all of these experiences, many of us have similar experiences more frequently than we wish. Our stomachs churn, we worry, we wonder how we can get our work done, and we question why everything seems to happen to us. When such things happen, we experience stress.

Types of Stress

Most of us recognize that we face various types of stress in our daily work and personal lives. Let's look briefly at what stress is and at four terms or conditions related to stress.

What is stress?

Stress may be defined as "a mental or emotional disquieting response to a difficult condition or situation." It may be thought of as a state of mental or emotional imbalance caused by a perceived difference between a person's capabilities and what is expected of that person. Extreme forms of stress can lead to physical conditions, such as hives, high blood pressure, stroke, and heart attacks.

Stress is an inherent part of life; it cannot be totally eliminated, nor should it be. Nevertheless, stress symptoms can be warning signals that changes need to be made in a person's life.

What are the positive aspects of stress?

Eustress refers to "a positive form of stress that helps a person recognize the need to make course corrections in his or her personal or professional life, or both." Eustress often accompanies growth and positive changes in a person's life.

What are some types of stress that affect people at work?

Technostress is a relatively new term that refers to "a computer-generated form of physical and emotional burnout" that is caused by an inability to adapt to rapidly changing technology.[1]

Burnout refers to physical or mental exhaustion that results from long-term, unrelieved stress.

Many middle-aged people experience a series of physical and psychological changes known as the **midlife crisis.** Symptoms include unhappiness, insecurity, depression, indecision, fear and anxiety, conflict, nervousness, and a feeling of entrapment. Dealing with people who experience this very real malady can be challenging for organizations.

When managers experience a midlife crisis, they have particular difficulty making decisions and commitments. They tend to withdraw into themselves.

Some Symptoms of Excessive Stress

Managers can help people through much work-related stress.

Excessive stress can manifest itself in some common physical symptoms: stomach pain, headache, hair loss, skin rashes, muscle tension, and the like. Some people experience a loss or increase of appetite.

Stress affects our thinking patterns, too. Psychological symptoms may include feelings of being distracted, forgotten appointments, frequently losing items, and sleep disorders. Finally, emotional reactions to stress may include moodiness or anxiety.

Everyone reacts to stress in different ways. We have all learned to cope with our unique forms of stress. But some people handle stress much better than others. The remainder of this chapter looks at the impact of stress on people at work, and some ways to improve coping skills.

Stressors Caused by Organizations

Do any of the following stressors have an impact on you?

1. *Ineffective communication.* Stress often results from a lack of the right kind of communication at the right time. For example, stress quickly emerges when you arrive at an appointment with your boss or a customer at the wrong time. You misunderstood the appointment hour, your boss or customer is upset, and you are edgy. Accurate communication could completely reduce this cause of stress. To reduce stress, people must do their best to make certain that they "get the message."

2. *Corporate mismanagement.* As corporate leaders make ineffective decisions, use ineffective management techniques, waste time, or see income falling or new products failing, they feel stress. Most people fear for their credibility and position. No one wants to fail. The level of stress tends to increase as employees take on greater organizational responsibility.

3. *Information overload.* **Information overload** means that an individual or an employee is given too much data in a certain period of time and is unable to deal with it. Letters can't be answered, phone calls aren't returned, appointments are rushed or missed, and a tremendous amount of stress falls on the employee.

4. *Inconsistent leader behavior.* Stress increases for subordinates when their leader functions in unpredictable ways. If people receive supportive behavior from a leader in some situations but nonsupportive behavior in others, a great deal of stress is created.

5. *Work overload.* A good way to determine if an organization is facing work overload is to measure the amount of the unfinished work. Work overload produces extreme stress when deadline pressures are put on employees. When employees feel bogged down because of too much work, they may have trouble deciding what to do first. Which task is the most important? Which deadlines can be missed?

6. *Job change.* As one type of work becomes extinct, another type becomes important. We are all forced to change, to take new jobs, to move into uncharted waters, a process that can trigger **change-produced stress.**

7. *Personal problems.* Although employers usually feel that one's personal problems should be left at home, this is an unrealistic expectation. Human nature does not allow people to divorce themselves from their personal lives while at the workplace. Any personal problem ranging from troubles with baby-sitters to the breakup of a marriage or relationship can add to the stress of the employee at work.

Stress can be caused by a lack of communication.

Stress can result from too much information or unpredictable leader behavior.

Some people create additional stress in others.

8. *Stress carriers.* Some people trigger stress in others. If a supervisor's style of management is stress-producing, subordinates and peers at all levels of the organization feel the effects. Many **stress carriers** have no idea of the negative impact they have on their coworkers. Other stress carriers are aware of what they are doing and for some reason enjoy creating stress in others.

9. *Company policies, salary, and working conditions.* Company policies, salary, and working conditions can cause stress. If people work in physically poor conditions, they can't function well. Workers are also stressed when they feel they are unfairly rewarded for their work or if company policy restricts them from doing things they feel they must do to be effective.

10. *Powerlessness associated with role changes.* Many people experience an increase in stress when they gain greater educational and career opportunities. They may panic from a sense of powerlessness as their roles in life change.

Technostress

Effects of human behavior must be considered when installing a management information system.

When organizations introduce new information technology (IT), they must consider how such changes will affect human behaviors. Implementing IT systems frequently results in changes to the formal structure of an organization (such as adjustments in department boundaries, individual responsibilities, and communication channels) or to the informal structure (work relations, workgroup norms, or status).

Changes in the organization almost always meet with resistance; people fear the unknown. In addition, people may fear that change will affect their status with colleagues. For example, today's managers often type their correspondence rather than have a secretary do so. If they do not know how to type, they may feel ignorant and embarrassed in front of their colleagues.

Some resistance stems from the fear of losing status.

People who work with computers for long periods of time can experience eyestrain or muscular discomfort such as carpal tunnel syndrome. This is a wrist problem directly associated with constant keyboard use.

All of these situations can create distress and resistance within a workforce.

The term "technostress" addresses the physical and emotional burnout that result from a person's inability to adapt to new technology. In extreme cases people show actual symptoms of a classic phobia—nausea, dizziness, cold sweat, and high blood pressure—as a result of their fear, distrust, or hatred of computers.

Phychological Reactions to Technostress   An early study of the use of computers in government finance organizations revealed that gender, age, and job title were related significantly to computer anxiety, or technostress. Twenty-three percent of female respondents experienced technostress, compared with 14 percent of male respondents. The percentage of technostressed respondents older than 50 was more than twice that of respondents younger than 30. The percentage of clerical workers classified as technostressed was twice that of professionals.[2]

Technostress has been linked to four major fears. First, some employees fear that as they rely more on computers and less on their job knowledge, their jobs will be "de-skilled" and they will be more easily replaceable and less secure. Second, other employees have a related fear that computers will replace people and lead to layoffs. Third, workers with low self-esteem fear that they will be unable to use computers. And fourth, some workers fear that the corporate

Source: By permission of Johnny Hart and Creators Syndicate, Inc.

power structure will be threatened as computers allow managers access to information that was previously jealously guarded by subordinates.[3]

Too often, managers and information specialists address the problems of technostress or emotional resistance to IT by showing employees that such technological advances will reduce costs, increase profits, decrease decision time, permit job streamlining, and improve the flow and accuracy of information. Even though these arguments are logical and reasonable, they usually fail to address (and often in fact *increase*) the emotional concerns of workers. When those concerns are not properly addressed, three kinds of resistance often occur.

Employee resistance cannot be reduced by logic alone.

1. *Aggression*—Attacking the information technology in an attempt to make it either inoperative or ineffective.

2. *Projection*—Blaming the system for anything that goes wrong in the organization.

3. *Avoidance*—Withdrawing from or avoiding interaction with the information system, often as a result of frustration.[4]

In a report on ways to overcome resistance to computers, Robert E. Callahan and Patrick C. Fleenor recommend the following four steps for overcoming employee fear of computers:

1. Have managers take the lead by buying and using computers to show how they can help performance.

2. Encourage and reward employees who show an interest in computers.

3. Establish a personal computer training center where employees can learn about and practice with computers.

4. Provide thorough employee computer training.[5]

Technostress may be seen as a healthy warning sign that we might be pushing technology without adequate concern for the human element at work.

Individual Techniques for Coping with Stress

The causes of stress are quite apparent, but effective **coping techniques** are not quite as obvious. The following ideas have proven to be useful in dealing with stress and tension. The application of these ideas depends entirely on the people who use them and the situations in which they are used. We do not suggest that each technique will work for every person in every situation, but a variety of techniques are listed so that individuals will be able to choose among them.

1. *Escape for a while.* If you find yourself encountering a stressful situation where you question how you are going to act, *just leave*—escape for the amount of time you need to get back to normal and get composed. If you think you might blow up and fight, it is better to escape for a while.

2. *Talk it out.* Don't hold things in or bottle up tension—confide in someone you trust. You can find great relief in sharing your feelings with someone else. Let others know why you are upset, tense, and nervous. Usually, the longer you talk, the more you reduce your stress.

3. *Work off your anger.* Play racquetball, walk around the block, run up and down stairs, jog a mile, or sock a punching bag. Physical activity is a good way to relieve stress. As you start to cool off, you can approach the situation in a more intelligent manner.

4. *Give in occasionally.* In interactions with supervisors and with family members, people find it difficult to accept being wrong. A good way to reduce stress about who is right and who is wrong is simply to give in occasionally. Besides, if you give in, the other person may respond by occasionally giving in to you.

5. *Do something for others.* When you find yourself in a high-stress situation where you are worrying and simply can't get anything done, you can sometimes reduce stress by doing a kind deed or helping someone else. When you are out buying a flower, a card, or carrot sticks to give to someone else, you can forget about your stress.

6. *Take one thing at a time.* Most of us have too many things to do and cannot possibly complete everything. One effective way to deal with this stressful condition is to rank all items that you have to do. Then take one item at a time and complete it. Don't worry about any items other than the one you are working on. This gives you a sense of accomplishment that you are completing some of your responsibilities, and it helps reduce stress. We'll talk more about time and task management in Chapter 17.

7. *Shun the superperson urge.* Don't go through life under the mistaken assumption that you can do everything for everybody all the time. This is a gigantic producer of stress. Be willing to do as much as you can, but don't accept more.

8. *Go easy with criticism.* Working with people who do not complete assignments is stress producing. Expecting too much from others can lead to disappointment and frustration. It is best to go easy with criticism. Expect the work to be done, but avoid **criticism stress** by keeping your expectations of others realistic.

9. *Take time for recreation.* Physical **recreation** and reducing mental stress go hand in hand. Recreation can take the form of demanding physical activities, such as jogging, or less strenuous activity, such as going to the movies or a concert. Recreation helps take your mind off all the stress-producing activities in your life.

10. *Organize your life.* A highly organized time schedule saves tension as well as helps you accomplish a great deal. Being organized can help

Source: © Tribune Media Services, Inc. All Rights Reserved. Reprinted with permission.

save the time necessary to complete more work. (However, being too organized can also cause stress in your life.)

11. *Establish a nutritious diet.* Include a balance of healthy foods while eliminating or reducing excessive calories, fats, alcohol, caffeine, and other unhealthy substances.

12. *Investigate stress-reduction programs.* Check out employee assistance programs or community agency programs that offer help in reducing stress.

13. *Discover your personality.* How stress affects one depends on certain aspects of personality. Complete and score the following activity entitled "Which Personality Type Are You?" and then read the section on job stress and personality to discover how your **personality-produced stress** might be causing difficulties in your life.

Job Stress and Personality

"Jobs, in and of themselves, are not necessarily the cause of stress," says Rosalind Forbes in an article entitled "Job Stress and Personality."[6] Forbes describes twelve personality characteristics and their relationship to stress:

Twelve personality characteristics that relate to stress . . .

1. *"I want to be left alone."* Introverts are not very social and do not cope well with tensions with other people. They usually do well working alone but are often hampered in team settings. Promotions trigger stress because they usually include assuming supervisory or additional interpersonal responsibilities.

2. *"Look at me; I'm here and I want to join you."* Extroverts are "people who need people" for a variety of reasons. They usually work well in jobs that require teamwork and interpersonal relationships. Extroverts are limited in that they require access to others if they are to perform adequately. Whereas the introvert is happy if left alone, the extrovert must be surrounded with people to maintain a healthy self-identity.

3. *"You'll do it this way or else!"* Rigidly structured individuals are interested in security and are afraid to take risks. They possess characteristics that are highly resistant to change. These people might crack under pressure while attempting to implement an inappropriate but accepted strategy, rather than risking the use of an innovative solution that has not been totally proven. They are stressed by anything that upsets the routine. They sometimes make it to supervisory or managerial positions, where their need for knowing and controlling details causes their employees to work out of fear. Rigid individuals rarely make good managers because they lack the flexibility required for effectively interacting with others.

4. *"Sure, I'm willing to try it."* People with the flexible personality type normally suffer very little job stress. They have healthy, mature egos and can usually adapt to changing situations while tolerating high degrees of stress. Individuals with this personality type can generally delegate authority and work well either alone or in a group.

5. *"Where there isn't any stress, I'll create it."* The stress-prone personality is often both a victim and a carrier of stress. Characterized as hard-driving, work-oriented, performance-conscious, or goal-oriented, individuals in this category constantly overwork and seldom enjoy the benefits of their efforts as they continuously seek greater and often unrealistic goals. They are also highly susceptible to physical repercussions and are three times more likely than others to suffer a coronary in middle age.

6. *"If there is no reason to be concerned, I won't worry about it."* Stress reducers may be as ambitious and work-oriented as stress-prone individuals. However, they are usually more aware of, and confident in, their capabilities and therefore are more patient and less concerned with what others think of their work. These people are seldom driven

ACTIVITIES

WHICH PERSONALITY TYPE ARE YOU?

This questionnaire is designed to help you determine if the personality you bring to work is the reason for most of your stress. Go through all 30 statements and rate yourself as to how you typically feel or react in each situation.

1. Never
2. Seldom
3. Sometimes
4. Frequently
5. Always

_____ 1. Meeting new acquaintances is very stressful for me.

_____ 2. My spouse or friends think I am hard-driving and work too hard.

_____ 3. What happens in my life is determined by fate and circumstances.

_____ 4. If given the chance, I prefer to work alone.

_____ 5. When a job is not clearly laid out for me, I begin to feel anxious.

_____ 6. A negative evaluation about my work makes me depressed for days.

_____ 7. I pride myself on accomplishing the most work in my department and being the first to meet quotas.

_____ 8. Having to make business decisions is particularly stressful for me.

_____ 9. There is little I can do to influence the decisions of those in authority.

_____ 10. My work is less productive when I have to interact with others.

_____ 11. I rely more on other people's opinions than on my own.

_____ 12. I would rather have a steady income I can count on than a stimulating but responsible job.

_____ 13. I usually work with frequent deadlines and time pressures.

_____ 14. Since it is impossible to try to change a large organization, I tend to go along with things as they are.

_____ 15. I tend to withdraw from people rather than confront them with problems.

_____ 16. If one method for getting the job done works, I am not likely to change it.

_____ 17. I need the praise of others to feel I am doing a good job.

_____ 18. Since I do not want to fail, I avoid risks.

_____ 19. I seldom feel good about myself.

_____ 20. I become particularly upset with any changes in my routine.

_____ 21. I personally do not reveal things about myself.

_____ 22. I tend to become overly cautious and anxious in new situations.

_____ 23. I have a tendency to produce more and more work in less time.

_____ 24. Because of my work, I have no opportunity to do the things I really want to do in life.

_____ 25. If someone criticizes me, I begin to doubt myself.

_____ 26. I pride myself on being orderly, neat, and punctual.

_____ 27. I do not like to go to parties or places where there are a large number of people.

_____ 28. Luck has a great deal to do with success.

_____ 29. I do a great deal of business during a game of golf or in the course of evening dinners with clients.

_____ 30. I become particularly upset if I am contradicted.

continued

ACTIVITIES

WHICH PERSONALITY TYPE ARE YOU?, CONTINUED

Evaluation

If your score is between 134 and 150, you possess personality characteristics that are likely to generate a great deal of stress for you on the job. Your personality causes you to create much of your own stress, and this may limit your ability to function well under pressure.

A score between 114 and 135 indicates there is room for improvement. You are usually unable to handle high amounts of stress for prolonged periods of time.

There is a good balance between 74 and 115. You will have to make a conscious effort, however, to keep your behavior on the positive end of the scale when going through stressful situations.

If your score is between 44 and 75, it is not likely that your personality aggravates your reaction to stress. You probably feel that you can handle and control most situations.

A score between 30 and 45 indicates you possess characteristics that defuse much of the stress in your life. You have the qualities that make you a candidate for a leadership position since you function well under pressure.

The statements you just responded to can be used to indicate more than just how you react to stress; they can also identify what personality trait is causing you to react that way.

To identify which personality type you are, the items on the questionnaire are grouped around personality clusters. Add up the score of each cluster and you will see which is more heavily weighted. It is not unusual to have more than one predominant trait.

Cluster	Pertinent Statements
Low/high self-esteem	6, 11, 17, 19, 25
Rigid/flexible	5, 16, 20, 26, 30
Introvert/extrovert	4, 10, 15, 21, 27
Outer-/inner-directed	3, 9, 14, 24, 28
Stress-prone/stress reducer	2, 7, 13 23, 29
Security seeker/risk seeker	1, 8, 12, 18, 22

Once you have determined which characteristics are creating your stress, you can begin changing those aspects of your behavior.

by the clock and do not take on extra work just to enhance their image or prestige. Nevertheless, they accomplish much and are more likely to enjoy the fruits of their accomplishments than will their driven, exhausted counterparts.

7. *"If I take a chance, I might fail."* Risk avoiders tend to be overly cautious and afraid to make a decision. These people are driven by feelings of inadequacy, insecurity, and dependency, which inhibit innovative thinking. They avoid new ideas, new jobs, transfers, and even promotions as they seek security while rarely feeling secure.

8. *"Hey, that sounds great! Let's risk it!"* Risk takers create action and provide the fuel for most business and professional endeavors. Usually logical thinkers, people with this personality type consider available facts, weigh alternatives, and take appropriate action. Risk takers have confidence in their decisions and enjoy a high level of success.

9. *"They set me up to fail."* People with an outer-directed personality tend to blame other people, things, or the organization when problems occur. Since they are outer-directed, their self-identities are tied to their work or organization and they have no sense of power or control. To compensate for this problem, their immediate action when faced with failure is to look for someone to blame. Outer-directed people often develop a high level of expertise in generating paperwork since paper can often be used to cover mistakes and failures. While outer-directed people are capable of success, they are sensitive to criticism, and because they often spend more time working on excuses than solutions, they limit their success potential.

10. *"I'm responsible."* Inner-directed people attribute their failures and successes to their own actions, attitudes, and inner resources. They are more adaptable than outer-directed people but often suffer higher stress levels. In extreme cases, they become preoccupied with details and obsessed with finding why they have not achieved desired results.

11. *"Tell me I'm okay."* Persons with low self-esteem tend to become overwhelmed and show a sharp decrease in performance when under stress. These people seldom succeed in high-pressure business situations, and if placed in such situations are likely to suffer severe depression.

12. *"That's all right; I'm okay."* Individuals with high self-esteem can usually deal with frustration and often perform better under pressure. These people have self-confidence based on internal qualities and tend to be optimistic about their ability to achieve desired results. High self-esteem is a vital quality for success in the rough-and-tumble business world.

Forbes's 12 personality types are not all mutually exclusive; more than one can apply to the same person in varying degrees. These types can serve as reference points to develop ideas for building on individual strengths and limiting or compensating for weaknesses in order to reduce negative stress and improve overall performance.

The Burned-Out Worker

Why do workers burn out?

Human relations problems arising from stresses on the job, as well as from social pressures, are increasing. We have been addressing these kinds of pressures for several chapters now. Certain symptoms show up in so-called burned-out workers—workers who have given their all for the company and become overly tired from it.

Why do workers burn out? A number of forces are at work here. Sometimes the frustrations emerge from a high achiever's expectations. When a person who has set very high goals suddenly finds that those goals are not achievable, that person may become very frustrated and burn out.

In other cases, workaholics may be set up as role models for other workers. Nevertheless, the problems of *workaholism*—that is, addiction to one's work—are very severe. They can readily lead not only to worker burnout but to all types of social, family, and other adjustment problems.

Many highly successful people come to feel that they have given too much to their organizations. Some of these people eventually face the reality that life is passing them by. They recognize that they have dedicated virtually all their time and efforts to their career pursuits while missing out on many other aspects of life. These people are burned out—they have little left to give.

In his article "Coping with Burnout," Kerry L. Johnson says that burnout may be caused by a compulsion for business or financial success. He also says

By recognizing the symptoms and taking positive action, burnout can be alleviated.

that burnout causes low self-esteem, decreased productivity, and sometimes failed relationships, but that burnout is not inevitable if recognized and treated in its early stages. The five stages of burnout, as identified by Randy Kunkel, are headaches, general body fatigue, severed communication to family and friends, overload, and disintegration of values. According to Johnson, burnout can be avoided or alleviated by preventing a career rut, staying physically active, focusing on nonbusiness relationships, stimulating the intellect, making spiritual discoveries, and consciously improving one's lifestyle.[7]

Management Approaches for Coping with Stress and Burnout

Management can reduce **environment stress** by bringing employees together in team meetings, using proper management techniques, establishing an effective communication system, and, above all, reducing uncertainty among employees.

"I think that maybe in every company today there is always at least one person who is going crazy slowly."

Joseph Heller

Team Meetings   Talking over problems helps people feel better about their coworkers. This can reduce the stress they have about their ability or inability to solve problems. **Team meetings** allow employees to get together and discuss problems.

If employees are feeling a tremendous amount of stress, team meetings can be an effective way to reduce it.

Some organizations use encounter groups to reduce stress. The members reduce strong feelings and emotions by telling others why they are upset. A professional group facilitator should lead the encounter so that people do not become too upset with what occurs.

Another approach is the deep sensing session, in which executives meet with employees and communicate face-to-face. This approach should not be just a gripe session, but a situation where problems associated with miscommunication can be cleared up. Usually with this approach a special outside consultant must be brought in to guide and direct the meeting. The consultant can direct misunderstandings without evoking too much defensive behavior.

Good Management Can Reduce Stress
Proper management does a great deal to reduce employee stress. For example, a manager can reduce stress related to time or overwork by allowing employees enough time to plan, organize, and complete the tasks they must do.

Rest breaks during the working day can also help reduce stress. Some organizations call these rest breaks "minivacations." All people need some time during the day to sit down, to daydream, to fantasize, and to deal with feelings.

Teaching people how to cope with stress is important to management. Employees can be taught to cope with difficulties and reduce their own tensions. Managers should help employees upgrade their life goals. Working toward strong, positive life goals can help people overcome small stressful circumstances much more quickly and effectively. The organization must help employees establish life goals.

Good managers can do much to reduce stress

Productive Communication
Effective communication within the organization and among employees is an important tool for reducing employee stress. When employees do not receive information, they wonder why, and they tend to become worried and suspicious. An effective communication system fosters openness and feedback at all levels and for all people in the organization.

One approach to increasing effective communication is to talk about the achievements of employees and to let word get out that people are doing well and that they are appreciated. This builds high employee expectations, self-esteem, and self-confidence—and reduces stress.

Also, make certain that people understand what they have been asked to do. Managers should continually ask for feedback so that they know what is happening.

Effective communication reduces stress.

A Final Statement

Anything that *can* be done to reduce employee stress *should* be done. More and more companies have established stress-reducing programs to increase productivity and efficiency in employees. Some managers will always support the idea that employees must be pressured to get them to complete their jobs. However, many organizations are now realizing that learning how to manage stress is important. As individuals and organizations learn to cope with and thrive on stress, supervisors and employees become happier, and workgroups become more productive. Team interaction, good management, and effective communication can help reduce uncertainty and help organizations function more effectively with less toll on employees.

As stress is reduced, employees become happier and organizations more productive.

Summary of Key Ideas

- The ten stressors are: ineffective communication; corporate mismanagement; information overload; inconsistent leader behavior; work overload; job change; personal problems; stress carriers; company policies, salary, and working conditions; and powerlessness associated with role changes.

- Techniques for coping with stress include: escape for a while, talk it out, work off your anger, give in occasionally, do something for others, take one thing at a time, shun the superperson urge, go easy with criticism, take time for recreation, organize your life, establish a nutritious diet, investigate stress-reduction programs, and discover your personality.

- Changes in information technology and other computer systems can create "technostress," resulting in physical and psychological reactions. As people become more familiar with technology, this stress becomes more manageable.

- Our personalities influence our susceptibilities to stress as well as our reactions to it. A greater awareness of personality types helps us deal more effectively with stress in ourselves and others.

- Burnout is a logical but avoidable response to prolonged stress. It can be avoided or relieved by avoiding career ruts, staying physically active, focusing on nonbusiness relationships, stimulating the intellect, making spiritual discoveries, and consciously improving one's lifestyle.

- Management can help reduce stress in the work environment by holding team meetings, using proper management techniques, employing effective communication systems, and reducing uncertainty among employees.

Key Terms, Concepts, and Names

Burnout	Midlife crisis
Change-produced stress	Personality-produced stress
Coping techniques	Recreation
Criticism	Stress
Environment	Stress carrier
Eustress	Team meetings
Information overload	Technostress

Questions and Exercises

1. Answer the introductory questions at the beginning of the chapter.

2. Give an example of each technique for coping with stress listed in this chapter.

3. Discuss why you agree or disagree with the way you scored on the stress and personality inventory.

4. Read the following statement by St. Augustine. How does it relate to stress? Does the statement relate to or disagree with the information presented in this chapter on stress?

> For the world is like an olive press, and men are constantly under pressure. If you are the dregs of the oil you are carried away through the sewer, but if you are true oil you remain in the vessel. To be under pressure is inescapable. Pressure takes place through all the world: war, siege, the worries of state. We all know men who grumble under these pressures, and complain. They are cowards. They lack splendor. But there is another sort of man who is under the same pressure, but does not complain. For it is the friction which polishes him. It is pressure which refines and makes him noble.
>
> St. Augustine
> First Archbishop of Canterbury
> Seventh century A.D.

5. Compare the ten personal stressors listed in this chapter against your own experiences. What items would you add to the list? What items would you delete?

6. Often one of the best approaches for dealing with stress is simply to escape for a while. The following escape techniques have been advocated at one time or another. Check off the ones that appeal to you, and then store them in your memory to use the next time you find yourself in a stressful situation.

Checklist of Temporary Escape Techniques

_____ Spend time reading those books you've been promising yourself to read.

_____ Go to the movies.

_____ Listen to good music.

_____ Work it off by exercising.

_____ Avoid striving.

_____ Give in more often.

_____ Create a quiet scene.

_____ Use "not now" buttons.

_____ Plan your work.

_____ Do something for someone else.

_____ Write a letter.

_____ Take an adult education course.

_____ Take a walk.

_____ Talk it out.

_____ Cry.

_____ Take a bubble bath.

_____ Focus on enjoyment.

_____ Avoid making too many big changes at once.

_____ Be realistic.

_____ Tackle one task at a time.

_____ Hit a tennis ball against a wall.

_____ Engage in ten-minute "pity parties."

Notes

1. Victoria B. Elder, Ella P. Gardner, and Stephen R. Ruth, "Gender and Age in Technostress: Effects on White Collar Productivity," *Government Finance Review* 3, December 1987, pp. 17—21.

2. Ibid.

3. Robert E. Callahan and Patrick C. Fleenor, "There Are Ways to Overcome Resistance to Computers," *Office* 106, October 1987, pp. 78–80.

4. James A. Senn, "Essential Principles of Information Systems Development," *MIS Quarterly* 2, June 1978, p. 24.

5. Callahan and Fleenor, p. 80.

6. Rosalind Forbes, "Job Stress and Personality," *Western World* 10, 1970, pp. 41–43, 64–67.

7. Kerry L. Johnson, "Coping with Burnout," *Broker World* 8, December 1988, pp. 88–96.

Another Look: Handle Stress by Eliminating Negativity from Your Life

Motivational speaker and best-selling author, Charles J. Givens describes this strategy for dealing with stress:

I was teaching a success program in Lynchburg, Virginia, and we were discussing negativity as a cause of stress and physical problems. A woman told the group, "I get violently ill every night, and I have for the last ten years. I get sick to my stomach, and I end up vomiting. Night after night, it's always the same."

"All effects have preceding causes," I said. "Let's see if we can make the connection. Tell me exactly what you do from the moment you get home until the time you go to bed, since your illness occurs only during that one period of time."

"Well," she said, "every day I come home from work, feed the cat, put dinner on, and then sit down and watch the news on TV."

"Do you ever miss a broadcast?" I asked her.

"Oh, no," she replied. "I just have to watch the news because I feel so sorry for those people who are starving or in auto accidents, but I thank my lucky stars that it's not me."

"You may be getting mentally and emotionally involved in the events shown on the screen," I told her. "When there's a wreck, you're feeling and experiencing the wreck as if you were there. You're thinking about what might happen to you and how you might suffer, or how your family would feel if you weren't around anymore."

"That's right," she said. "The things that happen to people are just awful.'

I asked her to do an experiment. For one week she was not to watch or listen to the news—no matter what was happening or how badly she wanted to. She agreed, and the following week when she returned to class, she said, "I didn't watch the news for a whole week, and you won't believe what happened. No problems. The nausea went away, the upset and the sickness, and for the first time in ten years I experienced positive productive evenings!"

This true story illustrates the immense immediate impact of negativity from any source in your life. Even if negativity does not cause you to throw up or feel noticeably ill, it is eating away at you like an undetected cancer. Negativity causes intense stress. Events in your own life and in the lives of others, if you get sucked into them, affect you for as long as your mind dwells on them, producing emotional and physical stress reactions. Not only can reactions to events affect your life, but they can even control it. That's why you must become aware of and begin to eliminate the negative events, thoughts, emotions, and even the negative people in your life.

Source: Reprinted with the permission of Simon & Schuster from *Superself* by Charles J. Givens. © 1993 by Charles J. Givens.

A Case in Point: Screw Up, and Get Smart

WHO Katie Paine, founder and CEO, the Delahaye Group Inc., a reputation measurement firm.

WHAT'S YOUR PROBLEM? "We all make mistakes. But what really makes mistakes expensive is not admitting them right away. How do I get people not only to fess up but also to learn from their missteps?"

TELL ME ABOUT IT "Business culture teaches us never to admit to our mistakes but to bury them instead—or to blame somebody else. And most personnel and project reviews don't really do much to uncover mistakes. If we wait until we've finished a project to conduct a postmortem, people will forget the mistake, or they'll build up a grudge

against a coworker. Either way, we lose a learning opportunity."

WHAT'S YOUR SOLUTION? "Mistake of the Month. Several years ago, I overslept and missed a flight to a big client meeting. I walked into my next staff meeting, plunked 50 bucks down on the table, and said, 'If you can top my mistake, that money is yours.' Well, people started to own up to mistakes, and suddenly we had a flood of them: One of our sales guys had gone on a sales call without business cards; two of our people had arrived at Coca-Cola without their presentation materials. At every staff meeting since, we've set aside 30 minutes to write up the mistakes of the month on a whiteboard. Then we cast a vote on two categories: the mistake

continued

Screw Up and Get Smart, *continued*

from which we've learned the most, and the one from which we've learned the least. The prize for the first category is access to a coveted downtown parking space for the following month. The person who made the mistake from which we've learned the least has to talk at the next meeting about why it will never happen again.

"Since 1989, we've recorded more than 2,000 mistakes. Once a mistake hits the whiteboard, it tends not to happen again. This practice has had a real impact on our work. Mistake of the Month also helps set my agenda as a leader. As mistakes go on the whiteboard, I ask myself, 'Do I need to be concerned about

this?' Plus, it has become a bonding ritual. Once you go through it, you're a member of the club."

Questions

1. In light of this chapter's discussion of stress, what do you think of this approach?
2. Would such mistake discussions work in your organization? Why or why not?
3. What does this article say about the culture of the Delahaye Group and about the management philosophy of its CEO, Kathy Paine?

Source: Reprinted with permission. *Fast Company* Issue 19, November 1998, p. 58. Author Polly LaBarre.

A Case in Point: Bonne Bell: Dress Is Optional

This beauty-aids company bends office rules and adds financial incentives to promote good health among its employees. President Jess Bell brought the spirit of fitness to Bonne Bell. After sponsoring ski and tennis events throughout the 1960s, he started encouraging his employees to ride bikes to work and arranged for them to purchase bikes at cost. Today, the company sponsors races such as the Cleveland Heart-A-Thon and the Cystic Fibrosis Benefit Run.

In 1976, Bonne Bell began its first official fitness program, building tennis and volleyball courts, a track and shower and locker facilities. The company also constructed exercise rooms at both of its office locations in Ohio. To get and keep employees interested, Bonne Bell has set up generous incentives: Workers can use the facilities for free, they get an extra 30 minutes at lunch if they want to exercise, and workout clothes are acceptable attire after lunch. Employees can also purchase running suits and shoes at discount prices. Its newest incentive promises a check for $250 to employees who exercise four days a week from January to June.

Bonne Bell also pays $250 to employees who stop smoking for six months and $5 for each pound

(up to 40) a worker loses over six months. Going back to bad health habits cost double. The company requires people who start smoking again to give $500 to the corporate charitable foundation. For every pound gained back within six months of its loss, that donation is $10.

The company has noted many positive changes since the program began. Records of sick days, for example, show much less absenteeism. "Everyone enjoys it," says Connie Schafer, a spokesperson for Bonne Bell. "We've seen people start to take care of themselves." And, she adds, many employees—especially Jess Bell—wouldn't miss Wednesday morning early-bird runs.

Questions

1. Why do Bonne Bell's programs make "dollars and sense"?
2. If you worked for the ideal organization, what would you like to see it do for employee stress management?

Source: Reprinted from "Bonne Bell: Dress Is Optional," *Psychology Today* May 1989, p. 56. Reprinted with permission from *Psychology Today* magazine © 1989 (Sussex Publishers, Inc.).

Your Career in the Information Age

- How is the business landscape changing, and why is that important to you?

- What can managers reasonably expect from their companies?

- Why is the clarification of expectations an important step to becoming successful?

- How can you become an effective subordinate by managing your manager?

- How can you better manage yourself, your time, and your tasks?

- What do organizations expect from their managers?

- What do companies *not* expect from a new manager or employee?

- What is arguably the number-one job of any employee or manager?

- Why is getting work done on time not in itself a mark of good self-management?

The answers to these and other questions are coming up next in Chapter 17 . . .

If you've read this entire book, you will recognize that accomplishing meaningful work through the efforts of others is a complex process. We hope you now better understand more about human relationships and their effects on people at work.

Managerial leadership is not a job for everyone. Directing the work efforts of other employees can be frustrating and difficult. Nevertheless, people feel a great sense of satisfaction when they accomplish organizational work in a spirit of cooperation and teamwork.

There are all kinds of managers: some are highly successful, some are dismal failures, and most are somewhere in between. Since you have had the good sense to select our book as a guide to your study of human relations, we are confident that you are a person of discriminating taste and impeccable judgment. You, we suspect, will be satisfied with nothing less than becoming highly successful! A few key ideas can help you achieve this, and we'll share them with you in the following pages.

Successful employees and leaders in today's organizations will:

- Understand the changing business landscape

- Clarify expectations on the job

- Manage not only their subordinates, but their boss as well

- Develop excellent self-management skills

Understanding the Changing Business Landscape

Once upon a time, young people graduated from school and eagerly sought employment with large and prosperous companies. They considered themselves most fortunate if they were hired by a major and "secure" corporation. They were able to assume that they would systematically move up in the organization, eventually retiring with a gold watch and a comfortable pension.

If the phrase "once upon a time" sounds like a fairy tale, you understand why we used it. The lifetime employer with secure jobs is no longer a reality in the modern business landscape. There are exceptions, of course, but by far the more realistic picture of a typical career today involves job changes, extensive organizational restructuring (often with job cuts), and a greatly diminished sense of loyalty. Companies seldom feel deeply obligated to provide long-term work, and employees rarely feel loyalty to the company. Part of the reason for these dramatic shifts is the nature of the business world. The age of technology and information has created a fluid and dynamic economy where companies must make frequent and often radical changes to compete successfully. These changes have an impact on people. Some cannot adjust. Some lack skills to deal with a company's changed mission. And some feel betrayed by "big business" when they are downsized or laid off.

Career planning used to involve assessing your personal goals and seeing how you could make these work with a current employer or a similar business. It used to involve seeing how to set goals that would help you be promoted in the company. Even people who followed the advice of leadership gurus to develop a "vision" often did so within the context of existing organizations.

The Information Age has changed organizations and their people more dramatically than has any shift since the economy evolved from agricultural to industrial. At one time, the vast majority of Americans were employed in producing agricultural products. Today, less than 4 percent of the economy produces all the food we can eat. But the industrial revolution is also a thing of the past. Less than 20 percent of all workers are now employed in manufacturing. Some futurists predict that in the not-too-distant future, fewer than 10 percent of employees will produce all the manufactured goods we can use. So what will the other 85 percent of us be doing? We are, and increasingly will be, working with information.

"Muscle power, machine power, even electrical power are steadily being replaced by brain power," says Thomas A. Stewart in *Intellectual Capital.* He quotes management guru Peter Drucker, who says that the amount of labor needed to produce an additional unit of manufacturing output has fallen 1 percent per year (99 percent) since 1900 when machines took over what muscles once did. The years since World War II show similar drops in the amount of energy needed to increase manufacturing levels. What has taken the place of matter and energy is intelligence. Since 1900 the number of educated workers on the payroll has risen at about the same rate. The major economic powers are no longer "the industrialized world," but the knowledge world. Agriculture, construction, manufacturing, and mining employ fewer than one in four Americans, and even those people work principally with their heads rather than their backs and hands. We are all **knowledge workers** now, working for knowledge companies.[1]

If all this is true, how can we manage our careers in this new world? Many of the concepts taught throughout this book will prepare you for success in any type of organization, including the knowledge businesses.

Clarifying Expectations on the Job

Successful employees and managers create better understanding among people by clarifying **job expectations.** Theory X managers miss many opportunities to help subordinates grow because of their unclear and generally pessimistic expectations of others. Likewise, communicators or motivators who fail to clarify what arouses interest in others operate in a hit-and-miss fashion. The frequent result is wheel spinning and unproductive management. Successful managers spend time and effort clarifying what is expected of them and of the organization.

Why is clarifying expectations so important?

What Organizations Expect of Management Employees

Typically, when people begin new jobs, some uncertainties are involved. The level of uncertainty is especially high for the recent graduate who is going into his or her first full-time employment. Both the new employee and the organization must first come to agreement about what each expects from the other. Typically, companies expect the following kinds of things from their management employees.

Representation of the Company   Management employees at all levels are expected to represent their company on and off the job. The people we meet socially, in community activities, as neighbors, or within the scope of our business dealings develop an impression of our company based on our behavior. If we come across as shifty or suspicious, others may well question the ethics of our corporation. If we are aboveboard, honest, optimistic, and direct about our organization, we reflect a more positive image in the eyes of our friends and neighbors.

Managers expect their people to behave in ways that reflect positively on the company. They expect people to avoid activities or behaviors that might compromise or embarrass the organization in the eyes of the public. Although public relations (PR) is often a specialized function within an organization, in a very real sense, all employees are involved in PR. The public judges a company by the people it keeps.

The public judges a company by the people it keeps.

Open communication is important in establishing realistic expectations between employers and prospective employees.

Companies want managers who want to succeed as an organization.

A Desire for Success   Companies expect their employees to truly want to be successful. Few organizations want to hire people who have negative self-images or severe reservations as to what they can accomplish. Companies want to recruit winners. They typically look for people with proven track records. However, past successes are not enough. The ongoing desire to be successful within the organization is a very positive characteristic.

We once had lunch with a highly successful young executive who had formed a small conglomerate with his two brothers. Their growth rate had been highly impressive—all three had become self-made millionaires while still in their twenties. In our conversation, this individual identified his desire to be successful as a key to their organization's growth. All three brothers sincerely wanted their organization to be successful. There was no questioning of each other's desire. Each knew that the other two were working just as hard as he to make the corporation thrive. Organizational success was the first priority. The point is that these men had a true desire to succeed *as an organization,* not just as individuals. This is one key to becoming a highly successful manager.

People who work short hours are seen as doing less than their share.

Time Spent on the Job   Most companies expect their employees to spend time on the job each day. Normally, workers are expected to come to work at a certain time and to remain there until quitting time. Employees who habitually show up late or leave early create the impression of doing less than their fair share. This negative impression may be difficult to overcome, even if the employee is quite successful. Some individuals in sales, for example, accomplish a great deal of work in a short period of time. They meet their company objectives while only working a few hours a day in active sales. Nevertheless, they are regarded with some suspicion. The question is, "If they can attain company objectives working half a day, how much could they do if they worked a full eight-hour day?"

The old adage of "An honest day's work for an honest day's pay" still makes sense to most employers. Highly successful managers are typically generous with the time and effort they give to the organization. Clockwatchers seldom succeed.

Creativity and Innovation Most organizations expect their management employees to be creative. Creativity here does not necessarily mean coming up with a brand-new concept or idea that changes the entire direction of the corporation. It can, however, mean using ingenuity and initiative to do work in different, more productive, or more effective ways. We have talked throughout this book about the importance of motivating employees to participate in the creative process of doing the work of the organization more effectively. Good managers use creativity. They are not bound to "the way we've always done it" but constantly look for a better, more creative way of accomplishing the organization's work.

In today's knowledge companies, using brainpower to solve problems and develop creative procedures is a standard requirement of managers. If leaders cannot "think outside the box" (apply real ingenuity), they may have a difficult time innovating. Without innovation, companies are left in the competitive dust.

A Long-Term Commitment Executives are realistic about the nature of today's workforce. They don't honestly expect a worker to sign on for life. Nevertheless, the best companies will provide all kinds of creative incentives to keep the people it views as critical to organizational success. For managers, the most frustrating mark of "Generation X" is their typical lack of loyalty to employers. They largely hold a free-agent mentality and will quickly move to a new job if a slightly better opportunity appears. In fairness, this mentality is a natural outgrowth of the lack of loyalty companies have shown to their employees in recent decades with downsizing and frequent layoffs.

When accepting a new position, keep in mind that recruiting, training, and developing employees are costly processes. Few employees carry their own weight immediately on joining an organization. The training period costs the company far more than the immediate return that those employees can make to the organization's profitability.

Organizations may spend from $40,000 to $100,000 training key employees. Ethically, employees are bound to stay with a company at least until they are contributing members of the organization. Don't take a job with a company if you don't intend to give it your best shot for a reasonable period of time.

Customer Service Developing customer service skills provides the most significant arena for career success. Whether you work for a huge corporation or run a lemonade stand, the principles of customer service are largely the same. You live and die by what your customers think of you.

In fact, we believe that your number-one task, regardless of your job title, organizational position, experience, or seniority, will always be to attract, satisfy, and preserve loyal customers.[2]

In organizations, customers take two forms, *internal* and *external. Internal* customers are those people, departments, or organizations served by what we do. The only person who might have no internal customers is the individual who works completely alone. For the rest of us, internal customers are a fact of life.

For example, a word processing clerk or copy center worker within a company serves other workers' document-handling needs. A human resources office worker serves employees' need for benefits information, management's need for staffing, and the legal staff's need for handling various government paperwork requirements.

As individuals, we all have at least one internal customer: our boss. As managers, we also have internal customers in the form of the people we supervise. They rely on us to meet their needs.

Managers are expected to be somewhat creative in solving organizational problems.

Managers should make a long-term commitment to their organizations.

External customers are those people or departments who are the end users of our organization's product or services. This is, of course, the traditional use of the term "customer."

Arguably, the key to your success is your ability to meet and exceed customer expectations.

What Companies Do Not Expect from a New Manager

New employees are not expected to know it all.

Organizations do *not* expect a new employee to know it all. Clearly, new employees do not have a basis for making all the right decisions and performing all the right actions. This is why employee development programs are provided in all major organizations.

By the same token, new employees are not typically expected to produce immediate or profitable results for the company. As we've said, most organizations take a loss in productivity initially on hiring new employees. They hope to regain that initial loss by developing productive contributors to the organization as time goes on.

Having a realistic understanding of these expectations up-front can help avoid problems later. You must also have a realistic picture of what you as an employee can expect from your company.

What Employees Should Expect from the Company

Clarifying expectations is a two-way street. Not only must employees understand what is expected of them, but the organization's leaders must understand what employees normally expect from the company. Basic obligations to employees normally include the following.

Companies should give applicants a clear picture of the organization before hiring them.

Openness and Honesty in the Recruiting Process   Organizations have an obligation to tell potential employees what the company is all about. The individual being recruited should have some grasp of the company's management philosophy, the nature of the products or services it offers, and clear statements about what it expects from its employees. Sharing this information during the recruiting process is the responsibility of both the applicant, who should seek it out, and the potential employer, who should readily provide it.

Training is at the heart of the management process.

Appropriate and Adequate Training   Organizations need to provide both new and current employees with the training necessary for them to skillfully complete the tasks to which they've been assigned. Training is not and should not be regarded as a fringe benefit; it is at the heart of the organization's functions.

Reasonable Compensation and Benefits   Organizations have an obligation to provide fair and equitable compensation, as well as reasonable benefit plans.

Employees have a right to know how they are doing.

Performance Reviews and Periodic Raises   In addition to receiving pay and benefits, employees have a right to know how they are doing. The performance review is widely expected in industry. People who perform well also expect to receive additional compensation. An individual who produces more is worth more to the organization and therefore should be paid more.

A Good Working Environment   Corporations have an obligation to provide a safe, healthy, and reasonably pleasant working environment for their

Organizations must provide training to their employees.

employees. Although some tasks must be performed under less-than-desirable conditions, employees who do difficult, dangerous, or unpleasant work should receive additional compensation.

Managing Your Manager

Norman C. Hill and Paul H. Thompson wrote an article titled "Managing Your Manager: The Effective Subordinate." In it, they suggested a number of ideas that can be useful in becoming successful managers.

Building initially on the idea of expectation clarification that we have already discussed, they suggest some specific areas where understanding needs to be established. We've paraphrased a number of their ideas in this section.[3]

Little attention has been paid to the important art of managing your manager.

Resolving Key Issues

One way to avoid some problems of expectations is to sit down with your boss and talk things out. One successful manager described doing this: "Whenever I get a new boss, I sit down with him and ask him to make his expectations explicit. We try to list not my job activities, but the main purposes of my job. To do that, we continue each statement of activity with 'in order to . . .' and try to complete the sentence. By recording my job purposes, we get a clear picture of what I should be accomplishing; and that's what counts—results."

Sit down with your boss and talk things out.

You can excel in your organization by taking the initiative to resolve certain issues with your boss directly. This will be an ongoing process. The kinds of things that need to be discussed include:

Repeated conversations are often required.

- The content of your job

- The degree to which you should take initiative on your job

- How to keep the boss informed

- How to ask for help

Job descriptions often need to be flexible.

Clarifying Job Content   Reach an agreement on your responsibilities. Having a clearly written job description is more useful in some companies than in others. If, for example, your company is experiencing unusual growth or a rapidly changing environment, job descriptions may be less useful. In other words, people need to be able to react to changes and be flexible.

Taking Initiative   One manager describes a good subordinate as one who "thinks of the things I would do before I do them. What this means is that he or she tries to adopt my perspective and look at things from my position in the organization."

Just reporting back may not be enough.

Some employees think that just reporting back their efforts, successful or not, is enough. But good intentions are no substitute for what the boss needs. Individuals need to take initiative on the job; but the degree of initiative taken needs to be talked out with the boss. Some bosses may be threatened by subordinates who anticipate their desires; others welcome such enterprise.

Don't overdo your reporting to the boss; report progress, not activities.

Keeping the Boss Informed   Keeping the boss informed is closely tied to taking initiative, but some aspects deserve separate consideration. Subordinates need to learn how to keep the boss advised on *appropriate* matters. But don't overdo it and report everything. One rule of thumb is to let the boss know about the progress being made on a particular project and to avoid reporting all the *activities* engaged in or problems encountered to achieve those results.

Asking for Help   Some bosses want to be deeply involved in a project, and they use requests for help as an opportunity to teach their subordinates. Others only want to see the final product and do not want to be bothered with frequent questions.

Asking for help too often can undermine your boss's confidence in you.

A bank manager presented his views on the issue: "Some subordinates will take an assignment, work as hard on it as possible, then come back to you when they get stuck or when it is completed. Other people start coming back to you to do their work for them. People in the second group don't do very well in our bank."

Guidelines for when to go to the boss for help.

Asking for help too often can undermine the boss's confidence in you. When you're stuck, seek out the help of more experienced people on your own level first. This suggests some important guidelines for deciding when to go to the boss for help and when to handle a situation alone:

- Take risks, not gambles (and recognize the differences between the two).
- Handle the details, but keep the manager informed.
- Check with the boss on decisions that will affect work units outside the department.
- Give the boss a recommendation each time he or she asks for an analysis of a project.
- Ask for an appointment only when you are prepared to suggest some action that should be taken.

Developing Trust with the Boss

Four conditions are necessary for **superior-subordinate** trust to develop: accessibility, availability, predictability, and loyalty. Let's look at each briefly.

Accessibility An accessible person receives ideas easily and offers them freely. If two people are going to develop a productive relationship, they must respect each other's ideas and give those ideas careful thought and consideration. A subordinate who does not respect the boss's ideas will never be trusted and will not obtain needed help to develop his or her own ideas. You don't have to agree; just be respectful of each other's point of view.

Availability **Availability** is crucial. The subordinate should be attentive and available physically, mentally, and emotionally when the manager is under pressure and needs support.

Predictability **Predictability** means one is able to reliably handle delicate administrative circumstances with good judgment and thoroughness. If subordinates have been given appropriate assignments—ones that allow them to develop their personal skills—they will acquire the ability to handle even sensitive situations. However, if a subordinate lacks sensitivity or interpersonal skills and jeopardizes relationships with customers, in the future this subordinate will not be trusted and thus will be of much less value to the boss.

Predictability also means reliability in meeting important deadlines and doing work of high quality. Managers don't like to be let down. Surprises or failures to meet deadlines embarrass them, make them look bad, and do not help build manager-subordinate trust.

Loyalty Personal loyalty to one's boss and to one's subordinate is important. A manager is not likely to trust a subordinate with important information if there is reason to fear it might be used to further the subordinate's own interests at the manager's expense.

Once again, we suggest being up-front with managers. The relationship between two individuals in a superior-subordinate relationship is critical, and mutual expectations must be achieved if the individual is to become a valued subordinate. Herein lies the key to becoming a highly successful manager.

To recap some key thoughts, certain issues should be evident to any worker, regardless of organizational level:

- Very few bosses will do all that is necessary to clarify expectations in a superior-subordinate relationship.

- Most managers will respond favorably to a discussion of the manager-subordinate relationship. However, managers have varying styles, so an individual is well advised to find out how your boss is *likely* to respond.

Managing Yourself

Ultimately, success is a "do-it-yourself" project.

Regardless of where you work, *how* you work is equally important. And of all the resources you work with, *time* is the most valuable.

Identifying Time-Saving Techniques

It's ironic that some managers pay lip service to time management (after all, "time is money," they are quick to say) but fail to help subordinates be productive with their time. Indeed, the manager may be the employee's worst enemy when it comes to using time.

Four conditions for trust on the job are as follows:

- **Accessibility**
- **Availability**
- **Predictability**
- **Loyalty**

Embarrassing surprises do not help build trust.

Leaders pay lip service to time management but fail to help others be productive with time.

In a recent article in the cutting-edge business magazine *Fast Company,* Robert E. Kelly, Professor of Management at Carnegie Mellon University's Graduate School of Industrial Administration reveals what it takes to become a "star" at work. Among his conclusions he distinguishes between time management and self-management. Average workers see these as the same thing. Not so, says Kelley:[4]

> "If I get my work done on time, then I'm a good self-manager." To stars, that's just the beginning. You're *expected* to manage your time well. You're *expected* to manage your projects well. Real self-management means managing not only your work but also your relationships with people, your career, and your career assets over time.
>
> Here's an example of how average performers and stars differ in this category. The average performer finishes a project, and then goes to the boss and asks, "What do you want me to do next?" The star starts looking around six months before a project is done and asks, "What experiences do I have in my portfolio? What assignment should I tackle next that would make me more valuable for the company and more valuable in the marketplace?" Stars select their next project before they finish the one they're working on.
>
> There are some core skills that you can develop to do a better job of managing yourself. Start by understanding the company. What is its critical path? Then align yourself with its core business, so you contribute more directly to its larger purpose. Second, understand who you are and how you work best. Too many people think they're going to become a star by changing who they are—but that almost never works. It's more important to recognize how you work and then to turn that into an advantage. There are plenty of stars who have messy desks, for instance. They know how to be productive *and* have a messy desk. How do they do it? You can find out by talking to them—and then figuring out how to apply their techniques.

We need to be constantly jealous of our own and others' time.

Supervisors can and should develop time-saving techniques that show others they value time. We need to be *constantly jealous* of our time as well as our subordinates' and coworkers' time. Consistent awareness of time doesn't mean you become a slave to the clock. Quite the contrary. It means you more productively use your time so that you can have more leisure as well as better results.

Working with people can be particularly time-consuming. And working with people is a central task of managers. People are time consumers. And most people are time wasters—to some extent. We need to develop a sensitivity to others that tells us when to spend more time with people and when to cut back.

Time and Task Management Tools and Skills

The best tool for making the most of your time is a planner system. Bookstores and office supply stores are well stocked with a wide variety of planners, to-do list forms, and calendars. While formats differ, the purpose is the same: to help you get organized and better spend your daily 86,400 seconds.

A planner needn't be elaborate or expensive. Some people succumb to the status symbolism of certain planners, but any appropriately designed planner can tremendously boost your power to be productive.

A planner needs five things to make it work for you:

1. A place to list and assign priorities to tasks. (We'll show you how to develop a **priority task list** in just a moment.)

2. A place to record notes and follow-up information.

3. A place for goals and values. Having these incorporated into your planning tool is a powerful way to make sure they are realized.

It's important to find a time management system that works for you.

4. A place for frequently referred-to information, especially addresses, phone numbers, perhaps birthdays, and so forth.

5. Flexibility to meet your needs.

Some people resist planning. Some say they don't like to feel bound by a plan—they want to stay "flexible." They live by wandering around. Others claim to do all their planning in their heads.

Time management experts claim that as a general rule, spending only 5 percent of the day planning can help managers achieve 95 percent of their goals. Planning prevents managers from doing the wrong things the wrong way at the wrong time, and it forces them to answer the question, "What really needs to be accomplished?"

The Nuts and Bolts of Time and Task Management

Devote a minimum of ten minutes a day solely to planning. Use a planner system you like. Then apply the steps described below, and you will see a significant increase in your personal effectiveness.

Step 1. Develop a priority task list for each day

Prioritizing tasks helps us sort them out and determine which need to be attacked first and which can be saved for later.

Here's how: List the specific tasks you want or need to spend your time on for a particular day. List the items you wish to accomplish. It might read something like this: "Complete the XYZ report, get stamps, attend Billy's softball game, eat more fish, keep date with Chris."

At this stage, don't be concerned with the *importance* of the items; just get in the habit of listing *all* nonroutine tasks that you want to accomplish that day.

Step 2. Assign a letter priority to each item on your list

Use the **A-B-C System** to assign priorities. Place the letter A next to items that *must* be done. These are critical to you, though you alone determine this based on your values and goals. Tasks required either by outside forces (e.g., your boss) or internal ones (e.g., a strong personal commitment) will normally receive an A priority. Be careful not to assign A's to *every* task. Giving everything an A defeats the purpose of prioritizing.

Use the letter B to indicate *should-do* items. These tasks aren't quite as critical as the A tasks, yet it is worth spending time to achieve them.

The letter C is for *could-do* items. These tasks are worth listing and thinking about—and, if you complete your A's and B's, worth doing.

Step 3. Assign a number to your task

Your plan of attack can be further sharpened by assigning a number to each task. Some people, however, see little value in numbering tasks once the priority letter has been assigned. You can decide what works best for you.

The best use of the numbering system is as a chronological indicator. Ask, "Which task should I do first?" If you have a meeting at 2:00 P.M. and it's an A item, the meeting may not be A-1 simply because other A-priorities must be attended to earlier in the day.

Step 4. Use completion symbols: the payoff

After you complete the tasks listed in your planner, you deserve a reward. This reward takes the form of a completion symbol.

Here are several completion symbols:

- (✔) The check mark symbol indicates that a task has been completed. That should feel good. Many people prefer to make their check marks in red as a reminder of how productive they have been.

- (→) A second symbol, an arrow, is used when a task needs to be rescheduled. Perhaps a meeting has been canceled or an appointment changed, or the task simply could not be completed because you were wrapped up in another matter.

  IMPORTANT: Whenever you use the arrow, be sure to reschedule the task to another day in the planner. This earns you the right to forget that task for awhile. You'll be reminded of it automatically on the new day on which you scheduled it.

- (O) A third symbol often used is a circle placed in the margin to the left of the completion symbol column to indicate that the task has been delegated to someone else.

  It may be that you've asked your spouse to pick up a book of stamps on the way home from work or assigned a child to clean out the garage. Or it may be a more formal kind of delegation, in which you've asked a colleague or subordinate to complete a task. If several people are reporting to you, you may want to insert the initial of the person to whom the task has been delegated in the circle. When the task has been completed, you should then place a check mark in the "completed" column.

- (✕) A fourth symbol is an X, to indicate that a task has been deleted. It may mean that you blew it and it just didn't get done, or it may mean that you've reconsidered and determined that this task simply isn't worth doing. Remember, you are in charge. If you schedule a task but later decide it really isn't what you want to do—so be it. You X it out.

Incorporating Goals and Values in Your Daily Planning

Your priority task list should provide an overview of your daily activities. But how well do these activities tie in with your long-term values and goals?

For most people, they don't. And that's why people often fail to achieve what's really important to them. The challenge is to *make your daily activities consistent with your goals and values.*

The best planner system is more than just a calendar. It should have a place to record your core values and goals.

While planning your daily priority tasks, make sure that your goals and values are evident. It is very important to refer to them. The more often these are reviewed, the more likely they will become a part of your being.

Blocking out time-wasters   There is no foolproof formula to use when time-wasters and interruptions arise. Indeed, an interruption now, although aggravating, may clarify a worker's task or solidify a relationship that will prevent more serious problems down the road. Let's hope we never become so perfectly organized that we cannot take unplanned time to help another person in need. Here is where the *art* of managing comes into play. There are no scientific ways to teach people sensitivity to the needs of others. There are times when you'll need to waste a little time. And there are times to avoid such distractions.

> Don't get so well organized that you can't take some time for others.

Time-wasting mail is easy to handle. "When in doubt, throw it out." Rather than let reports, memos, letters, and ads pile up on your desk, ask these questions: "What would happen if I threw this out?" "Will I need to refer to this later?" "Will someone else keep a file copy if, by some chance, I do need to see it later?"

> Handle each piece of mail only once.

Don't let paperwork pile up. Handle each piece of incoming mail only once. Look at it, decide what to do with it, and get it out of sight. Either

- file it,
- respond to it,
- pass it on to someone else, or
- throw it away.

People are trickier to deal with than mail. If you determine that someone is wasting your time, be up front about it. Simply say, in a matter-of-fact tone (don't sound accusing or sarcastic):

> Be candid with those who try to waste your time.

- "Tom, I'd like to talk with you more about that issue, but I have some other work I need to do first," or
- "Carmelita, I think I understand what you are saying. Can we pursue this more after I've had a chance to think through a few ideas?" or
- (When the interrupter is a telephone caller) "I have someone else here with me. Can we talk this out later?"

Once the interruption is set aside, you can determine whether the issue is worth following up on. If you are concerned, you can initiate contact. If not, you can use selective forgetfulness to let the latter drop.

Delegating to Save Time
The more we can delegate, the more time we'll have for other activities.

Why some managers hesitate to delegate   Delegating work to others always involves some risk. Sometimes the job doesn't get done as well as you'd like—or doesn't get done at all. A few bad experiences with delegated tasks

> Most supervisors have no choice. Work **must** be delegated.

"falling through the cracks," and a supervisor can easily become gun-shy. But some work *must* be delegated.

Common reasons supervisors don't delegate include the following:

- *I-can-do-it-myself reasoning.* Sure, you probably can do virtually anything you ask others to do. That's not the issue. The real question isn't whether or not you *can* do it, but whether you *should*. Is doing it yourself a productive use of your time? If not, delegate.

- *Lack of confidence in subordinates.* If you are hesitant to delegate because you think people will foul up the job, you either are insufficiently aware of what your people can do, or you have failed to provide sufficient training. Your supervisory task here is not to avoid delegating but to *increase* it until you find out the limitations of your workers. Then work to upgrade employee capabilities through training and job enrichment.

- *Fear of not getting credit and recognition.* We all like to get credit for our efforts. And to some extent, we fear that someone else—perhaps someone we see as a competitor—will get the honor and glory for a job well done.

- *Lack of time, skills, or both at turning work over to others.* Sometimes it seems to take more time to delegate than to do the work yourself. But that is a short-range viewpoint. You could spend quite a bit of time teaching a secretary how to handle routine incoming correspondence initially. But eventually that secretary will be able to handle what had been a significant time-eating task.

You can spend time and effort now. Or you can keep on spending it forever. It's your choice.

Why you may not delegate   Most of us hesitate to delegate in some cases. But if this hang-up applies to you consistently, you'll have considerable difficulty in being effective in your career.

To be an effective delegator, you must be willing to do the following:

- Entrust others with responsibilities.

- Give subordinates the freedom necessary to carry out expanded tasks.

- Spend the time to bring people along from easy to more complex tasks.

- Let subordinates participate increasingly in decisions that affect them.

How delegation can sometimes go wrong   The most common reasons that delegation sometimes fails to produce the desired results follow, with some suggestions for overcoming the problems.

- *The delegator fails to keep the communication channels open.* Look for feedback about delegated jobs. Create a climate where the worker can ask you for clarifying instructions or periodically check on how he or she is doing.

- *The delegator fails to allow for mistakes.* Workers will make mistakes when doing delegated work. Allow for these. Don't jump all over the worker or make him or her feel inadequate. Let him or her learn from the inevitable—and forgiven—mistakes.

- *The delegator fails to follow up on delegated tasks.* Periodic checking to keep up-to-date on a job conveys a sense of continued interest and also provides communication opportunities.

- *The delegator fails to delegate enough authority to complete the task.* If you ask one of your workers to research a particular problem that involves interviewing other workers, for example, be sure those other employees know that the interviews are authorized. Often a memo announcing that employee X has been given such-and-such a task and asking others to cooperate will suffice.

- *The delegator is unclear.* Be sure the expected results or outcome is understood by both boss and worker. Specify the nature of the finished product. Do you want a written report or an oral briefing? Should the worker review parts shortages for the entire year or just for the third quarter? Be specific.

In this chapter, we've stressed the importance of understanding the changing business landscape, clarifying organizational and personal expectations, managing the manager, and managing one's own time and tasks. As a closing thought, we encourage you to *now take charge!* You can indeed find a rewarding career in people management by applying the principles we've discussed in this book.

Summary of Key Ideas

- The highly successful manager understands the ever-changing landscape of business, develops clear job expectations, manages both subordinates and superiors, and manages himself or herself.

- Few people spend an entire career with one company.

- Almost all workers are now "knowledge workers"—employed to use brainpower more than horsepower.

- Clarifying one's expectations requires understanding what organizations do and do not expect of managers as well as what managers can expect from companies.

- The art of managing one's superior is often overlooked in management texts but is nonetheless important for success at work.

- Managing upward requires that one understands job responsibilities, takes the initiative, keeps the boss informed, asks for help when needed, and above all, develops a trusting relationship with the boss.

- The four conditions for establishing trust with one's boss are accessibility, availability, predictability, and loyalty.

- Managing your own time and tasks is critical to overall success.

- Prioritizing tasks, writing "to-do" lists, delegating, and accepting responsibility for the use of your most precious resource—time—will make a huge difference in your success.

- Success is a "do-it-yourself" project.

- The highly successful manager recognizes the significance of a manager's role, applies human relations principles, and is willing to take charge.

Key Terms, Concepts, and Names

A-B-C System
Availability
Career planning
Creativity and innovation
Job expectations
Knowledge workers

Long-term commitment
Managing your manager
Predictability
Priority task list
Superior-subordinate trust

Questions and Exercises

1. What do you expect from your employer (present or future)? Discuss these expectations with a manager. How realistic have you been?

2. Read two or three current articles about knowledge workers and the Information Age. What does this information mean for your career planning?

3. How do "Generation X" workers differ from their predecessors?

4. How can a person show others that he or she values time?

5. What are some ways to reduce clutter and get organized?

6. How does the A-B-C system work to help organize time?

7. What are some common excuses people offer for not delegating enough?

8. How can a person be a more effective delegator?

9. Answer the introductory questions at the beginning of this chapter.

Notes

1. Thomas A. Stewart, *Intellectual Capital: The New Wealth of Organizations* (New York: Doubleday/Currency), 1997 p. v.

2. Paul R. Timm, *Customer Service: Career Success through Customer Satisfaction* (Upper Saddle River, NJ; Prentice-Hall, Inc., 1998), p. 16.

3. Norman C. Hill and Paul H. Thompson, "Managing Your Manager: The Effective Subordinate," *Exchange* Fall-Winter 1978.

4. Reprinted with permission. *Fast Company* Issue 15, June/July 1998 p. 114. Author Alan M. Webber. Robert E. Kelley is also author of the book, *How to Be a Star at Work: Nine Breakthrough Strategies You Need to Succeed* (Times Books, 1998).

Another Look: Your Career in the Information Age

The fundamental premise of the new model executive . . . is, simply, that the goals of the individual and the goals of the Organization will work out to be one and the same. The young men have no cynicism about the "system," and very little skepticism—they don't see it as something to be bucked, but as something to be cooperated with . . . they have an implicit faith that the Organization will be as interested in making use of their best qualities as they are themselves, and thus, with equanimity, they can entrust the resolution of their destiny to the Organization . . . [T]he average young man cherishes the idea that his relationship with the Organization is to be for keeps.

—William H. Whyte,
The Organization Man, 1956

Well, scratch that. If there's unanimity about any aspect of the Information Age economy, it's that you have a better chance of getting a gold watch from a street vendor than you do from a corporation.

Time was, and not long ago, employees mounted hierarchies as elegant and monumental as Aztec temples. The steps were clear, the path seemed obvious—forget that those who made it to the top were either priests or human sacrifices. Now the worker, the manager, the executive zigzag through organizations that resemble circuit boards more than pyramids, where lines of energy and control run every which way; where chutes are many, ladders few and short; where the organizing principle is ceaseless reorganization; where it's hard to know what a career *is*, let alone how to get one. Asked about the future of middle management, that famously endangered species, David Robinson, president of the CSC Index consulting firm, offers a lonesome-pine of a word: "Extinction."

After more than a decade in which millions of working lives have been disrupted—downsized, outsourced, flattened, reengineered—corporations and people have learned, often at awful cost, new clichés. "We cannot offer job security, but through challenging work you can learn marketable skills." "Act as if you are self-employed, working for 'Me, Inc.'" "Any

given job is temporary." "You are responsible for managing your own career." Like mother's milk, these make a nourishing beginning. But then what?

It is one thing to mouth the new truths, another to live them. How can you tell if your career is on track if there is no track? How can you conceive and execute a career strategy when corporate mores and institutions trail behind economic reality? Says Gary Knisley, CEO of Johnson Smith & Knisley Accord, a New York executive recruiter: "Companies haven't accepted the view of temporary employment the way employees have. They're talking about 'this great career opportunity in this great and growing company.' They honestly think they're offering an old-fashioned job, while across the desk the candidate is thinking, 'I know better.'" If you believe otherwise, ask yourself this Hobbesian question: How comfortable would you be if you went to your boss, or if a key subordinate came to you, and candidly said: "Since lifetime employment is no more, I want to discuss how to change what I do here so that I will be attractive to the next company that hires me?"

Take heart. (Take Prozac, too.) There is a new model for careers in the Information Age. True, confusion and contradiction abound—the CEO who in one breath proclaims that he wants well-rounded managers with broad, generalist skills, next sighs about how vital and how hard it is to keep star technical talent. And true, job security is gone, maybe for keeps. Even if a tight labor market raises employee's' bargaining power, says Robert Saldich, chief executive of Raychem Corp., "We'll never slip back to the level of comfort and complacency of the past."

Today's economic seas therefore cannot be navigated by the old stars above, but by internal compasses and gyroscopes. Instead of security, seek resilience. Chart your contribution, not your position. Careers will be defined less by companies ("I work for IBM") and more by professions ("I design RISC chips"); they will be shaped less by hierarchies and more by markets. There are new rules for success and new warning signs of trouble. Because the risks are higher, so as always are the rewards.

New Signs of Trouble

The old trappings of success—a leather chair, your own secretary—are gone. So are the old signs of trouble. Says Richard Moran, a leader of the change-

continued

Your Career in the Information Age, *continued*

management practice for Price Waterhouse Consulting: "The rule used to be incremental promotions every year or two. If you missed one—hmm—that was a warning. You don't get the little clicks now." Warnings are subtler—many audible only to you, not your boss or colleagues. If several of these click, wake up:

1. *Are you learning?* If you can't say what you have learned in the past six months, nor what you expect to learn in the next, beware. Says Harvard Business School professor John Kotter: "When there's nothing you can learn where you are, you've got to move on, even if they give you promotions." If your job has become easy, someone else will do it for less.

2. *If your job were open, would you get it?* Benchmark your skills regularly. Look at want-ads for jobs in your field. If they ask for skills you don't have—with phrases such as "familiarity with Lotus Notes a plus"—get on the stick.

3. *Are you being milked?* When you sacrifice your long-term growth for short-term benefits, especially your employer's, you are living on intellectual capital. A salesman who wants to learn

marketing but keeps hearing, "You're so good we need you here" or a finance guy who is asked to keep the old system running while others learn the new software—these are people in whom the company has stopped investing.

4. *Do you know what you contribute?* If you can't give anyone a two-minute summary of what you do and why it matters, your boss probably can't either.

5. *What would you do if your job disappeared tomorrow?* If you can't answer that question, you haven't thought about what marketable skills you have. More and more, you have to sell yourself inside the company.

6. *Are you having fun yet?* Sure, they call it "work," but you'll be less eager for new challenges if your heart's not in it.

7. *Are you worried about your job?* Says Moran: "If you are, you probably should be."

Source: From INTELLECTUAL CAPITAL by Thomas A. Stewart. © 1997 by Thomas A. Stewart. Used by permission of Doubleday, a division of Random House, Inc.

Another Look: Life Lessons: There May Be a Job That You Were Born to Do

Mary Ann Liebert has succeeded as an entrepreneur in an arcane, male-dominated field—medical publishing—through a combination of chutzpah, persistence, outrageousness, charm and prescience.

If it's true, as I've claimed here, that some people just aren't cut out to be entrepreneurs, it's equally true that some people would be wasting their time doing anything else.

That is certainly the case for Ms. Liebert, who left her post as vice president of marketing for publisher Marcel Dekker Inc. in 1980 and formed Mary Ann Liebert Inc. to get in on what she saw as a huge opportunity in the fledgling genetic-engineering industry.

Ms. Liebert is an unabashed fan of medical research. "Scientists are my heroes," she says, flashing her trademark grin. She has twice married doctors—both named Peter Liebert (honest!). "I'll do anything

to keep from changing the company name," she says, again grinning.

She launched the company—when she was between Lieberts—in a corner of her apartment, where stunned job aspirants were often greeted by Ms. Liebert dressed in fuzzy pink slippers and a pink feather boa; it's a look she describes as "the real me."

She created a trade newspaper, Genetic Engineering News, and a research publication, the Journal of Interferon Research. She began schmoozing, cajoling and flattering top scientists to get them to edit those journals and to speak at conferences she put together to promote the field and, of course, her publications. She sent them flowers to seal the deals.

"If I'm talking to an editor on the phone," she says, "I'll tell him I'm persuasive over the phone, in person, I'm irresistible.'

continued

Life Lessons: There May Be a Job That You Were Born to Do, *continued*

Today, Mary Ann Liebert Inc. offers 60 publications and occupies nearly 11,000 square feet in Larchmont, N.Y; the company became profitable in its fourth year and has remained comfortably so since, although Ms. Liebert won't reveal specifics.

If ever there was a perfect match of career and person, this would seem to be it. It's the first of her Life Lessons for fellow entrepreneurs:

1. Do what you love.
"People say if I sold the company I'd be rich and could pursue hobbies," she says. But "a lot of money doesn't move me. This is my hobby. I don't vacation well. I love rhinestones as much as diamonds. I don't have to insure them."

And those slavish hours entrepreneurs moan about? Ms. Liebert thrives on them. She spent a vacation on a beach at Long Island Sound doing business on her cellular phone. "I was never happier," she says. "I hate to be away from the phone; if I have an idea, I have to act on it."

2. Find the right niche and get there first.
Because Ms. Liebert was the first publisher to establish a specialty in genetic engineering, she was able to win over key scientists. Since then, she has inhabited some of the narrowest niches imaginable, publishing journals on research areas such as laparoendoscopic surgery, aerosol medicine, and child and adolescent psychopharmacology. (A narrow-niche publication like Tissue Engineering reaches 750 subscribers and costs $65 a year for individuals.) "Finding and selling the right niche is everything today," she says.

3. Move and move fast.
"Big companies are the best to go up against," she said. "While they're up to their eyebrows in committee meetings and decisions, we're moving right along."

Consider her creation of an automobile investment newsletter, a rare departure from medicine. She asked her husband to sell one of the cars he collects to pay for a new kitchen, but he didn't know the value of his cars. "I said, 'There's no auto investment publication for collectors?'" she recalls. "He said no. I said there will be one tomorrow."

4. Stoop to conquer.
"I don't feel there's anything that's beneath me, whether it's answering the phone or opening the mail, because I get something out of that," she says. Until the recent acquisition of voice mail, everyone took a turn on the switchboard. "It really floored people when they asked who this is and I said Mary Ann," she says.

One strapped caller was given an impromptu discount rate by the owner-operator. He sent in his check with a note: "I hope it was really Mary Ann."

5. Take care of your people.
Ms. Liebert says she makes three promises to her journal editors: "That we will do a quality publication, that it will be marketed strongly and that I will become their favorite publisher," she says. "I treasure my editors. I know every one socially as well as professionally."

She is equally attentive to staff. Ms. Liebert hands out $100 savings bonds for cost-saving tips and has bought opera or ballet tickets for deserving employees. She even bought a brocade coat for a top performer who mentioned she wanted it.

6. Be resourceful.
Entrepreneurs have to marshal their resources efficiently. Once, when the company was looking for larger offices, Ms. Liebert didn't go to a commercial broker; she paid the postman to inform her when people moved out of nearby buildings.

7. God bless the woman who's got her own.
"I see women stuck in bad marriages who can't afford to get out. I see women who are widowed who had been totally dependent on their husbands," she says. "Having the company has given me choices."

Source: Hal Lancaster, "Managing Your Career," *The Wall Street Journal*, July 11, 1995, p. B1. Republished by permission of Dow Jones, Inc. via Copyright Clearance Center, Inc. © 1995 Dow Jones and Company, Inc. All rights reserved worldwide.

A Case in Point: The Brilliant Engineer

Donald Butler had earned straight A's in school and was apparently a brilliant young engineer. He hired on with an environmental engineering firm but was fired within a relatively short period of time. The reason? Everyone said he was brilliant at his work but he couldn't take directions. His supervisor would tell him how to do a design, and Don would instead do it his own way. When the supervisor would point out how the design didn't conform to specifications, Don would get defensive. He regarded any feedback as personal criticism.

Furthermore, Don wasn't a team player. When other engineers would ask him for help, he'd turn them down, saying he was too busy on his own project. He created so much animosity that when Don needed some help, no one would give it to him.

Daniel Goleman, in his book *Working with Emotional Intelligence,* says that "High IQ and technical expertise can have a paradoxical effect among seemingly promising people who fail. In a study of once-successful managers who failed, most were technically brilliant. And their technical skills were often the very reason they were promoted into management in the first place. But once they reached higher positions, their technical strength became a liability: Arrogance led some to offend their peers by acting superior, others to micromanage subordinates—even those with better technical expertise."

Questions
1. What skills seem to be needed to avoid the problems illustrated by this case?
2. Are technical skills necessarily less important than people skills?
3. What are the costs to the organization of an employee like Donald?
4. What would you do if you managed an employee like Donald?

Source: Reprinted from Daniel Goleman, *Working with Emotional Intelligence* (New York: Bantam Books, 1998), p. 43. Used with permission.

GLOSSARY

Glossary

A

A-B-C System   A method of organizing the relative importance of tasks by assigning each an A, B, or C value.

Accurate Understanding   A valid interpretation of one's own experiences or those of others. To understand what another person is saying, you might restate in your own words what that person's statement means to you.

Acquired Immunodeficiency Syndrome (AIDS) A disease transmitted between people through blood contact, generally through sex or needles during drug use; there is currently no cure.

Affirmative Action   An active effort to improve the employment or educational opportunities of members of minority groups, the disabled, and women.

Affirmative Action for Persons with Disabilities Programs now common in many organizations that encourage the hiring of disabled workers as a sound business practice.

Alcoholism   A complex chronic psychological disorder associated with excessive and especially compulsive drinking; a major cause of lost efficiency and profit in the workplace.

Americans with Disabilities Act   A law passed in 1990 to provide people with disabilities equal opportunity in employment, public accommodations, transportation, government services, and telecommunications.

Appearance   Our physical demeanor; the way we look to ourselves and others.

Assumption   Proposition, axiom, or notion that, while unproven, is taken for granted or considered true.

Attitude   A feeling or emotion regarding a fact, state, or condition.

Autocratic Style   A strategy in which the leader makes most of the decisions with very low employee participation; the autocratic leader rebuffs ideas.

Availability   A condition of being physically, mentally, and emotionally ready to do what is necessary for the good of an organization. An available person is present, qualified, willing, and ready for duty or use. Availability is a trait associated with successful people.

B

***Bakke* Decision**   The 1978 U.S. Supreme Court finding that affirmative action quotas that discriminate against whites violate the Civil Rights Act of 1964.

Basic Needs   Fundamental human necessities such as water, food, sleep, and air.

Behaviorism   An approach to psychology pioneered by John Watson and B. F. Skinner that assumes observed behavior provides the only valid data of psychology.

Belonging Needs   Normal psychological longings, yearnings, or desires to be accepted by others or to be a member of some group of organization.

Benevolence   Making employees happy, a traditional strategy used by supervisors.

"Best Companies to Work For"   An annual feature in *Fortune* magazine that identifies those companies that most value their employees.

Body Language   The subtle physical movements that people make that provide clues to their attitudes, feelings, or inclinations. Because it is open to interpretation, body language alone should not be used to draw conclusions; other nonverbal and verbal communications should also be considered.

Brainstorming   A group problem-solving strategy that involves the spontaneous contribution of ideas from all members of the group.

Burnout   Exhaustion of physical or emotional strength; the combined physical, mental, and emotional exhaustion caused by stress.

C

Captive Nation   A group such as Native Americans or an ethnic minority in another country that is encompassed by a larger, dominant group of people with whom the members of the "captive nation" do not easily assimilate.

Career Planning   Giving thought to one's career by selecting goals, gathering occupational information, and clarifying personal values.

Caring   Showing interest or concern for others; protecting or supervising; paying attention to detail.

Centralized Decision Making   The concentration of decision making in top-level management, who make even routine decisions.

Chain of Command   The arrangement of organizational authority that determines how many people report to each manager, the span of control of the organization, and the size and number of levels of authority.

Change-Produced Stress   Stress produced by changes in the work environment.

Circle or Network Organizations   Organizations arranged as a series of coordinating groups or teams linked by a center rather than the apex typical of the traditional pyramid arrangement.

Civil Rights Acts of 1964 and 1991   The federal legislation enacted in 1964 that prohibits employers, labor unions, and employees from discriminating against persons on the basis of color, religion, sex, or national origin; amended and strengthened in 1991 to provide damages in cases of intentional employment discrimination.

Civil Rights Movement   Grassroots campaign that began in the 1960s with the purpose of ending discrimination against African Americans; served as the catalyst for civil rights legislation.

Cognitive Dissonance   An imbalance created in the mind when an experience is inconsistent with what one already "knows"; perceived inconsistency between beliefs and knowledge or behavioral tendency.

Cohesiveness   A sense of teamwork, group morale, and team spirit that characterizes a group and often leads to high productivity; the act or state of sticking together tightly.

Communication   The process of information exchange between individuals through a common system of symbols, signs, or behavior; the ability to gain or relate understanding through the exchange of concepts and ideas.

Communication Climate   The overall climate created by the personal communication styles of all group members determined by subtle verbal and non-verbal behaviors occurring during interpersonal transactions.

Communication Conflict   Caustic, angry, defensive, and sarcastic reactions that occur during communication.

Conformity   Adherence to norms that often leads to feelings of satisfaction and increased personal value; action in accordance with some specific standard or authority.

Consensus   Group solidarity in sentiment and belief; unanimity; general agreement; the judgment arrived at by most of those concerned.

Consultative Style   A strategy in which the leader makes many of the decisions with some employee participation; the consultative leader welcomes ideas.

Content Reflection   The act of echoing or mirroring back in the form of a question what the other person said to make sure it is properly understood.

Contingency Approach   Using flexibility in adjusting to changing conditions, and factoring in where you are and what tools you have available in determining what must be done in a particular situation.

Continuous Reinforcement   The method in which an individual receives reinforcement every time he or she does the desired behavior; works best for quick learning when low levels of abilities are in use.

Controls   In an organization, these include budgets, interviews, quality inspections, performance reports, product specifications, time clocks, and progress reports.

Coping   Struggling with a problem, often by trial and error, until some degree of satisfaction is achieved.

Coping Techniques   Individual methods for dealing with stress, such as taking time for recreation and avoiding criticism.

Creativity and Innovation   Two of the most important traits companies look for in employees today; they help assure the success of both the company and the worker.

Credible People   Believable individuals who can influence a person to change; credible people and new experiences affect attitude.

Criteria   Standards or guidelines phrased as statements that indicate the minimal requirements that any suggestion or proposal must meet to be acceptable; a standard on which a judgment or decision may be based.

Criticism Stress   Stress produced by negative feedback, from a coworker or management.

Customer Departmentalization   Organization of a company along customer lines; for example, grouping together similar types of activities and responsibilities into sections, divisions, branches, or departments based on the types of customers served.

D

Defensive Climate   A situation in which the prevailing attitudes, standards, or conditions discourage open communication, undermine trust, and lead participants to feel that they are not appreciated and that their efforts will not be supported.

Development   The act or process of helping and encouraging organization members to grow and advance professionally; the process of natural growth, differentiation, or evolution by successive changes.

Development Level   A combination of four characteristics that shows the competence and commitment a person or group has in relation to a specific job to be accomplished.

Discrimination   The systematic restraining or prohibiting of an individual from occupying a position or performing an activity on the basis of sex, religion, race, or national origin.

Diversity   The cultural differences among people in the workplace, such as looks, beliefs, language, or customs.

Downward Communication   Communication that is directed vertically in an organization, from managers to employees, following the formal chain of command.

Drug Abuse   The repeated indulgence of an employee in drug use that reduces his or her effectiveness and dependability on the job.

E

Education   The process by which an employee becomes well-rounded and competent; mental, moral, or aesthetic development through instruction or other method.

Effective Listening   Listening to show support for the other person and to retain and evaluate information.

Ego Conflict   An intrapersonal stressful situation involving competing or conflicting needs or desires that threaten one's basic sense of being.

Employee Involvement   One of the crucial factors in smoothing organizational change.

Empowerment   The process of giving, or helping people discover, the power within themselves to satisfy their needs or wants.

Environment   In business, the context (physical surroundings, setting, or location) in which employees work; the circumstances, objects, or conditions by which one is surrounded and that influence the life of an individual or community.

Environment Stress   Stress caused by a lack of control over one's work environment.

Equal Employment Opportunity Commission (EEOC)   A federal agency established to carry out affirmative action programs.

Equipment or Process Departmentalization   Organization of a company by the kind of equipment manufactured or processes offered.

Equity Theory   A concept of job motivation emphasizing the role played by one's belief in the fairness of rewards and punishments associated with performance.

Esteem Needs   The human need to be recognized by others and to have a clear self-image.

Eustress   A positive form of stress that helps a person recognize the need to make course corrections in his or her personal or professional life, or both.

Expectancy Theory   A model designed by Victor Vroom that shows relationships between needs and motivations.

Extinguishing Behaviors   The result that occurs when reinforcement is withheld; the unrewarded behavior ceases over time.

Eye Contact   Direct visual contact with the eyes of another person; creates a sense of communication.

F

Facial Expressions   Of all the areas of the body, the face is the most complex, and its expressions give the most reliable external feedback of internal feelings.

Favorableness of the Situation   A state defined by Fred Fiedler as "the degree to which the situation enables the leader to exert his influence over his group."

Fear = Motivation   The idea that motivation may derive from fear, a negative and short-lived impetus in which action is the result of force rather than desire or will.

Fixation or Obsession   A persistent concentration on achieving a goal, sometimes beyond any logic.

Flat Versus Tall Organizations   In a flat organization, many people report to a particular manager, creating a broad span of control that encourages horizontal communication. In a tall organization, only a few people report to one manager, creating many levels of management.

Flextime   A system that allows employees to choose their own times for starting and finishing work within a broad range of available hours.

Frustration   The human response to being prevented from accomplishing a desired goal or objective; a deep chronic sense or state of insecurity and dissatisfaction arising from unresolved problems or unfulfilled needs.

Function Departmentalization   Organization of a company along function lines; for example, research and development, finance, personnel, marketing, and manufacturing.

Functional Disciplines   The wide array of components, both outsourced and in-house, that make up an organization and that core workers will need to be familiar with to succeed.

G

Generation X   Individuals born between 1968 and 1978, often unfairly overlooked for their employment potential due to stereotyping.

Goal-Consuming Activity   Actual participation in the goal itself; also called goal activity. For example, when going to a restaurant and ordering a pizza, the goal activity would be eating the pizza.

Goal-Directed Activity   Motivated behavior based on expectations that the goal is in fact attainable, worthwhile, and desirable.

Group Structuring   Getting a group together and arranging it so that the members are ready to work.

H

Hawthorne Experiments   Experiments conducted in Western Electric's Hawthorne Plant in the 1920s that are viewed as the starting point for the human relations movement.

Hot Groups or Hot Teams   Informal subgroups in an organization that emerge spontaneously to solve a problem or resolve an issue.

Human-Relations-Smart   The state of being aware of the basics of interpersonal relations and communications that preclude or reduce many stresses in the workplace.

Hygiene or Maintenance Factors   Dissatisfiers that relate to Maslow's lower-level needs.

I

Informal Organization   The "real," human side of an organization based on the way people actually interact.

Information Overload   The stressful condition created when an individual is given too much data to process in a given time and is unable to deal with it.

Interaction   The communication patterns among group members; mutual or reciprocal action or influence.

Intermittent Reinforcement   The method in which an individual receives reinforcement for desired behavior at particular intervals or at random times.

Interpersonal Communication   Communication that maintains close relationships, aids in self-understanding and personal growth, carefully deals with information, and creates a supportive climate.

Interpretation   The meaning one assigns to one's perceptions; a concept of another's behavior or words.

J

Job Design   The division of an organization's work among its employees.

Job Enrichment   A process in which, through talking together, subordinates and their supervisors come to an understanding of how the job could be made more meaningful. This involves delegating more responsibility and having more trust.

Job Expectations   Preconceived ideas that an employee holds regarding his or her job, or that an employer holds regarding a worker.

Job Satisfaction   Contentment with one's job that does not necessarily include personal motivation.

Job Satisfaction Questionnaire   A tool for helping employees improve their performance on specific jobs.

Job Training   Instruction that helps employees improve performance on specific jobs.

K

Knowledge   Familiarity, awareness, or understanding gained through experience or study; the fact or condition of knowing something with familiarity gained through experience or association.

Knowledge Workers   Educated workers geared to the modern, Information-Age workplace that is no longer based on manufacturing, construction, agriculture, or mining.

Kye   A method of pooling financial resources and providing substantial personal loans to members of the group that is used by Korean-Americans to finance new business ventures.

L

Laissez-Faire Style   A strategy in which the leader avoids interfering or guiding in decision making, giving the employees free rein.

Leader-Member Relations   One of the three variables that must be considered in determining the best leadership style.

Leadership   Behaviors that keep a group together and working to solve a problem; the office or position held by an individual who guides others.

Leadership Contingency Model   A system that helps determine the best leadership style by looking at three variables: leader-member relations, task structure, and position power.

Life Balance   The concept of placing the various aspects of one's life in equilibrium.

Line Workers   Those who are directly involved in producing the goods or services of an organization in its early stages.

Line-Management Positions   Jobs in which managers are in direct authority over the organization's primary output or product.

Linking-Pin Function   The role of a leader as a liaison between workers and top management.

Long-Term Commitment   Agreeing to stay with a company until one has become a contributing member of it for a reasonable length of time.

M

Maintenance Activities   Activities concerned with how group members perform a task.

Majority   A number greater than half of the total. Decisions are made with a majority by identifying the majority and minority viewpoints and then taking a poll or vote.

Management as Service   A method in which the manager sets direction and obtains the resources employees need to do a job; in this approach a manager leads but does not run an organization.

Managing Conflict   Taking action to deal with disagreements with subordinates or managers by using suppression, compromise, or confrontation.

Managing Your Manager   Practicing techniques that enable a worker to foster understanding with his or her supervisor.

Maslow's Hierarchy of Needs   A list of universal needs established by Abraham Maslow that includes physiological, safety, belongingness, esteem, and self-actualization needs.

Matrix Organizations   Those organizations arranged in a "matrix," with each employee reporting to both a functional or division manager and a project or group manager.

Mechanistic View of Organizations   An outlook that compares organizations to machines and breaks them down into separate special tasks.

Mentor Relationships   Associations in which new employees are helped by a more seasoned or higher-level worker.

Mentoring   The process by which one employee informally guides another, providing contacts and inside tips on how to succeed in an organization.

Message   Symbols assembled into units of meaning that are assigned to some experience; a communication in writing, speech, or signals; the encoded information sent by the sender to the receiver.

Midlife Crisis   A stressful event usually associated with males in their 40s or 50s, in which they seriously question long-held values; sometimes results in dramatic lifestyle changes.

Mixed Situation   A state in which the leader's relationship to the group has both positive and negative aspects.

"Mop Bucket Attitude (MBA)"   The idea that honesty and basic customer service are more important than elaborate theories and sophisticated business techniques.

Motivation   The process of providing reasons or motives for exerting effort and causing oneself or someone else to act in certain ways.

Motivational Faith   Employees' belief that management is fair and honest, that other workers share the workload, and that the job is important and can be done.

Motives   Personal wants, interests, and desires that affect perceptions; the facts that cause, channel, and sustain an individual's behavior.

Myths of Leadership   The incorrect notions that leaders are rare; that they are born, not made; that they arise only out of extraordinary events; that they exist only at the top of an organization; that they manipulate rather than persuade; that they are charismatic; and that leadership is inherently immoral.

N

Need for Achievement   The human urge to accomplish something, which is exerted by challenging and competitive work situations; to some extent can be taught and learned.

Need for Affiliation   The human desire to be accepted by others, which is important for job satisfaction.

Need for Power   The human need to win arguments, persuade others, and prevail in every situation.

Nominal Group   A structured group meeting in which participants alternate among silently thinking up ideas, listing them on a flip chart, and voting on them.

Nonverbal Symbols   Nonlinguistic (not using language) behavior to which people assign meaning.

O

Open Questions   Questions that cannot be answered with a simple yes or no statement.

Organization   The meaningful way in which people put selected information together; the arrangement of an organization's structure and coordination of its managerial practices and use of resources to achieve its goals.

Organizational Character   The ideas, beliefs, and hopes of people inside and outside the organization about the appropriate role of the organization and how it should fulfill that role.

Organizational Climate   The composite impression people get from such things as the work atmosphere, organizational objectives, and corporate philosophy.

Organizational Culture   The set of pervasive understandings, such as norms, values, attitudes, and beliefs, shared by organization members.

Organizational Development   A planned effort that is aided by a change agent (an organizational development specialist) to improve the efficiency and effectiveness of the organization and its people; a long-range effort supported by top management to increase an organization's problem-solving and renewal processes through effective management of work culture.

Organizational Development Through the Involvement of Employees (ODIE)   A planned program for organizational change that is contingent on the active involvement of employees at various levels.

P

Paralanguage   The study of how something is said (not what is said) by the words that are used (also called vocal cues); optional vocal effects such as tone of voice that accompany or modify the phonemes of an utterance and that may communicate meaning.

Parental Leave   Work leave granted to either males or females for the purpose of attending to important activities involving their children; a major expansion of the old maternity leave concept.

Participative Style   A strategy in which the leader permits a high degree of employee participation; this style takes advantage of the subordinates' willingness and ability to work by creating a motivating environment.

Peer-Group Pressures   Stresses in which individuals are influenced by their peers to see life as their peers would like them to.

Perception   How an individual sees the world through his or her experiences, expectations, and interests; a quick, acute, and intuitive cognition; a common source of communication barriers; a pattern of meaning that comes to the individual through the five senses.

Perception/Truth Fallacy   The erroneous tendency of people to believe that the way they see the world is closer to "the truth" than the way others see it.

Perceptual Expectancy   Mental anticipation about how people, events, or things will be.

Performance Review (Appraisal)   Formal process of providing feedback to employees regarding how their job performance matches established standards or objectives.

Personal Coaching   Organizational strategy in which an employee receives personalized help in goal setting, leadership skills, customer service, and time management; the average time for this process is 8–12 weeks.

Personal Power   An individual's status based on how he or she is perceived by others; usually emerges when one is seen as having expertise, skills, ability, or other characteristics a group considers important.

Personal Space   The distance people comfortably allow and demand between themselves and others.

Personal Style   One of the determinants of leadership success; influenced by expectations, the tasks to be accomplished, and power.

Personality-Produced Stress   Stress experienced by an individual as a result of certain personal traits.

Plurality   More than half of the whole majority. With a plurality, the acceptable decision is the one supported by the largest number of individuals as determined by a poll or vote.

Position Power   A recognized status based on one's position in the company; according to Fred Fiedler, the power that is inherent in the formal position the leader holds.

Predictability   The capacity for handling delicate administrative circumstances with good judgment and thoroughness; reliability in meeting deadlines and doing high-quality work; the state of accurately seeing ahead based on observation, experience, or scientific reasoning.

Prejudice   The prejudging of others that is often rooted in a misunderstanding of or lack of exposure to different types of people; damage resulting from some judgment or action of another in disregard of one's rights.

Priority Task List   An inventory of things that need to be done; crucial in today's fast-paced workplace.

Product Departmentalization   Organization of a company along product or service lines.

Profit Center   Subgroup responsible for its own decisions; organizational unit where performance is measured by numerical differences between revenues and expenditures.

Programmed Limitations   Self-perceptions of what one can or cannot achieve.

Pseudoconflict   A conflict in which people agree on an issue but are unable to communicate the agreement, which may seem apparent but is not stated.

Pyramid Structure   The traditional organizational arrangement in which responsibility and decision making flow from the top down.

Q

Quality Circles   Strategies in which employee participation helps determine how jobs should be designed for best results.

Quality of Work Life (QWL)   First introduced in the 1960s, the concept refers to the degree to which work should provide opportunities to satisfy a wide variety of workers' needs.

R

Rationalization   A coping response whereby a person discounts or tries to explain away how a goal can or cannot be achieved.

Receptiveness to Workers' Ideas   The state of leadership being ready to accept employees' suggestions or concepts.

Recreation   Refreshment of strengths and spirits after work.

Retention Listening   Listening to retain and evaluate information by doing such things as identifying the speaker's purpose, adapting to it, and developing note-taking skills.

Reverse Discrimination   Discrimination against white males resulting from preferential treatment of minorities.

Reward A While Hoping for B   Steven Kerr's concept of organizations' compensating workers for one thing with the expectation of another. For example, companies hope employees will work efficiently but pay them by the hour, essentially rewarding them for using up time.

Ripple Effects   In systems theory, the effects one system has on other systems.

Role Models   Persons whose behavior in a particular role is imitated by others.

Roles   The patterns that characterize a person's contributions to the group; a socially expected behavior pattern usually determined by a person's status in a particular society.

S

Scientific Management   Pioneered by Frederick W. Taylor, a style of management based on the belief that through science, a careful worker or manager could find the one best way to do any job.

Secondary Needs   Higher-level human wants and desires such as to be accepted by others, to achieve certain goals, or to have prestige.

Security Needs   Human wants and desires related to protecting oneself from physical or psychological loss.

Selection   The process of sifting through raw data to identify for use key information that holds importance for the individual.

Self-Actualization   The achievement of one's full potential.

Self-Directed Workgroup (SDW)   The idea that employees should be trained to learn and share jobs traditionally performed by a manager.

Self-Fulfilling Prophecies   Outcomes related to preconceived expectations. For example, one person's expectations of another person may influence the latter to behave in certain ways that make the expectations reality.

Seniority   The number of years an employee has been with a company; can determine responsibilities, benefits, and promotions.

Sex-Based Roles   Work positions that are filled on the basis of preconceived, often incorrect notions of what is appropriate for men and women.

Sexual Harassment   Unwanted sexual requests or advances or the creation of an intimidating atmosphere through sexual jokes and remarks.

Simple Conflict   The condition in which individuals or groups cannot satisfy their own goals or needs without blocking the goals or needs of some other individuals or groups.

Situational Leadership Theory (SLT)   Paul Hersey and Kenneth Blanchard's leadership model that describes the situational or contingent behaviors of directing, coaching, supporting, and delegating.

Situational Variables   Factors in a work environment that are likely to change; these must be considered when trying to determine the best leadership style.

Small Group   A gathering of two or more people, yet few enough in number to permit each member to communicate directly with all other members.

Small-Group Problem Solving   Employing a small group to solve specific problems by stating and analyzing questions, generating ideas, selecting the most useful ones, and deciding which will be used.

Social Needs   Human wants and desires for belonging, affiliation, love, and acceptance by others.

Social Service Leaves of Absence   Programs that give selected employees full pay and benefits while they perform volunteer service for a year or more.

Span of Control   The number of people who report to an individual supervisor or manager.

Personnel   Those workers who advise and assist the line organization; they offer advice but do not ~~orders.~~

Stereotype   A generalization about the nature of a person or group that is often incorrect or misleading.

Stress Carrier   One who triggers stress in another person.

Superior-Subordinate Trust   A state of trust between manager and employee developed through accessibility, predictability, and mutual loyalty and respect.

Support Listening   Hearing and attending to what others say with a minimum of emotional or observable reaction.

Supportive Climate   A situation in which the prevailing attitudes, standards, or conditions encourage participants to feel that they have a sense of worth and importance and that their efforts will be supported.

Supportiveness   The degree or extent to which one person or group is willing to aid or sustain another; one of Charles Redding's five components of organizational climate; the degree to which management encourages its employees' efforts.

Survival Needs   Human wants or desires associated with the will to live. According to Abraham Maslow and others, these basic needs have dominance over higher-level needs.

Symbol   Something used for or regarded as representing something else.

Systems Theory   The idea that nothing in nature exists in a vacuum, and that systems emerge from interdependency.

T

Task Activities   Activities concerned with what group members are doing to accomplish the specific work or tasks assigned to the group, as opposed to maintenance activities, which are concerned with how group members perform a task.

Task Integration   The process of linking or coordinating specialized work or tasks of various individuals or groups to ensure that an organization's overall goals are met.

Task Specialization   The process of assigning specific work or tasks to individuals or groups so they will become experts in dealing with a specific segment of the organization's overall mission.

Task Structure   The degree to which a task is defined. A clearly designed task is high in structure, whereas a vaguely designed task is low.

Team Meetings   Meetings where employees gather to discuss and solve problems and reduce stress.

Technostress   A form of physical and emotional burnout triggered by difficulty in adapting to rapid technological change.

Territory Departmentalization   Organization of a company along territorial or geographical lines.

Theory X   A pessimistic, traditional approach to managing people that was described but not espoused by researcher Douglas McGregor. This approach is based on assumptions that employees have an inherent dislike of work, will avoid it whenever possible, are lazy, lack ambition, avoid responsibility, and prefer to be directed.

Theory Y   An optimistic view of human nature that assumes that people will naturally expend physical and mental effort in work and direct themselves toward objectives if their achievements are recognized and rewarded. This theory, developed by Douglas McGregor (along with Theory X), holds that people are able and willing to seek responsibility and to apply imagination, ingenuity, and creativity to organizational problems.

Time Departmentalization   Organization of a company according to time schedules, as in the use of work shifts.

Timely Information   Information, conveyed when needed, that enables employees to do their jobs properly and to establish a feeling of belonging in the company.

Touch Behavior   Use of the sense of touch to communicate certain kinds of nonverbal symbols.

Training   Development associated with learning human and technical skills to make the employee more effective on a specific job.

Traits Approach to Leadership Studies   A theory based on the underlying assumption that leaders possess certain characteristics that make them effective.

Trust   Belief in and reliance on the ability, strength, and integrity of a person or thing; one of Charles Redding's five components of organizational climate. The degree of trust employees have in management depends on a number of factors including the respect and trust management offers them.

Two-Factor Theory of Motivation   Frederick Herzberg's motivational-hygiene theory, which suggests that people are motivated by one set of higher-level needs (such as achievement or recognition) and satisfied by the fulfillment of another set of lower-level needs (such as pay and working conditions).

U

"Uh-Huh" Technique   The method of focusing on the other person and verbalizing support by saying "uh-huh" or some equivalent nonjudgmental comment.

Unanimity   Total agreement that transcends differences and leads to harmony.

Unity of Command   The principle that each employee reports to only one boss.

Upward Communication   Communication that is directed vertically in an organization, from employees to managers, following the formal chain of command.

V

Verbal Symbols   Words or arrangements of words that are used to convey one's thoughts and experiences to others.

Virtual Organizations   Organizations that are a confederation of independent service providers rather than in-house workers.

Vocal Cues   Hints at the real meaning behind spoken words, which may differ from the words themselves.

W

Work Teams or Workgroups   Autonomous groups of employees who are collectively responsible for their output.

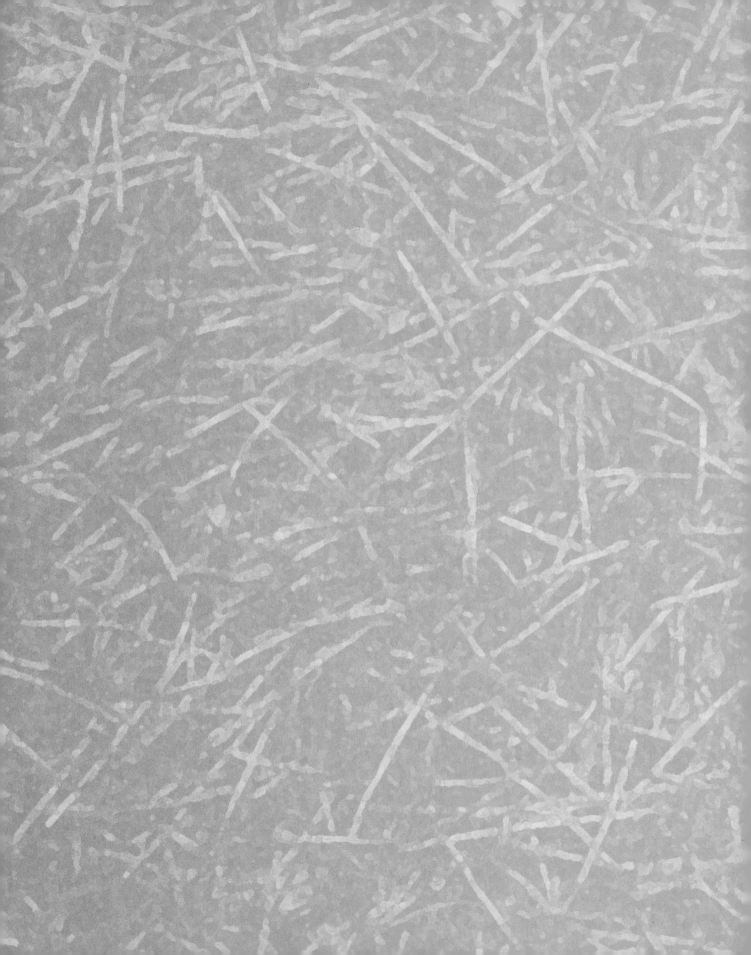

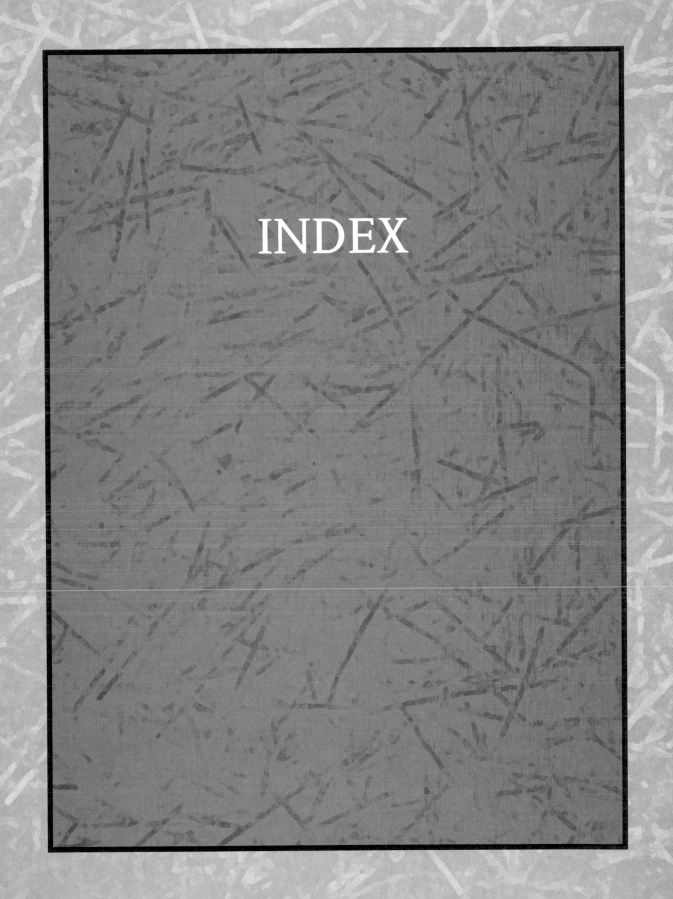

INDEX

Index

Photo Credits